Robert Burns

THE POET

Other Books by David Daiches:

The Place of Meaning in Poetry (1935)
New Literary Values (1936)
Literature and Society (1938)
The Novel and the Modern World (1939 [new edn. 1960])
The King James Bible: a Study of its Sources and Development (1941)
Virginia Woolf (1942)
Robert Louis Stevenson (1947)
A Study of Literature (1948)
Willa Cather: A Critical Introduction (1951)
Critical Approaches to Literature (1956)
Two Worlds [autobiographical] (1956)
Literary Essays (1956); *John Milton* (1957)
The Present Age (1958)
A Critical History of English Literature (1960)
George Eliot's Middlemarch (1963)
The Paradox of Scottish Culture (1964)
(ed) The Idea of a University (1964)
English Literature (Princeton Studies in Humanistic Scholarship) (1965);
More Literary Essays (1968)
Some Late Victorian Attitudes (1969);
Scotch Whisky (1969)
Sir Walter Scott and his World (1971)
A Third World (autobiographical) (1971)
(ed) The Penguin Companion to Literature; Britain and the Commonwealth (1971)
Robert Burns and his World (1971)
(ed with A Thorlby) Literature and Western Civilization, vol. I (1972),
vols. II and V (1973), *vols. III and IV* (1975), *vol VI* (1976)
Charles Edward Stuart: the life and times of Bonnie Prince Charlie (1973)
Robert Louis Stevenson and his World (1973)
Was (1975); *Moses* (1975)
James Boswell and his World (1976)
Scotland and the Union (1977)
Glasgow (1977); *Edinburgh* (1978)
(with John Flower) Literary Landscapes of the British Isles: a narrative atlas (1979)
(ed) Selected Writings and Speeches of Fletcher of Saltoun (1979)
(ed) Selected Poems of Robert Burns (1979)
(ed) A Companion to Scottish Culture (1981)
Literature and Gentility in Scotland (1982)
Robert Fergusson (1982)
Milton's Paradise Lost (1983)
God and the Poets (1984)
Edinburgh, A Traveller's Companion (1986)
A Wee Dram (1990)
General Editor, *Studies in English Literature* (1961-1985)

Robert Burns

THE POET

by
David Daiches

SCOTLAND
ALBA

SALTIRE
SOCIETY

First published in 1950 as *Robert Burns* by
G. Bell and Sons Ltd.
This paperback edition published 1994 by
The Saltire Society, 9 Fountain Close, High Street,
Edinburgh EH1 1TF

The publisher acknowledges subsidy from
the Scottish Arts Council towards the
publication of this volume.

A catalogue record for this book is available from
the British Library.

ISBN 0 85411 060 7

Detail from portrait of Robert Burns by Nasmyth
reproduced in front cover design by permission of the
Scottish National Portrait Gallery

Designed by Gourlay Graphics, Glasgow

Printed and bound in Great Britain by Bell & Bain Limited

PREFACE

This study of Burns is intended primarily as a critical examination of his poetic achievement rather than as a biographical work. However, in my endeavour to explain his development as a poet and the forces that helped to condition this development, I have been drawn to some degree into biography. Thus I have found it necessary to discuss at length his education and his early friendships and associations, for these were important factors in his poetic growth. I have tried to quote from primary sources wherever it is necessary to document my interpretation, and I have naturally drawn heavily on the letters and on such standard documents as the narratives of Gilbert Burns and of John Murdoch. My indebtedness to older editors of Burns, such as Currie, Cromek, Chambers, Wallace, and Scott Douglas, will be evident to any reader who is familiar with Burns scholarship, and I am indebted in a somewhat different way to a host of modern Burns scholars, among whom it should not be invidious to single out Professor J. DeLancey Ferguson, whose noble edition of Burns's letters, to say nothing of his other work in the field, put Burns studies on a new footing. I am further indebted to Professor Ferguson for his careful reading of my manuscript and for his many valuable suggestions.

I have tried to see Burns and his poetry in a wider context than that provided by traditional Burns studies. Interested as I am in contemporary developments in Scottish poetry and in the reassessment of Scottish literature that has been going on in Scotland for some time, I have perhaps given more attention to Burns's relation to the older Scottish 'makars' than most of his critics have done, and I have concerned myself, too, with the place of Burns in the Scottish literary tradition—a question much debated in Scotland these days. But my essential task has been to throw as much light as I can on Burns the poet, with a view to increasing understanding and appreciation of his poetry.

In quoting from Burns's poems I have in most instances used the latest published text with which Burns himself was directly concerned. Even in the chapter on the Kilmarnock edition I have as a rule used the 1793 text for the poems quoted, because the numerous italics and the excessive punctuation of the 1786 volume may confuse the modern reader. In quoting poems first printed after Burns's death I have used whatever appears to be the best text. In quoting from Watson's *Choice Collection* I have used the Glasgow reprint of 1869, and I have used the 1871 Glasgow reprint of the fourteenth edition of *The Tea-Table Miscellany*; in other instances where I have quoted from eighteenth-century works I have cited the editions in the text. In quoting from Burns's Commonplace Book I have used the facsimile edition of Ewing and Cook (Glasgow: 1938).

I have to thank Professor J. DeLancey Ferguson and the Clarendon Press, Oxford, for permission to quote from his edition of Burns's letters: *The Letters of Robert Burns*, edited by J. DeLancey Ferguson from the original manuscripts, 2 vols. (Oxford: Clarendon Press, 1931).

DAVID DAICHES

Ithaca, New York
August, 1950

PREFACE TO THE 1966 EDITION

In the sixteen years since this book was first published there has been a steady if hardly spectacular development of Burns scholarship and some interesting further attempts have been made to provide a re-valuation of Burns's poetic achievement in the light of modern critical ideas and of the recent history and present needs of Scottish poetry. The long needed definitive modern edition of Burns's poems is now under way, in the capable hands of James Kinsley; *The Merry Muses of Caledonia* is at last freely available, edited by James Barke and Sydney Goodsir Smith (1959); James Dick's long out-of-print edition of Burns's songs has been re-issued (1962) by Folklore Associates, Hatboro, Pennsylvania. Folklore Associates have also re-issued the *Orpheus Caledonius* (two volumes in one, 1962), and other contributions to the study of Burns's background have been made, including the extremely useful *Ayrshire at the Time of Burns* put out in 1959 by the Ayrshire Archaeological and Natural History Society. I myself, in *The Paradox of Scottish Culture: the Eighteenth Century Experience* (Oxford University Press, 1964), have both refined and elaborated many of the points made in the opening chapter of the present book; but I have let that chapter stand unaltered not because it is incapable of improvement but because it would require much more space to improve it. J. W. Egerer has produced the first complete bibliography of the works of Burns (1964) and R. D. Thornton has written a biography of James Currie, Burns's first biographer (1963), which has led me to alter two sentences in the first paragraph of chapter 7 of my own book. But in spite of advances in scholarship and criticism, the same sentimental rubbish about Burns tends to be spouted forth each year by hundreds of Burns Night orators. The need for a critical study of Burns's poetry and for an estimate of the man and his work in the light both of objective critical standards and of the problems and pressures of his own time—and for that matter of the problems and pressures of *our* time—has thus not abated; if anything, it has grown. And that is one reason for the re-issue of this book.

DAVID DAICHES

University of Sussex
December, 1965

PREFACE TO THE 1981 REPRINT

Since I wrote the Preface to the 1966 edition, James Kinsley's edition of the poems has appeared and established itself as the definitive text. Critical and scholarly work has continued to enrich our understanding of Burns both as man and as poet: a good cross-section of this is to be found in *Critical Essays on Robert Burns*, edited by Donald A. Low, London, 1975. I myself have published a selection of Burns's poems with a critical and biographical introduction (Deutsch, 1979 and Fontana, 1980). The whole situation with regard to Burns scholarship and criticism—particularly criticism—has developed in ways I hoped for but could not foresee when I originally wrote this book over thirty years ago. But I hope that it is not unduly complacent of me to believe that my book still has value as a

CONTENTS

THE SCOTTISH LITERARY TRADITION

No LYRIC poet has been as much talked about and as often misunder-stood as Robert Burns. In the conventional academic literary histories he is regarded as a 'pre-Romantic', the representative of a 'new spirit' which was to lead English poetry to greater glories in the nineteenth century; while in the annual Burns Night speeches of enthusiasts his significance as Scottish poet and literary craftsman is wholly obscured in mists of sentimental oratory. Burns was, in fact, neither a pre-Romantic nor the ideal Rotarian: his work represented the last brilliant flare-up of a Scottish literary tradition that had been develop-ing for centuries and that in the eighteenth century was in its final, disintegrating phase, and his character was to a large extent moulded by the impact of the rising world of urban gentility on the final phase of this tradition. Eighteenth-century Scottish culture was complex and confused, and though the period was the second 'Golden Age' of literary and intellectual Scotland, this distinction was won at the price of national schizophrenia – a price that Scottish culture is still paying. If we look at Burns, not through the teleological spectacles of the mappers of literary movements, but in the context of the social and cultural forces of the Scotland of his day, we shall be less likely to misunderstand his achievement and misread his poetry.

In order to see this context in proper perspective we must pay some attention to its development. To answer even such simple questions as why Burns chose to write largely in the Scottish vernacular or whether he properly belongs to the history of English literature requires some understanding of Scottish literary history. History will not tell us how good his poems are, but it will help us to account for their characteristic qualities and to see them for what they really are – the Indian Summer of a Scottish literary tradition rather than sports in the garden of English poetry. Let us begin, therefore, by looking briefly at the background of Burns's Scotland.

'Is it not strange,' wrote David Hume to Gilbert Elliot of Minto in 1757, 'that, at a time when we have lost our Princes, our Parliaments, our independent Government, even the Presence of our chief Nobility, are unhappy, in our Accent & Pronunciation, speak a very corrupt Dialect of the Tongue which we make use of; is it not strange, I say, that, in these circumstances, we shou'd really be the People most distinguish'd for Literature in Europe?' We may agree with Hume that it is strange, but it is still stranger to find a distinguished Scotsman taking pride in the literary eminence which his own people had attained and in the same breath stigmatizing the traditional written and spoken language of that people as 'a very corrupt dialect.' And the situation becomes even stranger when we discover that less than two years after Hume wrote this letter a poet was born who, using this 'very corrupt dialect,' was to achieve a universal fame eclipsing that of the great philosopher himself. To understand how this situation arose we must look back fifty years.

On January 28, 1707, Queen Anne announced to both Houses of Parliament that the Treaty of Union, merging the Scottish Parliament in the English, had been ratified by the Scottish Estates. On May 1, the treaty came into force. Instead of the 145 noblemen and 160 commoners who with their friends and families thronged the streets of Edinburgh when the Scots Parliament was in session, reminding the city of its importance as the capital of a proud if not always a fortunate country, there was from now on only the little hand-picked and subservient band of 16 representative peers and 45 members of the House of Commons to wend their bewildered way from Scotland to Westminster, where they would be sneered at for their accent and abused for their manners. 'The end of an auld sang', remarked Lord Chancellor Seafield, and historians have disagreed as to whether this remark of Scotland's last Lord High Chancellor was cynical or romantic.

It was indeed the end of an auld sang, and an inglorious one at that. The plots and intrigues which paved the way for the unprecedented act by which the Scottish Parliament voted itself out of existence, as well as the riots which followed, made it clear that the act was anything but the expression of the national will. The Kingdom of Scotland dissolved 'not with a bang but a whimper'. Even those who supported the Union could not help showing some embarrassment at the manner in which it was put through, and pleaded shabbily that the end justified the means. The fact is, however, that the Union of 1707, was the end rather than the beginning of a movement – a movement which had begun in 1568 when Mary Queen of Scots crossed the Solway Firth into England to seek the dubious protection of Queen Elizabeth; a movement which had begun when John Knox recognized that a Protestant Scotland could gain more from association with Protestant England than with Catholic France; which had begun when the rich culture of medieval Scotland succumbed to the cold theology of reforming zealots and the 'auld alliance' with France gave place to a series of shifty and evasive overtures to England which certainly did no good either to the Scottish or to the English character.

At this point one must push one's vision still further back. In the Middle Ages Scotland had been an independent country with a vigorous, if chequered, cultural and political life of her own. Her ties were then much more with the continent of Europe, particularly France, than with England, the hereditary enemy whose rulers had made many vain attempts to subdue permanently their northern neighbour. In the fifteenth century Scotland produced a literature second none to in Europe and certainly more lively and more original than that produced by the lifeless representatives of a worn-out tradition who were for most of this period spinning out their endless verses in England. This was the period of the so-called 'Scottish Chaucerians' – of the *Kingis Quair*, that remarkable narrative poem which infused into the love-allegory convention a delicacy of expression and a tenderness of personal feeling unknown in other examples of its kind; of the lively and shrewdly humorous fables of Robert Henryson, who produced also in his *Testament of Cresseid* a moving and original continuation to Chaucer's story; of the skilful and versatile lyrics of William Dunbar, with his arresting grey-and-silver portraits of medieval Edinburgh, his rich and sonorous religious and courtly poetry and his strangely powerful poems of satire and abuse.

Scotland received a setback in 1513, when the disastrous Battle of Flodden undid at a blow most of the work of the early Stuarts, but in spite of political and other difficulties Scottish literature was moving towards a new efflorescence when the Reformation plunged the country into a series of civil disputes in the course of which much of its culture vanished and the very character of the people seems to have become permanently gruffer. The peculiarly violent form which the Reformation took in Scotland not only interrupted the course of the country's culture for generations but also destroyed numerous monuments of its existing art. Folk dance and drama were alike proscribed (so that we have virtually no Scottish drama, in spite of the immense promise of Sir David Lyndsay's bold and humorous *Satyre of the Thrie Estaitis*), and the great abbeys and cathedrals were destroyed. When Boswell, accompanying Dr. Johnson on his visit to Scotland in 1773, asked Johnson, as they were looking at the ruins of St. Andrews Cathedral, where John Knox was buried, 'Dr. Johnson burst out, "I hope in the highway, I have been looking at his reformation".'

The fact that Knox turned to England and abandoned the traditional ties with France, that he wrote his *History of the Reformation* in a language which abandoned most of the traditionally Scottish forms of the old Anglian speech (or, to put it less historically, in a language that was more English than Scots), and that the versions of the Bible which were circulated among the Scottish Protestants (first the Geneva version and later the King James version) were in English and not in Scots, all contributed to the weakening of Scottish national culture. When in 1603 a Scottish king inherited the throne of England and came south to London to rule as king of both countries, the confusion in Scottish cultural life became worse confounded. The Scots language (developing from the northern form of the old Anglian speech, and in its first phase identical with the northern English dialect) began to give way more and more, in literary productions, to the English. Drummond of Hawthornden (1585–1649), though he spoke Scots, wrote all his poetry in English, and in this he is symbolic of what was happening to the nation, which continued to talk in Scots and to do its formal writing in English. The Scots language gradually ceased to be a language and became a series of dialects; for when there is no literary standard of purity a language will always so disintegrate.

Scottish political life became equally confused. In the reigns of Charles II and of James II of England and VII of Scotland – that is, from 1660 to 1688 – Scottish national feeling was, at least in the Lowlands, largely Protestant, Whig, and often what we today would call 'leftist' – or became so in opposition to the English attempts to force Episcopacy on Scotland. But with the 'glorious revolution' of 1688, the establishment in Scotland the following year of a national Presbyterian Church, and the emergence as the dominant political party in England of the 'Revolution Whigs' whose cry was 'Peace, Protestantism, and Plenty', the pattern of Scottish political life changed rapidly. One section of the Scottish Whigs joined the Jacobites to oppose the movement for an 'incorporating union' with England, while another section joined the Revolution Whigs of England to foster union between the two countries and to eliminate Jacobite Scottish nationalism.

As the eighteenth century developed, the number of those who looked back to the exiled Stuart line and sentimentalized over Scotland's glorious past came to include even those who, like Burns, were strong democrats in politics and hated all that the later Stuart kings had in fact stood for; they adopted a Jacobite attitude as a form of Scottish patriotism. In a very short time Scottish patriotism, from being sternly Protestant, Whiggish and even antimonarchist, had become, at least in imagination, anti-Whig and Jacobite. Paradoxically enough, the lost Stuart line, which in the seventeenth century had stood for absolutism and the *Gleichschaltung* of Scotland and England, became identified by Scottish patriots of both the left and the right with the lost liberties of their country. This working of a sentimental patriotic imagination in the romantic implications of a lost cause (and the Jacobite cause became romantic only when it was lost) helps to explain why Burns could welcome the French Revolution and at the same time write powerful Jacobite lyrics which implied that all would be well if the old monarchical absolutism could be restored.

But let us look again at the Reformation and its effect on Scottish culture. The peculiar form which the Reformation took in Scotland not only helped to frustrate the development of Scottish culture for more than a hundred years but also succeeded in achieving what was equally unfortunate for Scottish civilization: it drove a wedge between Lowland and Highland Scottish culture, that is, between Lowland Scots and Highland Gaelic culture, at a time when the ties between these two elements in the country had been growing steadily closer. The question of the relation between the Gaelic (or Celtic) and the non-Gaelic elements in Scottish civilization is far too elaborate to be treated adequately in a bird's-eye view of the Scots literary tradition, but a few relevant points might be made. These two distinct elements in the country had existed from very early times; the Gaelic element was older and had been the primary one till the end of the eleventh century, when the pious Queen Margaret began a policy of Anglo-Normanizing the country. Nevertheless, the Celtic element held its own for a much longer period than is generally believed, and in Sir Walter Scott's day the Gaelic-speaking area of the country was still larger than the rest of the country. In the fifteenth century, under the Stuart kings, the Gaelic and Lowland Scots elements were fusing into a really national Scottish culture; the Reformation stopped this process of fusion and drove a new wedge between the predominantly Catholic Highlands and the now predominantly Protestant Lowlands. The Revolution of 1688 enlarged this wedge; for the Highlands associated their welfare with the exiled Stuart cause, and the Lowlands, moving closer to England both politically and economically, soon ceased to understand the Highlands at all.

Thus at the beginning of the eighteenth century we find Lowland Scotland losing the basis for any distinctively Scottish political life and turning more and more towards England; while the Highlands remained forgotten and neglected, a prefeudal society precariously surviving on the fringe of a civilization rapidly advancing into modern industrialism. The Union of Parliaments did not immediately bring Scotland the prosperity its advocates had promised; but the Lowlands, or at least the cities, did eventually share in the general rise in the standard of living which developed in the latter part of the century. Material conditions in Lowland Scotland did improve, if not as a demonstrable result of the Union, throughout the eighteenth century. But political life was dead, or, if it lived at all, hopelessly corrupt. The Scots had fought their last real political fight in 1707, against the Union of Parliaments, and they had lost. There was little more to be said or done. Fletcher of Saltoun, that passionately patriotic Scotsman, who had fought so hard to prevent the measure from going through, would not stay in Edinburgh a moment after its passing. It is recorded that 'on the day of his departure his friends crowded around him, entreating him to stay. Even after his foot was in the stirrup, they continued their solicitations anxiously crying, 'Will you forsake your country?' He reversed his head and darting on them a look of indignation, keenly replied: "It is only fit for the slaves who sold it": then leaped upon the saddle and put spurs to his horse.'[1]

The opening of the eighteenth century thus found the fortunes of Scotland at an extremely low ebb. The country was poor, confused, corrupted, betrayed. Its cultural prospects seemed particularly low; on the very level of language there was a basic difficulty. A nation which speaks in Scots and writes (sometimes painfully) in English, which feels in Scots and thinks in English (as Mr. Edwin Muir has argued), is surely in no position to produce integrated works of literature. And not only was there confusion between Scots and English; as we have seen, there was a much deeper (and, as time was to show, a much more serious) split between Lowland Scotland and Gaelic Scotland. How could a country in this confused and divided state produce a lively culture? We know that it did. We know that, if the first great age of Scottish literature was the fifteenth century, when the Scottish Chaucerians wrote some of the best poetry then being produced in Europe, its second and hardly less great age was the Golden Age of the eighteenth century. Between 1740 and 1830 Scotland produced an astonishing galaxy of talent – poets, philosophers, men of letters, scientists, engineers, architects.

What, we might well ask, happened in the early part of the eighteenth century to make this extraordinary revival possible?[2] Was the re-establishment of an intellectual climate hospitable to such varied activity the result of a final abandonment of Scottish traditions and the complete merging with English civilization, or did the threat of the total submergence of Scots culture rally the dying forces of national culture to a final splendid effort? And what is humble Robert Burns doing in that glittering company of philosophers, doctors, chemists, and professors? Or do these varied activities represent no single movement but a chance juxtaposition of utterly different phenomena caused by a variety of forces? These are significant questions for an understanding of Burns's social and intellectual environment.

There are two ways in which a baffled and frustrated nation can attempt to satisfy its injured pride. It can attempt to rediscover its own national traditions, and by reviving and developing them find a satisfaction that will compensate for its political impotence; or, accepting the dominance of the culture of the country which has achieved political ascendancy over it, it can endeavour to beat that country at its own game and achieve distinction by any standard the dominant culture may evolve. Eighteenth-century Scotsmen chose both these ways. Francis Hutcheson, Adam Smith, David Hume, and Hugh Blair were among those who chose the second way; James Watson, Allan Ramsay, David Herd, Robert Fergusson, and Robert Burns were among those who chose the first. To the latter group we owe the revival of interest in older Scottish literature, in Scottish folk traditions, and in Scottish antiquities; to the former we owe the philosophical and scientific movements that made eighteenth-century Edinburgh perhaps the most distinguished intellectual centre in Europe.

It is not simply that, defeated politically, the Scots turned to non-political activities to restore their faith in their own national genius; for such a diagnosis will not explain the profound division between the critical and the creative activities of eighteenth-century Scotland. But it does seem to be true that the different kinds of cultural life which Scotland produced at this period can to some degree be attributed to different ways of reacting to the same situation. One remembers that W. B. Yeats, caught up in the furious rush of Irish politics in the time of Parnell, waited patiently for 'the first lull in politics' when the claims of literature might be vindicated; and it was precisely during that lull

in politics that followed the death of Parnell in 1891 that the so-called
'Irish Revival' began to manifest itself.

The situation in Scotland at the beginning of the eighteenth century
was in some ways analogous. After well over a century of furious
political and religious disputes, during which Scottish culture had all
but perished, the Scottish people suddenly found that the disputes had
all been settled, and though many regarded the settlement as both
unfair and unfavourable, there was a breathing spell, there was a kind
of empty quiet, and there was vitality enough left in the country to fill
this emptiness.

In 1706, the year before the Union of Parliaments was finally
effected, the first important sign of the way in which one of the new
currents was going to flow became visible. James Watson, Edinburgh
printer and Scottish patriot with (if we may believe his enemies)
Jacobite inclinations, brought out a book entitled *A Choice Collection of
Comic and Serious Scots Poems Both Ancient and Modern*, the first of three
volumes, of which the second and third appeared in 1709 and 1711
respectively. These are the words which the publisher addressed to the
reader at the beginning of the first volume:

> As the frequency of Publishing Collections of Miscellaneous
> Poems in our Neighbouring Kingdoms and States, may, in a great
> measure, justify an Undertaking of this kind with us; so 'tis hoped
> that this being the first of its Nature which has been publish'd in our
> own Native *Scots* Dialect, the Candid Reader may be the more easily
> induced, through the Consideration thereof, to give some Charitable
> Grains of Allowance, if the Performance come not up to such a Point
> of Exactness as may please an over nice Palate. . . .

These three volumes contained, without the scholarship or textual
accuracy which would be expected of a modern editor, a mixed collection of Scots poems, both old and new, some in the vernacular, some
in standard English. It is clear from Watson's introduction that the
poems in the vernacular constituted the *raison d'être* of the collection,
and the phrase he uses, 'our own native Scots dialect', shows national
pride transferred – for the first time, one might almost say, for well
over a century – from the realm of politics and religion to that of
literature. The most significant things in Watson's collection are the
popular poems and folk songs, earlier and contemporary imitations of
ballads and folk songs, and the few brilliant examples of sixteenth-
century verse, that is, of Scottish poetry written just before the swamp-

ing of Scots literature by the Reformation. These represented a definite turning back to the roots of Scottish culture, a turning back to the period when Scottish literature was still both Scottish and literary, and to the folk tradition which alone was able to survive the seventeenth-century blight.

That the folk tradition survived this blight was due largely to its adaptability, not to its being in any way exempt from the general suspicion cast by Scottish Calvinists on secular literature and particularly popular poetry. No better example of the adaptability of Scottish folk poetry can be found than in the mid-sixteenth-century *Gude and Godlie Ballatis*, in which secular love poems are transformed by a few judicious touches into vigorous antipapal satires or robust Protestant hymns. David Herd, one of the ablest eighteenth-century collectors of Scottish folk poems, included in his *Ancient and Modern Scottish Songs*,[3] the following old song:

> John, come kiss me now, now, now,
>   O John come kiss me now,
> John come kiss me by and by,
>   And make nae mair ado.
>
> Some will court and compliment,
>   And make a great ado,
> Some will make of their goodman,
>   And sae will I of you.
>   John come kiss, etc.

Herd had got behind the *Gude and Godlie Ballatis* to discover its original form. In the *Ballatis* it has been metamorphosed into:

> Johne, cum kis me now,
> Johne, cum kis me now;
> Johne, cum kis me by and by
> And mak no moir adow.
>
>   The Lord thy god I am
>   That Johne dois the call;
>   Johne representit man,
>   Be grace celestiall.[4]

And it continues in the vein of the second stanza for twenty-four verses more. It is also easy to see what has happened in the following

poem from the *Gude and Godlie Ballatis;* the refrain gives away its
origin:

Pope	The Paip, that pagane full of pryde,
has	He hes us blindit lang;
where	For quhair the blind the blind dois gyde,
go wrong	Na wonder baith ga wrang;

Lyke prince and king he led the ring
Of all iniquitie:
Hay trix, tryme go trix,
Under the grene wod-tre.[5]

Sometimes a secular love emotion has been successfully carried over
into a religious context, as in

leave	All my Lufe, leif me not,
	Leif me not, leif me not;
	All my Lufe, leif me not,
	Thus myne alone:
	With ane burding on me bak,
weak	I may not beir it I am sa waik;
	Lufe, the burding from me tak,
	Or ellis I am gone.

With sinnis I am ladin soir,
Leif me not, leif me not;
With sinnis I am ladin soir,
Leif me not alone.
I pray the, Lord, thairfoir
Keip not my sinnis in stoir,
Lowse me or I be forloir,
And heir my mone.[6]

By such metamorphoses the folk tradition survived even in print,
and where so much can survive in print we may guess how much more
survived orally.

This folk tradition, then, began to reappear at the beginning of the
eighteenth century in the work of compilers like Watson. Not only
did the folk tradition thus reappear, but also the art tradition of light,
occasional verse which never really died out in Scotland even in the

seventeenth century. It is to the seventeenth century that the half-comic epitaph on Habbie Simson the Piper of Kilbarchan belongs:

> Kilbarchan now may say alas!
> For she hath lost her game and grace,
> Both Trixie, and the Maiden Trace:
> _remedy_ But what remead?
> For no man can supply his place,
> Hab Simson's dead.

This poem, by a landed gentleman, Robert Sempill (or Semple) of Beltrees (_c._ 1595–_c._ 1668) is perhaps the most influential single poem in the whole of Scots literature; imitated by Allan Ramsay, Fergusson, and Burns, and called by Ramsay 'Standard Habbie' because he saw it as the norm of a certain type of Scots poetry, it has had a clear and obvious influence from the time of its reprinting by Watson up to the present day. Its verse form became a favourite of Scottish poets and is still associated with Scottish literature by the general reader. There were many other types of poetry represented in Watson's collection which were to inspire Ramsay, Fergusson, and Burns; for example, the rollicking sixteenth-century 'Christ's Kirk on the Green', a lively description of a rustic festivity, whose form both Fergusson and Burns copied exactly in poems on similar themes. And in printing Alexander Montgomerie's 'The Cherry and the Slae', Watson drew attention to the complex and fascinating forms that were prevalent in Scottish poetry just before its decline at the end of the sixteenth century. We shall have more to say of these poems in Chapter Three, where we discuss some of the poems of Burns which derive from them.

Watson printed works of almost all the relatively few representatives of Scottish poetry who lived in the barren century and a half preceding the publication of his collection. And barren and confused though the period was, the Scots poems that were written had all the advantage of the moulding of the language achieved by the Scottish Chaucerians and even seem – in the accomplished love lyrics of Alexander Scott and the technically brilliant work of Alexander Montgomerie, for example – to have been influenced by the French Pléiade. Alexander Scott (1547–1584), Mark Alexander Boyd (1563–1601), and Alexander Hume (d. 1609) are about the only significant poets of this period not represented in Watson. Boyd wrote one remarkable sonnet in Scots, and Hume, in his 'Of the Day Estival', produced a brilliant and fascinating long poem descriptive of a summer's day from dawn to dusk. Neither poem

affected the eighteenth-century Scottish tradition; nor did the varied
lyric forms of Alexander Scott, which reflect some of the same interest
in technical experimentation with lyric forms that is shown in *Tottel's
Miscellany* in England.

But poems of popular revelry like 'Christ's Kirk on the Green', and
'The Blythsome Wedding' were in Watson's collection, together with
'flyting' poems in the old Scots tradition, and poems in the English
tradition by Drummond of Hawthornden, Montrose and others;
echoes of street ballads and folk songs, including the charming 'Lady
Anne Bothwel's Balow'; poems which maintain the tradition of the
Scottish Chaucerians, like 'The Cherry and the Slae'; mock elegies like
'Habbie Simson'; and poems maintaining William Dunbar's tradition
of intricate craftsmanship and carefully chiming vowel sounds like
Alexander Montgomerie's remarkable and beautiful poem on the
marigold, 'The Solsequium'. When we add to these the medieval and
other works that Allan Ramsay was shortly to print in his *The Ever
Green*, and the oral folk literature which still persisted, we have the not
insubstantial basis for the revived Scots literary tradition of the
eighteenth century.

The date of Watson's first volume was 1706. It was not until 1725,
with the publication of Francis Hutcheson's *Inquiry into the Originals
of Our Ideas of Beauty and Virtue*,[7] that the other aspect of the Scottish
revival of the eighteenth century began to manifest itself. Watson was
interested in collecting what for the most part was characteristically
Scottish from the storehouse of his country's poetry; Hutcheson, in a
discourse 'in which the principles of the late Earl of Shaftesbury are
explained and defended', was endeavouring, in a sense, to rescue
Scotland from itself and to appear before the world simply as an
English-speaking philosopher. How clearly Hutcheson was abandoning
at least one Scottish tradition can be seen in his introductory statement
that philosophy and religion had been made 'too austere and ungainly
for the enjoyment of gentlemen', a state of affairs which he was taking
on himself to remedy. Gentlemanliness in religious, philosophical,
or poetic controversy had never before been considered a Scottish trait.
Earlier writers would probably have equated it with superficiality.

Watson, then, was interested in 'our native Scots dialect', while
Hutcheson's ambition was to argue for the benefit of gentlemen. It is
important to bear in mind the difference between these two aspects of
eighteenth-century Scottish culture, and their reactions on each other.
One must remember, too, that the tradition represented by Watson had
a start of eighteen years. Watson's tradition culminated in Burns;

Hutcheson's, shorter lived, in David Hume; and the fusion of the two in the work of Sir Walter Scott explains many otherwise puzzling characteristics of his work. When in 1822 George IV, dressed in what he had been told was the Royal Stuart tartan, visited Edinburgh and was proudly greeted by Sir Walter arrayed in the tartan of the Campbells, Scotland had become British in a sense that neither Whigs nor Tories could have foreseen in 1707. One might add that the dramatic and in a sense tragic conflict of which this was the uneasy resolution can be seen in many of Scott's novels.

The desire to revive and imitate the older Scots literature, especially the folk literature, which Watson's *Collection* so clearly revealed, was manifesting itself in other ways, too. Well-born ladies of leisure began to write poems in Scots in the style of the older folk lyrics or of the ballads. Lady Wardlaw (1677–1727) produced in her 'Hardyknute' the most successful imitation ballad of the eighteenth century; Lady Grizel Baillie (1665–1746) wrote 'Werena My Heart Licht I Wad Dee', a charming lyric in the true folk tradition; Jane Elliot (1727–1805) produced, later in the century, one of the two famous versions of 'The Flowers of the Forest', the other of which was written by Mrs. Cockburn (1712?–1794). Landed gentlemen, too, showed their skill in writing imitations of the older popular poetry: William Hamilton of Gilbertfield (1665?–1751) produced in his 'Last Dying Words of Bonnie Heck, a Famous Greyhound in the Shire of Fife' a fine rollicking poem in the 'Habbie Simson' tradition; Burns imitated it more than once. Further, Hamilton, in his verse letters to Allan Ramsay, began the tradition of familiar verse epistles in the dialect, a tradition that Burns was to bring to its culmination towards the end of the century. Hamilton's third contribution was his modernizing of the old patriotic poem *Wallace* by the fifteenth-century poet Blind Harry; this was the version Burns borrowed from Candlish the blacksmith, the reading of which, in his own words, 'poured a Scottish prejudice in my veins which will boil along there till the flood-gates of life shut in eternal rest'.

Watson's *Collection* was thus anything but an isolated symptom. Scotsmen and Scotswomen were turning more and more from the barren political life of the country to a rediscovery of a characteristically Scottish literature. (Even when they did engage in politics, as in Jacobite activity, it was politics seen through a folk emotion, unrealistic and often literary in its application; thus the Jacobite movement was more successful in encouraging a revival of folk song and imitation folk song than it was as a political movement.) Older works, both folk and art literature, began to be collected and imitated; that is to say, both an antiquarian and a creative movement developed, and both played an important part in determining the course of eighteenth-century Scottish poetry. A greater man than Watson, and a man much wider of influence, was Allan Ramsay (1684 or 1685–1758); with Ramsay we can see the new movement well under way.

Ramsay came from his native Lanarkshire to Edinburgh about 1700 and, with nothing but his enthusiasm and good humour to help him, developed from an obscure wigmaker's apprentice to be the 'Scottish Horace'. About Ramsay's work as bookseller, antiquarian, poet, patron of the arts, and general literary busybody, an entire book could be written; in an introductory chapter of this kind it must suffice to note that his characteristic activities were directed towards the enrichment of the nationalist literary movement on both its antiquarian and its creative sides. He was largely instrumental in bringing closer together social and literary life, and he is thus to some degree responsible for that host of clubs, societies, literary associations and similar organizations which made later eighteenth-century Edinburgh so distinguished for its unique combination of literature, conversation, and drink. He restored Scots literature to its natural place in the daily life of the people by associating it with the normal activities of the citizen.

Ramsay's creative work is perhaps less important than his work as an editor. In *The Tea-Table Miscellany*, of which the first of four volumes appeared in 1724, he brought together a mixed collection of old and new songs and ballads by authors living and dead, known and unknown, among which were many hitherto unprinted specimens of Scottish folk literature. But Ramsay was less interested in restoring the true texts of older works than in presenting them in such a way that they would be wholly acceptable to the taste of his day, and this well-meaning but unfortunate intention resulted in the wholesale tampering with old songs, comparatively few of which survived his attempts to polish them up a bit. Not possessing the genius of Burns, Ramsay, when he attempted to polish up a folk song, generally just spoiled it.

But in this mixed bag of genuine, improved, and imitated work there is an abundance of riches. There are several of the pieces which Watson printed, including one beginning, 'Fy let us a' to the bridal' (entitled 'The Blythsome Wedding' in Watson and 'The Blythsome Bridal' in Ramsay) and 'Lady Anne Bothwel's Lament' (which Watson called 'Lady Anne Bothwel's Balow' from the lullaby's first line, 'Balow my boy, lie still and sleep'); there are numerous rollicking drinking songs, such as 'Up in the Air' (which Scott put into the mouth of Madge Wildfire in *The Heart of Midlothian*), 'Todlen Butt, and Todlen Ben' (better known by the words of the chorus, 'Todlen hame', and much admired by Burns), and 'The Tippling Philosophers'; there is a version of 'The Bonny Earl of Murray' and of the even better-known 'Barbara Allen'; there is a pre-Burns version of 'Auld Lang Syne' differing from another pre-Burns version to be found in Watson's *Collection*; there are scores of folk songs which Burns was later to make use of in one way or another, including (I give Ramsay's titles and spelling in each case) 'The Bob of Dumblane', 'The Mill, Mill-O', 'This is no mine ain House', 'My Daddy forbad, my Minny forbad', 'Tak your Auld Cloak about ye', 'The auld Man's best Argument', 'Willy was a wanton Wag', and many others; there is the 'Merry Beggars', which almost certainly gave Burns the idea for 'The Jolly Beggars'; there is Robert Fergusson's favourite song, 'The Birks of Invermay' – and a wealth of similar material.

The Tea-Table Miscellany was immensely popular and ran into many editions during Ramsay's lifetime. In his preface to the fourteenth edition, Ramsay wrote:

Although it be acknowledged that our SCOTS tunes have not lengthened variety of music, yet they have an agreeable gaiety and natural sweetness, that make them acceptable wherever they are known, not only among ourselves, but in other countries. They are, for the most part, so chearful, that, on hearing them well played, or sung, we find a difficulty to keep ourselves from dancing. What further adds to the esteem we have for them, is their antiquity, and their being universally known.

He adds in a later paragraph:

In my compositions and collections, I have kept out of all smut and ribaldry, that the modest voice and ear of the fair singer might meet with no affront; the chief bent of all my studies being to gain their good graces; and it shall always be my care to ward off those frowns that would prove mortal to my muse.

The avoidance of 'smut and ribaldry' was not, however, the only motive for the changes Ramsay or the 'ingenious young gentlemen' who 'generously lent [him] their assistance' made in old poems; it is indeed difficult to find any consistent principle of emendation in the collection. Some indication of the various degrees of emendation and alteration is given in Ramsay's note before the index: 'The SONGS marked C, D, H,

L, M, O, &c., are new words by different hands; X, the authors unknown; Z, old songs; Q, old songs with additions.'

In the year which saw the publication of the first volume of *The Tea-
Table Miscellany*, Ramsay brought out *The Ever Green: A Collection of
Scots Poems Wrote by the Ingenious before* 1600, containing poems mostly
taken from the Bannatyne Manuscript, a collection made in 1568 of
earlier Scottish poetry, including much of the work of the Scottish
Chaucerians. This volume introduced his readers to the work of
Scotland's first Golden Age, poetry produced at a time when the nation
was independent and its culture, though national, was at the same time
truly European. The patriotic intention is made clear in Ramsay's
preface:

> When these good old *Bards* wrote, we had not yet made Use of
> imported Trimming upon our Cloaths, nor of foreign Embroidery in
> our Writings. Their *Poetry* is the Product of their own Country, not
> pilfered and spoiled in the Transportation from abroad: Their *Images*
> are native, and their Landskips domestick; copied from those Fields
> and Meadows we every Day behold.
>
> The *Morning* rises (in the Poets Description) as she does in the
> *Scottish* horizon. We are not carried to *Greece* or *Italy* for a Shade, a
> Stream or a Breeze. The *Groves* rise in our own Valleys; the *Rivers*
> flow from our own Fountains, and the *Winds* blow upon our own
> Hills. I find not Fault with those Things, as they are in *Greece* or *Italy*:
> but with a *Northern Poet* for fetching his Materials from these Places, in
> a Poem, of which his own Country is the Scene, as our *Hymners* to the
> *Spring* and *Makers* of *Pastorals* frequently do.

In this last phrase we find a clue to Ramsay's purpose in writing his
dramatic pastoral, *The Gentle Shepherd*: like the older Scottish poets, he
was trying to domicile European traditions in a Scottish environment.
The point that Ramsay is making in this introduction – that the older
Scots poets used native settings in their descriptive poetry – is a shrewd
and interesting one. It is in fact true that the poetry of the medieval
Scottish poets is the only medieval poetry in Europe which consistently
keeps its eye on the poet's native landscape. All the English romances
written in the *Romance of the Rose* tradition have landscapes and gardens
which are Italian or French. Even Chaucer's *Troilus and Criseyde* is set
in a Mediterranean climate. But Robert Henryson's *Testament of Cresseid*
is set in an unmistakable Scottish environment, from the opening where
the poet describes how he built up the fire and closed the door against

the cold winds outside, to the conclusion when, after lamenting 'in ane dark corner of the hous allone' while outside 'the cloudis blak ouirquel-mit all the sky', Cresseid meets Troilus outside the leper house. This interesting characteristic of Scots poetry, to be found in Dunbar's pictures of Edinburgh as well as in Henryson, is revived in the eighteenth century, and for that revival Ramsay is to a considerable extent responsible.

In Ramsay's original poetry we first see clearly the tradition which, for convenience, one might call the Hutcheson tradition – the tradition of a polite, non-Scottish culture in Scotland – interacting with the tradition represented by Watson. Ramsay, after all, bookseller and avid reader that he was, was keenly aware of what was going on in con-temporary London. And so were a considerable number of the Edin-burgh gentry. For all his love of Scottish traditions, he was susceptible to the taste of his generation, and that taste was formed in London, not in medieval Scotland. It is not surprising, therefore, to find among Ramsay's original poems a large number of verses in the neoclassic English diction of his southern contemporaries. These poems are for the most part undistinguished; frigid, formless, imitative, they show Ram-say writing in what was for him almost a foreign tongue – certainly one in which it was impossible for him to perform with grace. His most successful original poems are racy, familiar poems in Scots: drinking songs, verse letters, descriptions of Edinburgh low life, and easy adapta-tions of Horace's less ambitious odes. For it was in such poetry that an eighteenth-century Scot would be least likely to adopt the standards of taste and diction that prevailed in London.

But Ramsay's importance is not confined to the books he produced or edited. His good-humoured, sociable attitude to his native literature helped to close the gap between life and letters which might well have developed to preposterous proportions under the influence of the pecu-liar cultural and political situation – a situation in which an educated man spoke in Scots but felt it his duty to make any formal utterance in English. After he retired to his octagonal house beside the Castle – the Goose Pie, as contemporaries called it – he remained for years an enliven-ing and humanizing element in the literary life of Edinburgh. It is in large measure thanks to his influence that the movement of Scots poetry in the eighteenth century is from a Ramsay to a Burns, not from a Pope to a Shenstone; that is, it is a movement towards greater, not less, vitality.

Ramsay's work included and went beyond that of Watson, and from now on the movement went steadily forward. Numerous collections of

Scots songs, with and without music, were published. The *Orpheus Caledonius*, published in London in 1725, contained about fifty Scottish songs with the music, and was followed in 1733 by a greatly enlarged edition in two volumes. Its editor, William Thomson – 'who', says Allan Ramsay, 'is allowed to be a good teacher and singer of *Scots songs*' – selected most of his songs from *The Tea-Table Miscellany*. This was the début of Scottish popular literature in London; the collection was beautifully produced, 'the music for both the voice and the flute, and the words of the songs finely engraven in a folio book, for the use of persons of the highest quality in *Britain*, and dedicated to the late Queen'.[8] Similar collections followed in Scotland, culminating in the *Scots Musical Museum*, of which the first volume appeared in 1787 and to whose subsequent volumes Burns contributed so much. Of the books of Scots songs without music the most important was the collection by David Herd already referred to; Herd's first edition appeared in 1769 and a second enlarged edition in two volumes in 1776. There were also many collections of the tunes alone, arranged for a variety of instruments. The pioneer volume here was the *Collection of Scots Tunes* made by the violinist Adam Craig in 1730, and the most impressive such collection was James Oswald's *Caledonian Pocket Companion*, of which the first of many volumes appeared in 1740. Burns's career as a song writer was made possible to a large degree by the work of these earlier collectors; as in so many other fields, his work here represented the culmination of a tradition, not the birth of a new one.

Eight years before Ramsay's death there was born in Edinburgh the poet who was to continue the tradition of Scottish popular poetry which Ramsay revived and who produced in his brief career a small but impressive collection of Scots verse which directly inspired Burns to emulation. This was Robert Fergusson, whose death in the public Bedlam of Edinburgh in October, 1774, when he had just completed his twenty-fourth year, was one of the greatest losses Scottish literature has ever suffered. Fergusson, son of an Aberdeenshire family who had moved south to Edinburgh a few years earlier, was the only one of the trilogy of eighteenth-century Scots vernacular poets who had a formal academic education, although the death of his father while he was still a student at the University of St. Andrews cut short his academic career and compelled him to take an ill-paid job as a legal copyist in Edinburgh in order to support his mother and himself. From 1768, when he left St. Andrews, until 1774, he lived frugally but not miserably in Edinburgh, spending his days in the drudgery of copying legal manuscripts and his nights in the 'howffs' of Edinburgh amid song and poetry and mild dissipation.

He soon discovered a remarkable talent for rendering the life of the city in racy Scots verse, and in 1771 he became a regular contributor of Scots poems to the *Weekly Magazine or Edinburgh Amusement* (otherwise known as *Ruddiman's Magazine*), which had been founded by the brothers Ruddiman in 1768. Making use of many of the Scottish verse forms found in Ramsay, he took phase after phase of Edinburgh life and described them in a verse which combined liveliness, a sure and crafts-manlike use of imagery, and a classical sense of form. His poems, although much narrower in range than those of Burns, are often more perfect of their kind; the street life of eighteenth-century Edinburgh lives with all its warmth and colour in such poems as 'The Daft Days', 'The King's Birthday in Edinburgh', 'Hallow Fair', 'The Rising of the Session', 'The Sitting of the Session', 'Leith Races', and others. Although – unlike Burns – essentially an urban poet, he knew the countryside, too, partly because eighteenth-century Edinburgh was set in the midst of the countryside, and partly because he knew the fields of Fife from his student days in St. Andrews and the Aberdeenshire country scene from his visits to relatives there. 'The Farmer's Ingle', both in inspiration and in integrity of feeling superior to Burns's 'Cotter's Saturday Night', is one of the finest descriptions of rural life in either English or Scottish poetry, while his 'Ode to the Gowdspink' (goldfinch) has the combina-tion of fresh natural description and underlying melancholy which Burns was to achieve in such poems as 'To a Mouse'. The language of Fergusson's Scots poems is Edinburgh Scots with a dash of his parents' Aberdeenshire; he uses it with flexibility and verve, and with a sureness of taste quite lacking in Allan Ramsay. He wrote a fair number of English poems, too, but these, like the English poems of Ramsay and many poems of Burns, have little distinction. It was as a Scots poet that he attained real stature, and as a Scots poet that he inspired Burns.

The liveliness, the sense of colour and richness in daily popular life, the wit and irony and sense of fun which we find in Fergusson are all qualities to be found to some degree in Ramsay and to a great degree in Burns. Fergusson drew his inspiration not only from the Scots folk tradition as he found it in Ramsay and from the art tradition of the older Scots poets but also from the remnants of the traditions of the medieval 'Goliards', the songs of the wandering scholars as they lingered on at St. Andrews University – and they lingered there perhaps longer than at any other British university – and from a tradition of academic horseplay of which both Ramsay and Burns were innocent.

In 1772, Fergusson became a member of the 'Cape Club', a society of talented Edinburgh men which included David Herd the editor and antiquary, Alexander Runciman the painter, and other men of distinction who were nevertheless not in the upper ranks of genteel Edinburgh society. Members of the Cape Club were all designated 'knights', and Fergusson, who had an excellent singing voice, became 'Sir Precentor' on election. His convivial meetings with the Cape Club – and the records show that he seldom missed a meeting until his last melancholy illness – were only part of the lively night life in which Fergusson indulged and which was such an important feature of eighteenth-century Edinburgh life. The more genteel scholars and philosophers whose work was giving Edinburgh an international reputation at this time moved as a rule in other circles; what we have called the Watson tradition rarely came together socially with what we have called the Hutcheson tradition. When Burns was in Edinburgh in 1786–1787, and later, he relaxed after formal parties with the literati by visiting the more popular taverns of the city in the company of friends who included several Knights of the Cape.

While Ramsay and Fergusson were reviving a native vernacular literature, the genteel tradition we have associated with the name of Hutcheson was also developing apace. Francis Hutcheson was a professor at the University of Glasgow when Ramsay was writing and editing in Edinburgh. It was Hutcheson who 'rang the bell which called the wits together' in eighteenth-century Scotland. Who were these wits, and what, if anything, had they to do with the revival of interest in Scottish poetry and Scottish literary traditions which Ramsay did so much to encourage?

The wits were, of course, that group of philosophers, critics, and historians whose work made eighteenth-century Scotland famous throughout the world. They were for the most part European rather than purely Scottish in outlook; and in this one respect they were continuing the older Scottish tradition, for before the Reformation Scotland had been much more European than England, largely because of its close ties with France. Their interests were devoted to the handling of ideas which were common property in eighteenth-century Europe. If they owed any of their characteristic mental qualities to their Scottish background or heredity, they were not eager to publicize the fact. If Ramsay and those whom he represented can be said to have had as their ideal the re-establishment of a genuinely Scots culture so that Scotland could again take its place with honour among the nations of Europe, one might define the aim of the wits whom Hutcheson called together as the establishment of themselves, not as Englishmen, but as Europeans. In other words, while the first group wished to become Europeans by becoming genuinely Scottish again, the second group, abandoning peculiarly Scottish characteristics (such as the Scottish vernacular) as provincial and limiting their audience, wished to make the jump more directly.

Each group was patriotic in its own way. Men like Adam Smith, David Hume, and Hugh Blair were not, in spite of all their attempts to purge their works of Scotticisms, in any sense ashamed of being Scots or eager to become Englishmen. They lived and worked in Scotland and were leaders of Edinburgh social and intellectual life. If their aim had simply been to assimilate with England, they could have gone, as many a Scot had done before and has done since, to London. There were careers open to Scotsmen in eighteenth-century London – far too many, if we are to trust the enemies of Lord Bute, who attacked this Scottish Prime Minister of Britain for giving all the positions at his disposal to fellow Scotsmen. Lord Bute himself, a Scotsman if ever there was one, was the most influential statesman in England at the beginning of the reign of George III; he became Secretary of State in 1761. The Scottish John Home, author of the tragedy, *Douglas*, lived with him in London in the capacity of glorified secretary. No, it was not that the Scottish literati – as they liked to call themselves, though one of their wives suggested that 'eaterati' would be a more appropriate term – were ashamed of being Scots. It is true that they regarded Scots as a provincial or even a corrupt dialect of English, which ought to be kept out of written work, but at this period in Scottish history there was some excuse for the misconception. Their ambition, however, was not to be English but to be European. David Hume was more at home in Paris than in London. But for Allan Ramsay Edinburgh was the world, just as for Burns, Scotland was the world.

That the literati could be patriotic Scotsmen and yet ashamed of their native speech is clearly shown not only by Hume's statement quoted earlier but also by the part Hume played as patron of Scottish letters. Hume did his utmost to emphasize the significance of the Scottish poets who followed the English neoclassic tradition, and he trumpeted their claims as loudly as he could, but he seems to have completely ignored those who worked in the Watson-Ramsay tradition. Hume hailed Dr. Wilkie, author of the unbelievable *Epigoniad*, an epic poem in nine books, as 'the Scottish Homer', and the wholly worthless poems of the blind poet Dr. Blacklock were similarly regarded by the literati as the work of 'the Scottish Pindar'. Macpherson's Ossian (a rendering of Gaelic poetry in terms of sentimental English assumptions about the nature of primitive poetry and the natural man) was also viewed by the literati as Scotland's

Homeric poems, although the genuine Gaelic poets who were writing at this time were wholly ignored.

In James Beattie's privately printed edition of the works of his son, James Hay Beattie (Edinburgh, 1794), he gives us a sketch of his son's life which includes the following statement:

> At home, from his Mother and me, he learned to read and write. His pronunciation was not correct, as may well be supposed: but it was deliberate and significant, free from provincial pecularities, and such as an Englishman would have understood; and afterwards, when he had passed a few summers in England, it became more elegant than what is commonly heard in North Britain. He was early warned against the use of Scotch words and other similar improprieties; and his dislike to them was such, that he soon learned to avoid them; and, after he grew up, could never endure to read what was written in any of the vulgar dialects of Scotland. He looked at Mr. Allan Ramsay's poems, but he did not relish them.

This passage provides a good commentary on the attitude of the Scottish literati of the middle and late eighteenth century towards the literary tradition of their own country. The very term 'North Britain', with its implicit denial of the separate existence of Scotland, is eloquent.

Developments in mathematics, medicine, and other scientific subjects represent a large part of the achievement of the literati, but perhaps the most impressive achievement was in philosophy. In philosophy, as in the other activities of the literati, the attitude was antiprovincial, and the aim was European. That the important Scottish philosophers of this century did not build on the theology which had, in most cases, their nominal allegiance is an important and significant fact. Not only sceptics like Hume but professedly religious men like Hutcheson and Hugh Blair (the latter a minister of the Church of Scotland) adapted their religious ideas to an independently conceived philosophy, and not the other way round. That is why philosophy had an extremely important influence on eighteenth-century religion in Scotland, but religion, dominant as it was in so many aspects of the nation's life, had not any considerable influence on philosophy. Thus throughout the century we get a series of liberalizing movements in the Scottish Church which tended more and more to split off the Moderates from the more conservative elements and to make even the conservative elements split again and again among themselves.

Scottish philosophy in the eighteenth century thus had its origin in a professedly non-Scottish mood; a mood which impelled the philoso-phers to reject the official religious ideas of their country (so hotly debated and so keenly expounded) as a basis for the foundation of a new philosophical system, in favour of general principles which could be proved from common sense, individual introspection, or arguments from history and psychology.

By the middle of the century this new intellectual life in Scotland, more especially in Edinburgh, was beginning to show itself in full vigour. Hume had published his *Treatise on Human Nature* in 1739 and his *Essays Moral and Political* (with more success) in 1741–1742. His *Essay on Human Understanding* in 1748 established his reputation as a European philosopher. In 1753, William Robertson began his *History of Scotland*, published in 1759; his other histories followed (of Charles V, 1769, and of America, 1777). Principal of the University of Edinburgh and leader of the Moderate party in the Church of Scotland, Robertson was also Moderator of the General Assembly in 1763, thus demonstrating vividly the extent to which the Church of Scotland had become liberalized. Hugh Blair was appointed professor of rhetoric at Edinburgh in 1760 and of belles-lettres in 1762; his *Lectures on Rhetoric and Belles Lettres* appeared in 1783. Adam Smith, professor of moral philosophy at Glasgow from 1752 to 1763 but an Edinburgh resident from 1777, published his *Theory of Moral Sentiments* in 1759 and his *Wealth of Nations* in 1776. And this is only a microcosm of a much longer catalogue.

In 1754 the original *Edinburgh Review* was founded by a group of the literati (including Blair and Adam Smith), and though it ran only for two numbers, its contents are most illuminating for anyone interested in the intellectual life of the period. Writing in the second and final number, Adam Smith remarked: 'This country, which is just beginning to attempt figuring in the learned world, produces as yet so few works of reputation, that it is scarce possible a paper which criticizes upon them chiefly, should interest the public for any considerable time'. He advised the editors, therefore, to review foreign works, and, by way of example, himself embarked on an account of the French *Encyclopedia*. By 'foreign', Smith meant continental rather than English; so here again we find that the aim is to make Scotland European. And in the remark of Hume's quoted at the beginning of this chapter we can see that interesting com-bination of shame, at the Scots 'corrupt dialect', and the desire to make Scotland a European rather than an English country. Hume is proud of the place that Scotland has won in Europe. 'This is the historical age and we are the historical people', he exclaims proudly.

We might say, then, that the contrast between the Hutcheson tradition and the Watson tradition in eighteenth-century Scottish culture is not between English assimilationists and Scottish patriots, but between two kinds of Scottish patriots, each of which tried in different ways to enhance the culture of their country. And both groups can to some degree be explained as the reaction of sensitive and intelligent men to the political condition in which the Scotland they knew found herself.

If, therefore, we wish to see Burns in the cultural context of the Scotland of his day, we have to take all these elements into account. The total picture was, in fact, threefold. There was the native Lowland-Scots tradition, revived first by Watson and continued by Ramsay and Fergusson. This tradition was represented equally well by scholarly, creative, and social activities (David Herd, Robert Fergusson, the Cape Club). There was the ancient Gaelic tradition, representing a rather different Scotland from that of either the Hutcheson or the Watson tradition, and largely cut off from both of these; it was nevertheless very much alive in the middle of the century, in the poetry of Alexander Macdonald, Duncan Ban Macintyre, Dugald Buchanan, and Rob Donn. Jerome Stone called attention to this tradition in 1756 with his publication in the *Scots Magazine* of the first translations of Gaelic poetry ever printed in Scotland. Lastly, there was the new eighteenth-century tradition of the Edinburgh literati, who preserved the older Scottish 'European' outlook – the ties with France, the metaphysical habit – and thought of Scotland as the part of Britain that could best represent the British Isles in Europe. The literati were anxious to avoid all traces of any characteristically Scottish element in their speech or outlook, for they believed that Scotland would be greater in proportion as her distinguishing features were obliterated.

These three strands in eighteenth-century Scottish culture never really came together. It is true that in their own activity occasionally men like Henry Mackenzie seemed to unite them, but theirs was a superficial unification. The literati accepted Macpherson's Ossian partly because of Scottish patriotism and partly because the view Macpherson presented of a noble and primitive people coincided with their philosophy's a priori conceptions about such people. (And Hume was suspicious just because *his* philosophy justified no such view of the 'natural man'.) Similarly, Burns was hailed by Henry Mackenzie in 1787 as the 'Heaven-taught ploughman' and as an illustration of contemporary theories concerning the natural man. The literati were more suspicious of the results of an education from heaven in practice, however, than they were in theory – like the eighteenth-century clergyman mentioned by Mackenzie in his *Anecdotes*, who, crossing the Forth in a storm and being told by the ferryman, in answer to his inquiry if they were in danger, that 'we are in the hand of God', replied indignantly, 'Man, what kind of a hand is that to be in!'

Fergusson was not patronized and petted by the literati, although he did write quite a number of poems in regular neoclassic English. He made no real attempt to reconcile his literary activity with the sentimentality of Henry Mackenzie or the rhetorical theories of Hugh Blair. In fact, he laughed at Mackenzie, and in his poem, 'The Sow of Feeling', implicitly ridiculed Mackenzie's famous sentimental novel, *The Man of Feeling*. Burns, however, as we shall see, did for a time attempt a *rapprochement* with the literati and the tradition they represented, and this impact of the Watson tradition on the Hutcheson tradition was not altogether fortunate. Unlike Fergusson, Burns *was* to some degree taken up by the literati, and in studying his work and his literary career we have to take this fact into consideration. Fergusson, aloof from the literati yet as well educated as they, had no inferiority complex about his education and was therefore less likely to play into their hands. Burns, who was always self-conscious about his rustic upbringing, sometimes tried to present himself to genteel Edinburgh as the kind of natural man which some of the literati liked to talk about in their theoretical works, and it was not a comfortable role. In following Burns's career and development as a poet, therefore, we are led into the genteel atmosphere of cultured Edinburgh as we are not in dealing with Fergusson. The literati for a while took Burns to their heart and it was not good for him.

Any discussion, therefore, of Edinburgh's Golden Age, leads at some point to Burns but ignores Fergusson. In books about David Hume and John Home and James Beattie and Hugh Blair we hear about the *Scots Magazine* but not of Ruddiman's *Weekly Magazine*, because the literati read the former but not the latter. We hear, too, of Macpherson, who faked Gaelic poetry, and not of Jerome Stone, who genuinely translated it, or of Alexander Macdonald, whose poems, published in Edinburgh in 1751, represented the first book in Scottish Gaelic ever printed; we hear of the Select Society, where the wits of Edinburgh debated problems in philosophy, but not of the Cape Club, where Rab Fergusson and his cronies were singing over their modest ale old Scottish songs that were to quicken the imagination of Burns and produce the great, though short-lived, culmination of the one phase of Scottish literature in which the literati consistently failed – that of poetry.

It is not easy to see why the literati did so consistently fail in the field of poetry – why the work of John Home, Wilkie, Blacklock, and Beattie was so downright bad. The reason is partly that, although the insistence on English diction and the deliberate avoidance of a parochial attitude worked excellently in the purely intellectual disciplines, they were no recipe for producing poetry. Fergusson and Burns achieved success only when they repudiated the poetic tradition of the literati. The Scottish poets who worked in the fringes of the English neoclassic tradition did not as a rule achieve anything more than frigid exercises in a foreign idiom. Anyone who looks at that preposterous collection of poems published in Edinburgh in 1760 under the title *A Collection of Original Poems by The Rev. Mr. Blacklock, and other Scotch Gentlemen* will see this truth at once.

One should also note that many of the Scottish philosophers of the period explained their philosophical or literary principles with reference to the passions, and this made for a certain kind of corruption in literary and critical practice which was to prove dangerous for Scottish literature. However ingenious or adequate as a theoretical statement of the position a work like Blair's *Lectures on Rhetoric* or Kames's *Elements of Criticism* might be, the practical application of the critical ideas implied in these works was peculiarly liable to abuse, even by people like Blair and Kames themselves. The abuse lay in estimating the value of a work by the degree of emotional response it aroused and in combining with this rhetorical approach a precise analytic method of determining what elements in language and in style contribute to the various kinds of rhetorical effect; it also lay in rigid notions of what constitute (in Blair's phrase) 'good sense and refined taste'. When serious critics praise a play by saying that 'the ladies [in the audience] distinguished themselves by their virtuous distress', or assess a poem by the number of tears it arouses in the moral reader, obviously something has gone far wrong. This cult of critical sensibility (it affected literary practice, too, as Mackenzie's *Man of Feeling* shows, but the attitudes underlying Mackenzie's work are much more complicated than this) tended to result in the complete collapse of critical standards. When serious critics put the preposterous and trivial poems of Dr. Blacklock beside the work of Pope – or John Home's *Douglas* above Shakespeare, or the impossible *Epigoniad* of Dr. Wilkie beside the *Iliad*; when the literati of Edinburgh advised Burns to give up writing in Scots and model himself on Shenstone or Homer; when the same literati some years earlier wholly ignored the remarkable and to this day underestimated Scots poems of Fergusson – obviously something was very wrong with critical practice, however brilliant Scottish critical theory might be at this time.

We should remember also that standard English was in large measure a foreign tongue to many of the literati (even David Hume submitted his manuscripts to correction on these grounds; James Currie, Burns's first editor, maintained that Burns 'had less of the Scottish dialect than Hume'), and in judging it they had all the disadvantages of the man who judges literature written in a language which he knows but in which he is not at home. Therefore those writers and critics who avoided the dualism by sticking to the native tradition in which they were really at home produced both better poetry and better criticism of that poetry. Intellectual works, such as philosophies and histories, are not affected by such a linguistic problem; in fact, the discipline of turning a philosophical discourse into a carefully polished formal language is wholly beneficial; but it is different with poetry and the criticism of poetry. The literati were better philosophers than literary critics and better critical theorists than practical critics.

Not that the language of Burns was the spontaneous vernacular; in his best poems it is often English sprinkled with Scots. But the compromise language in which Burns so often wrote represented a natural and effective poetic vocabulary for him. It was not tailored to fit preconceived principles about what constitutes a 'liberal and elegant turn of mind' or to illustrate how 'a cultivated taste increases sensibility to all the tender and humane passions' or how the author is 'not deficient in elegance or ornament'. When Burns did so tailor his verse, with his eye on the genteel tradition in eighteenth-century Scottish criticism, the results, as we shall see, were not happy.

Such, then, was the intellectual atmosphere of the Scotland which produced Burns. We have seen something of the literary tradition that lay behind the revival led by Watson and Ramsay and noticed the other factors that contributed to the cultural climate of the period. It is time to introduce Burns himself and to trace his development as a poet.

GROWTH OF A POET

> There was a lad was born in Kyle,
> *which*   But whatna day o' whatna style,
> I doubt it's hardly worth the while
> To be sae nice wi' Robin.

So WROTE Robert Burns in 1785, when he was twenty-six years old, already a poet, but as yet known only in the neighbouring countryside through the circulation of his poems in manuscript and by word of mouth. 'Kyle' is the central district of Ayrshire, the county in southwest Scotland where Robin was born on January 25, 1759:

> Our monarch's hindmost year but ane
> Was five-and-twenty days begun,
> *January*   'Twas then a blast o' Janwar win'
> *wind*
> Blew hansel in on Robin.
> *first gift*

It was stormy weather that week, and a few days after Robert's birth in the clay cottage which his father had built with his own hands in the village of Alloway the wind blew out part of the gable, and the baby had to be carried through the storm to a neighbour's house where he stayed until his father could repair the damage. Alloway lies a few miles south of the county town of Ayr. William Burnes (so the poet's father always spelled his name) had left his native Kincardineshire, on the other side of Scotland, considerably further north, to find work; he went first to Edinburgh and soon after to Ayrshire, where he found employment as head gardener on the estate of Dr. Fergusson, 'a worthy gentleman' of some small fortune. He married Agnes Broun, the daughter of a neighbouring tenant farmer, and prepared to found a family.

William Burnes had not come south from Kincardine in any spirit of idle adventure. He had come with reluctance, after his own father's farming prospects had been ruined by the uncertainties produced by the Jacobite Rebellion of 1745–1746. 'I have often heard my father', wrote Robert Burns's younger brother Gilbert many years later, 'describe the anguish of mind he felt when they [William and his brother] parted on the top of a hill, on the confines of their native place, each going off their several way in search of new adventures, and scarcely knowing whither he went.' Those were difficult times for farmers, and throughout his life William Burnes was dogged by ill-luck in his farming ventures, until he died, prematurely worn out, early in 1784. Not content to be a rich man's gardener, he leased the farm of Mount Oliphant, a few miles west of Alloway, in 1765, and when, through no fault of his own, he found himself unable to make it pay, he took in 1777, at a grossly inflated rental, the farm of Lochlie, some ten miles northeast of Mount Oliphant; his struggles to keep Lochlie going, under the most unfavourable circumstances, caused his bankruptcy and death seven years later.

William Burnes, a stern but fundamentally humane man, was ambitious both for himself and his children. Robert, writing an account of his own early life to Dr. John Moore in August, 1787, remarked that if his father had continued as a gardener, 'I must have marched off to be one of the little underlings about a farm-house: but it was his dearest wish and prayer to have it in his power to keep his children under his own eye till they could discern between good and evil; so with the assistance of his generous Master my father ventured on a small farm in his estate'. The Mount Oliphant venture seems to have been embarked on largely for the sake of the children, so that they would not need to hire themselves out as farm servants, which was the general lot of children of mere 'peasants' in the Scotland of the time. William was thirty-six by the time he married, and his character was by now firmly set in its mould of stern sobriety. His greatest ambition was to bring up his children to be both educated and God fearing. He himself was no illiterate peasant, and liked nothing better than to engage in philosophical and theological discourse. In this he was characteristic of his class. Writing some three years after Robert Burns's death, Dr. Currie, the first editor of Burns's works, made these observations:

A slight acquaintance with the peasantry of Scotland, will serve to convince an unprejudiced observer that they possess a degree of intelligence not generally found among the same class of men in the other countries of Europe. In the very humblest condition of the Scottish peasants every one can read, and most persons are more or less skilled in writing and arithmetic; and under the disguise of their uncouth appearance, and of their peculiar manners and dialect, a stranger will discover that they possess a curiosity, and have obtained a degree of information corresponding to these acquirements.

This was more true of the men than of the women. Agnes Broun, Burns's mother, was unable to write, though she could manage to read the Bible. The wife of a tenant farmer had more practical duties than acquiring book learning, and Agnes was well skilled in all the household duties of a farm when she married William Burnes, twelve years her senior. She was skilled in other things, too: she had a good voice and a great store of songs, and Robert was at least as much indebted to her as to his father for his education as a poet. He owed a still greater debt to another unconscious teacher. 'In my infant and boyish days', wrote Burns in his autobiographical letter to Dr. Moore, 'I owed much to an old Maid of my Mother's, remarkable for her ignorance, credulity and superstition. – She had, I suppose, the largest collection in the county of tales and songs concerning devils, ghosts, fairies, brownies, witches, warlocks, spunkies, kelpies, elf-candles, dead-lights, wraiths, apparitions cantraips, giants, inchanted towers, dragons and other trumpery. – This cultivated the latent seeds of Poesy. . . .'

In his sixth year young Robert was sent to the local school at Alloway Miln, about a mile from the cottage. The parish schools of Scotland, in spite of the admirable legislation on the statute book, were often pretty haphazard affairs, and this one does not seem to have been in a flourishing condition. It was, according to Dr. Currie, 'taught by a person of the name of Campbell; but this teacher being in a few months appointed master of the work-house at Ayr, William Burnes, in conjunction with some other heads of families, engaged John Murdoch in his stead'. Murdoch was a priggish and pedantic young man of eighteen, who was boarded in turns by William Burnes and his fellow farmers while he instructed their children. In a letter written in 1799, Murdoch gave his own account of his teaching:

In 1765, about the middle of March, Mr. W. Burnes came to Ayr, and sent to the school, where I was improving in writing, under my good friend Mr. Robison, desiring that I would come and speak to him at a certain Inn, and bring my writing-book with me. This was immediately complied with. Having examined my writing, he was pleased with it; – (you will readily allow he was not difficult) and told me that he had received very satisfactory information of Mr. Tennant, the master of the English school, concerning my improvement in

English, and in his method of teaching. In the month of May following, I was engaged by Mr. Burnes, and four of his neighbours, to teach,
and accordingly began to teach the little school at Alloway, which was
situated a few yards from the argillaceous fabric above-mentioned.
[That is, the clay cottage, which Murdoch had referred to in an earlier
part of his letter. This continuous search for pretentious synonyms was
characteristic of Murdoch's method of instruction.] My five employers
undertook to board me by turns, and to make up a certain salary at the
end of the year, provided my quarterly payments from the different
pupils did not amount to that sum.

My pupil, Robert Burns, was then between six and seven years of
age; his preceptor, about eighteen. Robert and his younger brother,
Gilbert, had been grounded a little in English, before they were put
under my care. They both made a rapid progress in reading; and a
tolerable progress in writing. In reading, dividing words into syllables
by rule, spelling without book, parsing sentences, &c. Robert and
Gilbert were generally at the upper end of the class, even when ranged
with boys by far their seniors. The books most commonly used in the
school were, the *Spelling Book*, the *New Testament*, the *Bible*, *Mason's
Collection of Prose and Verse*, and *Fisher's English Grammar*. They
committed to memory the hymns and other poems of that collection,
with uncommon facility. This facility was partly owing to the method
pursued by their father and me in instructing them, which was, to
make them thoroughly acquainted with the meaning of every word
in each sentence, that was to be committed to memory. By the bye,
this may be easier done, and at an earlier period, than is generally
thought. As soon as they were capable of it, I taught them to turn verse
into its natural prose order; sometimes to substitute synonimous
expressions for poetical words, and to supply all the ellipses. These,
you know, are the means of knowing that the pupil understands his
author. These are excellent helps to the arrangement of words in
sentences, as well as to a variety of expressions.

The *Collection of Prose and Verse* by Arthur Masson (not Mason, as
both Burns and Murdoch later wrote) contained no representatives of
Scottish literature: it was a purely English compilation, containing
extracts from eighteenth-century English poets, including Thomson,
Gray, and Shenstone, passages from Shakespeare, Milton, and Dryden,
and prose selections from Addison and from the *Letters Moral and
Entertaining* of Elizabeth Rowe. In his autobiographical letter to Dr.
Moore Burns wrote that the earliest compositions he recollected taking

pleasure in were 'the vision of Mirza and a hymn of Addison's beginning – "How are Thy servants blest, O Lord!" I particularly remember
one half-stanza which was music to my boyish ears –

> "For though in dreadful whirls we hung,
>   High on the broken wave" –

I met with these pieces in Mason's English Collection, one of my school-
books.'

Masson's *Collection* played a most important part in Burns's literary
education. From it he learned what serious and respectable literature
ought to be; it gave him an insight into the genteel taste of his day, and
it in large measure formed his own taste in non-Scottish prose and
poetry. Much of it he committed to memory, and in later years he was to
strew his letters with quotations from the pieces in Masson. The
anthology gave him a feeling for formal utterance and often led him, as
far as his epistolary style was concerned, to employ an excessive formality. Elizabeth Rowe's *Letters Moral and Entertaining* were hardly
models of epistolary ease, and the stiffness of many of Burns's letters is to
be attributed to his early introduction to this kind of epistolary style and
to his ignorance of the more intimate and less public style of eighteenth-
century correspondence. In the Scottish folk tradition and in the literary
tradition represented by Ramsay and Fergusson he was eventually to
find models to suit his own genius in poetry, but he never found the
happiest prose models. Nevertheless, writing to close friends in moments
of relaxation, he did develop a fluent, informal English prose style, which
shows that Burns could handle standard English with perfect ease and
confidence, and that it was the defects of his models, not any linguistic
barrier, which made him often such a relatively poor performer in
standard English prose.

If the literature to which Murdoch introduced young Robert tended
on the whole to be formal, rhetorical and sentimental, we must remember that it did include Shakespeare and Milton and also that Murdoch's
manner of teaching consistently encouraged the virtues of clarity and
precision. 'That Burns in later life never had any difficulty in saying
precisely what he meant', observes Professor DeLancey Ferguson, 'he
probably owed at root to Murdoch's severe drill; that his style of saying
it was frequently much too formal he likewise owed to the dominie and
to the prose selections of Arthur Masson'.[1]

Murdoch was clearly on the side of the genteel tradition of his day;
literature for him consisted mostly of eighteenth-century English

writers with a sprinkling from the seventeenth century, and of some of
the neoclassic writers of France. Though it included the Scottish writers
who followed English models and wrote in an English neoclassic idiom,
it ignored the entire body of Scottish writings from the Scottish Chaucerians to Allan Ramsay (Fergusson was still in his teens at this time), and
of course the folk tradition which was not regarded as a literary tradition
at all. Of English literature before the eighteenth century, Shakespeare,
Milton, and Dryden, were almost the sole representatives. If the influences represented by John Murdoch had proved dominant in Burns's
development as a poet, he would have grown up to be another John
Home or James Beattie. Fortunately, the Scottish folk tradition did not
require an introduction from a schoolmaster, and other aspects of the
Scottish literary tradition forced themselves on Burns's attention while
his poetic career was still in its earliest stage.

Murdoch's training in spelling and grammar was sound, and there
was never a trace of rustic illiteracy about Robert's speech, written or
spoken. We must not forget, also, that he read the Bible continuously
throughout his youth; he soon acquired that familiarity with both the
Old and the New Testament which, though common among all classes
in his generation, seems so remarkable to many members of ours.
Masson's *Collection*, the Bible, a spelling book, and an English grammar –
solid enough fare for a small child and not altogether the pabulum we
would expect to nourish the future author of 'Holy Willie's Prayer' and
'Tam o' Shanter'.

Murdoch preferred the docile and tractable Gilbert to the elder
brother, and he has left a record of his opinion of the two as children
which surprises the modern reader and makes him wonder how much
insight into character or even ability Murdoch had.

Gilbert always appeared to me to possess a more lively imagination,
to be more of the wit, than Robert. I attempted to teach them a little
church-music. Here they were left behind by all the rest of the school.
Robert's ear, in particular, was remarkably dull, and his voice un-
tunable. It was long before I could get them to distinguish one tune
from another. [This of the future poet who was to display an ability to
distinguish the subtlest variations between different versions of the
same folk tune, who was to collect and help transcribe popular
melodies, and scores of whose finest poems were written to be sung
to specific airs.] Robert's countenance was generally grave, and expressive of a serious, contemplative, and thoughtful mind. Gilbert's
face said, *Mirth, with thee I mean to live*; and certainly, if any person

who knew the two boys, had been asked, which of them was the most likely to court the muses, he would surely never have guessed that Robert had a propensity of that kind.

It seems probable that even at this early age Robert had a tendency to intermittent moodiness. Throughout his life he was visited by periodic fits of depression from which (like Dr. Johnson) he sought refuge in company and conviviality. Some of his earliest poems are records of these moods, done in the eighteenth-century rhetorical style he had learned from Masson's *Collection*.

Let Murdoch tell the rest of the story of Robert's early education:

In the year 1767, Mr. Burnes quitted his mud edifice [identical with the 'tabernacle of clay', 'humble dwelling', and 'argillaceous fabric' of earlier parts of the letter: it is amusing to trace these indications of Murdoch's pedagogical method], and took possession of a farm (Mount Oliphant) of his own improving, while in the service of provost Ferguson. This farm being at a considerable distance from the school, the boys could not attend regularly; and some changes taking place among the other supporters of the school, I left it, having continued to conduct it for nearly two years and a half.

In the year 1772, I was appointed (being one of five candidates who were examined) to teach the English school at Ayr; and in 1773, Robert Burns came to board and lodge with me, for the purpose of revising his English grammar, &c. that he might be better qualified to instruct his brothers and sisters at home. He was now with me day and night, in school, at all meals, and in all my walks. At the end of one week, I told him, that, as he was now pretty much master of the parts of speech, &c. I should like to teach him something of French pronunciation, that when he should meet with the name of a French town, ship, officer, or the like, in the newspapers, he might be able to pronounce it something like a French word. Robert was glad to hear this proposal, and immediately we attacked the French with great courage.

Now there was little else to be heard but the declension of nouns, the conjugation of verbs, &c. When walking together, and even at meals, I was constantly telling him the names of different objects, as they presented themselves, in French; so that he was hourly laying in a stock of words, and sometimes little phrases. In short, he took such pleasure in learning, and I in teaching, that it was difficult to say which of the two was most zealous in the business; and about the end of the second week of our study of the French, we began to read a little of the *Adventures of Telemachus*, in Fénelon's own words.

But Robert was needed at the farm, and, in Murdoch's fancy phrase he 'was summoned to relinquish the pleasing scenes that surrounded the grotto of Calypso, and, armed with a sickle, to seek glory by signalizing himself in the fields of Ceres'. This youthful heavy labour on the farm, when times were bad and food cut down to a minimum, laid the foundations of the rheumatic heart disease which was eventually to be the cause of Burns's death.

We can fill in the details of Murdoch's account of Burns's early education by going to the accounts given by Robert himself and by his brother Gilbert. 'The first two books I ever read in private', wrote Robert in his autobiographical letter, 'and which gave me more pleasure than any two books I ever read again, were, the life of Hannibal [lent to him, Gilbert tells us, by Murdoch] and the history of Sir William Wallace. – Hannibal gave my young ideas such a turn that I used to strut in raptures up and down after the recruiting drum and bagpipe, and wish myself tall enough to be a soldier [we shall meet this desire to be a soldier later on, in some interesting forms]; while the story of Wallace poured a Scottish prejudice in my veins which will boil along there till the floodgates of life shut in eternal rest.' The life of Hannibal was probably a chapbook bought from an itinerant pedlar, while the *History of Sir William Wallace* was the modernization of Blind Harry's late fifteenth-century poem done by William Hamilton of Gilbertfield: it was probably Burns's first introduction (and from the literary point of view a rather shabby one) to the nonfolk side of Scottish literature.

Gilbert gives us some idea of how he and his brother were educated after Murdoch's removal in 1768. 'There being no school near us' [after Murdoch's departure from the neighbourhood], 'and our little services being useful on the farm, my father undertook to teach us arithmetic in the winter evenings, by candle-light, and in this way my two elder sisters got all the education they received'. Gilbert proceeds to recount 'a circumstance that happened at this time', which is worth quoting as throwing some light on the young Robert:

Murdoch came to spend a night with us, and to take his leave when he was about to go into Carrick. He brought us as a present and memorial of him, a small compendium of English Grammar, and the tragedy of *Titus Andronicus*, and by way of passing the evening, he began to read the play aloud. We were all attention for some time, till presently the whole was dissolved in tears. A female in the play (I have but a confused remembrance of it) had her hands chopt off, and her tongue cut out, and was then insultingly desired to call for water to wash her hands. At this, in an agony of distress, we with one voice desired he would read no more. My father observed, that if we would not hear it out, it would be needless to leave the play with us. Robert replied, that if it was left he would burn it. My father was going to chide him for this ungrateful return to his tutor's kindness; but Murdoch interfered, declaring that he liked to see so much sensibility; and he left *The School for Love*, a comedy (translated I think from the French) in its place.

This incident gives us insight not only into Robert's character but also into Murdoch's views concerning what was proper reading for children (Robert, the eldest, was only nine years old at the time). We should like to know what was going on in the mind of grave William Burnes as he heard the young tutor reading that bloody play to his children and whether it was courtesy towards his guest or genuine displeasure at Robert's attitude which made him start to chide Robert; one suspects it was the former.

Life at Mount Oliphant after Murdoch's departure from the neighbourhood was hard and bare. 'Nothing', wrote Gilbert, 'could be more retired than our general manner of living'. They rarely saw anyone except members of their own family, and the children had no other children of their own age to play with. 'My father was for some time almost the only companion we had. He conversed familiarly on all subjects with us as if we had been men, and was at great pains while we accompanied him in the labours of the farm, to lead the conversation to such subjects as might tend to increase our knowledge, or confirm us in virtuous habits.'

William Burnes provided what books he could for his children. He borrowed Salmon's *Geographical Grammar* and 'endeavoured to make us acquainted with the situation and history of the different countries in the world'. From 'a book-society in Ayr' he obtained William Derham's *Physico-Theology* and *Astro-Theology* (works which explore the wonders of astronomy in order to prove, by the well-known 'argument from design', the existence and beneficence of God) and John Ray's *The Wisdom of God Manifested in the Works of the Creation*. 'Robert read all these books', records Gilbert, 'with an avidity and industry scarcely to be equalled'. William Burnes also subscribed to Thomas Stackhouse's *New History of the Holy Bible*, first published in London in 1737 in two folio volumes, published in a revised second edition in 1742 and re-printed at Edinburgh in 1765 in six volumes (presumably the edition subscribed to by Burnes). This impressive work, which was biblical history rather than history of the Bible, helped to give Robert the solid understanding of biblical narrative which is evidenced so often in his letters. 'From this', wrote Gilbert, 'Robert collected a compe-tent knowledge of ancient history; for no book was so voluminous as to slacken his industry, or so antiquated as to damp his researches.'

A further contribution to the reading of the Burns family was 'a small collection of letters by the most eminent writers, with a few sensible directions for attaining an easy epistolary style', as Gilbert describes it, or, in Robert's words, 'a collection of letters by the Wits of Queen Anne's reign', obtained by a brother of Mrs. Burnes by mistake, when he thought he was buying a *Complete Letter-Writer*. This volume Robert 'pored over most devoutly', and it joined with other influences in making his epistolary style excessively formal. (Though Gilbert tells us that it included directions for attaining an easy epistolary style, it appears to have contained only stiff and formal letters written with an eye on the public by Pope, Bolingbroke, and others; the precise volume has never been identified.)

The next step in Robert's education was taken when he was 'about thirteen or fourteen'. 'My father', wrote Gilbert, 'regretting that we wrote so ill, sent us week about, during a summer quarter, to the parish school of Dalrymple, which, though between two and three miles distant, was the nearest to us, that we might have an opportunity of remedying this defect'. At about the same time the boys were able to borrow two volumes of Richardson's *Pamela* from 'a bookish acquain-tance of my father's'; – 'the only part of Richardson's works my brother was acquainted with', comments Gilbert, 'till towards the period of his commencing author. Till that time too he remained unacquainted with Fielding, with Smollet (two volumes of *Ferdinand Count Fathom*, and two volumes of *Peregrine Pickle* excepted) with Hume, with Robertson, and almost all our authors of eminence of the latter times'. Gilbert had a vague recollection of a book of English history that his father borrowed about this time 'from Mr. Hamilton of Bourtreehill's gardener', which seems to have dealt with the reigns of the later Stuarts. This brings us to the period of Murdoch's reappearance at Ayr, which produced Robert's second, though brief, period of discipleship. Murdoch seems to have taken a genuine interest in the Burns family. 'He sent us Pope's works', records Gilbert, 'and some other poetry, the first that we had an oppor-tunity of reading, excepting what is contained in *The English Collection*, and in the volume of *The Edinburgh Magazine* for 1772; excepting also *those excellent new songs* that are hawked about the country in baskets, or exposed on stalls in the streets.'

Robert seems to have acquired a smattering of Latin from 'Mr. Robinson, the established writing-master in Ayr, and Mr. Murdoch's particular friend', but, though he learned enough to quote a few tags in later poems and letters, he never took the study very seriously. He was, however, reading avidly whatever he could lay hands on, partly because of genuine eagerness to acquire an education and partly because of some vague sense that he wanted to equip himself to play a more important role in the world that would normally be expected of the son of a struggling tenant farmer.

At an early period Robert seems to have begun to resent all social distinctions, particularly those which divided his own class from the landowners and the wealthy merchants. In Scotland, there has always been a tradition of close association of all classes during childhood, with the social divisions manifesting themselves only in adult life; and it irked Robert to realize that youngsters who might regard him as an equal now would one day look down on him as a mere peasant.

> My vicinity to Ayr was of great advantage to me [he wrote in his autobiographical letter to Dr. Moore]. – My social disposition, when not checked by some modification of spited pride, like our catechism definition of Infinitude, was 'without bounds or limits'. – I formed many connections with other Youngkers who possessed superior advantages; the youngling Actors who were busy with the rehearsal of PARTS in which they were shortly to appear on that STAGE where, Alas! I was destined to drudge behind the SCENES. – It is not commonly at these green years that the young Noblesse and Gentry have a just sense of the immense distance between them and their ragged Play-fellows. – It takes a few dashes into the world to give the young Great man that proper, decent, unnoticing disregard for the poor, insignificant, stupid devils, the mechanics and peasantry around him; who perhaps were born in the same village. – My young Superiours never insulted the clouterly appearance of my ploughboy carcase, the two extremeties of which were often exposed to all the inclemencies of the seasons. – They would give me stray volumes of books; among them, even then, I could pick up some observations; and ONE, whose heart I am sure not even the MUNNY BEGUM's scenes have tainted, helped me to a little French.

*   *   *

Though Burns wrote this in 1787, looking back on his childhood after the experience of being patronized by the Edinburgh gentry, we can be fairly sure that he is right in laying emphasis on his youthful pride and class consciousness; for there is abundant evidence pointing in the same direction. His earliest poems, his earliest letters, and the opening entries in the Commonplace Book he began in the spring of 1783 all sound this note.

By 1771, there were seven children living in the Mount Oliphant farm house with William and Agnes Burnes. Robert and Gilbert had to take their share of the farm work; Murdoch testified that Robert was doing a man's work on the farm by the time he was fifteen. He must have been doing heavy enough 'boy's work' long before this; Gilbert tells us that he was threshing at the age of thirteen. But in spite of their efforts, the farm did not prosper. From 1774 until 1777, when William Burnes moved from Mount Oliphant to Lochlie, things were especially bad. Robert recalls these days in his letter to Dr. Moore:

> My father's generous Master died; the farm proved a ruinous bargain; and, to clench the curse, we fell into the hands of a Factor who sat for the picture I have drawn of one in my Tale of two dogs. – My father was advanced in life when he married; I was the eldest of seven children; and he, worn out by early hardship, was unfit for labour. – My father's spirit was soon irritated, but not easily broken. – There was a freedom in his lease in two years more, and to weather these two years we retrenched expences. – We lived very poorly; I was a dextrous Ploughman for my years; and the next eldest to me was a brother, who could drive the plough very well and help me to thrash. – A Novel-Writer might perhaps have viewed these scenes with some satisfaction, but so did not I: my indignation yet boils at the recollection of the scoundrel tyrant's insolent, threatening epistles, which used to set us all in tears.

Gilbert's account is even more vivid:

> To the buffetings of misfortune, we could only oppose hard labour and the most rigid economy. We lived very sparingly. For several years butcher's meat was a stranger in the house, while all the members of the family exerted themselves to the utmost of their strength, and rather beyond it, in the labours of the farm. My brother at the age of thirteen assisted in threshing the crop of corn, and at fifteen was the

principal labourer on the farm, for we had no hired servant, male or female. The anguish of mind we felt at our tender years, under these straits and difficulties, was very great. To think of our father growing old (for he was now above fifty) broken down with the long continued fatigues of his life, with a wife and five other children, and in a declining state of circumstances, these reflections produced in my brother's mind and mine sensations of the deepest distress.

In spite of the hard life and the family distresses – 'the chearless gloom of a hermit with the unceasing moil of a galley-slave', as Burns described it in his autobiographical letter – during this period (although just before things began to get really bad) he 'first committed the sin of RHYME'. Again, the story is best told in his own words:

You know our country custom of coupling a man and woman together as Partners in the labours of Harvest. – In my fifteenth autumn, my Partner was a bewitching creature who just counted an autumn less. – My scarcity of English denies me the power of doing her justice in that language; but you know the Scotch idiom, She was a bonie, sweet, sonsie lass. – In short, she altogether unwittingly to herself, initiated me in a certain delicious Passion, which in spite of acid Disappointment, gin-horse Prudence and bookworm Philosophy, I hold to be the first of human joys, our dearest pleasure here below. – How she caught the contagion I can't say; you medical folks talk much of infection by breathing the same air, the touch, &c. but I never expressly told her that I loved her. – Indeed I did not well know myself, why I liked so much to loiter behind with her, when returning in the evening from our labors; why the tones of her voice made my heartstrings thrill like an Eolian harp; and particularly, why my pulse beat such a furious ratann when I looked and fingered over her hand, to pick out the nettle-stings and thistles. – Among her other love-inspiring qualifications, she sung sweetly; and 'twas her favorite reel to which I attempted giving an embodied vehicle in rhyme. – I was not so presumtive as to imagine that I could make verses like printed ones, composed by men who had Greek and Latin; but my girl sung a song which was said to be composed by a small country laird's son, on one of his father's maids, with whom he was in love; and I saw no reason why I might not rhyme as well as he, for excepting smearing sheep and casting peats, his father living in the moors, he had no more Scholarcraft that I had. –

Thus with me began Love and Poesy; which at times have been my only, and till within this last twelvemonth have been my highest enjoyment.

'Thus with me began love and poesy': Burns here laid his finger on an important aspect of his art. Love (by which Burns clearly meant physical passion) and poesy were to go together for him whenever he worked in the Scots folk tradition, and particularly when he wrote songs. It is significant that he wrote this youthful poem to the girl's favourite reel tune; the full trilogy was love, poesy, and melody. But there was another factor, too, of which he was equally aware when he wrote this account. Though he was aware of his lack of Latin and Greek and felt that as a result he could not write verses to compete with printed ones (the fact that he felt this, however, indicates that he had an ambition to do so), he was stirred to emulation by learning that a 'small country laird's son' with no more education than he had written a song for the girl *he* was in love with. And Robert Burns could do as well as any small country laird's son! There was clearly a pride at work here – one of the many aspects of the pride which he himself diagnosed as one of the main constituents of his character – and the pride in this case was both social and literary. He, the son of a tenant farmer, would not be outdone by the son of a landowner. The literary emulation is of course easier to see. It played an important part in Burns's development as a Scottish poet. Some years later, when he came across Fergusson's Scots poems, he 'strung anew [his] wildly-sounding rustic lyre with *emulating* vigour'. The trilogy is thus to be expanded further, into a tetralogy – love, poesy, melody, and emulation. He did not, of course, always require all four elements, but they were all important in his career as a poet.

The girl for whom Burns wrote his first poem was Nelly Kilpatrick, and in 1783 he entered it in his Commonplace Book under the title SONG. – (*Tune* – 'I Am a Man Unmarried'), though it was never published in his lifetime. The entry in the Commonplace Book is preceded by this note:

There is certainly some connection between Love, and Music & Poetry; and therefore, I have always thought it a fine touch of Nature, that passage in a modern love composition

'As towards her cot he jogged along
Her name was frequent in his song – '

For my own part I never had the least thought or inclination of turning Poet till I got once heartily in Love, and then Rhyme and Song were, in a manner, the spontaneous language of my heart.

The song written for Nelly Kilpatrick has no special merit, but it has directness and simplicity, and it has a lilt to it. Unfortunately, the tune 'I Am a Man Unmarried' is unknown, so we cannot judge the success with which Burns wedded the words to the music in this his first song. It appears in the Commonplace Book with a 'Fal lal de dal' chorus:

> O once I lov'd a bonny lass
> Ay and I love her still
> And whilst that virtue warms my breast
>   I'll love my handsome Nell
>   Fal lal de dal &c.

> As bonny lasses I hae seen,
>   And mony full as braw;
> But for a modest gracefu' mien,
>   The like I never saw.

The fifth verse, which was Burns's favourite, gives, as he said, his idea of 'a sweet sonsy Lass':

> She dresses ay sae clean and neat
>   Both decent and genteel;
> And then there's something in her gate
> *makes*   Gars ony dress look weel.

The seventh and last verse might have been written by a minor English poet of the period; it derives as much from Masson's reader and from the collection of English songs he acquired about this time as from any Scottish source:

> 'Tis this in Nelly pleases me;
>   'Tis this inchants my soul;
> For absolutely in my breast
>   She reigns without controul.

It is interesting to find in this first poem by Burns a mingling of English and Scottish influences, with the English on the whole predominating. The vocabulary alternates between English and Scots. The first verse starts off with a genuine Scots folk feel about it, but the third line – 'And whilst that virtue warms my breast' – is pure English neoclassic in its idiom. (It should be noted, however, that Burns clearly intended a Scots *pronunciation* – witness his rhyming of 'still' with 'Nell'; in Scots the short 'i' of still is almost indistinguishable from the short 'e' of 'Nell'.) Burns's development as a poet was not from untutored Scots country bard to cultivated poetic craftsman; it would be truer to say that his progress was marked by his shedding of many of the influences that came from Masson and similar sources and his discovery of his native Scots literary tradition as well as of a more congenial and less conventional English idiom. But he never completely shed the traces of Murdoch's education, and they weave in and out of his later poetry unpredictably.

Hard times at Mount Oliphant also turned his thoughts to tragedy, and 'the bursting cloud of family misfortunes' led him to write a 'tragic fragment', or, as he describes it in the Commonplace Book, 'a penitential thought, in the hour of Remorse, Intended for a tragedy', which begins on a suitably melodramatic note:

> All devil as I am, a damned wretch;
> A hardened, stubborn, unrepenting villain:
> Still my heart melts at human wretchedness;
> And with sincere, though unavailing sighs
> I view the helpless children of distress.
> With tears indignant I behold th' Oppressor
> Rejoicing in the honest man's destruction
> Whose unsubmitting heart was all his crime.

Towards the end of the Mount Oliphant period, in the summer of 1775, Robert was sent to learn 'Mensuration, Surveying, Dialling, &c.' at a 'noted school' in Kirkoswald, about eight miles to the southwest and near the coast. Hugh Rodger, the schoolmaster, had the reputation of an expert in these subjects, and presumably William Burnes thought that it would help his son to learn the art of the surveyor and also that he would benefit generally from the mathematical training that he would receive. Though Robert later maintained that he acquired no formal knowledge at Kirkoswald, he must have learned enough mathematics to enable him in later life to handle the fairly complicated problems of measurement that faced an excise officer. His stay there also taught him what life was like in a smuggling town and provided him with the second of his recorded love affairs:

The contraband trade was at that time very successful; scenes of swaggering riot and roaring dissipation were as yet new to me, and I was no enemy to social life. – Here, though I learned to look unconcerned on a large tavern-bill [he cannot have meant any such bill of his own, for he certainly did not have the money to pay any large tavern-bills], and mix without fear in a drunken squabble, yet I went on with a high hand in my Geometry; till the sun entered Virgo, a month which is always a carnival in my bosom, a charming Fillette who lived next door to the school overset my Trigonomertry [sic], and set me off in a tangent from the sphere of my studies. – I struggled on with my Sines and Co-sines for a few days more; but stepping out to the garden one charming noon, to take the sun's altitude, I met with my Angel,

> ——'Like Proserpine gathering flowers,
> Herself a fairer flower'——

It was vain to think of doing any more good at school. – The remaining week I staid, I did nothing but craze the faculties of my soul about her, or steal out to meet with her; and the two last nights of my stay in the country, had sleep been a mortal sin, I was innocent.

Burns returned home 'having seen mankind in a new phasis'. He had arranged to correspond regularly with some of his schoolfellows; and he had enlarged his reading 'with the very important addition of Thomson's and Shenstone's works'. He kept copies of such of his letters as pleased him and flattered himself on being engaged in correspondence like a flourishing man of the world. It is unlikely, however, that, as he alleged in his letter to Dr. Moore, 'every post brought me as many letters as if I had been a broad, plodding son of Day-book & Ledger', for postage had to be paid by the recipient, and Burns could not have afforded such frequent luxuries.

At Whitsun, 1777, the Burns family moved to Lochlie, a farm of 130 acres which William Burnes leased from an Ayr merchant at the inflated yearly rental of one pound per acre. 'The nature of the bargain', wrote Burns to Dr. Moore, 'was such as to throw a little ready money in his hand at the commencement, otherwise the affair would have proved impracticable'. Whatever kind of advance William Burnes received from his landlord, the affair did prove 'impracticable' in the long run.

. . . For four years we lived comfortably here; but a lawsuit between him and his Landlord commencing, after three years tossing and

whirling in the vortex of Litigation, my father was just saved from
absorption in a jail by phthisical consumption, which after two years
promises, kindly stept in and snatch'd him away – 'To where the
wicked cease from troubling, and where the weary be at rest'.

But the difficult years at Lochlie had their compensations for Robert.
The first four years seem to have been happy enough, perhaps (as
tradition affirms and Dr. Snyder agrees) the happiest ever enjoyed by
the Burns family as a whole. The villages of Tarbolton and Mauchline
were both near by, and they provided for Robert companionship, a
social atmosphere, and an audience, three most important factors in his
development. Here he made friends with some of the characters whom
he was later to immortalize in his verse epistles. None of them was in any
way distinguished – David Sillar was a poor enough poetaster, John
Rankine a coarse if witty farmer, and 'Saunders' Tait an indifferent local
versifier, though he had his lively moments – but they all possessed the
essential quality of vitality, and because two of them had pretensions to
poetic fame and one had a reputation as a wit, they operated on Burns's
pride and produced in him the emulation he needed in order to embark
seriously on a poetic career.

Robert's education progressed. Let us turn again to his own account,
in his letter to Dr. Moore:

It is during this climacterick [the years at Lochlie] that my little story
is most eventful. – I was, at the beginning of this period, perhaps the
most ungainly, aukward being in my parish. No solitaire was less
acquainted with the ways of the world. – My knowledge of ancient
story was gathered from Salmon's and Guthrie's geographical
grammars; my knowledge of modern manners, and of literature and
criticism, I got from the Spectator. – These, with Pope's works, some
plays of Shakespear, Tull and Dickson on Agriculture, The Pantheon,
Locke's Essay on the human understanding, Stackhouse's history of
the bible, Justice's British Gardiner's directory, Boyle's lectures, Allan
Ramsay's works, Taylor's scripture doctrine of original sin, a select
Collection of English songs, and Hervey's meditations had been the
extent of my reading. – The Collection of Songs was my vade
mecum. – I pored over them, driving my cart or walking to labor,
song by song, verse by verse; carefully noting the true tender or
sublime from affectation and fustian. – I am convinced I owe much
to this for my critic-craft such as it is.

*   *   *

His reading is expanding, but it is still mostly in the neoclassic English tradition, though we note the significant exception of Allan Ramsay's poems. The list he gives here is a curious mixture – Pope, Shakespeare, theology, agriculture, geography, philosophy, and a smattering of varied belles lettres. Andrew Tooke's *Pantheon* was an account of Greek and Roman mythology, which was to serve him in lieu of a classical education.

It is significant that at this time (apparently in 1779, and not, as he states in his autobiographical letter, in his 'seventeenth year') he felt the need of 'giving his manners a brush', and attended a country dancing school for that purpose. 'My father had an unaccountable antipathy against these meetings', wrote Burns to Dr. Moore, 'and my going was, what to this hour I repent, in absolute defiance of his commands.' Ill-luck in his farming ventures was not improving William Burnes's temper, and it seems clear that in the years immediately preceding the death of the prematurely old farmer there developed a certain tension in the relations between father and son. 'My father, as I said before, was the sport of strong passions: from that instance of rebellion he took a kind of dislike to me, which, I believe was one cause of that dissipation which marked my future years'. But he hastens to add, 'I only say, Dissipation, comparative with the strictness and sobriety of Presbyterian country life; for though the will-o'-wisp meteors of thoughtless whim were almost the sole lights of my path, yet early ingrained Piety and Virtue never failed to point me out the line of Innocence.'

Robert, in fact, was growing more and more restless, increasingly dissatisfied with his lot and his prospects as the son of a struggling tenant farmer. Yet he did not quite know what he did want.

. . . The great misfortune of my life was, never to have AN AIM. – I had felt early some stirrings of Ambition, but they were the blind gropins of Homer's Cyclops round the walls of his cave: I saw my father's, situation entailed on me perpetual labor. – The only two doors by which I could enter the fields of fortune were, the most niggardly economy, or the little chicaning art of bargain-making; the first is so contracted an apperture, I never could squeeze myself into it; the last, I always hated the contamination of the threshold.

His undirected ambition was not made any easier to bear by the periodic fits of depression with which he was visited and which seem to have been the result of his cardiac trouble, which in turn was the product of over-work during the lean years towards the end of the Mount Oliphant period. He was alternately gay and morose, and growing ever more resentful of his station and his prospects.

> . . . Abandoned of aim or view in life; with a strong appetite for sociability, as well from native hilarity as from a pride of observation and remark; a constitutional hypochondriac taint which made me fly solitude; add to all these incentives to social life, my reputation for bookish knowledge, a certain wild, logical talent, and a strength of thought something like the rudiments of good sense, made me generally a welcome guest; so 'tis no great wonder that always 'where two or three were met together, there was I in the midst of them.'

Although at this period male companionship meant most to Burns – and indeed, he always depended on it – he was becoming more and more interested in the opposite sex as he matured sexually. His early affairs were wholly innocent, but there seem to have been many of them. 'My heart was completely tinder, and was eternally lighted up by some Goddess or other.' He soon achieved a reputation as a rustic gallant, and one well qualified to assist others in their amours. 'A country lad rarely carries on an amour without an assisting confident,' he explained to Dr. Moore. There was no privacy in the crowded farmhouses where Burns and his friends lived, and courting was done in the open air, with the help of suitable messengers.

> . . . I possessed a curiosity, zeal and intrepid dexterity in these matters which recommended me a proper Second in duels of that kind; and I dare say, I felt as much pleasure at being in the secret of half the amours in the parish, as ever did Premier at knowing the intrigues of half the courts of Europe.

Burns seems to have written love letters for his friends and to have thoroughly enjoyed his position as assistant to the parish in matters of love.

> . . . To the sons and daughters of labour and poverty they are matters of the most serious nature: to them, the ardent hope, the stolen interview, the tender farewell, are the greatest and most delicious part of their enjoyments.

Love-making, in fact, was the only relaxation which the hard-working Scottish peasant could afford. 'Puir bodies hae nothing but mow', as

Burns summarized the position bluntly but effectively in one of his bawdy songs.

Love-making, as we have seen, was associated for Burns with poetry; his feeling for Nelly Kilpatrick inspired his first poem and it was to be expected that his later experiences with women would inspire him in a similar way. The second of the songs in the Kilmarnock edition was the result of his affair with Peggy Thomson, the Kirkoswald girl who overset his trigonometry, and it is possible that other early love poems have not been preserved. The extant early poems that follow Nelly's song are, however, mostly 'occasional' pieces arising out of a variety of incidents and moods; it did not take him long to extend his poetic activities beyond the love song. What encouraged him most was his audience. He now had friends and companions to whom he could recite his verses and whose applause and appreciation fired his ambition. Clear evidence of his need and use of an audience can be seen in the founding of the Tarbolton Bachelors' Club in November, 1780. The prime mover here was clearly Burns, and the club's rules and regulations, printed by Dr. Currie from a 'curious document, evidently the work of our poet', give us an interesting insight into his state of mind at this time:

Rules and Regulations to be observed in the Batchelor's Club

1st. The club shall meet at Tarbolton every fourth Monday night, when a question on any subject shall be proposed, disputed points of religion only excepted, in the manner hereafter directed; which question is to be debated in the club, each member taking whatever side he thinks proper.

2nd. When the club is met, the president, or he failing, some one of the members till he come, shall take his seat; then the other members shall seat themselves, those who are for one side of the question on the president's right hand, and those who are for the other side on his left. . . .

3rd. The club met and seated, the president shall read the question out of the club's book of records, . . . then the two members nearest the president shall cast lots who of them shall speak first. . . .

4th. The club shall then proceed to the choice of a question for the subject of next night's meeting. The president shall first propose one, and any other member who chuses may propose more questions; and whatever one of them is most agreeable to the majority of the members, shall be the subject of debate next club-night.

5th. The club shall lastly elect a new president for the next meeting. . . . Then after a general toast to the mistresses of the club, they shall dismiss.

6th. There shall be no private conversation carried on during the time of debate, nor shall any member interrupt another while he is speaking, under the penalty of a reprimand from the president for the first fault, doubling his share of the reckoning for the second, trebling it for the third, and so on in proportion for every other fault; provided always however that any member may speak at any time after leave asked and given by the president. All swearing and profane language, and particularly all obscene and indecent conversation, is strictly prohibited, under the same penalty as aforesaid. . . .

7th. No member, on any pretence whatever, shall mention any of the club's affairs to any other person but a brother member, under pain of being excluded; and particularly if any member shall reveal any of the speeches or affairs of the club with a view to ridicule or laugh at any of the rest of the members, he shall be for ever excommunicated from the society; and the rest of the members are desired, as much as possible, to avoid, and have no communication with him as a friend or comrade.

8th. Every member shall attend at the meetings, without he can give a proper excuse for not attending, . . .

9th. The club shall not consist of more than sixteen members, all batchelors, belonging to the parish of Tarbolton; except a brother member marry, and in that case he may be continued, if the majority of the club think proper. . . .

10th. Every man proper for a member of this Society, must have a frank, honest, open heart; above any thing dirty or mean; and must be a professed lover of one or more of the female sex. No haughty, self-conceited person, who looks upon himself as superior to the rest of the Club, and especially no mean-spirited, worldly mortal, whose only will is to heap up money, shall upon any pretence whatever be admitted. In short, the proper person for this Society is, a cheerful, honest-hearted lad; who, if he has a friend that is true, and a mistress that is kind, and as much wealth as genteely to make both ends meet – is just as happy as this world can make him.

This is an extraordinary document to come from the pen of the son of a struggling Scottish tenant farmer living in a relatively remote part of the country. (Burns at this time had never been in any city larger than Ayr, which, though a moderately busy town, was hardly a cultural centre.) The inspiration here is clearly English; these young men were trying to domicile the English genteel tradition in rural Scotland. The careful formality, the insistence on parliamentary procedure, the pure neoclassic English of the statement – these show an ambition to emulate the kind of thing Burns had read about in English novels and essays. The fear of ridicule, the remarkable sensitivity to the potential sneers of any 'haughty, self-conceited person, who looks upon himself as superior to the rest of the Club', are thoroughly characteristic of Burns, and we recognize his hand, too, in the insistence that members should have 'a frank, honest, open heart' and in the curious stipulation that every member 'must be a professed lover of *one or more* of the female sex.' We see here the germ of those views on morality which are to be found later in Burns's poems and letters.

'After agreeing on these, and some other regulations', wrote Burns (if it was Burns) in the account of the club printed by Dr. Currie, 'we held our first meeting at Tarbolton, in the house of John Richard, upon the evening of the 11th of November 1780, commonly called Hallowe'en, and after choosing Robert Burns president for the night, we proceeded to debate on this question – *Suppose a young man, bred a farmer, but without any fortune, has it in his power to marry either of two women, the one a girl of large fortune, but neither handsome in person, nor agreeable in conversation, but who can manage the household affairs of a farm well enough; the other of them a girl every way agreeable, in person, conversation, and behaviour, but without any fortune: which of them shall he choose?'* There can be no doubt about who suggested this question or about the answer its author would have given. Here is Burns's class consciousness again, his pride, his sensitivity about his station in life. Other questions debated by the club reflect a similar state of mind: 'Whether is a young man of the lower ranks of life likeliest to be happy who has got a good education, and his mind well informed, or he who has just the education and information of those around him?' One young man in the lower ranks of life was certainly worrying about these matters.

Burns got some relief in discussing these things with his friends. In the first of his extant letters (it is in a fragmentary state), dated July 29, 1780, he writes to his friend William Niven about pride (which properly joined with other qualities is 'part of the noblest virtues'), and phrases like 'generous, frank, open' emerge from the torn page to suggest that Burns was discussing human nature and his ideal of good character. In another letter to Niven, later in the same year, he is asking him how he is progressing 'in the cultivation of the finer feelings of the heart'; for by this time he had discovered Henry Mackenzie's *Man of Feeling* and had been precipitated into the mainstream of eighteenth-century sentimentalism.

'My life flowed on much in the same tenor till my twenty third year', says the autobiographical letter, speaking of this period. 'Vive l'amour et vive la bagatelle, were my sole principles of action. – The addition of two more Authors to my library gave me great pleasure; Sterne and Mackenzie. – Tristram Shandy and the Man of Feeling were my bosom favourites.' These two works, with Macpherson's Ossian, were the last important representatives of the eighteenth-century English literary tradition (for Mackenzie, though a patriotic Scot, wrote his *Man of Feeling* in an English tradition, and Ossian was written for English sentimentalists) which were to influence Burns. Their influence was to remain with him all his life, for the simple reason that they provided him with a literary pose in which he could express his feelings of pride, ambition, and sensitivity without giving himself away directly. The sententious moralizing letters about human character and sensibility in which he was indulging in the early 1780's show him in this pose. It remained a favourite pose; yet it was a constant threat to his integrity as a poet, and he did his best work only in periods when he cast it off. That he did cast it off more and more often, and assumed it in his later years only half-ironically or when deliberately playing a part before somebody with whom for one reason or another he could not be himself, made possible his achievements of real poetic stature.

Meanwhile, he continued to write poetry. 'Poesy was still a darling walk for my mind, but 'twas only the humour of the hour. – I had usually half a dozen or more pieces on hand; I took up one or other as it suited the momentary tone of the mind, and dismissed it as it bordered on fatigue. – My Passions when once they were lighted up, raged like so many devils, till they got vent in rhyme; and then conning over my verses, like a spell, soothed all into quiet.' He mentions as having been written in this period, 'Winter, a Dirge', 'The Death of Poor Mailie', 'John Barleycorn', and three of the songs in the Kilmarnock edition.

These are the earliest of the pieces printed at Kilmarnock; there were many more written at this time that were not published until much later.

In 1780 or 1781 Burns seems to have had a love affair with a girl who worked on a neighbouring farm. Alison Begbie, the third recorded name among Burns's loves, remains a shadowy figure; yet the affair was apparently his most serious to date. If the five letters he addressed to 'My dear A.'[2] were, as seems very probable, really written to her, it is clear that he proposed marriage to her and was rejected. The letters are curiously formal and stilted. The third opens with the young farmer's remarking, 'I do not remember, in the course of your acquaintance and mine, ever to have heard your opinion on the ordinary way of falling in love amongst people of our station in life: I do not mean the persons who proceed in the way of bargain, but those whose affection is really placed on the person' – and Alison must have been thoroughly bewildered by them. We gather from the final letter, which maintains a tone of proud sorrow and an astonishing objectivity ('It would be weak and unmanly to say that without you I never can be happy; but sure I am, that sharing life with you, would have given it a relish, that, wanting you, I can never taste'), that the affair ended with a formal proposal on his part and a formal rejection on hers. After this rebuff he was careful to conduct his wooing in a more direct manner, except in the instance of Mrs. M'Lehose ('Clarinda'), the grass widow whom he met later in Edinburgh and with whom he had a long epistolary affair; but Clarinda was a special type, a passionate lady full of genteel inhibitions, who could be approached only in this artificial way.

The songs 'Bonie Peggy Alison' and 'Mary Morison' may have been written for Alison Begbie. The first is a simple love song in the pure folk tradition, based on an old fragment and set to a reel tune; one can hear the dancing steps in the chorus:

> And I'll kiss thee yet, yet
> And I'll kiss thee o'er again
> And I'll kiss thee yet, yet
> My bonie Peggy Alison.

'Mary Morison' is a more serious and polished performance, with considerable influence from the English tradition. The interesting eight-line stanza he employs (with the second, fourth, fifth, and seventh lines rhyming, binding the stanza together) makes possible a slowness of movement and a gravity of utterance which distinguish the poem sharply from the tripping liveliness of 'Bonie Peggy Alison'; there is an elegiac strain both in the words and the melody, which is reinforced by a fine sense of phrasing and a carefully controlled note of self-pity. Altogether, 'Mary Morison' is the most successful of his early songs.

Meanwhile, Robert and his brother Gilbert were giving thought to methods of improving conditions on the farm. They rented about three acres of land from their father to try their hand at cultivating flax. William Burnes seems to have thought that the entire farm might be turned over to flaxgrowing and thus made more of an economic success. In any event, it was proposed in the summer of 1781 that Robert go to Irvine, a flourishing seaport some twelve miles north of Ayr and a centre of the flax-dressing industry, to learn how to dress flax so that they could save money by taking care of the flax at home. Robert's stay at Irvine was a turning point in his development. This is how he described it in his letter to Dr. Moore:

My twenty third year was to me an important era. – Partly thro' whim, and partly that I wished to set about doing something in life, I joined with a flax-dresser in a neighbouring town, to learn his trade and carry on the business of manufacturing and retailing flax. – This turned out a sadly unlucky affair. – My Partner was a scoundrel of the first water who made money by the mystery of thieving; and to finish the whole, while we were giving a welcome carousal to the New year, our shop, by the drunken carelessness of my Partner's wife, took fire and was burnt to ashes; and left me like a true Poet, not worth sixpence. – I was oblidged to give up business, the clouds of misfortune were gathering thick round my father's head, the darkest of which was, he was visibly far gone in a consumption; and to crown all, a belle-fille whom I adored and who had pledged her soul to meet me in the field of matrimony, jilted me with peculiar circumstances of mortification. [This is apparently a reference to his affair with Alison Begbie, but if the letters we have referred to were written to Alison, Burns was not telling the truth in saying that she jilted him: she simply refused him when he proposed. Burns's pride and sensitivity must have made him change the story, consciously or unconsciously.] – The finishing evil that brought up the rear of this infernal file was my hypochondriac complaint being irritated to such a degree that for, three months I was in a diseased state of body and mind. . . .

From this adventure I learned something of a town-life. – But the principal thing that gave my mind a turn was, I formed a bosom-friendship with a young fellow, the first created being I had ever seen, but a hapless son of misfortune. – He was the son of a plain mechanic; but a great Man in the neighbourhood taking him under his patronage gave him a genteel education with a view to bettering his situation in life. – The Patron dieing just as he was ready to launch forth into the world, the poor fellow in despair went to sea; where after a variety of good and bad fortune, a little before I was acquainted with him, he had been set ashore by an American Privateer on the wild coast of Connaught, stript of everything. . . .

This gentleman's mind was fraught with courage, independence, Magnanimity, and every noble, manly virtue. – I loved him, I admired him, to a degree of enthusiasm; and I strove to imitate him. – In some measure I succeeded: I had the pride before, but he taught it to flow in proper channels. – His knowledge of the world was vastly superiour to mine, and I was all attention to learn. – He was the only man I ever saw who was a greater fool than myself when WOMAN was the presiding star; but he spoke of a certain fashionable failing with levity, which hitherto I had regarded with horror. – Here his friendship did me a mischief. . . . My reading was only encreased by two stray volumes of Pamela, and one of Ferdinand, Count Fathom, which gave me some idea of Novels. – Rhyme, except some religious pieces which are in print, I had given up; but meeting with Fergusson's Scotch Poems, I strung anew my wildly-sounding, rustic lyre with emulating vigour.

Irvine was at this time a prosperous seaport, larger and busier than the county town of Ayr itself. (At the end of the seventeenth century it was considered the third seaport in Scotland, but the slow silting-up of the harbour gradually reduced its importance.) The town was full of sailors, smugglers, and other picturesque characters, as well as followers of less adventurous occupations, including (according to the article on Irvine in the *Statistical Account of Scotland*, written by the parish minister in 1791) weavers, shoemakers, smiths, tailors, coopers, masons, wrights, maltsters, butchers, bakers, cloth merchants, chandlers, physicians (but only one), surgeons, writers (that is, lawyers), saddlers, druggists, coppersmiths, tinkers, barbers, coal hewers, carters, and carriers, not to mention three master shipbuilders, a tan work, a rope work, a bleach field, a distillery, and 'one small brewery'. While, according to the *Statistical Account*, 'manufactures, as yet, are not carried on here to any extent', and 'the young men, in general, are sailors, or go abroad to the West Indies and America as storekeepers and planters', the beginnings of the Industrial Revolution can be seen in the report that 'last year a spinning

Jenny was erected, which employs about 80 hands.' Irvine was the busiest town Burns had yet seen, and it fascinated him.[3]

Burns arrived at Irvine in a mood of bitterness and recklessness. He had been rejected (if not jilted) by the first girl to whom he had proposed marriage; the economic position at Lochlie was getting steadily worse; his health was not good, and as a result he was becoming more and more subject to fits of acute depression. The rheumatic endocarditis, of which he eventually died, was already creeping up on him, and the 'dull headache' and 'palpitation of the heart' of which Gilbert speaks in his account of his brother's life were symptoms of this disease, not, as he himself believed, mere hypochondria. But none of these circumstances could dampen his curiosity about life in the bustling town or his interest in observing his fellow men. Moods of gaiety and excitement seem to have alternated with fits of depression. Such was his general state when he met Richard Brown, the educated sailor, the man of the world, the romantic figure who had really seen life and could act as a guide to the young farmer in his exploration of city customs. The space he devotes to Brown in his autobiographical letter is clear evidence of Brown's importance to him.

The story of the New Year's Eve carouse and the failure of Burns's ambitions as a flax dresser is less significant than the general effect on him of life in Irvine and his friendship with Brown. His earlier love affairs had been ardent, but they remained innocent; it was Brown who taught him to lose his horror at the idea of fornication. (Brown later denied this, and some biographers have attributed this step in Burns's education to his stay in Kirkoswald; but when Brown denied it he had become a respectable and happily married middle-class husband, who would not have liked it noised about that he had first taught Robert Burns how to seduce the girls. Further, Burns always tried to tell the truth about himself, and he had no reason for lying here.) Brown stimulated his ambition and increased his discontent with his present lot. Writing to Brown in December, 1787, Burns looked back on this period and wrote:

I have met with few things in life which has given me more pleasure than Fortune's kindness to you, since those days in which we met in the vale of misery; as I can honestly say, that I never met with a man who more truly deserved it, or to whom my heart more truly wish'd it. – I have been very much indebted, since that time, to your story and sentiments, for steeling my heart against evils of which I have had a pretty decent share. – My will-o'-wisp fate, you know: do you recollect a sunday we spent in Eglinton woods? you told me, on my repeating some verses to you, that you wondered I could resist the temptation of sending verses of such merit to a magazine: 'twas actually this that gave me an idea of my own pieces which encouraged me to endeavour at the character of a Poet.

The poem which Brown admired was probably the song 'I Murder Hate by Field or Flood', which in one manuscript has the title 'On the great recruiting during the American War', which would date it not later than 1781. It is a song of sexual swagger, English rather than Scots in inspiration:

> I murder hate by field or flood,
>   Tho' Glory's name may screen us.
> In wars at hame I'll spend my blood—
>   Life-giving wars of Venus.
> The deities that I adore
>   Are Social Peace and Plenty:
> I'm better pleased to make one more
>   Than be the death of twenty.
>
> I would not die like Socrates,
>   For all the fuss of Plato;
> Nor would I with Leonidas,
>   Nor yet would I with Cato;
> The zealots of the Church and State
>   Shall ne'er my mortal foes be;
> But let me have bold Zimri's fate
>   Within the arms of Cozbi.

If, as seems probable, this was the song which aroused Brown's enthusiasm (and it is just the type of thing Brown would have enjoyed), the fact will explain Burns's own later fondness for it; many years after he had written it he inscribed its first stanza on a windowpane in Dumfries, and he included the entire poem in the manuscript collection of a number of his poems which he made for Robert Riddell between 1789 and 1791.

At Irvine, then, he first met serious encouragement to publish his poems, and the prospect of becoming something more than a rustic bard like Sillar or Lapraik was opened to him; but at Irvine also his fits of depression, accompanied by a sense of being doomed to an early death, first became really serious. A letter he wrote to his father on December 27, 1781, is full of gloom and foreboding, and though it is couched in a deliberately artificial language and actually includes a sentence lifted without acknowledgment from Mackenzie's *Man of Feeling*, it seems to reflect his real state of mind at the time. 'The weakness of my nerves has so debilitated my mind,' he writes, 'that I dare not, either review past events, or look forward into futurity; for the least anxiety, or perturbation in my breast, produces most unhappy effects on my whole frame'. He talks of looking forward to death, quotes from Pope and from the Bible, and continues: 'As for this world I despair of ever making a figure in it – I am not formed for the bustle of the busy nor the flutter of the Gay [this is the echo from *The Man of Feeling* – from the hero's speech on his death bed]. I shall never again be capable of it'. But another current of thought is evident when he adds: 'I foresee that Poverty & Obscurity await me & I am, in some measure prepared & daily preparing to meet & welcome them'. Although his melancholy was in part the effect of physiological causes, it was also in some degree the result of frustrated ambition; he was becoming more and more distressed at the thought of living out his life a struggling tenant farmer. It was not the hard work he objected to; he wanted a wider stage.

At this time he composed several religious and melancholy poems, wholly in the English tradition, which we discuss in the next chapter. Copying one of these into his Commonplace Book in March, 1784, he noted:

> There was a certain period of my life that my spirit was broke by repeated losses & disasters, which threatened, & indeed effected the utter ruin of my fortune. My body too was attacked by that most dreadful distemper, a Hypochondria, or confirmed Melancholy: in this wretched state, the recollection of which makes me yet shudder, I hung my harp on the willow trees, except in some lucid intervals, in one of which I composed the following—

Burns returned from Irvine in the early spring of 1782, his flax-dressing venture abandoned presumably as a result of his having been burned out on New Year's Eve. Things at Lochlie were getting worse and worse. William Burnes became involved in a dispute over the amount of his rent and the person to whom it was legally payable. The resultant legal proceedings impoverished and exhausted him; he was ill and prematurely old, and these troubles helped to bring about his death in February, 1784.

Robert, in the midst of the hard work at the farm, comforted himself by adopting the pose of the sardonic observer of men and manners – a pose which he managed to combine with that of the Man of Feeling (a combination which may seem paradoxical but which Henry Mackenzie himself had managed to maintain). 'I have nothing to tell you of news', he wrote to Thomas Orr in September, 1782, '—studying men, their manners & their ways, as well as I can. Believe me Tom, it is the only study in this world will yield solid satisfaction.' Writing again to Orr the following November, he remarked how he loved 'to see a man who has a mind superiour to the world and the world's men, a man who, conscious of his own integrity, and at peace with himself, despises the censures and opinions of the unthinkable rabble of mankind. The distinction of a poor man and a rich man is something indeed, but it is nothing to the difference between either a wise man or a fool, or a man of honor and a knave'.

He had become a Freemason before leaving for Irvine, joining the St. David's Lodge of Tarbolton partly for the insurance that membership automatically brought (for the prime purpose of such local Scottish lodges was assistance to distressed members) but also for social reasons. He liked an audience, and he continued to seek it wherever he could find it. David Sillar, the 'brother poet' with whom he exchanged verse letters, later gave an account of Burns at this period in a letter to Robert Aiken of Ayr:

Mr Robert Burns was sometime in the parish of Tarbolton prior to my acquaintance with him. His social disposition easily procured him acquaintance; but a certain satirical seasoning, with which he and all poetical geniuses are in some degree influenced, while it set the rustic circle in a roar, was not unaccompanied by its kindred attendant – suspicious fear. I recollect hearing his neighbours observe he had a great deal to say for himself, and that they suspected his *principles*. He wore the only tied hair in the parish; and in the church, his plaid, which was of a particular colour, I think *fillemot*, he wrapped in a particular manner around his shoulders. . . .

After the commencement of my acquaintance with the bard, we frequently met upon Sundays at church, when, between sermons, instead of going with our friends or lasses to the inn, we often took a walk in the fields. In these walks I have frequently been struck by his facility in addressing the fair sex; and many times, when I have been bashfully anxious how to express myself, he would have entered into conversation with them with the greatest ease and freedom; and it was generally a death-blow to our conversation, however agreeable, to meet a female acquaintance. Some of the few opportunities of a noontide walk that a country life allows her laborious sons, he spent on the banks of the river, or in the woods in the neighbourhood of Stair. . . . Some book (especially one of those mentioned in his letter to Mr Murdoch) he always carried, and read when not otherwise employed. It was likewise his custom to read at table. In one of my visits to Lochlie, in time of a sowen supper, he was so intent on reading, I think 'Tristram Shandy', that his spoon falling out of his hand, made him exclaim, in a tone scarcely imitable, 'Alas, poor Yorick!'

He had in his youth paid considerable attention to the arguments for and against the doctrine of original sin, then making considerable noise in the neighbourhood of Ayr; and having perused Dr Taylor's work on that subject, and also a book called 'Letters concerning Religion essential to Man', his opinions, when he came to Tarbolton, were consequently favourable to what you Ayr people call the 'moderate side'. The religion of the people of Tarbolton at that time was purely that of their fathers, founded on the Westminster Confession, and taught by one generation to another, uncontaminated by reading, reflection, and conversation; and, though divided into different sectaries, the Shorter Catechism was the line which bounded all their controversies. The slightest insinuation of Taylor's opinions made his neighbours suspect, and some even avoid him, as an heretical and dangerous companion.

The letter to Murdoch to which Sillar referred was written by Burns in January, 1783, and though he is probably showing off a little to his former teacher, it is worth quoting because it shows the attitude he liked to adopt at this time, as well as the books he was reading:

. . . I do not doubt, Sir, but you will wish to know what has been the result of all the pains of an indulgent father, and a masterly teacher; and I wish I could gratify your curiosity with such a recital as you would be pleased with; but that is what I am afraid will not be the case. I have, indeed, kept pretty clear of vicious habits; & in this respect, I hope, my conduct will not disgrace the education I have gotten, but, as a man of the world, I am most miserably deficient. . . . – I seem to be one sent into the world, to see, and observe; and I very easily compound with the knave who tricks me of my money, if there be any thing original about him which shews me human nature in a different light from anything I have seen before. In short, the joy of my heart is to 'study men, their manners, and their ways'; and for this darling subject, I chearfully sacrifice every other consideration. I am quite indolent about those great concerns that set the bustling, busy Sons of Care agog. . . . However, I am under no apprehensions about that, for though indolent, yet so far as an extremely delicate constitution permits, I am not lazy; and in many things, especially in tavern matters, I am a strict economist; not, indeed, for the sake of the money; but one of the principal parts in my composition is a kind of pride of stomach; and I scorn to fear the face of any man living: above every thing, I abhor as hell, the idea of sneaking in a corner to avoid a dun – possibly some pitiful, sordid wretch, who in my heart I despise and detest. 'Tis this, and this alone, that endears economy to me. In the matter of books, indeed, I am very profuse. My favourite authors are of the sentim[1] kind, such as Shenstone, particularly his Elegies, Thomson, Man of Feeling, a book I prize next to the Bible, Man of the World, Sterne, especially his Sentimental journey, Macpherson's Ossian, &c. these are the glorious models after which I endeavour to form my conduct, and 'tis incongruous, 'tis absurd to suppose that the man whose mind glows with sentiments lighted up at their sacred flame – the man whose heart distends with benevolence to all the human race – he 'who can soar above this little scene of things' – can he descend to mind the paultry concerns about which the terrae-filial race fret, and fume, and vex themselves? O how the glorious triumph swells my heart! I forget that I am a poor, insignificant devil, unnoticed and unknown, stalking up and down fairs and markets when I happen to be in them, reading a page or two of mankind, and 'catching the manners living as they rise', while the men of business jostle me on every side, as an idle encumbrance in their way. . . .

This is a remarkable self-portrait of Burns revelling in sentimental literature and posing as the proud yet benevolent observer of mankind. Yet it is not the complete picture. The other side is revealed in the poetry he was writing at this time, which included such lively songs as

> My father was a farmer upon the Carrick border O
> And carefully he bred me, in decency & order O

which he entered in the Commonplace Book in 1784, noting that it was 'a wild Rhapsody miserably defficient in Versification, but as the sentiments are the genuine feeling of my heart, for that reason I have a particular pleasure in conning it over.' This Commonplace Book – the First Commonplace Book, as it is known to Burns's biographers – Burns began early in 1783, and it constitutes a fascinating record of his mental development from the latter part of the Lochlie period until the end of 1785.

The Commonplace Book reveals that Burns's dissatisfaction with his station in life had led him to hope for some kind of fame; for the opening of the book, and many other passages in it, were clearly intended eventually for the public eye. It begins with a flourish:

> Observations, Hints, Songs, Scraps of Poetry &c. by Robt Burness; a man who had little art in making money, and still less in keeping it; but was, however, a man of some sense, a great deal of honesty, and unbounded good-will to every creature rational or irrational. – As he was but little indebted to scholastic education, and bred at a plough-tail, his performances must be strongly tinctured with his unpolished, rustic way of life; but as I believe, they are really his own, it may be some intertainment to a curious observer of human-nature to see how a plough-man thinks, and feels, under the pressure of Love, Ambition, Anxiety, Grief with the like cares and passions, which, however diversified by the Modes, and Manners of life, operate pretty much alike, I believe, in all the Species—

This introduction concludes with two quotations from Shenstone.

In August, 1783, he entered the note on the relation between love, music, and poetry which we have already quoted, and his song for Nelly Kilpatrick. He added a 'critisism' of the song, in order to demonstrate that he was aware of its faults. In September, he noted that he entirely agreed 'with that judicious Philosopher Mr Smith [Adam Smith] in his excellent Theory of Moral Sentiments, that remorse is the most painful sentiment that can embitter the human bosom', and added several indifferent blank-verse lines elaborating this point. The 'penitential thought, in the hour of Remorse' was entered the following March, and was followed by reflections on the modicum of goodness even in the worst of men and an expression of views on our judging of others similar to those he was to express in his 'Address to the Unco Gude, or the Rigidly Righteous'.

By this time he was no longer Robert Burns, son of the tenant farmer of Lochlie, but 'Rab Mossgiel', head of the family and himself tenant of the farm of Mossgiel. On the death of his father in February, 1784, Robert and Gilbert, who had for some time been negotiating with Gavin Hamilton, liberal-minded Mauchline 'writer', with a view to leasing from him the farm of Mossgiel, moved with the rest of the family to their new home. It had been a tricky business, for William Burnes had died heavily in debt and it did not at first look as though the sons would be able to save anything from the wreck. But they had taken the precaution of having every member of the family properly recognized as employees of William ('During the whole of the time we lived in the farm of Lochlea', wrote Gilbert, 'he [William Burnes] allowed my brother and me such wages for our labour as he gave to other labourers') and so they were preferred creditors. This device enabled them to extricate themselves from their father's bankruptcy and to remove to Mossgiel free of debt and even with a small amount of ready cash. Preparations for the move had been carefully and quietly made in William Burnes's last days. 'When my father's affairs grew near a crisis', wrote Gilbert, 'Robert and I took the farm of Mossgiel, consisting of 118 acres, at the rent of £90 per annum . . . from Mr. Gavin Hamilton, as an asylum for the family in case of the worst.'

Mossgiel was only a few miles from Lochlie, in the adjoining parish of Mauchline. The new landlord was well disposed and friendly, the rent was more reasonable than the pound per acre William had paid for Lochlie, and altogether it looked as though they had left misfortune behind them.

> I entered on this farm with a full resolution, 'Come, go to, I will be wise!' [wrote Burns in the autobiographical letter]. – I read farming books; I calculated crops; I attended markets; and in short, in spite of 'The devil, the world and the flesh', I believe I would have been a wise man; but the first year from unfortunately buying in bad seed, the second from a late harvest, we lost half of both our crops: this overset all my wisdom, and I returned 'Like a dog to his vomit, and the sow that was washed to her wallowing in the mire'. [He is presumably referring to what he had called earlier his 'social and amorous madness'.]

So after all it looked as though they were never going to escape bad luck. 'The farm of Mossgiel lies very high, and mostly on a cold wet bottom', wrote Gilbert. 'The first four years we were on the farm were very frosty, and the spring was very late. Our crops in consequence were very unprofitable, and notwithstanding our utmost diligence and economy, we found ourselves obliged to give up our bargain, with the loss of a considerable part of our original stock'. It is clear that this bad luck was the fault of neither Robert nor Gilbert. The farm, Gilbert explained, 'was stocked by the property and individual savings of the whole family, and was a joint concern among us. Every member of the family was allowed ordinary wages for the labour he performed on the farm. My brother's allowance and mine was seven pounds per annum each. And during the whole time this family concern lasted, which was four years, as well as during the preceding period at Lochlea, his expenses never in any one year exceeded his slender income. As I was intrusted with the keeping of the family accounts, it is not possible that there can be any fallacy in this statement, in my brother's favour. His temperance and frugality were every thing that could be wished.'

But that 'temperance and frugality' hardly extended to his emotional life. The death of his father – whom he loved and admired but whom illness and misfortune had rendered irascible and not easy to get on with in his last years – had removed a moral anchor; and with his head confused by inarticulate ambitions, his sexual urges growing ever more imperious, and his need, nurtured by his reading as well as by his temperament, to make some kind of impression on the countryside, there was no telling what course of action he might plunge into. The friendship of Gavin Hamilton, who admired Burns's poems and encouraged his revolt against the sterner aspects of Calvinist church discipline which were still dominant in rural Scotland, and his proximity to Mauchline, where he found other friends and enemies to challenge and excite him, helped to increase his restlessness and his desire to be conspicuous. Above all, it encouraged him to write poetry and to formulate his poetic ambitions more precisely than he had hitherto done.

Mauchline was a lively village which boasted several lively characters: Gavin Hamilton, liberal, friendly, opponent of the old order in Church discipline; 'Daddy Auld', the parish minister, elderly and zealous upholder of good old-fashioned doctrine, a stern but not fundamentally unkind man whom Burns seems to have respected; John Richmond, a clerk in Hamilton's law office, six years the poet's junior and ready to join him in 'social mirth' and to provide him with an admiring if not a very understanding audience; James Smith, the linen draper, whom he hailed in terms of the most intimate friendship in a verse epistle written in 1786; Dr. John Mackenzie, whom Burns first met when the physician was called in to attend William Burnes in his last illness and who eventually served as one of the links between Burns's immediate environment and the world of gentility and formal culture; John Goldie, the heterodox wine merchant whose *Essays on Various Subjects* had scandalized the orthodox; Robert Muir, also a wine merchant, generous and erratic, who was to die of tuberculosis in 1788; and, perhaps most important of all, Robert Aiken, 'orator Bob', the genial and eloquent Ayr lawyer who, though twenty years older than Burns, became his friend and patron and served as another important link between Moss-giel and the genteel world.

Richmond, Smith, and Burns became the lads of the village, out to 'épater les bourgeois', in which enterprise they were on the whole successful. Neither Richmond nor Smith was in fact possessed of much ability or character. Burns at this time needed their friendship and needed to believe that they were more 'sympathique' than they in fact were; and so he welcomed their friendship and made something of it. Hamilton, Aiken, and Dr. Mackenzie were less intimate with Burns but no less important for him. Hamilton was, after all, his landlord, and, friendly and convivial though he was, there was a social difference between landlord and tenant which the latter was never able wholly to forget, as is made clear at the conclusion of his dedicatory poem to Hamilton in the Kilmarnock volume. But Hamilton was in church matters a Moderate, a man who believed in humanitarian behaviour rather than in Calvinist doctrine, and, further, he had become involved in a dispute with the Kirk Session; this helped to endear him to Burns and Burns to him, for the poet was ready with his poetic ammunition to support Hamilton's cause and make his persecutors ridiculous through-out the countryside. Aiken was both a man of the world and a senti-mentalist; he was genuinely fond of the young farmer-poet and helped his poetic ambitions both with applause and with shrewd, practical advice. Dr. Mackenzie, a close friend of Hamilton, a keen Freemason, and amateur philosopher and liberal thinker, had been attracted to Burns from the beginning and had deliberately sought out and cultivated his friendship. Writing a brief account of Burns in 1810 for inclusion in Josiah Walker's edition of the poems (1811), Dr. Mackenzie remarked that 'before I was acquainted with his poetical powers, I perceived that he possessed very great mental abilities, an uncommonly fertile and lively imagination, a thorough acquaintance with many of our Scottish poets, and an enthusiastic admiration of Ramsay and Fergusson'. He added an observation which was echoed by many other friends of Burns: 'Indeed I have always thought that no person could have a just idea of the extent of Burns's talents, who had not an opportunity to hear him converse'. He also paid tribute to 'his discrimination of character', which was 'great beyond that of any person I ever knew'. 'I seldom ever knew him to make a false estimate of character, when he formed the opinion from his own observation.'

The 'persecution' of Gavin Hamilton by the Kirk Session (which accused him of such crimes as 'unnecessary absence from Church two Sabbaths in December and three Sabbaths in January together' and 'setting out on a journey to Carrick on the third Sabbath of January') helped to bring to a focus Burns's own discontent with the traditional Presbyterian method of church discipline and, more fundamentally, with the entire Calvinist doctrine of total depravity and of the pre-destined salvation of a tiny minority who were 'elected' by an arbitrary manifestation of God's grace in order to justify His reputation for mercy. To this theory that the vast majority of mankind was predestined to eternal damnation because of man's total depravity arising out of Adam's fall, and the corollary that the few who were predestined to salvation owed that good fortune to no good deeds of their own (for the best of actions performed by depraved man were no better than filth and wickedness in the sight of God), Burns opposed a common-sense humanitarianism, insisting on salvation by good works rather than by prior election, and meaning by good works those acts of kindness and humanity, those qualities of frankness and generosity, which he considered the highest of human virtues. In taking this view Burns was not, of course, developing an original position; his was in large measure the view of the age, and in some degree the view implied by the theory of 'moral sense' first put forward in Scotland by Francis Hutcheson and developed by a variety of philosophers throughout the century. Such views, though they had by this time exerted considerable influence in Edinburgh and Glasgow and played a large part in producing the Moderate party in the Scottish Church, had not yet penetrated to rural areas; certainly the Kirk Session at Mauchline was innocent of them. Burns was thus in continual conflict with the ecclesiastical authorities in his immediate neighbourhood. The farther from that immediate neighbourhood he got, the less unpopular his views would appear; it is significant that when Hamilton appealed from the Kirk Session to the Presbytery of Ayr the Presbytery found in his favour, and when the Kirk Session in turn appealed to the Synod of Ayr and Glasgow to reverse the decision of the Ayr Presbytery, the Synod again found in Hamilton's favour and upheld the Presbytery's decision. The battle that Burns was fighting from Mossgiel and Mauchline had already been in large measure won outside these rural areas; but this fact did not make Burns's satiric poems on these matters any less effective or any less valuable.

It may seem strange that a church which believed that salvation is granted to a tiny minority by a predestinate decree of God should be so anxious to insist on rigid standards of orthodox behaviour; if men are predestined to salvation or (in the vast majority of cases) to damnation and if their own actions are incapable of changing that decree (though of course they can *illustrate* it, because the rare man predestined to salvation

of his welcome to his daughter ('his bastart wean', as Burns called her; 'his love-begotten daughter', as the editors politely phrase it) shows him defying public opinion, but the poem returns at once to a note of fatherly affection, and it is on that note that it rests:

Tho' now they ca' me fornicator,
country An' tease my name in kintra clatter,
gossip The mair they talk, I'm kent the better,
tattle E'en let them clash;
feeble An auld wife's tongue's a feckless matter
give one To gie ane fash.
annoyance

Welcome! my bonie, sweet, wee dochter,
Tho' ye come here a wee unsought for,
And tho' your comin' I hae fought for,
Baith kirk and queir;
Yet, by my faith, ye're no unwrought for—
That I shall swear. . . .

For if thou be what I would hae thee,
And tak the counsel I shall gie thee,
I'll never rue my trouble wi' thee—
The cost nor shame o't,
But be a loving father to thee,
And brag the name o't.

Burns handed his daughter over to his mother to rear, and that long-suffering woman received the child kindly, as she did other illegitimate offspring of her unpredictable son. Elizabeth Paton, who seems to have borne no grudge against Robert, had returned to her home at Largieside when the Burnses moved to Mossgiel, and after the birth of the baby the relationship came to an end, except for one more appearance on Bessy's part in 1786, when she made a claim against Burns and was bought off with twenty pounds out of the profits of the Kilmarnock edition.

Although Burns was not temperamentally a rake and was never happy for long in this role, he occasionally expressed his general feelings of unrest and of dissatisfaction with his environment by melodramatically playing the part of one. A song he wrote shortly after settling in Mossgiel shows him posturing in this way; it is rather an absurd poem, in which

the influences are English and 'literary' in the bad sense of that word, but
it is revealing:

> O leave novéls, ye Mauchline belles,
>   Ye're safer at your spinning-wheel;
> Such witching books are baited hooks
>   For rakish rooks like Rob Mossgiel;
> Your fine Tom Jones and Grandisons,
>   They make your youthful fancies reel;
> They heat your brains, and fire your veins,
>   And then you're prey for Rob Mossgiel.
>
> Beware a tongue that's smoothly hung,
>   A heart that warmly seems to feel;
> That feeling heart but acts a part—
>   'Tis rakish art in Rob Mossgiel.
> The frank address, the soft caress,
>   Are worse than poisoned darts of steel;
> The frank address, and politesse,
>   Are all finesse in Rob Mossgiel.

It may be true, as an early biographer of Burns comments, that 'to warn
the young and unsuspecting of their danger, is only to stimulate their
curiosity'. At any rate, 'the belles of Mauchline' (he celebrated six of
them in a poem of that title) seemed interested in the unconventional
young farmer, and one of them, Jean Armour, precipitated a crisis in
Burns's life which changed its entire course.

   In the summer of 1784 Burns had the most serious bout of illness he had
thus far suffered; like his illness in Irvine, it was one of the recurring
effects of his rheumatic endocarditis. He was attended by Dr. Mackenzie,
but his real condition could not be diagnosed without the stethoscope,
which had not yet been invented, and he was advised to take the preposterous course of keeping a tub of cold water at his bedside and
plunging into it whenever he felt a fainting fit coming on. This illness
brought its usual moods of depression and remorse and several poems
expressing these emotions. 'His sensations', writes Sir James Crichton-
Browne, who has examined the records of Burns's life from the point of
view of the expert medical man, 'which only those who have thus
suffered can fully realise, were terrible, kept him in fear of sudden death,
and led to acute compunction for errors real or imaginary'.[4]

   All this time his poetic output was mounting steadily, and the entries in the Commonplace Book (though a far from adequate record of this output) were becoming increasingly interesting. In April, 1784, he notes the 'peculiar pleasure' he took 'in the season of Winter, more than the rest of the year'. He adds:

> There is scarcely any earthly object gives me more – I don't know if I should call it pleasure, but something which exalts me, something which enraptures me – than to walk in the sheltered side of a wood or high plantation, in a cloudy, winter day, and hear a stormy wind howling among the trees & raving o'er the plain. – It is my best season for devotion; – my mind is rapt up in a kind of enthusiasm to Him who, in the pompous language of Scripture, 'walks on the wings of the wind'.

He proceeds to transcribe a song he had composed 'in one of these seasons, just after a tract of misfortunes', indicating that it is to go to the tune of 'McPherson's Farewell':

> The wintery West extends his blast
>   And hail & rain does blaw;
> Or the stormy North sends driving forth
>   The blinding sleet & snaw:
> And tumbling brown, the burn comes down,
>   And roars frae bank to brae;
> And bird & beast in covert rest,
>   And pass the weary day. . . .

The song moves from a description of nature to an account of the poet's own troubles and ends with a prayer to the 'Power Supreme'—

> Since to enjoy, Thou dost deny,
>   Assist me to resign.

Here he is writing like any minor English poet of the period, and the influence of his reading of such poets is clear.

In the same month, however, he transcribes 'My Father was a Farmer' and 'My Nanie, O'. The latter is preceded by this note:

> Shenstone observes finely that love-verses writ without any real passion are the most nauseous of all conceits; and I have often thought that no man can be a proper critic of Love composition, except he

himself, in one, or more instances, have been a warm votary of this
passion. – As I have been all along, a miserable dupe to Love, and have
been led into a thousand weaknesses & follies by it, for that reason I
put the more confidence in my critical skill in distinguishing foppery
& conceit, from real passion & nature. – Whether the following song
will stand the test, I will not pretend to say, because it is MY OWN; only
I can say it was, at the time, real.

SONG————(Tune As I came in by London O)

Behind yon hills where Stincher flows
    'Mong muirs & mosses many, O
The weary sun the day has clos'd
    And I'll awa' to Nanie, O

Chorus

And O my bonny Nannie O,
My young, my handsome Nannie O
Tho' I had the world all at my will,
    I would give it all for Nanie, O

The westlin win' blaws loud & shrill,
    The night's baith dark & rainy O;
But I'll get my plaid & out I'll steal
    And o'er the hill to Nanie O.

The song continues in this simple folk idiom for another seven verses,
the last verse with the chorus rising to the kind of climax which Burns
was to employ so often in his later love songs and which he was soon to
learn to use so much more adroitly:

Come weel, come woe, I care na by,
    I'll tak' what Heaven will sen' me O;
Nae other care in life have I
    But live and love my Nanie O.

And O my bonny Nannie O,
My young, my handsome Nannie O
Tho' I had the world all at my will,
    I would give it all for Nanie, O.

This is not one of Burns's best songs, but it has a lilt to it, a fine flowing quality, and a sense of structure; and it shows a gift for finding words to fit a melody.

The April entries, which are numerous, continue with some epigrams on Tarbolton characters and an eight-line 'Epitaph on my ever honoured Father'. The next entry consists of observations on human character – a favourite study of Burns – which he divides into 'the Grave, and the Merry', with a curious intermediate type, 'very like blockheads, but generally, on a nearer inspection, [they] have somethings surprisingly clever about them'. He then elaborates on the character of the merry, and this leads him to another favourite theme, the man of spirit condemned to a life of 'poverty and obscurity'. 'The Merry, are the men of Pleasure, of all denominations; the jovial lads who have too much fire & spirit to have my settled rule of action; but without much deliberation, follow the strong impulses of nature: the thoughtless, the careless, the indolent; and in particular He, who, with a happy sweetness of natural temper, and a cheerful vacancy of thought, steals through life, generally indeed, in poverty & obscurity; but poverty & obscurity are only evils to him, who can sit gravely down, and make a repining comparison between his own situation and that of others; and lastly to grace the quorum, such are, generally, the men whose heads are capable of all the towerings of Genius, and whose hearts are warmed with the delicacy of Feeling'.

The next entry is in August; the long gap was presumably due to illness. 'The foregoing was to have been an elaborate dissertation on the various species of men', it begins; 'but as I cannot please myself in the arrangement of my ideas, I must wait till farther experience, & nicer observation throw more light on the subject. – In the mean time I shall set down the following fragment which, as it is the genuine language of my heart, will enable any body to determine which of the Classes I belong to—'. There follows the song, 'Green Grow the Rashes, O', the first of the great expressions of total abandonment to the moment of which he was to write so many. He writes the chorus first:

> Green grow the rashes – O
> Green grow the rashes – O
> The sweetest hours that e'er I spend
> Are spent among the lasses – O
>
> There's nought but care on ev'ry hand
> In ev'ry hour that passes – O

> What signifies the life o' man
>> An' 'twere na for the lasses - O
> Green grow &c.

The version in the Commonplace Book (four verses and the chorus) lacks a final verse which he apparently added later.

Immediately following the song there is an interesting defence of its philosophy:

> As the grand end of human life is to cultivate an intercourse with that Being, to whom we owe life, with ev'ry enjoyment that renders life delightful; and to maintain an integritive conduct towards our fellow creatures; that so by forming Piety & Virtue into habit, we may be fit members for that society of the Pious, and the Good, which reason and revelation teach us to expect beyond the grave – I do not see that the turn of mind, and pursuits of such a one as the above verses describe – one who spends the hours & thoughts which the vocations of the day can spare with Ossian, Shakespeare, Thomson, Shenstone, Sterne &c. or as the maggot takes him, a gun, a fiddle, or a Song to make, or mend; and at all times some hearts-dear bony lass in view – I say that I do not see that the turn of mind & pursuits of such a one are in the least more inimical to the sacred interests of Piety & Virtue, than the, even lawful, bustling, & straining after the worlds riches & honours: and I do not see but he may gain Heaven as well, which by the bye, is no mean consideration, who steals thro the Vale of Life, amusing himself with every little flower that fortune throws in his way; as he, who straining strait forward, & perhaps spattering all about him, gain[s] some of Life's little eminences, where, after all, he can only see & be seen a little more conspicuously, than, what in the pride of his heart, he is apt to term, the poor, indolent, devil he has left behind him.—

We must not consider that Burns was hypocritical in making such observations. His opposition to Calvinist theology and his attacks on it and on methods of church discipline in country parishes should not suggest a completely sceptical outlook; Burns was, in fact, genuinely religious, but his theology was deistic rather than Christian. He was fond of the Bible, he believed in a benevolent and paternal God and in the paramount duties of kindness and openness. He is not simply rationalizing in suggesting that a man who reads poetry and goes with the lasses may be more fundamentally religious than those who practice the 'lawful, bustling,

& straining after the worlds riches & honours.' This was a central part
of his creed.

After two despondent entries, both poetic, we find the first September
entry very different in tone – a lively, self-assertive song, set to an
equally lively reel tune. It clearly reveals Burns's social sensitivity as it
operated in his love affairs. If he grew interested in a girl who came from
a family of greater wealth or higher social pretensions than his own, his
pride began to assert itself immediately, and he was careful, after
apparently having experienced early rebuffs, never to put himself in a
position where he could be rejected on such grounds. This song, 'Tibby,
I Hae Seen the Day' (which, like many of the songs entered in the
Commonplace Book, was written some years before its entry) has a
taste of 'sour grapes' about it.

CHORUS

Tibby I hae seen the day
  Ye wad na been sae shy
An' for laik o' gear ye lightly me
  But fien' a hair care I. —

lack;
wealth;
scorn
devil

Yestreen I met you on the Moor
Ye spak'na but gaed by like stoor
Ye lightly me because I'm poor
  But fien' a hair care I. —

spoke not;
went by
like blow-
ing dust

When comin' hame on Sunday last
Upon the road as I cam' past
Ye snufft an' gae your head a cast
  But trouth I caretna by. —

I doubt na lass, but ye may think
Because ye hae the name o' clink
That ye can please me at a wink
  Whene'er ye like to try. —

wealth

But sorrow tak' him that's sae mean
Altho' his pouch o' coin were clean
That follows ony saucy Quean
  That looks sae proud & high. — . . .

But Tibby lass tak' my advice
Your father's gear mak's you sae nice
ask   The de'il a ane wad speir your price
Were ye as poor as I. —

There lives a lass beside yon park
shift   I'd rather hae her in her sark
Than you wi' a' your thousand mark
makes   That gars you look sae high. —

The contempt reaches its climax in that almost epigrammatic final verse.

The last entry in 1784 is the song 'John Barleycorn', a reworking of an old fragment in the purest folk idiom. The theme itself is one of the oldest and most ubiquitous of all folk themes, that of death and resurrection used to symbolize the cycle of the seasons and the sprouting in the summer of seeds planted in the early spring. Burns adds to this another folk motif, a symbolic account of the brewing of the grain, so that to death and resurrection are added the further stages of killing yet again (cutting the grown barley), roasting, and grinding, and John Barleycorn's 'heart's blood' is extracted. The poem ends on a bacchanalian and patriotic note which hardly suits the elemental quality of the subject and the simple ballad form in which Burns handles it.

The next entry is in June, 1785, and it consists of 'The Death and Dying Words of Poor Mailie', and this is followed by two verse letters to John Lapraik. 'Man Was Made to Mourn' follows in August. Discussion of these poems, which appear in the Kilmarnock volume of 1786, is deferred to the next chapter, where the poems in that volume are considered.

Following these poems, and still in August, there appear remarks that we have been expecting for a long time. We have by now read much of Thomson and Shenstone in the Commonplace Book but have so far seen no indication in Burns's critical remarks of his awareness of the Scottish poetic tradition. But we have it in this entry:

However I am pleased with the works of our Scotch Poets, particularly the excellent Ramsay, and the still more excellent Ferguson, yet I am hurt to see other places of Scotland, their towns, rivers, woods, haughs, &c. immortalized in such celebrated performances, whilst my dear native country, the ancient Baileries of Carrick, Kyle, & Cunningham, famous both in ancient & modern times for a gallant, and warlike race of inhabitants; a country where civil, & particularly religious Liberty have ever found their first support, & their last asylum; a country, the birth place of many famous Philosophers, Soldiers, & Statesmen, and the scene of many important events recorded in Scottish History, particularly a great many of the actions of the GLORIOUS WALLACE, the SAVIOUR of his Country; Yet, we have never had one Scotch Poet of any eminence, to make the fertile banks of Irvine, the romantic woodlands & sequestered scenes on Aire, and the healthy, mountainous source, & winding sweep of Doon emulate Tay, Forth, Ettrick, Tweed, &c. this is a complaint I would gladly remedy, but Alas! I am far unequal to the task, both in native genius & education. – Obscure I am, & obscure I must be, though no young Poet, nor young Soldier's heart ever beat more fondly for fame than mine—

We see here the mixture of patriotism, ambition, and interest in the earlier Scottish poets which was to prove so powerful a spur to his poetic activity.

Two song fragments follow, and then, in September, another most illuminating example of his interest in the Scottish tradition. This time he is discussing the characteristic of Scots songs:

There is a certain irregularity in the old Scotch Songs, a redundancy of syllables with respect to that exactness of accent & measure that the English Poetry requires, but which glides in, most melodiously with the respective tunes to which they are set. For instance, the fine old Song of the Mill Mill O, to give it a plain prosaic reading it halts prodigiously out of measure; on the other hand, the Song set to the same tune in Bremner's collection of Scotch Songs which begins 'To Fanny fair could I impart &c.' it is most exact measure, and yet, let them be both sung before a real Critic, one above the biasses of prejudice, but a thorough Judge of Nature, – how flat & spiritless will the last appear, how trite, and tamely methodical, compared with the wild-warbling cadence, the heart-loving melody of the first. – This particularly is the case with all those airs which end with a hyper-metrical syllable. – There is a degree of wild irregularity in many of the compositions & Fragments which are daily sung to them by my compeers, the common people – a certain happy arrangement of old Scotch syllables, & yet, very frequently, nothing, not even *like* rhyme, or sameness of jingle at the ends of the lines. – This has made me sometimes imagine that perhaps, it might be possible for a Scotch Poet with a nice, judicious ear, to set compositions to many of our most favourite airs, particularly that class of them mentioned above, independent of rhyme altogether.—

These are not the comments of a 'Heaven-taught ploughman', who breaks spontaneously into song without fully knowing what he is doing. They are the observations of a careful craftsman, and of a poet particularly interested in the problem of setting words to music. They point forward to Burns's remarkable later activity in rescuing, rehabilitating, and recreating Scottish folk song.

It is true that Burns was indebted to his careful study of English poetry and of English songs for much of his understanding of the craft of verse making, and this aspect of his debt to English literature is perhaps too often ignored; but the more important fact is that Burns found himself as a poet only when he was able to identify himself with a Scottish literary tradition and to throw off what to him were fundamentally the affectations and artificial gestures he learned from Shenstone and others. The First Commonplace Book, as it draws to a close, reflects his progress towards this identification.

In transcribing his song, 'Montgomerie's Peggy', in September, he remarks that it is 'something in imitation of the manner of a noble old Scottish Piece called McMillan's Peggy, and sings to the tune of Galla Water'. ('Galla Water' is a very tricky tune indeed, and it required skill and courage to try to write a song to it.) 'I have even tried to imitate', he adds, 'in this extempore thing, that irregularity in the rhyme which, when judiciously done, has such a fine effect on the ear.' The song was composed a long time before its entry in the Commonplace Book; it was the result of a fairly serious love affair which lasted six or eight months and ended rather abruptly when Burns discovered that Peggy had during all this time been engaged to another. Later in the same month he transcribes 'Another Fragment in imitation of an old Scotch Song, well known among the Country ingle sides'. He remarks at this point:

By the way, these old Scottish airs are so nobly sentimental that when one would compose to them; to south the tune, as our Scotch phrase is, over & over, is the readiest way to catch the inspiration and raise the Bard into that glorious enthusiasm so strongly characteristic of our old Scotch Poetry.

Discussion of Scots songs now becomes mixed up with remarks on the 'heavy train of misfortunes' which inspired some of his productions. The final entry is in October: Burns starts to give advice to 'any young man, on the vestibule of the world', who may 'chance to throw his eye over these pages'. 'In the first place', he begins, 'let my Pupil, as he tenders his own peace, keep up a regular, warm intercourse with the Deity'. But he gets no further than this opening. The rest of this page, the last in the Commonplace Book, is blank.

Among the fragments of song which Burns entered in the Common-place Book in August, 1785, was the following:

> When first I came to Stewart Kyle
>   My mind it was nae steady,
went; rode Where e'er I gaed, where e'er I rade,
>   A Mistress still I had ay:
> But when I came roun' by Mauchlin town,
>   Not dreadin' any body,
> My heart was caught before I thought
>   And by a Mauchlin Lady —

The Mauchline Lady was Jean Armour, daughter of a highly respectable Mauchline master mason; she was about six years younger than the poet. There are various traditions about how she and Burns first met, but all we can say for certain is that they became acquainted in 1784 and by the summer of 1785 were in the midst of a very serious affair. Early in 1786 it became clear that Jean was pregnant, but Robert's intentions were 'honourable', and it seems that he took it for granted that he and Jean would marry until Jean's family made it clear that they would not tolerate him for a son-in-law, even in order to 'make an honest woman' of Jean. It is probable that Jean and Robert went through some form of irregular marriage and that only Jean's later repudiation of this marriage under pressure from her family prevented it from standing. Under Scots law, it was possible to enter into the marriage relationship merely by mutual promise sealed by either previous or subsequent consummation; but of course if either party later were to deny the promise, the marriage could not be proved. Whatever the precise nature of the form which the two lovers appear to have gone through, it is clear that had they subsequently mutually acknowledged each other as husband and wife the marriage would have been wholly legal. Eventually, that is what they did do, but Burns had some rough sailing before he entered those smooth waters.

Burns did more than make a verbal promise to Jean: he gave her a written document of some kind to reinforce it. But James Armour, horrified at finding that his daughter had been made pregnant by a struggling tenant farmer with a reputation for rhyming and blasphemy, persuaded Robert Aiken – Burns's friend but also the Armours' lawyer – to cut the names out of the paper, evidently assuming that this would end all suggestion that Jean and Robert were married. Why the paper was mutilated rather than destroyed is difficult to understand; nor is it easy to see why Aiken, with his expert legal knowledge, did not persuade Armour of the irrelevance of this action. But this is in fact what happened: Jean was bullied by her father into surrendering the paper, and Aiken was then persuaded to mutilate it.

To Burns it appeared that Jean had betrayed him, and he was both hurt and angry. Writing to Gavin Hamilton on April 15, 1786, he informed him that 'old Mr Armour prevailed with [Aiken] to mutilate that unlucky paper yesterday. – Would you believe it? tho' I had not a hope, nor even a wish, to make her mine after her damnable conduct; yet when he told me, the names were all cut out of the paper, my heart died within me, and he cut my very veins with the news. – Perdition seize her falsehood and perjurious perfidy! but God bless her and forgive my poor, once-dear, misguided girl. – She is ill-advised'. An account of the affair was included in a letter to John Arnot about the same time, and Burns prefixed his own transcript of the letter with this note:

> . . . I had got deeply in love with a young Fair-One, of which proofs were every day *arising* more & more to view. – I would gladly have covered my Inamorata from the darts of Calumny with the conjugal Shield, nay, had actually made up some sort of Wedlock; but I was at that time deep in the guilt of being unfortunate, for which good & lawful objection, the Lady's friends broke all our measures, & drove me au desespoir.

The letter itself is an extraordinary document. It is written with a passion which borders on hysteria, and at the same time with a literary skill, a deft and apt use of quotation and allusion, an immense speed and vividness, which show how well Burns could write English prose when he forgot his more formal models.

> I have been all my life, Sir, one of the rueful-looking, long-visaged sons of Disappointment. – A damned Star has always kept my zenith, & shed its baleful influence, in the emphatic curse of the Prophet – 'And behold whatsoever he doth, it shall not prosper!' – I rarely hit where I aim: & if I want anything, I am almost sure never to find it where I seek it. – For instance, if my pen-knife is needed I pull out twenty things – a plough-wedge, a horse-nail, an old letter or a

tattered rhyme, in short, everything but my pen-knife; & that at last, after a painful, fruitless search, will be found in the unsuspected corner of an unsuspected pocket, as if on purpose thrust out of the way. – Still, Sir, I had long had a wishing eye to that inestimable blessing, a wife. – My mouth watered deliciously, to see a young fellow, after a few idle, common-place stories from a gentleman in black, strip & go to bed with a young girl, & no one durst say, black was his eye; while I, for just doing the same thing, only wanting that ceremony, am made a Sunday's laughing-stock, & abused like a pick-pocket. – I was well aware though, that if my ill-starred fortune got the least hint of my connubial wish, my schemes would go to nothing. – To prevent this, I determined to take my measures with such thought & fore-thought, such a caution & precaution, that all the malignant planets in the Hemisphere should be unable to blight my designs. – Not content with, to use the words of the celebrated Westminster Divines, 'The outward & ordinary means', I left no *stone* unturned; sounded every unfathomed *depth*; stopped up every *hole* & bore of an objection: but, how shall I tell it! notwithstanding all this turning of stones, stopping of bores, &c. – whilst I, with secret pleasure, marked my project *swelling* to the proper crisis, & was singing te Deum in my own fancy; or, to change the metaphore, whilst I was vigourously pressing on the siege; had carried the counter-scarp, & made a practicable breach behind the curtin in the gorge of the very principal bastion; nay, having mastered the covered way, I had found means to slip a choice detachment into the very citadel; while I had nothing less in view than displaying my victorious banners on the top of the walls – Heaven & Earth must I 'remember'! my damned Star wheeled about to the zenith, by whose baleful rays Fortune took the alarm, & pouring in her forces on all quarters, front, flank, & rear, I was utterly routed, my baggage lost, my military chest in the hands of the enemy; & your poor devil of a humble servant, commander in chief forsooth, was obliged to scamper away, without either arms or honors of war, except his bare bayonet & cartridge-pouch; nor in all probability had he escaped even with them, had he not made a shift to hide them under the lap of his military cloak.—

In short, Pharaoh at the Red Sea, Darius at Arbela, Pompey at Pharsalia, Edward at Bannockburn, Charles at Pultaway, Burgoyne at Saratoga – no Prince, Potentate, or Commander of ancient or modern unfortunate memory, ever got a more shameful or more total defeat—

'O horrible! O horrible! Most horrible!'

How I bore this, can only be conceived. - All powers of recital labour far, far behind. - There is a pretty large portion of bedlam in the composition of a Poet at any time; but on this occasion I was nine parts & nine tenths, out of ten, stark staring mad. - At first, I was fixed in stuporific insensibility, silent, sullen, staring like Lot's wife be-saltified in the plains of Gomorha. - But my second paroxysm chiefly beggars description. - The rifted northern ocean when returning suns dissolve the chains of winter, and loosening precipices of long accumu-lated ice tempest with hideous crash the foaming Deep - images like these may give some faint shadow of what was the situation of my bosom. - My chained faculties broke loose; my maddening passions, roused to ten-fold fury, bore over their banks with impetuous, resistless force, carrying every check & principle before them - Counsel, was an unheeded call to the passing hurricane; Reason, a screaming elk in the vortex of Moskoestrum; & Religion, a feebly-struggling beaver down the roarings of Niagara. - I reprobated the first moment of my existence; execrated Adam's folly-infatuated wish for that goodly-looking, but poison-breathing, gift, which had ruined him, & undone me; & called on the womb of uncreated night to close over me & all my sorrows.—

Burns was, it is clear, severely shaken by the discovery that the Armours would rather see their daughter bearing an illegitimate child than have him as their son-in-law. His pride, always on the alert, received the most resounding blow it had yet suffered. There were also more practical results of the affair:

But this is not all. - Already the holy beagles, the houghmagandie pack, begin to snuff the scent, & I expect every moment to see them cast off, & hear them after me in full cry: but as I am an old fox, I shall give them dodging and doubling for it; & by & bye, I intend to earth among the mountains of Jamaica.

He had still to reckon with the Church, and the elders of Mauchline were only too glad to be able to say, 'I told you so' about the wild and irreverent young man who had been circulating satirical poems about them and their beliefs. It is significant that in the autobiographical letter he links together his account of his ecclesiastical satires with the story of his affair with Jean:

. . . The first of my poetic offspring that saw the light was a burlesque lamentation on a quarrel between two rev^d Calvinists, both of them dramatis person in my Holy Fair. – I had an idea myself that the piece had some merit; but to prevent the worst, I gave a copy of it to a friend who was very fond of these things, and told him I could not guess who was the Author of it, but that I thought it pretty clever. – With a certain side of both clergy and laity it met with a roar of applause. – Holy Willie's Prayer next made its appearance, and alarmed the kirk-Session so much that they held three several meetings to look over their holy artillery, if any of it was pointed against profane Rhymers. Unluckily for me, my idle wanderings led me, on another side, point blank within reach of their heaviest metal. – This is the unfortunate story alluded to in my printed poem, The Lament. – 'Twas a shocking affair, which I cannot yet bear to recollect; and had very nearly given [me] one or two of the principal qualifications for a place among those who have lost the chart and mistake the reckonings of Rationality.

One more quotation from his letters will complete the picture of Burns's state of mind at this time. This was written to David Brice in June:

. . . Poor, ill-advised, ungrateful Armour came home on Friday last. – You have heard all the particulars of that affair; and a black affair it is. – What she thinks of her conduct now, I don't know; one thing I know, she has made me compleatly miserable. – Never man lov'd, or rather ador'd, a woman more than I did her: and, to confess a truth between you and me, I do still love her to distraction after all, tho' I won't tell her so, tho' I see her, which I don't want to do. – My poor, dear, unfortunate Jean! how happy I have been in her arms! – It is not the losing her that makes me so unhappy; but for *her* sake I feel most severely. – I foresee she is in the road to, I am afraid, *eternal* ruin; and those who made so much noise, and showed so much grief, at the thought of her being *my wife*, may, some day, see her connected in such a manner as may give them more real cause of vexation. – I am sure I do not wish it: may Almighty God forgive her ingratitude and perjury to me, as I from my very soul forgive her! and may His grace be with her and bless her in all her future life! – I can have no nearer idea of the place of eternal punishment than what I have felt in my own breast on her account. – I have tryed often to forget her: I have run into all kinds of dissipation and riot, Mason-meetings, drinking matches, and other mischief, to drive her out of my head, but all in vain: and now for a grand cure: the Ship is on her way home that is to take me out to Jamaica; and then, farewell dear old Scotland, and farewel, dear ungrateful Jean, for never, never will I see you more!

It was at this time that he began to talk of emigrating to Jamaica as a remedy for his woes. But there were many things to be done first. Jean acknowledged her fault to the Kirk Session and awaited the public admonition in church which both she and Burns would eventually have to face. Burns, struggling with a variety of moods from despair to hysterical gaiety, and regarding Jean as having betrayed him (though he admitted it was under pressure from her parents), sought comfort in the arms of Mary Campbell, the 'Highland Mary' of Burns legend. The truth about Burns's relations with this Highland servant girl will probably never be known. He himself was unusually reticent about the affair, and we have to construct his side of the story from a few songs and several other cryptic references in his letters. It seems probable that he promised her marriage; one of the Bibles which they appear to have exchanged, its end papers containing inscriptions in Burns's hand dealing with the sanctity of promises, is extant, though the names of Robert and Mary have been mutilated.

In the midst of this emotional turmoil – raging against the Armours, making love to Mary, making his peace with the ecclesiastical authorities, planning to emigrate to Jamaica – he was also concerning himself with a more important project, the publication of a volume of his poems. The resolution to try to get his poems published must have been forming for some time, and by early April, 1786, he had concluded arrangements with John Wilson, the Kilmarnock printer, for bringing out a volume of 'Scotch Poems', to be 'elegantly printed in one volume, octavo'. In the latter half of 1785 and the early months of 1786 he had been writing poetry fast and furiously, and he had by now more than enough to fill a substantial volume. The decision to publish may have been in part the reaction of his pride to the attitude of the Armours, though since the date of the 'Proposals' for publishing the volume is April 14, 1786, and there is a reference to his sending the proposals to the press in a letter of April 3, it seems clear that he had been thinking about publishing before the crisis with the Armours. (It is impossible to date exactly Burns's first awareness of the Armours' hostility, but the letter to Hamilton talking of the mutilation of 'that unlucky paper' was written on April 15, a fact which suggests that the storm first broke shortly before.) In the auto-biographical letter Burns himself alleged that he decided to publish in order to leave Scotland a memento of himself before he emigrated; but, again, if we look at the date of the publication of the proposals and realize that the decision to publish must have been arrived at a considerable time before the proposals were drawn up, it seems clear that Burns had determined to bring out a book of his poems some time before he thought of emigrating to Jamaica. He does not seem to have considered emigration as a solution to his problems until April, 1786. Further, it is difficult to believe that Burns was ever wholly serious in his intention to go to Jamaica; he continually kept postponing his passage, and though each time the reasons he gave for postponement sounded plausible enough, they may well have been rationalizations. Going to Jamaica was a noble and proud gesture, like forsaking society and going into the countryside to beg. Burns was fond of such gestures, and his poetry is full of them:

> O why the deuce should I repine,
>   And be an ill foreboder?
> I'm twenty-three, and five feet nine,
>   I'll go and be a sodger!

I'll go and be a soldier – I'll go to Jamaica – I'll take the road; these announcements were essentially ways of thumbing his nose at society.

But he could not thumb his nose at the Church. On June 25, he appeared before the Kirk session and admitted his responsibility for Jean's pregnancy. He was quite ready to humble himself before the ecclesiastical authorities if it would mean that he would be cleared of all obligation to marry Jean; for if he admitted fornication and accepted suitable reproof, he could not be held to be married to her. On July 9, he wrote to his friend John Richmond:

> I have waited on Armour since her [Jean's] return home, not by – from any the least view of reconciliation, but merely to ask for her health; and – to you I will confess it, from a foolish hankering fondness – very ill-plac'd indeed. – The Mother forbade me the house; nor did Jean shew that penitence that might have been expected. – However, the Priest, I am inform'd will give me a Certificate as a single man, if I comply with the rules of the Church, which for that very reason I intend to do.

He added later:

> Sunday morn:
> I am just going to put on Sackloth & ashes this day. – I am indulged

so far as to appear in my own seat. Peccavi, Pater, misere [sic] mei. –
My book will be ready in a fortnight.

The juxtaposition is significant. By public penitence he could get his
freedom, and then his thoughts turn to his book. The following week he
wrote to David Brice:

I have already appeared publickly in Church, and was indulged in the
liberty of standing in my own seat. – I do this to get a certificate as a
bachelor, which Mr Auld has promised me. – I am now fixed to go for
the West Indies in October. – Jean and her friends insisted much that
she should stand along with me in the kirk, but the minister would not
allow it, . . .

Robert and Jean appeared three times in Church to receive public
reproof for the sin of fornication. After their third appearance, on
August 6, they were free of further obligation. It should be added that
such appearances were frequent in Scottish churches at this time;
fornication was among the commonest sins, especially in rural areas,
while premarital intercourse among the peasant and farming people was
very common. Burns and Jean were doing what many another young
man and woman in Mauchline and elsewhere had done and were to do
again. Burns was conspicuous to the orthodox less as a fornicator than as
a wild rhymster with a satirical pen and heretical ideas whose sinning was
to be expected and gloated over.

Although Burns had made his peace with God, he had still to reckon
with man, in the person of James Armour, who, hearing of Burns's
proposed emigration, tried to secure legal means of compelling him to
put up money for the support of the yet unborn child. Burns, in a panic,
and fearing imprisonment if he were unable to raise the sum demanded,
left Mossgiel and described himself on July 30 in a letter to Richmond as
'wandering from one friend's house to another'. In the meantime he
took the precaution of assigning his share in the Mossgiel farm and
property to his brother Gilbert for the support of his daughter by
Elizabeth Paton; he also assigned to Gilbert, in trust for his daughter,
'the profits that may arise from the Publication of my Poems presently
in the Press' and the copyright of the poems. This would put his property
outside the reach of any legal process brought by the Armours.

Burns's state of mind on the eve of his public debut as a poet must have
reached an extraordinary pitch of confusion and excitement. He was
expecting the repudiated Jean to bear his child very shortly; he was in

the midst of a passionate affair with Mary Campbell, who was also (if we correctly interpret the not too conclusive evidence on this point) getting ready to bear his child; he was ostensibly making plans for an early departure from his native land; he was trying to extricate himself from any legal process James Armour might institute against him; and he was seeing his book through the press and making strenuous efforts to circulate the proposals and get subscribers. His letter to Richmond of July 30 shows something of this confusion:

My hour is now come. – You and I will never meet in Britain more. – I have orders within three weeks at farthest to repair aboard the Nancy, Cap^n Smith, from Clyde, to Jamaica, and to call at Antigua. – This, except to our friend Smith, whom God long preserve, is a secret about Mauchlin. – Would you believe it? Armour has got a warrant to throw me in jail till I find security for an enormous sum. . . . – I know you will pour an execration on her head, but spare the poor, ill-advised girl for may sake; tho', may all the Furies that rend the injured, enraged Lover's bosom, await the old harridan, her Mother, untill her latest hour! May Hell string the arm of Death to throw the fatal dart, and all the winds of warring elements rouse the infernal flames to welcome her approach! For Heaven's sake burn this letter, and never show it to a living creature. – I write it in a moment of rage, reflecting on my miserable situation – exiled, abandoned, forlorn. . . .

He was in an ugly mood with respect to Jean. 'Against two things however, I am fixed as Fate: staying at home, and owning her conjugally', he wrote to James Smith at about the same time. 'The first, by Heaven I will not do! the last, by Hell I will never do!' But he concludes the same letter with: 'If you see Jean tell her, I will meet her, So help me Heaven in my hour of need!'

How far his affair with Mary Campbell was responsible for his reiterated determination not to own Jean conjugally, it is impossible to say. None of his surviving letters of this time makes any explicit reference to Mary, and neither Smith nor Richmond seems to have been aware of the affair; if they were, neither seemed to consider it serious enough to mention. (Yet Richmond long afterwards gave a circumstantial and unflattering account of Highland Mary and of Burns's relations with her at this time to James Grierson of Dalgoner, when the latter was collecting information about Burns.) It is even impossible to say with any certainty that Burns turned to Mary Campbell only after his repudiation by Jean's family. That his relations with Mary were platonic is hard to believe;

all the evidence points the other way. Even if we reject Richmond's story, which paints Mary's character as 'loose in the extreme' (and there seems to be no reason for rejecting it except that it is inconsistent with the legend and that it apparently conflicts with the tone of Burns's later references to Mary), it is hard to explain away the discovery in 1920 that a newborn infant had been buried at the foot of Mary's grave. When Mary died, in October, 1786, she may well have died in giving birth to Burns's child. If this conjecture is sound, we have ample explanation of the tone of all Burns's later references to her, of his self-reproach, his mystifications and his morbid exaggerations.

The fact is that, in spite of the romantic Highland Mary legend, Burns's permanent interest was with Jean rather than with Mary. Jean produced twins on September 3, and called them Robert and Jean. In spite of Burns's rather histrionic anger with the Armour family, he was touched at finding himself a father again. 'A very fine boy and girl have awakened a thousand feelings that thrill, some with tender pleasure, and some with foreboding anguish, thro' my soul', he wrote to Robert Muir, but this somewhat studied speech expressed his immediate feelings less effectively than the joyous letter he wrote to Richmond immediately after the birth. This letter opens with an older bawdy version of 'Green Grow the Rashes O', which Burns was later to rewrite:

> Green grow the rashes O
> Green grow the rashes O
> The lasses they hae wimble bores,
> The widows they hae gashes O.

There are three verses, in addition to this chorus, and the note of exultation and happy bawdry in them must have corresponded to Robert's own mood:

> In sober hours I am a priest;
> A hero when I'm tipsy, O;
> But I'm a king and ev'ry thing,
> When wi' a wanton Gipsey, O.

The climax ('An' ceremony laid aside,/I fairly fun' her c-ntie, O') leaves no doubt of the direction to which his thoughts were turned at this moment. The manuscript of the letter is not complete; there is much missing between the poem and the brief announcement of the birth, and it may be that the poem was on paper before the news of the birth was actually confirmed, for the end of the poem reads like a postscript:

Sept: 3ᵈ Armour has just now brought me a fine boy and a girl at one throw. – God bless them poor little dears. —— ⁵

Burns had already expressed his feelings for the mother in a poem written probably before the quarrel with the Armours, a poem which treats man in the combined roles of father and lover in a manner unique in literature. Tenderness and protection for the girl, affection and physical love for her, pride in paternity, happy unity in defying the outside world – these notes are all sounded, and they are so deftly harmonized that they sound like a single strain. This is the poem of a 'free' lover who was also a family man at heart; yet at the same time it is humourous and wholly unsentimental. Burns is laughing at himself, laughing even a little at the girl, but he is proud of himself, too, and above all he is happy. He puts the poem into the girl's mouth with an audacity few male poets would risk, and the resulting indirect picture of the poet's attitude flowers out of the poem magnificently:

O wha my babie-clouts will buy?

care for   O wha will tent me when I cry?

Wha will kiss me where I lie?

rollicking   The rantin dog, the daddie o't.

fault   O wha will own he did the faut?

ale for the nurse   O wha will buy the groanin maut?

name it   O wha will tell me how to ca't?

The rantin dog, the daddie o't.

stool of re-pentance   When I mount the creepie-chair,

Wha will sit beside me there?

Gie me Rob, I'll seek nae mair,

The rantin dog, the daddie o't.

talk; alone   Wha will crack to me my lane?

eager and excited   Wha will make me fidgin fain?

Wha will kiss me o'er again?

The rantin dog, the daddie o't.

He wrote no such poem for Mary. He asked her in fairly conventional poetic language if she would go to the Indies with him:

> Will ye go to the Indies, my Mary,
> And leave auld Scotia's shore?
> Will ye go to the Indies, my Mary
> Across the Atlantic's roar?

And in the same song he protested (too much?) that he would keep his oath of faithfulness:

> I hae sworn by the Heavens to my Mary,
> I hae sworn by the Heavens to be true;
> And sae may the Heavens forget me
> When I forget my vow!

He celebrated her, too, in a lively, carefree song in which she figures anonymously as the 'Highland lassie':

> Nae gentle dames, tho' ne'er sae fair,
> Shall ever be my muse's care:
> Their titles a' are empty show;
> Gie me my Highland lassie, O.

In the final chorus he takes leave of her with a lightheartedness that contrasts sharply with the protestations of the other poem:

> Farewell the glen sae bushy O!
> Farewell the plain sae rushy O,!
> To other lands I now must go,
> To sing my Highland lassie, O.

The fact is that during her lifetime he wrote for Mary nothing that has the personal urgency and the note of protective tenderness of some of the songs he wrote for Jean, and what he wrote after Mary's death sounds a note of passionate self-reproach in an oddly conventional manner:

> See'st thou thy lover lowly laid?
> Hear'st thou the groans that rend his breast?

Mary's story was soon to close. The account had better be given in what appear to be Burns's own words. It is in the form of a note to 'My Highland Lassie, O', said by R. H. Cromek when he first printed it in his

Reliques of Robert Burns, 1808, to have been written by Burns in the interleaved copy of the *Scots Musical Museum* which Burns prepared for his friend Robert Riddell. Although the note is not discoverable in the interleaved *Museum* and apparently was never there, Cromek may well have taken it (as was his custom) from another genuine source, now lost:

> This was a composition of mine in early life, before I was known at all in the world. My Highland lassie was a warm-hearted, charming young creature as ever blessed a man with generous love. [This does not suggest a Platonic relationship!] After a pretty long tract of the most ardent reciprocal attachment, we met by appointment, on the second Sunday of May, in a sequestered spot by the Banks of Ayr, where we spent the day in taking a farewell, before she should embark for the West-Highlands, to arrange matters among her friends for our projected change of life. At the close of Autumn following she crossed the sea to meet me at Greenock, where she had scarce landed when she was seized with a malignant fever, which hurried my dear girl to the grave in a few days, before I could even hear of her illness.

She must have died soon after Jean had given birth to the twins. If we agree that Mary was with child by Burns and died in giving birth to it, we can imagine in what a harassed state Burns must have been while awaiting the birth, at around the same time, of two of his children by different mothers. If Mary's death in childbirth solved, in the most ruthless way imaginable, *that* particular problem, we can imagine the horror and remorse such a solution must have brought to the poet. He had decided not to sail for Jamaica on the 'Nancy'; nor did he sail, in accordance with his next plans, on the 'Bell', which left later. He stayed in Scotland, wrote to Robert Aiken about the possibility of a job in the Excise, and gave evidence of being in a most anguished state of mind:

> I have been feeling all the various rotations and movements within (he wrote to Aiken in October), respecting the Excise. There are many things plead strongly against it; the uncertainty of getting soon into business; the consequence of my follies, which may perhaps make it impracticable for me to stay at home; and besides I have for some time been pining under secret wretchedness, from causes which you pretty well know – the pang of disappointment, the sting of pride, with some wandering stabs of remorse, which never fail to settle on my vitals like vultures, when attention is not called away by the calls of

society, or the vagaries of the Muse. Even in the hour of social mirth, my gaiety is the madness of an intoxicated criminal under the hands of the executioner. . . .

Dr. Snyder explains that this outburst was the result of Burns's having 'two luckless women on his hands at once, and the father of one loosing "the pack of the law" at his heels',[6] and he may be right; but it is possible that the letter (which is undated) was written just after Burns had received the news of Mary's death, and that 'the madness of an intoxicated criminal under the hands of the executioner' reflected his feeling of remorse in this connection. The reference to 'some wandering stabs of remorse' earlier in the letter may be considered too slight an expression of his feelings under such circumstances, but one must remember that neither Aiken nor any other of his friends appears to have known how he stood with Highland Mary, and Burns did not intend to be too explicit.

In any event, Burns found himself, some time in October, 1786, a free man as far as marital obligations went. And he was also a poet. His *Poems Chiefly in the Scottish Dialect* was published on July 31, 1786. The book was an immediate success. It swept the countryside, simple and gentle joining in its praises. The Reverend George Lawrie, minister in the parish of Loudon, a few miles from Mossgiel, a Moderate clergyman with friends among the Edinburgh literati, sent a copy to Dr. Blacklock, and Blacklock wrote back to Lawrie on September 4, expressing his enthusiasm and indicating that such distinguished critics as Professor Dugald Stewart were equally interested. Lawrie gave the letter to Gavin Hamilton, who in turn showed it to Burns. 'The Doctor', wrote Burns in his autobiographical letter, 'belonged to a set of critics for whose applause I had not even dared to hope'. From the confusions, emotional crises, insecurities, and guilt feelings of his position at Mossgiel he heard the learned and genteel world of Edinburgh beckon. In spite of everything, in spite of humble position, lack of formal education, poverty, disgrace, and illness, he had become a real poet.

The Kilmarnock volume contained only a selection of Burns's output up to 1786, and some of his best pieces were omitted from it. It was, nevertheless, a remarkable volume – one of the most remarkable first volumes ever published by a British poet – and left no doubt of Burns's poetic stature. A fair conception of the kind of poet Burns had by this time become, as well as some idea of the impact he made on the literary world in 1786, can be gained by an examination of the Kilmarnock poems. Let us therefore inquire rather carefully into the nature of the book which turned 'Rab Mossgiel' into 'Caledonia's bard'.

THE KILMARNOCK VOLUME

'Before leaving my native country for ever, I resolved to publish my Poems. – I weighed my productions as impartially as in my power; I thought they had merit; and 'twas a delicious idea that I would be called a clever fellow, even though it should never reach my ears a poor Negro-driver, or perhaps a victim to that inhospitable clime gone to the world of Spirits'. So Burns explained the origin of the Kilmarnock volume; it was to be his legacy to his native country before he left it for Jamaica, something by which Scotland might remember her lost poet. That the volume would be remembered, he seems never to have doubted. 'I can truly say', he adds in the same letter, 'that pauvre Inconnu as I then was, I had pretty nearly as high an idea of myself and my works as I have at this moment [August, 1787]'.

We have, however, already remarked that Burns's emigration to Jamaica played a part in his imagination comparable to his more vaguely conceived plans to run away and join the army or to wander through the countryside as a beggar, and it is hard to believe that he really intended to leave Scotland after the publication of his poems. Publication was essentially an assertion of his abilities, a vindication of 'Rab the rhymer' both to his friends and his enemies, a claim to be something more than a provincial versifier. It was his public bow as a poet, and that he meant it from the first as an opening rather than a farewell gesture is clear from the whole pattern of his behaviour with respect to the book.

Burns seems early to have formed the habit of thinking of himself as a Poet with a capital 'P'. As early as 1784 he wrote his 'Epistle to Davie, a Brother Poet', and according to Gilbert Burns 'the first idea of Robert's becoming an author was started on this occasion'. In both letters and poems he was more and more to refer to himself as 'the poet' or 'the bard'. 'Poets are such outré beings . . .' he began a letter to Miss Wilhelmina Alexander of Ballochmyle in November, 1786, by way of explanation and apology for having written a song in her honour. He clearly enjoyed thinking of himself in the capacity of poet. The Kilmarnock volume was intended primarily to justify, to a wider audience than friends and neighbours, his right to this title.

The printed Proposals for publishing his poems also present interesting evidence of the attitude with which Burns contemplated publication. They run as follows:

APRIL 14TH, 1786

PROPOSALS,

FOR PUBLISHING BY SUBSCRIPTION,

SCOTCH POEMS

BY ROBERT BURNS.

The Work to be elegantly Printed in One Volume, Octavo, Price Stitched *Three Shillings.*

As the Author has not the most distant *Mercenary* view in Publishing, as soon as so many Subscribers appear as will defray the *necessary* Expence, the Work will be sent to the Press.

> Set out the brunt side o' your shin,
> For pride in *Poets* is nae sin;
> *Glory's* the Prize for which *they* rin,
>   And *Fame's* their jo;
> And wha blaws best the Horn shall win:
>   And wharefore no?
>
> RAMSAY.

Modern scholars have pointed out that Burns was not being strictly truthful in disclaiming any mercenary view in publishing, because in July, 1786, as we have noted, he had signed a deed of assignment in which he made over to Gilbert 'the profits that may arise from the Publication of my Poems presently in the Press' in order to help him support his (Robert's) illegitimate daughter by Elizabeth Paton, and in any event he needed all the money he could get and was glad to collect it when it came. But we must not be too literal in interpreting Burns's statement. The essential reason for publishing was certainly not to make money but to claim glory as a poet. The quotation from Ramsay makes perfectly clear what he is most anxious to win from the publication of his poems: 'pride', 'glory', and 'fame' are precise words, and they appear in three successive lines of the Ramsay quotation. 'Pride in poets is nae sin.' Pride, as we have seen, is a key word in Burns's vocabulary and a key factor in his emotional make-up.

Burns published, in short, in order to gain as poet a wider recognition than his status as local bard could grant him. 'We, Robert Burns, by virtue of a Warrant from Nature . . . Poet-Laureat, and Bard in Chief, in and over the Districts and Counties of Kyle, Cunningham and Carrick, of old extent' was how he described himself in a humorous letter to two of his friends in November, 1786; but, as he wrote to John Ballantine the following January, he was soon to be hailed at a Masonic meeting in Edinburgh as 'Caledonia's Bard, brother Burns'. That was the measure of what the Kilmarnock volume had achieved for him and it was what Burns had intended it to achieve.

If the Kilmarnock volume represented a deliberate public appearance, it was inevitable that he should dress for the part. The dress he chose was perhaps unfortunate, but it was understandable. A country poet whose audience had hitherto been restricted to friends and neighbours in his own corner of Scotland, a poet, moreover, with little of the formal education which he understood, from a study of Masson's reader and similar books, to be an orthodox prerequisite for a man of letters, had one obvious recourse: to fall back on that growing sentimentalism which, in one of its aspects, could be used to idealize the simple rustic. Burns knew all about that sentimentalism – Henry Mackenzie's *Man of Feeling* was his favourite novel from the first time he set eyes on it – and he deliberately took advantage of it in dressing himself to make his opening bow before the genteel world of the late eighteenth century. He begins his Preface in costume, as it were:

> The following trifles are not the production of the Poet, who with all the advantages of learned art, and perhaps amid the elegancies and idlenesses of upper life, looks down for a rural theme, with an eye to Theocrites (*sic*) or Virgil. To the Author of this, these and other celebrated names their countrymen are, in their original languages, 'A fountain shut up, and a book sealed'. Unacquainted with the necessary requisites for commencing Poet by rule, he sings the sentiments and manners, he felt and saw in himself and his rustic compeers around him, in his and their native language.

If this bait (to vary the metaphor) was designed for Henry Mackenzie, it was shrewdly done, for Mackenzie grabbed it, as his review in the *Lounger* of December 9 made clear. 'Whoever will read his lighter and more humorous poems . . . will perceive with what uncommon penetration and sagacity this Heaven-taught ploughman, from his humble and unlettered station, has looked upon men and manners'. It was hardly fair to Murdoch, or to William Burnes, or to the other varied sources that contributed to Burns's education, to call him a 'Heaven-taught ploughman'; but if Burns was misunderstood in Edinburgh it was in some measure because of the part he had deliberately chosen to play in his Preface.

But Burns was unable to sustain the part throughout the Preface. He did not wish to rest his claims on his rusticity alone, for he felt that his poems were good by any reasonable standard. He did not wish to be dismissed by those who had no interest in children of nature as 'an impertinent blockhead, obtruding his nonsense on the world; [who] because he can make a shift to jingle a few doggerel, Scotch rhymes together, looks upon himself as a Poet of no small consequence forsooth', and so he proceeded, in a very unploughmanlike manner, to quote the 'divine Elegies' of 'that celebrated Poet' Shenstone to the effect that 'Humility has depressed many a genius to a hermit, but never raised one to fame' and then defended his use of the word 'genius' with reference to himself. He then disclaimed equality with either Ramsay or Fergusson, though he admitted imitating them. (To move from Shenstone to Fergusson in one paragraph was indication of the confused role he was playing). He ended the Preface with a reiteration both of his desire for fame, and of his lack of mercenary intention, and an almost hysterical appeal to be judged fairly:

> To his Subscribers, the Author returns his most sincere thanks. Not the mercenary bow over a counter, but the heart-throbbing gratitude of the Bard, conscious how much he is indebted to Benevolence and Friendship, for gratifying him, if he deserves it, in that dearest wish of every poetic bosom – to be distinguished. He begs his readers, particularly the Learned and the Polite, who may honour him with a perusal, that they will make every allowance for Education and Circumstances of Life: but, if after a fair, candid, and impartial criticism, he shall stand convicted of Dulness and Nonsense, let him be done by, as he would in that case do by others – let him be condemned, without mercy, to contempt and oblivion.

Here we see his characteristic touchiness and pride, which, incidentally, led him so to disregard the most elementary laws of rhetoric as to leave the reader with strong (though hypothetical) abuse of the poet ringing in his ears: 'Let him be condemned, without mercy, to contempt and oblivion'. The poet wanted no favour or special consideration; he was an illiterate ploughman, but he was convinced of his own genius, uninterested in making money out of his poems, and full of a proper pride. And with this not wholly consistent picture of himself he left the stage and rang up the curtain on his poems.

The Kilmarnock volume opens with 'The Twa Dogs, a Tale'. This poem was not one of Burns's earliest but was written (or at least completed) in February, 1786, after he had almost decided on publication. It shows Burns under the influence neither of the sentimental English models which inspired, unfortunately, so much of his earlier work nor of the pure folk tradition, but of the older Scottish literary tradition which descended to him through Ramsay and Fergusson. Scottish literature has always had a particular aptness for handling animal stories: Robert Henryson in the fifteenth century had in his *Fables* treated his animal characters with a much more lively human feeling than was usual in the medieval beast fable, and later poets maintained a tradition of comic or mock-heroic treatment of animals which Burns seized on with gusto. The immediate model of the poem was probably Fergusson's 'Mutual Complaint of Plainstanes and Causey', which, like 'The Twa Dogs', was written in octosyllabic couplets and takes the form of a dialogue (between the footpath and the main part of the road) after a preliminary description of the general setting. Burns had caught from Fergusson the conversational ease in handling this verse form which was to be such a feature of his best verse letters. Fergusson begins the dialogue part of his poem in this relaxed manner (Plainstanes is speaking):

> My friend, thir hunder years and mair,
> *tired out*   We've been forfoughen late and air,
> In sun-shine, and in weety weather,
> *harsh*   Our thrawart lot we bure thegither.

This is the accent that Burns caught and improved on in 'The Twa Dogs'. He moves into the poem with a splendid ease:

> 'Twas in that place o' Scotland's isle,
> That bears the name o' auld king Coil,
> Upon a bonie day in June,
> When wearing thro' the afternoon,
> *busy*   Twa Dogs, that were na thrang at hame,
> *met by*
> *chance*   Forgather'd ance upon a time.

The reader finds himself accepting the human characteristics of the dogs before he is aware of it. 'Two dogs, that were na thrang at hame' – the explanation of how they happened to be free to forgather and chat convinces us by its sheer matter-of-factness. The note of complacent gossip continues:

> The first I'll name, they ca'd him Caesar,
> Was keepit for His Honor's pleasure;
> *ears* His hair, his size, his mouth, his lugs,
> Shew'd he was nane o' Scotland's dogs,
> But whalpet some place far abroad,
> Where sailors gang to fish for Cod.

—He was a Newfoundland dog, in fact, and a gentleman—

> His locked, letter'd, braw brass-collar
> Shew'd him the gentleman an' scholar.

Burns preserves a straight face as he proceeds to catalogue Caesar's qualities, and the smooth, flexible trot of the rhymed octosyllables helps him to do so. The other dog, Luath, modelled on a faithful animal of his own that had recently been killed, was no aristocrat, but, like the poet himself, 'a rhyming, ranting, roving billie':

> *wise* He was a gash, an' faithfu' tyke,
> *leaped; ditch* As ever lap a sheugh or dyke.
> *stone fence*
> *pleasant;* His honest, sonsie, baws'nt face,
> *whitestriped* Ay gat him friends in ilka place;
> *every* His breast was white, his towzie back,
> *shaggy* Weel clad wi' coat o' glossy black;
> *joyous* His gawsie tail, wi' upward curl,
> *buttocks* Hung owre his hurdies wi' a swirl.

There is a sense of triumph in those last two lines, with its joyful description of Luath's up-curling tail keyed to poverty and democracy, by the use of the familiar vernacular word 'hurdies'. This is no ploughman poet artlessly warbling of what he sees around him, but a conscious artist deliberately exploiting the resources of his native dialect and a literary tradition of his people to present a picture, half-humorous, half-ironic, both of animals as men and (by implication) of men as animals. (The irony glances obliquely from 'hurdies'; the description had started off like that of a knight's plume or a coat-of-arms, but comes slyly to earth on this word. We are reminded that Burns had written to Dr. Moore: 'I have not the most distant pretensions to what the pye-coated guardians of escutcheons call, A Gentleman'.)

The dialogue that follows is most artfully constructed. Caesar begins by pitying the kind of life led by poor dogs such as Luath, and Luath agrees that life among the poor has its disadvantages but that it also has its compensations:

knew	But how it comes, I never kent yet,
	They're maistly wonderfu' contented;
stout lads;	An' buirdly chiels, and clever hizzies,
young women	Are bred in sic a way as this is.

Caesar replies by pointing out that nevertheless the poor are contemptuously treated by the gentry – and by now we have an idea of where the poem is going: it is going to be a social satire. Caesar's picture of the treatment of the poor by the rich is drawn from Burns's own memories of his father's treatment by his landlord in the last years of his life, and behind the lively description there is a grim note. Luath replies with a moving picture of the bright side of rustic life, which is nevertheless (unlike 'The Cotter's Saturday Night') utterly free from sentimentality:

	The dearest comfort o' their lives,
thriving	Their grushie weans an' faithful wives;
	The prattling things are just their pride,
	That sweetens a' their fire-side.
sometimes;	An' whyles twalpennie worth o' nappy
ale	Can mak the bodies unco happy;
	They lay aside their private cares,
	To mind the Kirk and State affairs;
	They'll talk o' patronage and priests,
	Wi' kindling fury in their breasts,
	Or tell what new taxation's comin,
marvel	An' ferlie at the folk in Lon'on.
	As bleak-fac'd Hallowmass returns,
harvest-homes	They get the jovial, ranting Kirns,
	When rural life, o' ev'ry station,
	Unite in common recreation;
glances	Love blinks, Wit slaps, an' social Mirth
	Forgets there's Care upo' the earth.

That merry day the year begins,
They bar the door on frosty win's;
smokes; froth   The nappy reeks wi' mantling ream,
An' sheds a heart-inspiring steam;
smoking;   The luntin pipe, an' sneeshin mill,
snuffbox   Are handed round wi' right guid will;
cheery;   The cantie, auld folks, crackin crouse,
talking merrily   The young anes ranting thro' the house —
romping   My heart has been sae fain to see them,
That I for joy hae barkit wi' them.

Then comes the unexpected turn in the poem. Luath makes a reference to the great man going to London to attend Parliament, 'for Britain's guid his saul indentin', when he is interrupted by Caesar:

faith   Haith, lad, ye little ken about it;
For Britain's guid; guid faith! I doubt it.
going   Say, rather, gaun as Premiers lead him,
An' saying *aye* or *no's* they bid him:
At operas an' plays parading,
Mortgaging, gambling, masquerading:
Or maybe, in a frolic daft,
To Hague or Calais taks a waft,
To mak a tour, an' tak a whirl,
To learn *bon ton* an' see the worl'.

There, at Vienna or Versailles,
tears   He rives his father's auld entrails;
Or by Madrid he taks the rout,
fight; cattle   To thrum guitars an' fecht wi' nowt;
Or down Italian vista startles,
Whore hunting amang groves o' myrtles:
drinks; muddy   Then bouses drumly German water,
To mak himsel look fair and fatter,
An' clear the consequential sorrows,
Love-gifts of Carnival Signoras.

For Britain's guid! for her destruction!
Wi' dissipation, feud an' faction.

The dog who had begun by pitying the poor now leads the attack on the rich, and henceforth it is Luath who does the tut-tutting. It's true, says Caesar, that great folks need not starve or sweat,

> But human-bodies are sic fools
> For a' their colledges an' schools,
> That when nae real ills perplex them,
> They mak enow themsels to vex them.

By now the ambling, conversational quality of the verse which we found in the earlier part of the poem has changed into a brisk, sharp-toned, satirical style. The indictment flashes forth with wit and point, and Burns achieves in octosyllables something of what Pope achieved with the heroic couplet. The fine contempt of 'For a' their colledges and schools' (deriving in part from the key word 'schools' rhyming with the earlier key word 'fools') and the sneer suggested by the double rhyme of 'perplex them' with 'vex them' show a complete mastery of the art of satirical verse.

The contemptuous picture is built up to a climax:

> The Ladies arm-in-arm in clusters,
> As great an' gracious a' as sisters;
> But hear their absent thoughts o' ither,
> *downright*   They're a' run deils an' jads thegither.
> Whyles, owre the wee bit cup an' platie,
> They sip the scandal potion pretty;
> *livelong*   Or lee-lang nights, wi' crabbit leuks
> *playing*
> *cards*   Pore owre the devil's pictur'd beuks;
> Stake on a chance a farmer's stackyard,
> An' cheat like ony unhang'd blackguard.

It has been fancy swordplay up to this point, but with that last couplet the victims are hit over the head with a club. There is a pause, then a slight modification of the indictment in a couplet that stands in a verse paragraph of its own—

> There's some exceptions, man an' woman;
> But this is Gentry's life in common —

before the poet rounds off his poem with a perfect little coda:

> By this, the sun was out o' sight,
> An' darker gloamin brought the night:
> The bum-clock humm'd wi' lazy drone,
> The kye stood rowtin i' the loan;
> When up they gat an' shook their lugs,
> Rejoic'd they were na *men*, but *dogs*;
> An' each took off his several way,
> Resolv'd to meet some ither day.

beetle

cattle; low-ing; lane

The two dogs melt quietly into the evening landscape, in lines that remind one of the opening of Gray's 'Elegy'; then the poet makes a final ironic gesture ('Rejoic'd they were na *men* but *dogs*') before ending with the quiet matter-of-factness with which he had opened.

We turn from the accomplished octosyllables of 'The Twa Dogs' to 'Scotch Drink', the second poem in the Kilmarnock volume (again, not one of the earliest poems, but written at the end of 1785 or early in 1786), and at first sight we might imagine we have come face to face with the rustic bard in simple bacchanalian mood. It is true, of course, that the poem is a bacchanalian poem, with a deliberately induced and not very profound roistering mood. But like 'The Twa Dogs' it ends in a rather different mood from that in which it began; there is a careful progress here from mere baccchanalianism to a presentation of an ideal of the simple life. Both poems are concerned with poverty and the possibility of happiness for the poor – a favourite topic with Burns. And though 'Scotch Drink' is neither as skilful nor as appealing as 'The Twa Dogs', it shows Burns's mastery of the difficult 'Standard Habbie' verse form and his ability to maintain a conversational tone while manipulating it. Burns seems to have taken the idea of the poem from Fergusson's 'Caller Water', a charming and ironic piece, beginning with praise of water and deftly turning into a celebration of the girls of his native city. (It is probably from Fergusson that Burns learned to 'turn' a poem with such dexterity, moving it from its ostensible to its real subject without the reader's being aware of the shift.)

The poem opens with a rousing statement of its theme. The first three stanzas form a kind of introduction, and in each there is a pause after the fourth line, where the poet takes breath, as it were, before rising to a more passionate utterance:

Let other Poets raise a fracas
'Bout vines, an' wines, an' druken Bacchus,
torment   An' crabbit names an' stories wrack us,
ear   An' grate our lug,
barley   I sing the juice Scotch bear can mak us,
In glass or jug.

O thou, my Muse! guid, auld Scotch Drink!
winding   Whether thro' wimplin worms thou jink,
dodge   Or, richly brown, ream owre the brink,
cream   In glorious faem,
foam   Inspire me, till I lisp an' wink,
To sing thy name!

meadows   Let husky Wheat the haughs adorn,
oats;   An' Aits set up their awnie horn,
bearded   An' Pease and Beans, at een or morn,
Perfume the plain,
blessings   Leeze me on thee, John Barleycorn,
on   Thou king o' grain!

In the first verse, the pause after 'An' grate our lug' is obvious and emphatic (many modern editors print a colon after the line), and the last two lines begin with a joyful emphasis on the first personal pronoun:

I sing the juice Scotch bear can mak us,
In glass or jug.

The pause is less emphatic in the second stanza, but it is there, and again marks the poet's turn towards his subject with magnificent passion:

Inspire me, till I lisp an' wink,
To sing thy name!

The third stanza, which concludes the invocation, ends with the ecstatic

Leeze me on thee, John Barleycorn,
Thou king o' grain!

The leaning on the first, long monosyllable ('Leeze'), the introduction at the end of the line of the term 'John Barleycorn' with all its rich folk undertones, and the climactic 'Thou king o' grain' take this aspect of the subject as far as it can go. He has hailed Scotch drink with as passionate

a gesture as poetry is capable of – we almost see the poet with out-
stretched arms and upturned face in that last line, abandoning himself to
welcoming his subject – and if the poem is to develop at all he must turn
it in another direction.

He turns it ably and quietly by introducing a series of scenes describing
the application of Scottish drink to Scottish life:

often; chews
her cud   On thee aft Scotland chows her cood,
pliable; choice   In souple scones, the wale o' food!
                     Or tumbling in the boiling flood
greens   Wi' kail an' beef;
                     But when thou pours thy strong heart's blood,
                               There thou shines chief.

For ten verses he develops this aspect of the subject, etching one after
another little scenes of conviviality which range from the domestic
warmth of

silver dress   Aft, clad in massy, siller weed,
                     Wi' Gentles thou erects thy head;
                     Yet humbly kind, in time o' need,
                               The poor man's wine;
porridge   His wee drap parritch, or his bread,
seasons   Thou kitchens fine

to the harvest merrymaking of

foams in the   That merry night we get the corn in,
horn cup   O sweetly, then, thou reams the horn in!
smoking   Or reekin on a New-year mornin
wooden   In cog or bicker,
vessels
whisky   An' just a wee drap sp'ritual burn in,
tasty sugar   An' gusty sucker!

with its effective double rhymes. This section ends with a picture of
liquor cementing quarrels:

law-case   When neebors anger at a plea,
angry   An' just as wud as wud can be,
-brew   How easy can the barley-brie
                               Cement the quarrel!
                     It's aye the cheapest Lawyer's fee
                               To taste the barrel.

The third section of the poem now begins, and here he strikes a patriotic note. In four stanzas he castigates those who prefer imported brandies and wines to their native drink, and ends with a fine curse:

bladder   May gravels round his blather wrench,

face;   An' gouts torment him, inch by inch,

frown   Wha twists his gruntle wi' a glunch

                        O' sour disdain,

over   Out owre a glass o' whisky punch

                        Wi' honest men!

Then he returns to whisky and himself:

         O Whisky! soul o' plays an' pranks!

         Accept a Bardie's gratefu' thanks!

         When wanting thee, what tuneless cranks

                  Are my poor Verses!

         Thou comes – they rattle i' their ranks

                  At ither's arses!

The sublime vulgarity of that last line is almost a climax in itself, but Burns cunningly moves the poem through two transitional stanzas (lamenting the loss of the privileged tax-free still of Ferintosh and cursing the 'horse leeches of the Excise') to end on a note descriptive of his own ideal:

whole   Fortune! if thou'll but gie me still

breeches   Hale breeks, a scone, an' whisky gill,

abundance   An' rowth o' rhyme to rave at will,

                     Tak a' the rest,

         An' deal't about as thy blind skill

                     Directs thee best.

This stanza, which parallels the opening invocation, stands by itself at the end of the poem, throwing a new light on the earlier descriptions of rustic content and merrymaking, while serving as the true climax of the poem. Just as Fergusson's 'Caller Water' started as a poem in praise of water and ended as a tribute to the beauty of the Edinburgh girls, Burns's 'Scotch Drink' turns from a bacchanalian poem into a poem on the nature of happiness.

     One might generalize at this point and observe that Burns is always at his best as a moralist when the moralizing is implicit, when it emerges unobtrusively from a sharply etched picture of a certain kind of life or from a simple outburst of emotion (as in 'John Anderson My Jo'). His overt moralizing, nearly always done with an eye on a genteel and sentimental audience, is often offensive and generally inappropriate poetically. Sentiment to Burns (this was one of the lessons he imbibed from his reading in eighteenth-century English literature) was the bridge that could connect the Ayrshire farmer with the genteel tradition of his day, the link between rusticity and sophistication; but he was happier when he forgot about the necessity of crossing this gap. The bridge led to an area of eighteenth-century civilization which had nothing helpful to offer him.

Before we move on to the other poems in the Kilmarnock volume, a word should be said about the epigraph to 'Scotch Drink', which is a paraphrase in Scots verse of the sixth and seventh verses of the thirty-first chapter of Proverbs. This is how the verses go in the King James Bible (which was, of course, the version Burns knew):

> Give strong drink unto him that is ready to perish, and wine unto those that be of heavy hearts.
> Let him drink, and forget his poverty, and remember his misery no more.

And here is Burns's epigraph:

> Gie him strong drink until he wink,
>   That's sinking in despair;
> An' liquor guid to fire his bluid,
>   That's prest wi' grief an' care:
> There let him bouse, an' deep carouse,
>   Wi' bumpers flowing o'er,
> Till he forgets his loves or debts,
>   An' minds his griefs no more.

> SOLOMON'S PROVERBS, xxxi. 6, 7

Burns has here done to the stately prose of the King James Bible precisely what he did to the theological concept of the Devil in his 'Address to the Deil'. He has changed the key of the passage, transposed it into an idiom that is partly derived from folklore and partly based on a Scots literary tradition that owes nothing to the Bible. This is an aspect of Burns's *implicit* attack on Calvinism that is worth attention. His explicit attacks were never so successful, because they were directed from a some-what insecure base – a sentimental deism which was neither profound nor clearly thought out. But by setting theological concepts beside the daily lives and problems of ordinary people, by showing what they meant in terms of 'the loves or debts' of a struggling farmer, he was able both to reinterpret and to criticize much in the theological thought of his day that had till then remained dead formulas or mere shibboleths.

'Scotch Drink' is followed in the Kilmarnock volume by 'The Author's Earnest Cry and Prayer, to the Right Honorable and Honour-able, the Scotch Representatives in the House of Commons'. This is a lively appeal to the Scottish Members of Parliament to repeal the heavy taxation of Scotch whisky, done in the 'Standard Habbie' verse form with a fine ease and vivacity. It is one of Burns's slighter works but shows him the complete master of his medium, treating the subject with a laughing abandon while retaining a sure hold of his technique. He uses the traditional poetic properties with humorous realism:

worn out with
shouting;
hoarse

Alas! my roupet Muse is hearse!
Your Honor's hearts wi' grief 'twad pierce,
To see her sittan on her arse
      Low i' the dust,
An' scriechan out prosaic verse,
      An' like to brust!

This poem, too, has a turn and moves skilfully from a lament over the state of whisky into a patriotic effusion:

Arouse, my boys! exert your mettle,
To get auld Scotland back her kettle!

wager;
ploughstaff

Or faith! I'll wad my new pleugh-pettle,
      Ye'll see't or lang,

smoking
knife

She'll teach you, wi' a reekin whittle,
      Anither sang.

fretful

This while she's been in crankous mood,
Her lost Militia fir'd her bluid;

may
trick

(Deil na they never mair do guid,
      Play'd her that pliskie!)

stark mad

An' now she's like to rin red-wud
      About her Whisky.

to it

An' L——d, if ance they pit her till't,
Her tartan petticoat she'll kilt,
An' durk an' pistol at her belt,
     She'll tak the streets,
An' rin her whittle to the hilt,
     I' the first she meets!

The poem dies away in a final compliment to the Members of Parliament he is supposed to be addressing, in which with deliberate mischief he domiciles them in a rustic environment by using humble phrases like 'sowps o' kail and brats o' claise' and referring to St. James's as 'St. Jamie's':

sups; broth
scraps; clothes
jackdaws

God bless your Honors, a' your days,
Wi' sowps o' kail and brats o' claise,
In spite o' a' the thievish kaes
     That haunt St. Jamie's!
Your humble Bardie sings an' prays
     While Rab his name is.

We have in this poem a characteristic mixture of humorous exaggeration, swaggering patriotism, and implicit social criticism. There is no conflict between these elements, all sit comfortably together in a fine, swinging verse, whose apparent effortlessness conceals a remarkable prosodic skill.

     The 'Postscript' which follows is really a separate poem, a roistering drinking song, a glorified toast to Scotland and the ordinary working Scotsman:

eyes; shut
smoke

Sages their solemn een may steek,
An' raise a philosophic reek,
An' physically causes seek,
     In clime an' season,
But tell me Whisky's name in Greek,
     I'll tell the reason.

sometimes

lose;
water

Scotland, my auld, respected Mither!
Tho' whyles ye moistify your leather,
Till whare ye sit, on craps o' heather,
     Ye tine your dam;
Freedom and Whisky gang thegither
     Tak aff your dram!

The swagger here is sometimes a little forced, the poem as a whole is rather feverish (and wavers badly into a conventional neoclassic idiom at the beginning of the second stanza), and there is a ring of the inferior kind of street ballad about some of the passages; but as an expression of democratic male conviviality keyed to a liquorish patriotism it is as good as can be done. And the final couplet is as effective a toast as anybody has yet contrived.

The next poem, 'The Holy Fair' (which is perhaps earlier than any of the preceding, though its date is uncertain), is the first of those in the Kilmarnock volume which show the full stature of Burns as a poet working in the Scots literary tradition. We have already said something of the Scottish poems describing popular celebrations which play such a central part in the older Scottish poetry; 'The Holy Fair' belongs in this category, with 'Peblis to the Play', 'Christ's Kirk on the Green', and many others. The tradition descended to Burns through Watson's *Choice Collection*, Ramsay's *Ever Green*, and Fergusson, whose 'Leith Races' and 'Hallow Fair' he clearly had in mind. Here is the opening of 'Leith Races':

> In July month, ae bonny morn,
> > Whan Nature's rokelay green

cloak
every

> Was spread o'er ilka rigg o' corn
> > To charm our roving een;
> Glouring about I saw a quean,

staring; girl
sky
silver

> > The fairest 'neath the lift;
> Her een were o' the siller sheen,
> > Her skin like snawy drift,
> > > Sae white that day. . . .

> 'An' wha are ye, my winsome dear,
> > That takes the gate sae early? . . .

fresh

> 'I dwall amang the caller springs
> > That weet the Land o' Cakes,

cheerful

> And aften tune my canty strings
> > At bridals and late-wakes:
> They ca' me Mirth; I ne'er was kend
> > To grumble or look sour,
> But blyth wad be a lift to lend,

try

> > Gif ye wad sey my pow'r
> > > An' pith this day.'

Burns follows his model fairly closely:

Upon a simmer Sunday morn,
    When Nature's face is fair,
I walked forth to view the corn,
    An' snuff the caller air,
The rising sun, owre Galston muirs,
    Wi' glorious light was glintin;
The hares were hirplin down the furs
    The lav'rocks they were chantin
         Fu' sweet that day.

As lightsomely I glowr'd abroad,
    To see a scene sae gay,
Three Hizzies, early at the road,
    Cam skelpin up the way.
Twa had manteeles o' dolefu' black,
    But ane wi' lyart lining;
The third, that gaed a wee a-back,
    Was in the fashion shining
         Fu' gay that day.

The twa appear'd like sisters twin,
    In feature, form, an' claes;
Their visage wither'd, lang an' thin,
    An' sour as ony slaes:
The third cam up, hap-step-an'-lowp,
    As light as ony lambie,
An' wi' a curchie low did stoop,
    As soon as e'er she saw me,
         Fu' kind that day.

Wi' bonnet aff, quoth I, 'Sweet lass,
    I think ye seem to ken me;
I'm sure I've seen that bonie face,
    But yet I canna name ye'.
Quo' she, an' laughin as she spak,
    An' taks me by the hauns,
'Ye, for my sake, hae gi'en the feck
    Of a' the ten commauns
         A screed some day.

Glosses (left margin):

fresh

hopping; furrows
larks

gazed

young women
spanking

grey
walked a
bit behind

clothes

shoes
hop; jump

curtsey

bulk

rip

'My name is Fun – your cronie dear,
　　The nearest friend ye hae;
An' this is Superstition here,
　　An' that's Hypocrisy.

going　　　　　I'm gaun to Mauchline Holy Fair,
merrymaking　　　To spend an hour in daffin:
if; wrinkled　　Gin ye'll go there, yon runkl'd pair,
　　We will get famous laughin
　　　　　　　At them this day.'

The stanza form, which is a simplified version of a very old Scottish form, used in 'Christ's Kirk on the Green' and 'Peblis to the Play', and the machinery come from Fergusson; but the development of the poem is Burns's own, as is the firm grasp on structure. The introduction of Fun as the figure who guides Burns through the Holy Fair[1] determines both the mood and the organization of the poem. With Fun presiding, this is no harsh satire, but good-humoured observation, narrated by one who relished the paradoxes and absurdities of human nature. Unlike some of his other satirical poems, 'The Holy Fair' shows no bitterness towards any of the characters held up for the reader's amusement, only a delighted acceptance of the bustling, crowded, variegated scene, and of the different kinds of hypocrisy, narrowness, confusion, enthusiasm, drinking, and love-making which are to be found there. The attack on the ministers he disliked is conducted with happy nonchalance:

In guid time comes an antidote
　　Against sic poison'd nostrum;
foot　　　　For Peebles,[2] frae the water-fit,
　　Ascends the holy rostrum:
See, up he's got the word o' God,
prim　　　An' meek an' mim has view'd it,
While Common-Sense has taen the road,
　　An' aff, an' up the Cowgate
　　　　　　Fast, fast that day.

One need hardly dwell on the appropriateness of that fine phrase 'meek an' mim', or on the comic significance of the image of common sense taking the road when the Reverend Mr. Peebles gets up to preach, or on the impression of the poet standing by, helpless with laughter, conveyed by the repetition of 'fast' in that concluding

Fast, fast that day.

Again, there is not a whit of malice in his account of 'Wee Miller'
professing strict orthodoxy,

> Tho' in his heart he weel believes,
>   An' thinks it auld wives' fables:
> *fellow; living*   But faith! the birkie wants a Manse,
> *artfully;*   So, cannilie he hums them;
> *humbugs*
>   Altho' his carnal wit an' sense
> *nearly half–* Like hafflins-wise o'ercomes him
>   At times that day.

The 'carnal' is, of course, a gibe at the orthodox jargon of the day.

The structure of the poem is worth remark. The opening stanzas
describe the general setting and the poet's encounter with Fun, who
offers to conduct him round the Holy Fair. He agrees to go, and returns
home to change his shirt:

> Quoth I, 'With a' my heart, I'll do't;
> *shirt*   I'll get my Sunday's sark on,
>   An' meet you on the holy spot;
> *we'll*   Faith, we'se hae fine remarkin!'

There follows a lively description of the sights and sounds of the Fair,
in which the verse gathers speed and the reader is given a vivid sense of
crowds and bustle. Burns takes every opportunity to point out the crazy
mixture of the religious and the secular which is so characteristic of the
scene:

> Here some are thinkin on their sins,
> *clothes*   An' some upo' their claes;
> *soiled*   Ane curses feet that fyl'd his shins,
>   Anither sighs an' prays: . . .

This section concludes with a hail from the poet to the one kind of
participator in the proceedings who is there for a single purpose and
knows exactly what it is:

> O happy is that man an' blest!
>   Nae wonder that it pride him!
> Wha's ain dear lass, that he likes best,
>   Comes clinkin down beside him!

> Wi' arm repos'd on the chair-back,
>   He sweetly does compose him;
>   Which, by degrees, slips round her neck,
> *palm*   An's loof upon her bosom
>   Unkend that day.

Now comes a change of tempo, and we move to the religious aspect of the Fair. The first stanza of this section opens slowly, but it has picked up speed by the time it concludes:

> Now a' the congregation o'er
>   Is silent expectation;
> *climbs*   For Moodie speels the holy door,
>   Wi' tidings o' damnation.[3]
> Should Hornie, as in ancient days,
>   'mang sons o' God present him,
> The vera sight o' Moodie's face,
>   To ain het hame had sent him
>   Wi' fright that day.

After the various preachers have been presented with tolerant irony, we move over to observe the 'yill-caup [ale-stoup] commentators' enjoying themselves in the change house, where they meet to discuss the preachers over their ale, and here the noise rises to its climax:

> While thick an' thrang, an' loud an' lang,
>   Wi' Logic, an' wi' Scripture,
> They raise a din, that, in the end,
>   Is like to breed a rupture
>   O' wrath that day.

Two transitional stanzas bring us back to the second bout of preaching, and by now, though the preachers are more violent than ever, the audience (doubtless under the influence of the ale) is inclined to be sleepy, and wakes up only when 'Black Russell' roars forth a hair-raising description of hell:

> A vast, unbottom'd, boundless pit,
> *full; flaming*   Fill'd fou o' lowin brunstane,
> *brimstone*
> Wha's ragin flame, an' scorchin heart,
> *whinstone*   Wad melt the hardest whun-stane!

The half asleep start up wi' fear,
An' think they hear it roarin,
When presently it does appear,
'Twas but some neebor snorin
Asleep that day.

The Fair then disintegrates into lunch parties, and the poem ends with a
brilliant summing-up of the incongruous elements of which the
'occasion' was composed:

How monie hearts this day converts
O' Sinners and o' Lasses!
by nightfall;   Their hearts o' stane gin night are gane,
gone   As saft as ony flesh is.
There's some are fou o' love divine;
There's some are fou o' brandy;
An' monie jobs that day begin,
fornication   May end in Houghmagandie
Some ither day.

The suggestion that the Holy Fair has been used by the young people
largely as an excuse for getting together and for making further appoint-
ments is made at intervals throughout the poem, but here in the final
stanza it is given new emphasis, as though to insist that nature will have
her way even in the midst of a theological jaunt – and this in turn is an
implicit criticism of Calvinism. But it is the calm juxtaposition of the
amorous, the bibulous, and the theological which gives this verse its
point and humour and which makes it a fitting conclusion of the whole.
There is a world of commentary on love, life, and religion in

How monie hearts this day converts
O' sinners and o' Lasses!

and

There's some are fou o' love divine;
There's some are fou o' brandy.

In using theological terms to describe the softening of the girls' hearts—

Their hearts o' stane gin night are gane
As saft as ony flesh is—

Burns is daringly reversing an old tradition in religious poetry – the practice of using secular love terms to denote divine love. This is the absolute antithesis of, say, the poetry of Crashaw: instead of starting from the natural and physical and moving up to the ecstatic and divine, Burns starts from the coldly theological and moves rapidly down to the physical and the earthy.

This is time's revenge on *The Gude and Godlie Ballatis*, which in the heyday of Calvinist enthusiasm had tried to make love poetry acceptable by presenting it in religious guise. The revolutionary implications of such poems as 'The Holy Fair' are best seen when they are put aside by side with the theologized love poems of the sixteenth century. Yet in a profounder sense Burns's position is conservative rather than revolutionary; he was reaching back to an earlier tradition, before the voice of John Knox was heard in the land, to the days of the 'merry world' sighed after by John Selden, before 'the Fairies left dancing and the Parson left conjuring'.

The next poem, 'Address to the Deil', another of the group composed late in 1785 or early in 1786, is also an example of Burns's indirect attack on the Calvinist attitude. His devil is the devil of folklore, of popular superstition, rather than of theology, and has more resemblance to Puck of *A Midsummer Night's Dream* than to Milton's Satan, for all the quotation from *Paradise Lost* at the head of the poem. Burns had made rather a parade of admiring Milton's Satan, professing to find in his character something of the pride which he himself felt it necessary to exhibit in the face of the genteel world. After his visit to Edinburgh he wrote a letter to William Nicol in which he expressed his scorn of the patronising 'patricians in Edinburgh' and 'the servility of my plebeian brethren' and went on immediately to discuss Milton's Satan:

I have bought a pocket Milton, which I carry perpetually about with me, in order to study the sentiments – the dauntless magnanimity; the intrepid unyielding independence; the desperate daring, and noble defiance of hardship, in that great personage Satan.

But this kind of gesture had nothing to do with his treatment of the devil in this poem, in which the Satan of *Paradise Lost* is reduced to earthy human dimensions much as the religious emotions are treated in 'The Holy Fair'. He sets the tone immediately by the names he gives the devil in the opening stanza:

Cloven-
foot

splashes;
brimstone
bowl
scald

> O thou! whatever title suit thee,
> Auld Hornie, Satan, Nick, or Clootie,
> Wha in yon cavern grim an' sootie,
>   Clos'd under hatches,
> Spairges about the brunstane cootie,
>   To scaud poor wretches.

One can hardly recognize the 'Chief of many throned powers', the prince 'that led th' embattled seraphim to war', in Auld Hornie or Clootie, still less in the Auld Hangie of the second stanza. There is a fine familiarity, a 'mateyness' in Burns's approach to the devil and in his treatment of his activities (with which most of the poem is taken up), and this is always his way when he seeks to undermine the contemporary theological approach to man and nature. The picture of Auld Nick spairging about the brunstane cootie to scaud poor wrteches is a humorous parody of the Devil's activities as described in innumerable sermons of the period. The devil is just a naughty boy having his fun, and Burns wags an amused but admonitory finger at him:

Hangman

> Hear me, auld Hangie, for a wee,
> An' let poor, damned bodies be;
> I'm sure sma' pleasure it can gie,
>   Ev'n to a deil,
> To skelp an' scaud poor dogs like me,
>   An' hear us squeel!

The picture of his own possible damnation as implying merely his suffering at the hands of a mischievous prankster is a much more effective (though implicit) attack on the hell-fire preachers than is the sentimental morality of Hutcheson. Burns proceeds to run through a list of the devil's activities in which he combines folk traditions with biblical references, but the biblical references are treated with a deliberate lack of reverence, as in his account of Satan's part in the temptation of Job:

bustle
smoky;
scorched wig
smutty

cast

> D'ye mind that day, when in a biz,
> Wi' reekit duds, an' reestit gizz
> Ye did present your smoutie phiz,
>   'Mang better folk,
> An' sklented on the man of Uzz
>   Your spitefu' joke?

The lack of reverence does not, however, imply any contempt for the Bible, rather the desire to see the Bible story as a series of human documents which can be immediately related to the daily life of contemporary man. His description of Adam and Eve in the Garden of Eden presents them as very human lovers with no theological aura around them:

long ago; Lang syne in Eden's bonie yard,
garden When youthfu' lovers first were pair'd,
An' all the Soul of Love they shar'd,
The raptur'd hour,
Sweet on the fragrant, flow'ry swaird,
In shady bow'r.

An earlier version, which Burns never published, illustrates this point more clearly:

Lang syne in Eden's happy scene
Adam's When strappin Edie's days were green
An' Eve was like my bonie Jean
My dearest part,
A dancin, sweet, young, handsome queen
Wi' guileless heart.

The poem has a clearly defined structure. After the invocation, in which, as we have noted, the names he applies to the devil set the tone for his treatment, he proceeds to define the devil's activities in terms of folklore (with more than once a mischievous suggestion that accidents popularly attributed to the devil have purely natural causes, such as the drunkenness of the victim – a device he uses again most happily in 'Tam o' Shanter') and then in terms of his biblical and theological activities. He sums up his catalogue thus:

But a' your doings to rehearse,
fighting Your wily snares an' fechtin fierce,
Sin' that day Michael did you pierce,
Down to this time,
beat; Low- Wad ding a Lallan tongue, or Erse,
land In prose or rhyme.

The third and concluding section expresses the poet's own view of the devil, with a cheerful insouciance that sums up the mood of the poem:

                An' now, auld Cloots, I ken ye're thinkin,
roistering   A certain Bardie's rantin, drinkin,
hurrying   Some luckless hour will send him linkin
                        To your black pit;
dodging   But, faith! he'll turn a corner jinkin,
                        An' cheat you yet.

                But fare you weel, auld Nickie-ben!
                O wad ye tak a thought an' men'!
perhaps   Ye aiblins might – I dinna ken –
                        Still hae a stake —
woe   I'm wae to think upo' yon den,
                        Ev'n for your sake!

The final suggestion that even the devil might perhaps repent and escape from 'yon den' is not the mere sentimentality that some critics have believed it to be: it is a satiric thrust at the Calvinist view adroitly disguised as a piece of sentimentalism. It is not, of course, a serious suggestion, but one made with the lighthearted airiness that characterizes the poem as a whole. But the picture of the poet wagging his finger at the devil in friendly admonition and suggesting that even he may be saved sets the entire theological conception of original sin in a context where it cannot survive; in such surroundings the doctrine dissolves or, one might say, blows up. And this method, too, is common in Burns's poetry – to reduce theological abstractions to daily realities in terms of the ordinary experience of ordinary people. The implied philosophy may not be profound, but the method is certainly effective.

The next poem in the Kilmarnock volume is 'The Death and Dying Words of Poor Mailie', one of the earliest of Burns's poems; Gilbert has described the occasion of its writing. Robert had bought a ewe and two lambs from a neighbour and kept the ewe in a field adjoining the house at Lochlie. 'He and I were going out with our teams, and our two younger brothers to drive for us, at mid-day, when Hugh Wilson, a curious-looking, awkward boy, clad in plaiding, came to us with much anxiety in his face, with the information that the ewe had entangled herself in the tether, and was lying in the ditch. Robert was much tickled with Huoc's appearance and posture on the occasion. Poor Mailie was set to rights, and when we returned from the plough in the evening he repeated to me her *Death and Dying Words* pretty much in the way they now stand.' Like 'The Twa Dogs', this poem is in the Scottish tradition of animal poems and gains its effect by the lively manner in which the human emotions are attributed to animals:

> . . . And now, my bairns, wi' my last breath,
> I lea'e my blessin wi' you baith:
> An' when ye think upo' your Mither,
> Mind to be kind to ane anither.

Whether Burns was thinking of Hamilton of Gilbertfield's 'Last Dying Words of Bonny Heck' (included in Watson's *Choice Collection*) or Ramsay's 'Lucky Spence's Last Advice' and 'Last Speech of a Wretched Miser' can hardly be determined and is not a point of much importance. 'Poor Mailie's Elegy', the poem immediately following, was certainly written with 'The Epitaph of Habbie Simson' and its imitations by Ramsay and Fergusson in mind. The significant fact is that Burns thus early in his career was working with traditional materials even when he was writing an 'occasional' poem prompted by a real incident. Already he had found in his native literature verse forms and other technical apparatus which he could effectively employ when he had something to say.

The gap we find in the Kilmarnock volume between such poems as those on Mailie and the poems written in the English tradition represents more than the difference between good and bad craftsmanship; rather, it represents the difference between a usable and an unusable literary tradition. It should be emphasized that Burns was no more an untaught child of nature when he wrote in 'Standard Habbie' than when he imitated Shenstone: in both instances he was following a literary mode. One mode helped him to find proper discipline for his inspiration; the other cramped his style. When we consider that 'The Death and Dying Words of Poor Mailie' was written long before he had decided to present himself to the world as a printed poet, that it was an early poem thrown off under the inspiration of a real incident in order to amuse himself and his friends, we cannot help being astonished at the sureness of instinct that led him to choose the literary form he used. That it *was* a literary form and no haphazard rhyming by a rustic versifier is made clear by any reasonably careful reading of the poem. 'The Death and Dying Words of Poor Mailie' is a mock testament – a form with a long tradition in Scottish and other European literatures – and it is done in smooth octosyllables that march with a conversational ease from the short but expressive introduction through the actual testament to the final brief description of Mailie's death. And throughout runs a warm human feeling saved from sentimentality by humour. Here is no Sterne venting his emotions over an ass, but a poet with a farmer's feeling for animals and a satirist's awareness of the weakness of human resolutions and institutions; here is rich comic sympathy for both man and beast.

'Poor Mailie's Elegy' was not contemporary with the 'Death and Dying Words' but was probably composed later with an eye to publication in the Kilmarnock volume. Its ancestry becomes apparent if we quote the opening of several earlier Scottish mock elegies. Here is the opening verse of Robert Sempill's 'Life and Death of the Piper of Kilbarchan or, the Epitaph of Habbie Simson' as printed in Watson's *Collection*:

> Kilbarchan now may say alas!
>> For she hath lost her game and grace,
> Both Trixie, and the Maiden Trace:
>> But what remead?
> For no man can supply his place,
>> Hab Simson's dead.

remedy

And here is the beginning of Hamilton of Gilbertfield's 'Last Dying Words of Bonny Heck', also from Watson:

> Alas, alas, quo' bonny Heck,
> On former Days when I reflect!
> I was a Dog much in Respect
>> For doughty Deed:
> But now I must hing by the Neck
>> Without Remeed.

And here is the first verse of Ramsay's 'Elegy on John Cowper':

> I wairn ye a' to greet and drone,
> John Cowper's dead, Ohon! Ohon!
> To fill his post, alake there's none,
>> That with sic speed
> Could sa'r sculdudry out like John,
>> But now he's dead.

smell im-
morality

Finally, here is the opening of Fergusson's 'Elegy on the Death of Mr. David Gregory, Late Professor of Mathematics in the University of St. Andrews':

Now mourn, ye college masters a'!
And frae your ein a tear let fa',
Fam'd Gregory death has taen awa'
    Without remeid;
The skaith ye've met wi's nae that sma',
    Sin Gregory's dead.

Coming to 'Poor Mailie's Elegy' after reading the earlier poems, we see at once the tradition in which Burns was working:

salt

copestone

Lament in rhyme, lament in prose,
Wi' saut tears trickling down your nose;
Our Bardie's fate is at a close,
    Past a' remead;
The last, sad cape-stane of his woes;
    Poor Mailie's dead!

The very rhyme words are the same – 'remead' and 'dead' (pronounced 'deed') – in 'Habbie Simson', the Fergusson poem, and in the Burns elegy. Burns shows the same mixture of mockery and genuine affection that we find in Fergusson, but Burns's poem has in addition that special unsentimental feeling of companionship for animals which he expresses with greatest success in 'The Auld Farmer's New-Year-Morning Salutation to His Auld Mare, Maggie'. It is, of course, a slight poem, but done with fluency and craftsmanship and a sense of joy in handling his subject – the joy of the artist who knows he is master of his medium – which shines out above the superficial melancholy of the subject matter.

Following the 'Elegy' in the Kilmarnock volume is the first of Burns's verse letters, the 'Epistle to James Smith'. It was not the first in order of composition – the other letters in this volume are all earlier – and shows the poet handling the 'Standard Habbie' form with remarkable ease and assurance. The poem progresses from an introductory expression of friendship to a statement of Burns's personal philosophy, reaches its climax in the fourth stanza from the end, and then dies away with a final appeal to his intimacy with Smith. These verse epistles of Burns – the best of them, at least, those written in Scots and addressed to genuine friends – combine a sense of rambling conversational discourse with a precise, though by no means an obvious, structure. They do read like letters, but they are not as inconsequential as most real letters are.

The opening three verses of compliment have a happy, humorous exaggeration which does not, however, detract from the genuineness of the emotion conveyed:

slyest;   Dear Smith, the sleest, paukie thief,
humorous   That e'er attempted stealth or rief,
plunder   Ye surely hae some warlock-breef
wizard-
spell   Owre human hearts;
proof   For ne'er a bosom yet was prief
                       Against your arts.

     For me, I swear by sun an' moon,
above   And ev'ry star that blinks aboon,
     Ye've cost me twenty pair o' shoon
going   Just gaun to see you;
     And ev'ry ither pair that's done,
taken   Mair taen I'm wi' you.

gossip   That auld, capricious carlin, Nature,
stunted   To mak amends for scrimpet stature,
     She's turn'd you off, a human creature
               On her first plan,
     And in her freaks, on ev'ry feature,
               She's wrote, *the Man.*

The poem comes to a temporary climax at this point, in a strong and decisive line. Burns pauses for breath, as it were, and then moves into the letter proper:

     Just now I've taen the fit o' rhyme,
fermenting   My barmie noddle's working prime,
brain   My fancy yerkit up sublime
jerked   Wi' hasty summon:
     Hae ye a leisure-moment's time
               To hear what's comin?

It becomes evident immediately that the poem is to be about himself and his personal attitude to life. People rhyme for various reasons, he goes on to say –

trouble   For me, an aim I never fash;
about   I rhyme for fun.

This leads him to a stanza of self-characterization, which in turn develops naturally into a discussion of one of Burns's favourite themes – his relation to the educated gentry. Poets far more learned than he have had their day and in subsequent ages been neglected; what, then, are his chances of poetic fame?

> Then farewel hopes o' laurel-boughs,
> To garland my poetic brows!
> Henceforth I'll rove where busy ploughs
> *busily*   Are whistling thrang,
> *hollows*   An' teach the lanely heights an' howes
>   My rustic sang.

He proceeds to describe himself as a careless, carefree wanderer through life, and eventually the philosophy emerges:

> This life, sae far's I understand,
> Is a' enchanted fairy-land,
> Where Pleasure is the Magic Wand,
>   That, wielded right,
> Maks Hours like Minutes, hand in hand,
>   Dance by fu' light.

> The Magic-wand then let us wield;
> *climbed*   For, ance that five-and-forty's speel'd,
> *age*   See, crazy, weary, joyless Eild,
>   Wi' wrinkl'd face,
> *coughing;* Comes hostin, hirplin owre the field,
> *limping*   Wi' creepin pace.

Then for a moment he goes beyond his simple hedonism to generalize on the inexperience of youth. It is significant that the stanzas in which he does this are written in pure English, without a trace of Scots. His theme has led him to overt moralizing, and overt moralizing belongs to the English neoclassic tradition rather than to the Scottish tradition of lively verse letters. And so the tone changes suddenly:

> O Life! how pleasant in thy morning,
> Young Fancy's rays the hills adorning!
> Cold-pausing Caution's lesson scorning,
>   We frisk away,
> Like school-boys, at th' expected warning,
>   To joy and play.

We wander there, we wander here,
We eye the rose upon the brier,
Unmindful that the thorn is near,
       Among the leaves;
And tho' the puny wound appear,
       Short while it grieves.

Some are lucky, he proceeds, and

       find a flow'ry spot
For which they never toil'd nor swat,

some are able to pursue and eventually capture Fortune, and others – and
with the reference to these others he returns to himself and to a Scots
diction – are less successful:

Poor wights! na rules nor roads observin;
To right or left, eternal swervin,
       They zig-zag on;
Til, curst with age, obscure an' starvin,
       They aften groan.

Still, this kind of life has its compensations, and he ends by glorifying it.
Poetry and poverty are all right (provided poverty is not too extreme):

My pen I here fling to the door,
And kneel, 'Ye Pow'rs!' and warm implore,
'Tho' I should wander *Terra* o'er,
       In all her climes,
Grant me but this, I ask no more,
plenty   Ay rowth o' rhymes.

dripping 'Gie dreeping roasts to countra Lairds,
Till icicles hing frae their beards;
clothes Gie fine braw claes to fine Life-guards
       And Maids of Honour;
ale; And yill an' whisky gie to Cairds,
tinkers
loathe it   Until they sconner.

'A Title, Dempster merits it;
A Garter gie to Willie Pitt;
Gie Wealth to some be-ledger'd Cit,
       In cent. per cent.;
But give me real, sterling Wit,
       And I'm content.

> 'While Ye are pleas'd to keep me hale,
> I'll sit down o'er my scanty meal,
> Be't water-brose, or muslin-kail,
> 　　　　Wi' chearfu' face,
> As lang's the Muses dinna fail
> 　　　　To say the grace.'

meal and water; thin broth

He has now reached the position where he can look back on the respectable folk whom he began by envying and where he can realize that they in fact get much less out of life than he does. The attack on them is the real climax of the poem:

> O ye douce folk, that live by rule,
> Grave, tideless-blooded, calm and cool,
> Compar'd wi' you – O fool! fool! fool!
> 　　　　How much unlike!
> Your hearts are just a standing pool,
> 　　　　Your lives, a dyke!

sober

wall

The attack becomes deftly turned against hypocrisy:

> Ye are sae grave, nae doubt ye're wise;
> Nae ferly tho' ye do despise
> The hairum-scairum, ram-stam boys,
> 　　　　The rattling squad:
> I see you upward cast your eyes –
> 　　　　– Ye ken the road.–

wonder

headlong

Then with immense speed he adroitly manoeuvers the poem to a conclusion and returns to the theme of his opening verses:

> Whilst I – but I shall haud me there –
> Wi' you I'll scarce gang ony where –
> Then, Jamie, I shall say nae mair,
> 　　　　But quat my sang.
> Content with You to mak a pair,
> 　　　　Whare'er I gang.

hold

quit

The poem is in a sense an impromptu, and the supple rhythms and swiftly moving verses carry the reader on with splendid ease; we have only to set it beside some of the older Scottish verse epistles to see the nature of Burns's technical achievement. The 'Familiar Epistles' between William Hamilton of Gilbertfield and Allan Ramsay, though lively enough, are thin, wandering things compared with the 'Epistle to Davie'; 'J.S.'s' verse letter to Fergusson is clumsy and often forced – the author obviously had difficulty in fitting his thought to the verse form – and even Fergusson's reply, which is the best Scottish verse epistle before Burns, is too exclamatory and jovial to rate very high as a poem. It should be added, though, that Burns seems to have got the basic structure of his verse letters from this poem of Fergusson's, which starts off with a warm expression of friendship and links that expression, in the penultimate stanza, with his carefree philosophy of life:

Lothian	I trow, my mettl'd Louden lathie,
laddie	Auld farran birky I maun ca' thee,
clever	
fellow	For whan in gude black print I saw thee
mouth	Wi' souple gab,
	I skirl'd fou loud, 'Oh wae befa' thee!
adept	But thou'rt a daub.'

There follows 'A Dream', a poem which offended some of Burns's genteel friends but which he retained in the Edinburgh edition nevertheless. The poem is interesting for the traces of Jacobite feeling to be found in it and for its sprightly use of the same stanza he used in 'The Holy Fair'. The poet imagines himself, in a dream, present at the royal birthday levee of June, 1786, and addressing the King; he is also indirectly attacking the birthday ode of Thomas Warton, the poet laureate. The mixture of controlled respect and avuncular advice in his attitude towards the royal family is not happy, and 'A Dream' is not one of Burns's most successful pieces. He had not adequately organized the various elements in his attitude towards royalty, and at intervals a note of vulgar familiarity emerges which would have been offensive even if the poem had been addressed to a fellow farmer.

'The Vision', the next poem in the Kilmarnock volume, was much worked over by Burns before it saw publication but, in spite of the brilliance of the opening, he never managed to weld it into a proper whole. It is divided into two 'Duans' ('Duan', Burns explained in his note, 'a term of Ossian's for the different divisions of a digressive poem') of which the first is by far the more successful. He opens with a picture of a winter evening as effective as anything he ever achieved:

The sun had clos'd the winter day,
quitted   The Curlers quat their roaring play,
hare   And hunger'd Maukin taen her way
kitchen-   To kail-yards green,
gardens
each   While faithless snaws ilk step betray
        Whare she has been.

The reader's eye moves with the poet's from a general contemplation of the winter scene to the curlers leaving their play and thence, growing ever more particular, to the tracks left by the hare on the snow as she makes her way to the green kail-yards. We proceed indoors with the poet:

flail   The thresher's weary flingin-tree,
livelong   The lee-lang day had tired me;
        And whan the Day had clos'd his e'e,
        Far i' the West,
back parlour   Ben i' the spence, right pensivelie,
        I gaed to rest.

These opening verses move with a deliberate slowness – contrasting with the lively handling of the same verse form in other poems – until the poem comes almost to a stop in the third stanza:

chimney   There, lanely, by the ingle-cheek,
corner   I sat and ey'd the spewing reek,
smoke
cough-;   That fill'd, wi' hoast-provoking smeek,
smoke   The auld, clay biggin;
building   And heard the restless rattons squeak
rats   About the riggin.

The precision of the imagery, the pensive movement of the lines, the vivid sense of change from a winter exterior to a warm, smoking fireside, draw the reader right into the poem to become identified with the poet. Sitting by the fire and listening to the rats squeak in the roof, he falls into a muse:

dusty   All in this mottie, misty clime,
        I backward mus'd on wasted time,
        How I had spent my youthfu' prime,
        An' done nae-thing,
nonsense   But stringin blethers up in rhyme,
        For fools to sing.

This most effective depreciatory description of his poetic activity is no
piece of rhetorical false modesty: it represents a mood appropriate to the
entire atmosphere of weariness and somnolence which Burns has by now
so compellingly brought into the poem. He proceeds to reproach himself for not having given more attention to practical matters and is about
to vow that he will never again waste time writing poetry –

latch	When click! the string the snick did draw;
	And jee! the door gaed to the wa';
–flame	And by my ingle-lowe I saw,
	Now bleezin bright,
young	A tight, outlandish Hizzie, braw,
woman	Come full in sight.

The visitor turns out to be Coila, one of the spirits of his native part of
Ayrshire, and she has come to hail him as her poet and give him advice
on what to write about. But the truth is that Burns does not quite know
what to do with her when he has brought her in. This is made clear by
the extent to which he tinkered with the verses describing her; but in
spite of omissions and additions they never came out quite right. She is
first described as a rustic beauty, reminding him of 'my bonie Jean', and
then it becomes apparent that her mantle contains a sort of aerial photo-
graph of the district of Ayrshire she represents, with rivers dashing down
to the sea, mountains tossed to the skies, and woods, towers, palaces, and
towns. Looking more closely, he discerns 'bold stems of heroes, here
and there' engaged in a variety of activities – Coila's mantle has now
turned into a moving picture. Clearly, Burns is confused about the kind
of symbolism he means to employ, and the mixture of neoclassic conventions with Scots realism is evidence of that confusion.

In 'Duan Second' the girl addresses the poet:

> All hail! my own inspirèd Bard!
> In me thy native Muse regard!
> Nor longer mourn thy fate is hard,
>   Thus poorly low;
> I come to give thee such reward
>   As we bestow.

She goes on to explain in more detail just who she is and what she is
doing, notes the varying functions of different classes–

The humbler ranks of human-kind,
The rustic bard, the laboring hind,
The artisan –

and proceeds to explain that she has followed the poet's career with interest. She describes at some length the principal subjects of his poems, and points out that for all his skill he cannot learn nor can she show him how 'to paint with Thomson's landscape glow / Or wake the bosom-melting throe / With Shenstone's art', nor can he hope to 'pour, with Gray, the moving flow warm on the heart.' Nevertheless, he should 'strive in [his] humble sphere to shine', for a rustic bard is not to be despised. Then she sums up her advice:

To give my counsels all in one:
Thy tuneful flame still careful fan;
Preserve the dignity of Man,
                With soul erect;
And trust the Universal Plan
                Will all protect.

Finally:

'And wear thou *this*' – she solemn said,
And bound the holly round my head;
And polish'd leaves and berries red
                Did rustling play;
And, like a passing thought, she fled
                In light away.

'The Vision' has rapidly moved into standard neoclassic English, both in vocabulary and in properties, and long before we hear of Shenstone's 'bosom-melting throe' we have become aware that the poem has become a piece of gesturing for a genteel audience. We do not need the overt, sentimental moralizing of the second-last stanza to inform us that he has succumbed to his temptation to strike attitudes. The tone of the latter part of the poem is far removed from that of the fine opening; there is not, in fact, any clearer example in Burns's poetry of the way in which, when he had his eye on the wrong audience, he was liable to go wrong.

We need say little of 'Halloween', the poem that follows in the Kilmarnock edition. It is an able enough piece, and in it Burns handles the old Scottish stanza form he used in 'The Holy Fair' with equal skill, but the poem remains of more interest to the expert in folklore than to the general reader; its accumulation of descriptions of Halloween folk customs, couched in a language containing a higher percentage of rustic Scots words than is found in any other of Burns's poems, becomes tedious in spite of the lively movement and the skilfully manipulated verse.

There follows 'The Auld Farmer's New-Year-Morning Salutation to His Auld Mare, Maggie', which has rightly been called 'the most simple and direct, the most free from any touch of egoism, burlesque, or self-criticism' of all Burns's animal poems. Here the farmer's attitude to his faithful work animal is presented with an emotion so carefully controlled that it never approaches sentimentality. The mare is old and worn out, and the poet (who is, of course, the farmer in fact as well as in the poem) has come to give her 'the accustomed ripp of corn to hansel in the New-Year'. The opening is direct and realistic:

handful of corn; belly hollow	A *Guid New-year* I wish thee, Maggie!
	Hae, there's a ripp to thy auld baggie:
backed; bony	Tho' thou's howe-backit, now, an' knaggie,
	I've seen the day,
gone; colt lea	Thou could hae gaen like onie staggie
	Out-owre the lay.

As he feeds the animal, the poet remembers what she once was:

drooping	Tho' now thou's dowie, stiff, an' crazy,
	An' thy auld hide as white's a daisie,
glossy	I've seen thee dappl't, sleek an' glaizie,
	A bonie gray:
alert; dared; anger	He should been tight that daur't to raize thee,
	Ance in a day.

stalwart, firm, and supple	Thou ance was i' the foremost rank,
	A filly buirdly, steeve, an' swank,
	An' set weel down a shapely shank,
earth	As e'er tread yird;
ditch	An' could hae flown out-owre a stank,
	Like onie bird.

As his mood of reminiscence grows on him, he thinks of his own youth:

father-in-
law's mare   It's now some nine-an'-twenty year,
                   Sin' thou was my Guid-father's Meere;
dowry   He gied me thee, o' tocher clear,
                          An' fifty mark;
money   Tho' it was sma', 'twas weel-won gear,
strong   An' thou was stark.

                   When first I gaed to woo my Jenny,
mother   Ye then was trottin wi' your Minnie:
sly   Tho' ye was trickie, slee, an' funnie,
vicious   Ye ne'er was donsie;
tractable;   But hamely, tawie, quiet, an' cannie,
easy   An' unco sonsie.
good natured

He returns to the mare, and thinks of all the occasions 'when thou an' I
were young and skeigh' (mettlesome) and of the years of faithful service
the mare has rendered, and the note of remembered companionship
grows stronger as the poem moves to its climax:

day's work   Monie a sair daurk we twa hae wrought,
world   An' wi' the weary warl' fought!
                   An' monie an anxious day, I thought
                          We wad be beat!
                   Yet here to crazy Age we're brought,
                          Wi' something yet.

The final verse, as Dr. Snyder has pointed out, has almost the quality of
the second stanza of 'John Anderson My Jo':

lived   We've worn to crazy years thegither;
totter   We'll toyte about wi' ane anither;
attentive;   Wi' tentie care I'll flit thy tether,
change   To some hain'd rig,
reserved   Whare ye may nobly rax your leather,
ridge   Wi' sma' fatigue.
stretch

Yet Burns keeps the emotion in superb control, and instead of turning
off into a note of self-pity, as in the poems on the mouse and the daisy,
he ends quietly and unaffectedly on a note of simple realism – the mare
will in its remaining days be kept in a special patch of grass and be given
plenty to eat. Though it is true that part of the effectiveness of the poem

derives from the subdued undertones concerning human companionship that set it going, there is no overt comparison of the horse to a human being, no romantic seeking after an animal soul, but simply the direct and vividly drawn account of what horse and owner had done in their youth. The subject is never anything more than a farmer and his mare: everything is kept concrete and realistic. Yet there is a deep underlying pathos, which Burns has the tact never to release or make artificial or ridiculous.

The poem which follows is one of the best known and most admired of all Burns's works, 'The Cotter's Saturday Night'. It was written in 1785 or early in 1786, very probably with an eye to publication. It is certainly directed at that genteel audience whom Burns never kept an eye on without loss. And in fact, though the poem contains several fine single stanzas, it is very imperfect. 'It is the most artificial and the most imitative of Burns's works', wrote Henley and Henderson in their notes to the Centenary Edition, with some exaggeration but with a great deal of truth; it is certainly the most imitative and artificial of his *major* works. 'Not only is the influence of Gray's *Elegy* conspicuous', these editors add, 'but also there are echoes of Pope, Thomson, Goldsmith, and even Milton; while the stanza, which was taken, not from Spenser, whom Burns had not then read, but from Beattie and Shenstone, is so purely English as to lie outside the range of Burns's experience and accomplishment'. These are severe words, but on the whole they are justified, even though the point is not that Pope, Thomson, Goldsmith, 'and even Milton' (why the influence of Milton should be surprising is not clear) influenced Burns's style in this poem but that in composing it he was writing with one eye on his subject and another squinting at the kind of audience whom he sought to please by imitating these poets. The original inspiration came from 'The Farmer's Ingle' of Fergusson, a more successful though a less ambitious poem. In expanding the scope of the work from a simple but moving picture of the Scottish farmer at home into a self-consciously moralistic poem, Burns has weakened the effect of his fine descriptive passages and spoiled the tone of the piece as a whole.

Here is the opening of 'The Farmer's Ingle':

sky	Whan gloming grey out o'er the welkin keeks,
oxen	Whan Batie ca's his owsen to the byre,
sore tired;	
shuts	Whan Thrasher John, sair dung, his barn-door steeks,
winnowing	And lusty lasses at the dighting tire;
defeats	
makes;	What bangs fu' leal the e'enings coming cauld,
snow-topped	And gars snaw-tapit winter freeze in vain;

sad
scared;
poverty

Gars dowie mortals look baith blyth and bauld,
  Nor fley'd wi' a' the poortith o' the plain;
Begin, my Muse, and chant in hamely strain.

pieces of
turf;
thatched
turfs
smoke;
sky

partition

every

neat

Frae the big stack, weel winnow't on the hill,
  Wi' divets theekit frae the weet and drift,
Sods, peats, and heath'ry trufs the chimley fill,
  And gar their thick'ning smeek salute the lift;
The gudeman, new come hame, is blyth to find,
  Whan he out o'er the halland flings his een,
That ilka turn is handled to his mind,
  That a' his housie looks sae cosh and clean;
For cleanly house looes he, tho' e'er sae mean.

ploughmen
meal;
draught
cannot

dish
broth
roof
seasoning

Weel kens the gudewife that the pleughs require
  A heartsome meltith, and refreshing synd
O' nappy liquor, o'er a bleezing fire:
  Sair wark and poortith douna weel be join'd.
Wi' butter'd bannocks now the girdle reeks,
  I' the far nook the bowie briskly reams;
The readied kail stand by the chimley cheeks,
  And had the riggin het wi' welcome steams,
Whilk than the daintiest kitchen nicer seems.

The praise of rustic good, the oblique criticism of luxurious living, is here in Fergusson as it is in 'The Cotter's Saturday Night', but it is brought in naturally and without posturing; this is true, also, of Fergusson's handling of the patriotic note, a note which is sounded too stridently in Burns's poem. 'The Farmer's Ingle' continues:

mouths;
learn
diligent
grow

drugs

Frae this lat gentler gabs a lesson lear;
  Wad they to labouring lend an eidant hand,
They'd rax fell strang upo' the simplest fare,
  Nor find their stamacks ever at a stand.
Fu' hale and healthy wad they pass the day,
  At night in calmest slumbers dose fu' sound,
Nor doctor need their weary life to spae,
  Nor drogs their noddle and their sense confound,
Till death slip sleely on, and gi'e the hindmost wound.

When Fergusson goes on to describe the family's conversation, he does not, as Burns does, suddenly begin moralizing about the possibility of 'a wretch, a villain, lost to love and truth' seducing one of the farmer's daughters and proceed to execrate this hypothetical character, but instead mentions casually how they gossip about the affairs and illegitimate children of their neighbours (and one must remember how common illiegitmate children were in the eighteenth-century Scottish countryside):

intimate
bowl;
chatter

farm's

stool of
repentance
scolding

The couthy cracks begin whan supper's o'er,
   The cheering bicker gars them glibly gash
O' simmer's showery blinks and winters sour,
   Whase floods did erst their mailins produce hash:
'Bout kirk and market eke their tales gae on,
   How Jock woo'd Jenny here to be his bride,
And there how Marion, for a bastard son,
   Upo' the cutty-stool was forc'd to ride,
The waefu' scald o' our Mess John to bide.

The children are ready for bed now, and have their bedtime story before they retire for the night:

never a
sound

cry

rows;
flame
witches;
hobgoblin
dwell
ruffles

The fient a chiep's amang the bairnies now;
   For a' their anger's wi' their hunger gane:
Ay maun the childer, wi' a fastin mou',
   Grumble and greet, and make an unco mane,
In rangles round before the ingle's low:
   Frae gudame's mouth auld warld tale they hear,
O' Warlocks louping round the Wirikow,
   O' gaists that win in glen and kirk-yard drear,
Whilk touzles a' their tap, and gars them shak wi' fear.

Finally, everybody is ready for sleep: the oil lamp is flickering low, conversation lags, and 'tacksman [farmer] and cotter eke to bed maun steer'. Fergusson ends the poem with a superb stanza of simple benediction:

ploughshare;
soil

harvests;
scouring
comfortable

Peace to the husbandman and a' his tribe,
   Whase care fells a' our wants frae year to year;
Lang may his sock and couter turn the gleyb,
   And bauks o' corn bend down wi' laded ear.
May SCOTIA's simmers ay look gay and green,
   Her yellow har'sts frae scowry blasts decreed;
May a' her tenants sit fu' snug and bien,
   Frae the hard grip of ails and poortith freed,
   And a lang lasting train o' peaceful hours succeed.

Burns is not content to stay within the limits of his model. The very fact that he dedicated 'The Cotter's Saturday Night' to Robert Aiken, the bustling, sentimental, but extremely practical Ayr lawyer, is an indication of his desire to keep an eye on a city audience; for, although 'Orator Bob' was a convivial and democratic soul who admired Burns's Scots poems and spoke the Doric himself, apparently his purpose in this poem is to stand for the genteel man of feeling. The opening stanza (which sounds as though it had been added to the poem as an after-thought) is full of the posturing which Burns was led into when he wrote with the genteel tradition too much in mind.

> My lov'd, my honor'd, much respected friend!
>   No mercenary Bard his homage pays;
> With honest pride, I scorn each selfish end,
>   My dearest meed, a friend's esteem and praise:
>   To you I sing, in simple Scottish lays,
> The lowly train in life's sequester'd scene;
>   The native feelings strong, the guileless ways,
> What Aiken in a Cottage would have been;
> Ah! tho' his worth unknown, far happier there, I ween!

Here is that touchy emphasis on pride again, that unnecessary disclaimer of mercenary motives – which appears quite ludicrous when embodied in a Spenserian stanza – and a preposterous sentimentalism which could actually suggest that the plump and prosperous little lawyer would have been happier in a cottage than in his comfortable house in Ayr! The two lines which contain this fantastic suggestion ring false even to the casual ear.

But if we forget this absurd opening and treat the second verse as the real beginning, we have at once what promises to be a grand poem:

moan

> November chill blaws loud wi' angry sugh;
>   The short'ning winter-day is near a close;
> The miry beasts retreating frae the pleugh;
>   The black'ning trains o' craws to their repose:
>   The toil-worn Cotter frae his labor goes,
> This night his weekly moil is at an end,
>   Collects his spades, his mattocks, and his hoes,
> Hoping the morn in ease and rest to spend,
> And weary, o'er the moor, his course does hameward bend.

This is a richer verse than the opening of 'The Farmer's Ingle': the line is slower and more musical, and fits perfectly the sense of weariness that hangs over the stanza and culminates in the long, slow last line. Burns is clearly reaching out to something more elaborate than the simpler (but effective) verse of Fergusson, and if he could have kept the whole poem in the key of this stanza the achievement would have been remarkable.

The third verse is not quite so successful (the 'aged tree' in the second line sounds rather like a stage property, and the last line is too propositional and lacks the weight such a line requires if it is to balance the stanza adequately). But the tone has not yet changed:

> At length his lonely Cot appears in view,
>   Beneath the shelter of an aged tree;
> *totter*   Th' expectant wee-things, toddlin, stacher through
> *fluttering*   To meet their Dad, wi' flichterin noise and glee.
>   His wee-bit ingle, blinkin bonilie,
> His clean hearth-stane, his thrifty Wifie's smile,
>   The lisping infant, prattling on his knee,
> Does a' his weary carking cares beguile,
> And makes him quite forget his labor and his toil.

In addition to the defects noted, one might object also to 'the lisping infant, prattling on his knee', as too stylized and conventional a picture to fit a realistically drawn cottage interior. We should prefer the 'bairnies' of 'The Farmer's Ingle'. Nevertheless, the poem has not yet gone off the rails. (We are ignoring the opening verse, and considering the poem as beginning with the second.)

In the next stanza the verse is lighter and not quite so well adapted to the elaborate Spenserian stanza (Burns would have done better to use Fergusson's simpler form):

> *by-and-by*   Belyve, the elder bairns come drapping in,
>   At service out, amang the Farmers roun';
> *drive;*
> *heedful;*   Some ca' the pleugh, some herd, some tentie rin
> *run*   A cannie errand to a neebor town:
> *quiet*   Their eldest hope, their Jenny, woman grown,
>   In youthfu' bloom, Love sparkling in her e'e,
> *hard-;*   Comes hame, perhaps to shew a braw new gown,
> *wages*   Or deposite her sair-won penny-fee,
>   To help her Parents dear, if they in hardship be.

The only serious fault to find here is the last line, which has a curious, stilted air, and like the final line of the preceding verse is not adequate to balance the stanza as a whole.

The next verse is a curious mixture of Scots realism and eighteenth-century convention, and it marks the beginning of a serious confusion in the poem:

With joy unfeign'd, brothers and sisters meet,

asks   And each for other's weelfare kindly spiers:

The social hours, swift-wing'd, unnotic'd fleet;

uncommon   Each tells the uncos that he sees or hears.
things

The Parents, partial, eye their hopeful years;

Anticipation forward points the view;

makes;   The Mother, wi' her needle and her sheers,
clothes;   Gars auld claes look amaist as weel's the new;
almost   The Father mixes a' wi' admonition due.

Terms like 'social hours' hardly sort well with such straightforward expressions as 'each tells the uncos that he sees or hears', while in the last four lines the juxtaposition of a personified Anticipation pointing the way like Washington crossing the Delaware and the simple, realistic statement that

> The Mother, wi' her needle and her sheers,
> Gars auld claes look amaist as weel's the new; . . .

is even more awkward.

There is something, too, rather overdeliberate and sententious about the picture of the father intervening in the conversation periodically in order to utter moral *sententiae:*

> The Father mixes a' wi' admonition due,

though this is very probably how William Burnes behaved. The development, in the following stanza, of the picture of the father giving advice in scriptural language may well be realistic enough, and it adds a note of gravity which is not forced or unprepared for; nevertheless, the presentation of the father as a biblical patriarch has a note of complacency about it which is faintly disturbing.

The picture which follows, of a 'neebor lad' coming in to see Jenny, is tight with self-consciousness, in spite of some happy touches. The mother seems overconcerned lest the boy be some 'wild, worthless rake', and the description of her inquiring his name 'with heart-struck, anxious care' is out of key with the general picture of a typical cotter's Saturday night, suggesting rather that this is a particular crisis in Jenny's life. The pose becomes more and more artificial, and when Burns, the greatest of all celebrators of the way of a man with a maid in its most unsophisticated form, pauses to contemplate the possibility of Jenny's seduction, we do not have to know anything of the history of the poet's own relations with women to notice at once the absurd artificiality of the stanza in such a context:

> Is there, in human form, that bears a heart –
>   A Wretch! a Villian! lost to love and truth!
> That can, with studied, sly, ensnaring art,
>   Betray sweet Jenny's unsuspecting youth?
> Curse on his perjur'd arts! dissembling smooth!
> Are Honor, Virtue, Conscience, all exil'd?
>   Is there no Pity, no relenting Ruth,
> Points to the Parents fondling o'er their Child?
> Then paints the ruin'd Maid, and their distraction wild!

The ruined maid, who comes from *The Man of Feeling* and other sentimental works of the period, is an artificial and melodramatic figure in this humble cottage. This verse is, in fact, full of melodramatic gestures, such as 'Curse on his perjur'd arts' – we almost see the villain in a black cloak and curled black moustachios – and the redundant, conventional language ('Is there no Pity, no relenting Ruth?') shows how far away from good writing Burns could get when he moved into a tradition in which he was not at home. The point was not that Burns was wrong to write in English; he could write excellent English verse, and some of his best songs are in English, but this is poetic diction of the worst kind and is clearly linked to the artificial pose which Burns, at this stage of the poem, was endeavouring to maintain.

It is perhaps not wholly irrelevant to add that in terms of the mores of the Scottish peasantry in Burns's day, a 'maid' was not 'ruined' if she was seduced before marriage; there were many cases of the birth of a child preceding the marriage of the lovers, who subsequently became perfectly respectable citizens, and the history of Burns's own relations with Jean Armour – by no means unique in this respect – bears this out. But there is no need to judge the stanza on the basis of sociological accuracy in order to see what is wrong with it. On purely technical grounds it can be seen to be impossible in this context.

It is with relief that we turn back, in the next verse, to the simple activities of the cottagers:

But now the Supper crowns their simple board,
wholesome   The healsome Parritch, chief of Scotia's food;
sup; cow   The soupe their only Hawkie does afford,
beyond;
partition   That 'yont the hallan snugly chows her cood:
-saved   The Dame brings forth, in complimental mood,
cheese;   To grace the lad, her weel-hain'd kebbuck, fell,
strong   And aft he's prest, and aft he ca's it guid;
The frugal Wifie, garrulous, will tell,
twelve
month;   How 'twas a townmond auld, sin' Lint was i' the bell.
flax; flower

This is admirable, and the subsequent picture of family prayers shows how Burns could introduce dignity and religion into his picture without artificial posturing. This is the true tone of rustic worship, and something on which Fergusson does not touch:

The chearfu' Supper done, wi' serious face,
    They, round the ingle, form a circle wide;
The Sire turns o'er, wi' patriarchal grace,
hall-   The big ha'-Bible, ance his Father's pride:
His bonnet rev'rently is laid aside,
grey side-   His lyart haffets wearing thin and bare;
locks   Those strains that once did sweet in Zion glide,
chooses   He wales a portion with judicious care;
'And let us worship God!' he says, with solemn air.

The next three verses, giving the theme of their prayers and praises, have no trace of Scots in their diction. This is perfectly appropriate, as well as historically accurate, for the Scottish rustic of the period would in fact move into the language of the King James Bible on such occasions. Burns makes this transition natural and effective, and we get a sense of a conscious move from the secular to the religious in the family behaviour. More questionable is the sixteenth verse of the poem, with its quotation from Pope's 'Windsor Forest' (duly acknowledged by Burns in a footnote) and the rather doubtful attempt at metaphysical sublimity in the last line,

While circling Time moves round in an eternal sphere.

Burns probably had in mind Addison's hymn:

> What though in solemn Silence all
> Move round the dark Terrestrial Ball
> What though nor real Voice nor Sound
> Amidst their radiant Orbs be found? . . .

There follows a somewhat intrusive stanza, also in standard English, in which Burns contrasts the simple 'language of the soul' with 'Religion's pride, / In all the pomp of method and of art', to the disadvantage of the latter. Here, again, Burns's attempt both to *be* his subject and to stand outside it and show it off to a genteel audience spoils the poem. We return from this moralizing to the cottage scene:

> Then homeward all take off their sev'ral way;
> The youngling cottagers retire to rest. . . .

That second line sounds rather forced beside Fergusson's

> The fient a chiep's amang the bairnies now,

and when we are presented with another picture of the parents at prayer, we begin to wonder impatiently whether these cottagers do not spend all their time at their devotions.

The poem moves into its conclusion, in the nineteenth stanza, with a fine line, simple and impressive, which promises well:

> From scenes like these old Scotia's grandeur springs,

but once again Burns moves into his exhibitionist moralizing:

> And certes, in fair Virtue's heavenly road,
> The Cottage leaves the Palace far behind;
>   What is a lordling's pomp! a cumbrous load,
> Disguising oft the wretch of human kind,
> Studied in arts of Hell, in wickedness refin'd!

The patriotic emotion which follows is genuine enough, and the expression has a certain power in spite of its conventional abstractions:

> O Scotia! my dear, my native soil!
>   For whom my warmest wish to Heaven is sent!
> Long may thy hardy sons of rustic toil
>   Be blest with health, and peace, and sweet content!

> And, O! may Heaven their simple lives prevent
> From Luxury's contagion, weak and vile!
> Then, howe'er crowns and coronets be rent,
> A virtuous Populace may rise the while,
> And stand a wall of fire around their much-lov'd isle.

But he overdoes the patriotic note, and in his final stanza seems to forget altogether the real theme of his poem:

> O Thou! who pour'd the patriotic tide,
> That stream'd thro' Wallace's undaunted heart;
> Who dar'd to, nobly, stem tyrannic pride,
> Or nobly die, the second glorious part,
> (The Patriot's God, peculiarly thou art,
> His friend, inspirer, guardian, and reward!)
> O never, never, Scotia's realm desert,
> But still the Patriot, and the Patriot-Bard,
> In bright succession raise, her Ornament and Guard!

There is probably no poem of Burns's in which the introduction of an artificial personality has spoiled a potentially fine work to the extent that it has in 'The Cotter's Saturday Night'. The main trouble is that the poet has kept shifting his attitude, and with it his diction, between several incompatible positions. He is at one time the sympathetic, realistic observer; at another he is almost the cotter himself; at still another he is the sophisticated moralist acting as guide, showing off his rustic character for the benefit of a sentimental, genteel audience. That audience appreciated the exhibition Burns prepared for them; Henry Mackenzie mentioned the poem as an 'advantageous' example 'of the tender and the moral', and *The English Review* of February, 1787, singled it out as 'the best poem in the collection'. 'It is written', wrote this reviewer, 'in the stanza of Spenser, which probably our bard acquired from Thomson's "Castle of Indolence" and Beattie's "Minstrel". It describes one of the happiest and most affecting scenes to be found in a country life, and draws a domestic picture of rustic simplicity, natural tenderness, and innocent passion that must please every reader whose feelings are not perverted.'

In spite of – perhaps because of – such praise, Burns must have known that there were incongruous elements in the poem, and known exactly what they were. It would be going too far to say that he must have known that these incongruous elements were faults, for his taste was never sure when he moved into the English sentimental tradition. He seems to have been trying to give scope and dignity to his work by grafting on these suggestions from Gray and Shenstone and Beattie. He was making the same mistake that Matthew Arnold made when he denied high seriousness to Burns; for neither realized that high serious-ness can be achieved in all sorts of ways (including the use of irony) without being overtly present. Burns imagined that these moral gestures, these melodramatic attitudes and self-conscious displays of himself as a man of feeling, would add that high seriousness. In fact, of course, they only spoiled the poem, and (as Matthew Arnold conceded) there is more real 'high seriousness' in

> We twa hae paidl'd in the burn,
>   Frae morning sun till dine;
> But seas between us braid hae roar'd
>   Sin' auld lang syne

than in any of the poems he wrote with an eye on the genteel tradition of his time. There is certainly a far more profound understanding of the relation between the sexes in 'The Ranting Dog, the Daddie O't', the poem he wrote for Jean when she bore his child out of wedlock, than in any of his remarks about Jenny and the risks she ran from country rakes in 'The Cotter's Saturday Night'. The critic of Burns can always appeal from Philip drunk to Philip sober, from Burns as a self-conscious man of feeling to Burns the inspired Scottish poet. If Burns did not know what was wrong with his picture of the cotter, there were dozens of his own poems that could have told him.

By this time the reader of the Kilmarnock volume will be able to discern clearly the three elements in Burns's poetry – the native Scots tradition, both folk and literary; the genteel tradition of his age; and of course his own taste and genius – and to see the relation of the three in Burns's poetic activity. We have seen how a combination of Scots literary influences and an exhibitionism directed at the literati and their tastes could spoil such a poem as 'The Cotter's Saturday Night'. There are other poems in the Kilmarnock edition which show the same un-happy results: some of them – for example, 'A Bard's Epitaph', which concludes the book – use a Scots literary form but are otherwise English in inspiration and timidly genteel in attitude. The group of five gloomy poems which are placed together in the latter part of the volume (three of them deriving, apparently, from the period of severe depression at Irvine in the winter of 1781–1782) show that, even when the mood is genuine and the stanza form native Scots, Burns can produce lugubrious platitudes like any minor 'pre-Romantic' poet of the period. Of the five – 'The Lament', 'Despondency, an Ode', 'Man Was Made to Mourn', 'Winter, a Dirge', and 'A Prayer in the Prospect of Death' – the first is of some slight biographical interest, since it was occasioned by his apparent desertion by Jean Armour; the second shows that Burns could write a complete poem of genteel despair in neoclassic English while employing throughout the old Scots stanza form of 'The Cherry and the Slae'; 'Man Was Made to Mourn' is based on an old folk song his mother used to sing, yet it employs a rhetorical neoclassic idiom; and 'A Prayer in the Prospect of Death' has something of the tone of the Scottish metrical version of the Psalms.

The various ways in which Burns handled some of the traditions available to him can be illustrated by comparing the wholly successful 'To a Mouse' with the less successful 'To a Mountain Daisy', in which he tried to repeat the success of the former poem but this time with his eye on the professional men of feeling in Edinburgh. 'To a Mouse' is quite different in tone from the animal poems we have already discussed. The mock-elegiac strain of the Mailie poems and the note of companionship in the new-year greeting to his old mare are alike absent from this friendly address to a mouse 'on turning her up in her nest with the plough November, 1785'. Though here as in the other animal poems he makes some kind of identification of the animal with the human world, the poem is essentially about himself, and the mouse is interesting to him because its plight reminds him of his own. The comparison, however, is neither forced nor sentimental, and the gap between the world of mice and that of men is bridged by a friendly compassion. The poem has charm and vigour, as well as technical skill. He opens with a direct address:

> Wee, sleekit, cowrin, tim'rous beastie,
> O, what a panic's in thy breastie!
> Thou need na start awa sae hasty,
> > Wi' bickering brattle!
> I wad be laith to rin an' chase thee,
> > Wi' murd'ring pattle!

hasty;
scamper
loath
ploughstaff

The effective pause after the first four lines adds emphasis to the statement of the poet's attitude in the last two and also prevents the stanza from dividing up in a purely mechanical way. Lesser practitioners of this verse form tended to make the pause consistently after the first two lines, so that the last four lines came together as a unit and the rhymes of the short lines jingled together too neatly. In the second verse there is no real pause at all:

> I'm truly sorry Man's dominion
> Has broken Nature's social union,
> An' justifies that ill opinion,
>   Which makes thee startle
> At me, thy poor, earth-born companion,
>   An' fellow-mortal!

We may wince a little at 'Nature's social union', a piece of neoclassic English which stands out from the Scots dialect of the poem as a whole, but in fact the sudden and brief introduction of a graver phrase is not inappropriate in its context; it gives us a momentary flash of a philosophical view of an order in nature, which is not made the subject of moralizing, but only lightly suggested. Light though the suggestion is, it swells out and provides an implicit moral basis for the poem.

The note of friendly compassion grows:

sometimes   I doubt na, whyles, but thou may thieve;
odd ear;   What then? poor beastie, thou maun live!
twenty-four   A daimen icker in a thrave
sheaves   'S a sma' request.
what's left   I'll get a blessin wi' the lave,
                    An' never miss't!

Having, at the end of both the second and the third verse, made the bridge between the mouse and himself, he is free to leave it unused for a while, returning to it at the end of the poem. He proceeds to build up a picture of the present plight of the mouse, contrasting it with the confident plans it had laid for the future:

            Thy wee-bit housie, too, in ruin!
feeble   Its silly wa's the win's are strewin!
build   An' naething, now, to big a new ane,
moss   O' foggage green!
            An' bleak December's winds ensuin,
biting   Baith snell an' keen!

One might note the effective use of the diminutive ('wee-bit housie') to strengthen the note of friendly concern, and the effective pause between

the first four lines and the strong close of the stanza. The suggestion of
'bleak December' is taken up in the following verses:

> Thou saw the fields laid bare an' waste,
> An' weary Winter comin fast,
> An' cozie here, beneath the blast,
>   Thou thought to dwell,
> Till crash! the cruel coulter past
>   Out thro' thy cell.

stubble

> That wee-bit heap o' leaves an' stibble
> Has cost thee monie a weary nibble!
> Now thou's turn'd out, for a' thy trouble,

without;
holding

>   But house or hald,

endure

> To thole the Winter's sleety dribble,

hoarfrost

>   An' cranreuch cauld!

In the seventh verse Burns returns to the bridge he had built earlier
and in a deft turn to the poem makes clear its real subject:

alone

> But, Mousie, thou art no thy lane,
> In proving foresight may be vain:
> The best-laid schemes o' Mice an' Men

awry

>   Gang aft a-gley,
> An' lea'e us nought but grief an' pain,
>   For promis'd joy!

The often quoted third and fourth lines of this stanza illustrate most effectively Burns's ability to cast a thought into the idiom of the folk proverb;
but the lines are more than that, for they mark a return to the bridge
between the two worlds of men and animals achieved effortlessly and
even with apparent casualness. Having linked 'mice an' men' in that
simple but telling phrase, he can proceed to speak of 'us', which now
means all mortal creatures. The comparison between the mouse and
himself is made explicit in the final stanza, where the autobiographical
nature of the poem at last becomes fully clear:

> Still thou are blest, compar'd wi' me!
> The present only toucheth thee:
> But, Och! I backward cast my e'e
>   On prospects drear!
> An' forward, tho' I canna see,
>   I guess an' fear!

'To a Mouse' provides an interesting contrast to 'The Cotter's Saturday Night', because in it Burns has made effective use of lessons he had
learned from English neoclassic poetry. He has not turned to the English
tradition for purposes of exhibitionism or overt moralizing, but in order
to sound, faintly and briefly, an occasional graver note which reverbe-
rates through the poem and expands its meaning. This point is worth
making, since it shows that the English neoclassic tradition was not
always or necessarily a corrupting influence on Burns.

'To a Mountain Daisy' (which comes near the end of the Kilmarnock
volume) is less successful. It lacks the ease and air of spontaneity which
mark the earlier poem, and we have a sense of emotion being deliberately
pumped up. The fault is not, as some critics have suggested, that a farmer
shows compassion for what his professional eye must have regarded as a
weed; farmers have no cause to love mice either, for that matter. But
after all, the mouse was a sentient being and was clearly discommoded
when Burns turned her up in her nest with the plough, whereas to pity
the feelings of the daisy involved the deliberate use of pathetic fallacy,
a legitimate enough figure of speech, but one which needs careful
handling. Throughout this poem Burns seems to be trying too hard to
express the pity of the daisy's situation. The opening is effective enough,
yet somewhat coy:

> Wee, modest crimson-tipped flow'r,
> Thou's met me in an evil hour. . . .

'Crimson-tipped' is perhaps a little heavy in this context, but the stanza
as a whole moves along with ease and conviction. The second verse
shows signs of strain:

> Alas! it's no thy neebor sweet,
> The bonnie Lark, companion meet! . . .

It is not the lark, it is Robert Burns with his plough; the contrast is not
wholly satisfactory, nor is the subsequent reference to the lark greeting
'the purpling east' appropriate in such a verse – it is too heavy and
elaborate.

The poem continues, building up (as in 'To a Mouse') the contrast
between the daisy before the plough crushed her and afterwards, with
some happy lines but never wholly sure of itself, until Burns, in a desperate effort to give the subject emotional quality by an impressive analogy,
strikes a completely false note:

Such is the fate of artless Maid,
Sweet flow'ret of the rural shade!
By Love's simplicity betray'd,
     And guileless trust,
Till she, like thee, all soil'd, is laid
     Low i' the dust.

From this ambiguous image of the betrayed maiden lying in the dust (done, it will be noted, in standard English) the poet moves to himself and thus becomes associated with both the daisy and the betrayed girl. After lamenting his own fate the poet proceeds towards the concluding climax of self-pity:

Ev'n thou who mournst the Daisy's fate,
That fate is thine – no distant date;
Stern Ruin's plough-share drives, elate,
     Full on thy bloom,
Till crush'd beneath the furrow's weight,
     Shall be thy doom!

It is significant that Burns changed the title of this poem from 'The Gowan' ('gowan' being the regular Scots word for daisy) to 'To a Mountain Daisy'. The new title has a touch of self-conscious sensibility about it, a quality with which the poem as a whole overflows. Writing to John Kennedy in April, 1786, Burns enclosed the poem and remarked:

I have here . . . inclosed a small piece, the very latest of my productions. I am a good deal pleased with some sentiments myself, as they are just the native querulous feelings of a heart which, as the elegantly melting Gray says, 'Melancholy has marked for her own.'

The elegantly melting Gray indeed! This is Burns in the mantle of the man of feeling. It should be added that he was successful in the role. 'To a Mountain Daisy' appealed to contemporary sentimental taste. Both Henry Mackenzie, in his *Lounger* review of December, 1786, and *The English Review* of February, 1787, quoted it in full. 'I have seldom', wrote Mackenzie, 'met with an image more truly pastoral than that of the lark in the second stanza. Such strokes as these mark the pencil of the poet, which delineates Nature with the precision of intimacy, yet with the delicate colouring of beauty and of taste. The power of genius is not less admirable in tracing the manners than in painting the scenery of

Nature'. The fact is, however, that Burns was not equipped to handle 'the scenery of Nature' as Mackenzie and those who thought as he did would have liked, and in trying to write for such an audience the poet only distorted his genius. His view of nature was equally different from that of the eighteenth-century dealers in the picturesque and the sublime and from that of the nineteenth-century Romantics. He was a farmer, and nature for him was associated with man's work and with the refreshment it might afford after such work.

If we wish to understand Burns's genuine view of humanity we should turn, not to his melodramatic poems of despair – such as the histrionic 'To Ruin', which follows 'To a Mountain Daisy' – or his expressions of sentimental morality, but to such a poem as the 'Epistle to a Young Friend', one of the most engaging and spontaneous of his poems, in which he jots down in a fine, flowing verse, for the benefit of Andrew Aiken, son of his good friend Robert Aiken of Ayr, his thoughts about life. (There is, however, a tradition that the poem was originally intended for another friend, William Niven of Kirkoswald, but this is very doubtful, and in any event is of no importance in a consideration of the value of the poem.)

The poem begins with an air of friendly casualness:

> I lang hae thought, my youthfu' friend,
>   A something to have sent you,
> Tho' it should serve nae ither end
>   Than just a kind memento:
> But how the subject-theme may gang,
>   Let time and chance determine:
> Perhaps it may turn out a sang;
>   Perhaps, turn out a sermon.

After this introductory stanza, Burns proceeds to moralize about man and his propensities for good and evil, but the moralizing proceeds so unselfconsciously, follows the curve of the verse so effectively, and is so free from any personal gesturing on the poet's part that the poem stands as a simple and eloquent testament of moral belief, without the slightest suggestion of exhibitionism or attitudinizing. The poem is of further interest as being one of the clearest statements of his own simple creed that he ever penned. Men are a sad lot, but the genuinely wicked are rare (one might contrast this view with some of the apostrophes to villainy in the more artificial poems); the most prevalent human weakness is selfishness:

Ye'll try the world soon, my lad;
 And, Andrew dear, believe me,
terrible   Ye'll find mankind an unco squad,
 And muckle they may grieve ye:
For care and trouble set your thought,
 Ev'n when your end's attainéd;
And a' your views may come to naught,
 Where ev'ry nerve is strainéd.

I'll no say men are villains a';
 The real harden'd wicked,
Wha hae nae check but human law,
 Are to a few restricked:
But och! mankind are unco weak,
 An' little to be trusted;
If self the wavering balance shake,
 It's rarely right adjusted!

The verse here is so organized as to suggest unpretentious conversation – it has the very ring of 'occasional' poetry – and even the rhymes, chiming so spontaneously together, give a sense of speed rather than of artificiality. The rhyming of 'attainéd' with 'strainéd' is perhaps a little forced, with its unconventional pronunciation, but the very fact that these words are the rhyme words gives them a kind of ease and appropriateness, as though the poet lengthens out his pronunciation in order to keep the trot of the verse going.

Burns proceeds to give sensible advice about helping out a neighbour and the proper limits of frankness – one should be free and off-hand with friends—

But still keep something to yoursel
Ye scarcely tell to onie.

And this leads him to give another very shrewd piece of advice, which he himself followed on his visit to Edinburgh and which resulted in his being acclaimed as the 'Heaven-taught ploughman':

Conceal yoursel as weel's you can
Frae critical dissection:
But keek thro' ev'ry other man
Wi' sharpen'd, sly inspection.

Burns always fancied himself as an observer of men and manners. 'I have nothing to tell you of news', he wrote to a friend as early as 1782; 'for myself I am going on in my old way – taking as light a burden as I can, of the cares of the world; studying men, their manners & their ways, as well as I can.' It was this continuous, careful examination of 'men, their manners and their ways' that helped to make him into such an effective satirist.

The sixth stanza is of particular interest to those concerned with Burns's attitude towards his own sexual adventures:

flame

> The sacred lowe o' weel-placed love,
>   Luxuriantly indulge it;
> But never tempt th' illicit rove,
>   Tho' naething should divulge it:
> I wave the quantum o' the sin,
>   The hazard of concealing;
> But, och! it hardens a' within,
>   And petrifies the feeling!

Those last four lines have the ring of a confession, though we may interpret them, with Andrew Lang, as revealing that 'Burns was never petrified enough to enjoy the role of Rab Mossgiel, of the rural Don Juan: hence arose most of his misery: he could love, and ride away, and repent'. Clearly, if Burns's own feelings had become petrified he would not have felt the horror of petrified feeling which he expresses here; the point seems to be that unless one's feelings do become petrified one cannot escape feelings of remorse and regret. It is interesting that Burns is prepared to 'waive the quantum o' the sin' – he is standing on psychological rather than explicitly moral grounds, though of course the eighteenth-century believers in the 'moral sense' would not have seen any real difference between the two.

At this point in the poem there is a stanza in the manuscript which Burns omitted from the printed version. It is interesting for the further light it sheds on Burns's attitude:

> If ye hae made a step aside,
>   Some hap-mistake o'er taen you,
> Yet, still keep up a decent pride,
>   An' ne'er owre far demean you.
> Time comes wi' kind, oblivious shade
>   An' daily darker sets it;

no more

> An' if na-mae mistakes are made
>   The warld soon forgets it.

The seventh stanza asserts that it is a good thing to be wealthy, if you can become so without recourse to dishonourable means, not in order to show off your wealth 'but for the glorious privilege of being independent'. He then proceeds to a discussion of one of his favourite subjects:

> The fear o' Hell's a hangman's whip
>   To haud the wretch in order;
> But where ye feel your honour grip,
>   Let that ay be your border. . . .

He is a deist, hates hypocrisy, warns against atheism:

> The great Creator to revere
>   Must sure become the creature;
> But still the preaching cant forbear,
>   And ev'n the rigid feature:
> Yet ne'er with wits profane to range
>   Be complaisance extended;
> And atheist-laugh's a poor exchange
>   For Deity offended.

This stanza shows perhaps more than any other how completely, in his moral and religious attitudes, Burns was a child of his period. His real quarrel with Scottish Calvinism was based on his attempt to apply to it the principles of a simple, humanitarian deism – the principles, that is, of perhaps the majority of cultivated Englishmen and of a considerable number of cultivated Scotsmen of his day. He got these ideas from the interaction between his own impulsive and humane temperament and his reading in neoclassic English literature.

The next stanza must surely refer to some of his own excesses while celebrating with his cronies:

> While ranting round in Pleasure's ring,
>   Religion may be blinded;
give > Or if she gie a random sting,
>   It may be little minded;
> But when on Life we're tempest-driven—
>   A conscience but a canker—
> A correspondence fix'd wi' heav'n
>   Is sure a noble anchor!

The poem ends with a simple blessing and a final twist in the tail which completely removes any suggestion of pomposity from the moralizing:

> In ploughman phrase, 'God send you speed,'
>   Still daily to grow wiser;
> And may ye better reck the rede,
>   Than ever did th' adviser!

Burns's success in achieving conversational rhythms in smooth-flowing verse is best illustrated in his verse letters, of which there are seven in the Kilmarnock volume. Two of them we have already looked at, but they are all worth attention. The 'Epistle to Davie, a Brother Poet' is one of the earliest, though Burns places it here after 'To a Mouse'. It was written, apparently, in January, 1785.[4] David Sillar, like James Smith, was a member of the Tarbolton Bachelors' Club and one of the friends to whom Burns turned in his early years at Mossgiel to satisfy his hunger for male companionship. Neither of these men possessed the character or personality Burns imagined he saw in them – this was true of nearly all of Burns's male friends – and Sillar was a pretty poor specimen of a poet. But it was important to Burns to consider Sillar a fellow poet, and to find himself in emulating and outstripping him. This letter sounds a note of true admiration and friendship. Burns's capacity for friendship was immense, and it was his tragedy that he too rarely found companions worthy of the affectionate intimacy he gave to them. At this stage of his career, however, companions like Smith and Sillar were of the greatest value to him: they gave him an audience and a sense of belonging, and, through no special abilities of their own, greatly assisted his development as a poet.

The 'Epistle to Davie' is written in the old Scottish stanza form used by Alexander Montgomerie in his remarkable poem, 'The Cherry and the Slae', first published in 1597, and reprinted in Watson's *Choice Collection* and in Ramsay's *Ever Green*. Here is the opening stanza as it appears in Ramsay:

boughs	About an Bank with Balmy Bewis,
	Quair Nychtingales thair Notis renewis
	With gallant Goldspinks gay;
thrush, blackbird	The Mavis, Merle, and Progne proud,
	The lintquyt, Lark and Lavrock loud,
	Salutit mirthful May.

Quen Philomel had sweitly sung,
To Progne scho deplored,
How Tereus cut out her tung
And falsly her deflourd;
Qhuilk story so sorie
seemed   To schaw hir self scho seimt,
To heir hir so neir hir,
I doutit if I dreimt.

Burns opens his poem with a characteristic contrast between a winter exterior and the indoor warmth of the 'chimla lug':

While winds frae aff Ben-Lomond blaw,
And bar the doors wi' driving snaw,
hang   And hing us owre the ingle,
I set me down, to pass the time,
And spin a verse or twa o' rhyme,
westland   In hamely, westlin jingle.
in to the   While frosty winds blaw in the drift,
chimney
corner   Ben to the chimla lug,
I grudge a wee the Great-folk's gift,
comfortable   That live sae bien an' snug:
heed   I tent less, and want less
Their roomy fire-side;
But hanker, and canker,
To see their cursed pride.

It is remarkable how far Burns has moved in this single stanza. Beginning with a brief but most effective description of the cold outside, in two slow-moving lines giving the impression of a whole landscape in snow and driving wind, he moves at once, in the third short line, to the contrasting image of himself huddled over the fire. The transition is most cunningly done, and shows how well Burns could mould his thought to the shape of this complicated verse form. In the second pair of long lines he is describing himself 'spinning a verse or twa o' rhyme', and after the word 'rhyme' comes the second short line, 'In hamely, westlin jingle', giving the very effect of rhyme by its deliberately tinny echoing of 'jingle' with 'ingle'. He has not, however, wholly excluded winter, for in the next two lines the 'frosty winds blaw in the drift, / Ben to the chimla lug', and he is reminded that he is not as comfortable as he might be. This reminder brings us to the turn of the stanza, the last four

lines with their internal rhyme, in which Burns, developing the suggestion that his fireside is not as comfortable as that of others may be,
registers his complaint against the rich. The movement from the description of a snowy landscape to an attack on the rich man's pride follows
the curve of the stanza, as it were, and the transitions are unforced and
effective.

Burns generally uses the last four lines of this complicated stanza – four
lines which stand somewhat apart from the main body of the verse – to
introduce a link with the following stanza. Having moved from a
description of the setting to his complaint against the pride of the rich,
he takes up the question of rich and poor in the second verse:

> It's hardly in a body's pow'r,
> To keep, at times, frae being sour,
>   To see how things are shar'd;
> How best o' chiels are whyles in want,
> While Coofs on countless thousands rant,
>   And ken na how to wair't:
> But Davie, lad, ne'er fash your head,
>   Tho' we hae little gear,
> We're fit to win our daily bread,
>   As lang's we're hale and fier:
>   'Mair spier na, nor fear na',
>   Auld age ne'er mind a feg;
>   The last o't, the warst o't,
>   Is only but to beg.

chaps;
sometimes
fools; revel
spend
trouble
wealth

sound
more ask not
fig

Here again, the poet moves a long way in a single stanza taking advantage of the stanza's structure. He begins by elaborating the point
about the 'great folk' which he had introduced in the final section of the
preceding verse, turns easily into a new thought with that 'But Davie,
lad, ne'er fash your head', and in the last four lines introduces his favourite
idea of turning beggar as a last resort. As in the first stanza, the last four
lines mark the transition to the next verse. He proceeds to elaborate his
idea of going begging:

> To lie in kilns and barns at e'en,
> When banes are craz'd, and bluid is thin,
>   Is, doubtless, great distress!
> Yet then content could make us blest;

bones

> Ev'n then, sometimes we'd snatch a taste
> 　Of truest happiness.
> The honest heart that's free frae a'
> 　Intended fraud or guile,
> However Fortune kick the ba',
> 　Has ay some cause to smile,
> 　　And mind still, you'll find still,
> 　　　A comfort this nae sma';
> 　　Nae mair then, we'll care then,
> 　　　Nae farther we can fa'.

Here the poet is not posturing for the benefit of the Edinburgh gentry, but letting the poem work itself easily into a lively expression of a careless, cheerful view of life. The theme is a mood rather than a philosophy, a mood of defiance of the rich and of happy acceptance of easygoing poverty. To seek for profundity of ethical thought here would be to miss the point of the poem, which seeks to capture a transitory state of mind rather than to state general principles.

　The 'Epistle' continues to develop the idea of freedom and poverty in a picture of the poet and his friend wandering at will through the countryside, and after reaffirming the contrast between the rich and the poor with reference to this question of which enjoys the greater freedom and happiness ('Nae treasures nor pleasures / Could make us happy lang; / The heart aye's the part ay / That makes us right or wrang') the poem comes to a momentary rest on a note of complete acquiescence:

> Then let us chearfu' acquiesce;
> Nor make our scanty Pleasures less,
> 　By pining at our state. . . .

After this the poem goes rather astray. Burns makes a new beginning in the eighth stanza, pointing out that both he and Davie enjoy the richest experience of all – love:

> Ye hae your Meg, your dearest part,
> 　And I my darling Jean!
> 　　It warms me, it charms me,
> 　　　To mention but her name:
kindles　　　It heats me, it beets me,
> 　　　And sets me a' on flame!

The conclusion of this verse is pretty tumty-tum stuff. Burns's inspiration seems to be flagging, and we have no doubt of it when in the succeeding stanza he moves into a prayer for his Jean wholly out of keeping with the tone of the earlier part of the poem:

> O all ye Pow'rs who rule above!
> O Thou, whose very self art love!
> Thou know'st my words sincere! . . .

This is in the stilted English he used in his least inspired moments, and there is a self-conscious attitudinizing about the verse which, especially when contrasted with the fine breeziness of the earlier parts of the poem, offends the reader. Burns becomes hypnotized by this sentimental projection of himself and continues in an orgy of sentimentality:

> All hail ye tender feelings dear!
> The smile of love, the friendly tear,
> The sympathetic glow. . . .

We have seen this sort of thing before, and we know what has happened to the poet. When we are told at the end of this stanza that love 'brightens the tenebrific scene' we are not in the least surprised. There is a partial recovery in the final verse, but the poem never really gets back into its stride after the seventh stanza. The first seven stanzas are Burns at his very best: in them he displays a masterly handling of this intricate verse form and moves with immense ease and flexibility from point to point, giving all the appearance of genuine spontaneity yet at the same time showing a fine craftsmanship both in the structure of the individual stanza and in the linking of the stanzas to one another. This craftsmanship is remarkable enough in such an early poem.

Near the end of the Kilmarnock volume the four remaining verse epistles are found together – two to John Lapraik, one to William Simpson, and one to John Rankine, the name in each case being indicated only by initials. Those to Lapraik and Simpson are in Burns's best style. The first epistle to Lapraik, dated April 1, 1785, was entered in the Commonplace Book in June of that year with the description: 'A letter sent to John Lapraik, near Muirkirk, a true, genuine, Scottish Bard'. Lapraik was at this time an elderly rustic poet of no great originality who was later inspired by the success of Burns's Kilmarnock poems to have his own poems also printed by John Wilson at Kilmarnock. He lived on a farm about fourteen miles east of Mossgiel.

Both poems to Lapraik follow the usual structure of Burns's verse epistles: first, the setting; then the movement towards the statement of attitude which is the core of the poem; finally, the swift turn to a concluding compliment. The earlier poem opens with a brief description of spring and proceeds in the same verse to state Burns's relation to his correspondent:

partridges
screaming
hare
scudding

> While briers an' woodbines budding green,
> And Paitricks scraichin loud at e'en,
> An' morning Poussie whiddin seen,
>   Inspire my Muse,
> This freedom, in an unknown frien',
>   I pray excuse.

The succeeding verses link Burns and Lapraik together in an atmosphere of sociability and conviviality – an atmosphere dear to Burns's heart and rarely absent from his best verse letters. From a description of the company talking about Lapraik over their ale, he moves on to describe his determination to write a rhyming letter to a fellow poet, and from this point the transition to a declaration of his own poetic ideals is easily managed:

> I am nae Poet, in a sense,
> But just a Rhymer, like, by chance,
> An' hae to Learning nae pretence,
>   Yet, what the matter?
> Whene'er my Muse does on me glance,
>   I jingle at her.

The stanzas that follow give Burns's account of himself as a popular poet, not in the self-conscious manner in which he presents himself in his introduction to this volume but with a passionate democratic feeling and with an awareness that his roots are with the folk tradition and with the Scottish literary tradition of Ramsay and Fergusson. He does, of course, exaggerate his illiteracy, but the essential point he makes is sound: he is *not* writing in an atmosphere of academic imitation and classical allusion as were 'The Rev. Mr. Blacklock and other Scotch gentlemen' who contributed to the *Collection of Original Poems* of 1760:

Your Critic-folk may cock their nose,
And say, 'How can you e'er propose,
You wha ken hardly verse frae prose,
   To mak a sang?'
But, by your leaves, my learned foes,
   Ye're maybe wrang.

What's a' your jargon o' your Schools,
Your Latin names for horns an' stools;
If honest Nature made you fools,

serves   What sairs your Grammars?
shovels Ye'd better taen up spades and shools,
stone-
breaking-   Or knappin-hammers.

dunder-
heads A set o' dull, conceited Hashes,
Confuse their brains in College-classes!
steers They gang in Stirks, and come out Asses,
   Plain truth to speak;
then An' syne they think to climb Parnassus
   By dint o' Greek!

Gie me ae spark o' Nature's fire,
That's a' the learning I desire;
puddle Then tho' I drudge thro' dub an' mire
   At pleugh or cart,
My Muse, tho' hamely in attire,
   May touch the heart.

To see the essential truth of Burns's description of himself we have only to put beside any of his numerous poems of male friendship and conviviality any poem on a similar subject from the collection by Blacklock and his friends – 'The Power of Wine', for example:

With roses and with myrtles crown'd,
I triumph; let the glass go round.
Jovial Bacchus, ever gay,
Come, and crown the happy day;
From my breast drive every care;
Banish sorrow and despair:
Let social mirth, and decent joy,
This delightful hour employ.

Haste, attend us, Wit refin'd,
Thou sweet enlivener of the mind!
And while the copious bumper's crown'd,
Bid the free jovial laugh go round.

Come, Good-nature, show thy face
With open smiles and sweetest grace. . . .

But to return to Burns, and the 'Epistle to J. Lapraik'. He has very
deftly brought the poem back to his friend in the last stanza quoted, and
the remainder of the letter chats about himself and his desire to meet
Lapraik in a proper atmosphere of conviviality (taking the hint from
Fergusson's 'Answer to J.S.'s Epistle'). He ends with an appropriate
generalization about friendship and a final protestation of his affection.
Burns never seems to be at a loss for a method of bringing his verse
letters to an end with a neat subscription; the ending here is one of his
neatest:

> But to conclude my long epistle,
> As my auld pen's worn to the grissle;
make;
tingle
> Twa lines frae you wad gar me fissle,
>   Who am, most fervent,
> While I can either sing, or whissle,
>   Your friend and servant.

We are reminded of the impromptu 'Reply to an Invitation' written
from Mauchline one 'Monday Night, 10 o'clock', in 1786:

> SIR,
> Yours this moment I unseal,
>   And faith! I'm gay and hearty.
> To tell the truth and shame the Deil,
drunk
>   I am as fou as Bartie.
Thursday
> But Foorsday, Sir, my promise leal,
>   Expect me o' your partie,
climb
> If on a beastie I can speel
ride
>   Or hurl in a cartie.
>   Yours,—
>   ROBERT BURNS.

The 'Second Epistle to J. Lapraik', dated April 21, 1785, was written
in reply to Lapraik's answer to the first epistle. It, too, begins with a

description of the seasonal setting and proceeds in the same stanza to state Burns's relation to his correspondent. In the three weeks that had elapsed since his first letter the season had advanced, and the imagery is one of spring activity:

newly driven
cattle low   While new-ca'd kye rowte at the stake,
smoke; harrow   An' pownies reek in pleugh or braik,
              This hour on e'enin's edge I take,
                      To own I'm debtor,
              To honest-hearted, auld Lapraik,
                    For his kind letter.

Burns proceeds to paint a picture reminiscent of the opening of 'The Vision'. He is tired with the spring ploughing, and his Muse begs to be excused from performing:

jaded   Forjesket sair, with weary legs,
ridges   Rattlin the corn out-owre the rigs,
nags   Or dealing thro' amang the naigs
                    Their ten-hours bite,
awkward   My awkart Muse sair pleads and begs,
                    I would na write.

A lively dialogue between himself and his Muse follows:

         'Shall bauld Lapraik, the king o' hearts,
         Tho' mankind were a pack o' cartes,
praise   Roose you sae weel for your deserts,
                  In terms sae friendly,
show   Yet ye'll neglect to shaw your parts
                  An' thank him kindly?'

         Sae I gat paper in a blink,
         An' down gaed stumpie in the ink:
         Quoth I, 'Before I sleep a wink,
                  I vow I'll close it;
rhyme   An' if ye winna mak it clink,
                  By Jove I'll prose it!'

The ease and fluency of the verse here shows Burns in perfect control over his medium. The tone is brisk and conversational, the idiom

familiar, the sense moulded to the curve of the stanza so that we are
hardly aware what an intricate verse form is employed. And how skilfully he gives the impression of halting the debate and getting down
resolutely to the job of writing:

> An' down gaed stumpie in the ink

gives us not only the clear picture of the poet plunging his stump of quill
into the inkwell but also the sense of resolution with which he does it.
For a brief moment we look at the situation from the point of view of the
overmastered pen.

As usual, it does not take long for Burns to work the poem into a
confession of faith. Before we quite realize how he has got there, Burns
is talking of fortune's uncertainties, of his own bad luck, and of the pride
and common sense which sustain him. He has not managed to become
rich, but his life has its compensations:

> Were this the charter of our state,
> 'On pain o' hell be rich an' great',
> Damnation then would be our fate,
>   Beyond remead;
> But, thanks to Heav'n, that's no the gate
>   We learn our creed.

way

> For thus the royal Mandate ran,
> When first the human race began,
> 'The social, friendly, honest man,
>   Whate'er he be,
> 'Tis he fulfils great Nature's plan,
>   And none but he.'

There is hope for the poor, and eventually the miserly rich will be cast
into outer darkness:

> Then may Lapraik and Burns arise,
> To reach their native, kindred skies,
> And sing their pleasures, hopes an' joys,
>   In some mild sphere,
> Still closer knit in friendship's ties
>   Each passing year!

The ending is perhaps rather too rhetorical – we prefer the quieter friendliness of the conclusion of the first letter – but it represents a genuine tying-up of the various thoughts in the poem.

The next epistle, 'To William Simpson of Ochiltree', is dated May, 1785; Burns was evidently in fine poetic fettle this spring. Here again the letter moves rapidly into a confession, this time of his poetic habits and ambitions. He is replying to a flattering letter from 'Winsome Willie', and from a deprecation of the excessive praise his correspondent has heaped on him he moves easily to an account of the kind of poetry in which he *can* take legitimate pride. He cannot compare himself 'wi' Allan, or wi' Gilbertfield' – that is, Ramsey or William Hamilton of Gilbertfield author of 'Bonnie Heck' and the rhyming paraphrase of Blind Harry's *Wallace* which had so inflamed Burns's patriotism – or with 'Fergusson, the writer-chiel'. On mentioning Fergusson, he digresses to pay a tribute to his 'glorious parts' and attacks the 'Edinburgh gentry' for having let him starve. Then he comes to his real point:

> Yet when a tale comes i' my head,
> Or lasses gie my heart a screed,
> As whiles they're like to be my dead,
> (O sad disease!)
> I kittle up my rustic reed;
> It gies me ease.

rent
sometimes;
death

tickle

He proceeds to give a picture of himself as the poet of his native Ayrshire:

> Ramsay an' famous Ferguson
> Gied Forth an' Tay a lift aboon;
> Yarrow an' Tweed, to monie a tune,
> Owre Scotland rings,
> While Irwin, Lugar, Ayr, an' Doon,
> Naebody sings.

up

Edinburgh and the east of Scotland have had their poets, and the Borders are celebrated in ballad and folk song; he will be the bard of his own part of Scotland.

There is a fierce ambition here, as well as modesty. He goes on to mention 'Th'Ilissus, Tiber, Thames, an' Seine' as other rivers that have been celebrated by poets, and in doing so he sets himself in a European tradition that reaches back to Rome. His subject matter may be local, but (so runs the implication) his stage will be universal. He will be doing for his own countryside what the great poets of old did for theirs – present it to the world.

The view of nature which Burns presents in describing the aspects of his native countryside which constituted the subject of his verse is not at all that of the Romantic poets. There is in Burns no feeling for sublimity (except in storms), no sense of grandeur in mountains or the sea, no discovery in nature of some spirit from which man can derive insight. The friendly woods and streams appeal to Burns, and he describes them with an affectionate intimacy. Fond as he was of water-falls, Burns could never have said with Wordsworth that the sounding cataract haunted him like a passion. For him the 'burnie' 'trots' or 'toddles' down the hill; nature is kept on a small scale and close to man. True, Burns has a strong feeling for a wild winter scene; but he is prone to think of naked trees etched in black against a sullen sky or the wind howling outside as he sits in the smoking ingle-nook rather than of any grand manifestation that might lead him, as it led Byron,

> To mingle with the universe and feel
> What I can ne'er express, yet cannot all conceal.

He is being simply autobiographical when he writes:

> The Muse, nae poet ever fand her
> Till by himself he learn't to wander
> Adown some trottin burn's meander.

The dominant images in Burns's nature poetry are streams, 'haughs, and woods', and the life among them is that of small animals like 'jinkin hares'. It has often been remarked that for one who lived so near the Ayrshire coast, with its fine seascapes and grand view across the water to the rugged island of Arran, Burns is surprisingly silent about the sea, nor does he dwell on the looming Arran mountains or on the Highland peaks visible in the distant northern horizon. Even in his Highland tours he was more interested in places of historical interest – which stirred his patriotic emotions – and in waterfalls than in the impressive views of the Grampians that surrounded them.

It is true that nature operated on Burns's sensibility, but in a direct and simple way: the sights and sounds of spring and summer made him feel cheerful, and the storms of winter made him relish his fireside the more:

O Nature! a' thy shews an' forms
To feeling, pensive hearts hae charms!
Whether the Summer kindly warms,
                    Wi' life an' light,
Or Winter howls, in gusty storms,
                    The lang, dark night!

The 'Epistle to Willie Simpson' moves from this discussion of nature
to a quick and simple conclusion:

too long   Fareweel, 'my rhyme-composing brither'!
unknown   We've been owre lang unkenn'd to ither:
                    Now let us lay our heads thegither,
                                        In love fraternal:
                    May Envy wallop in a tether,
                                        Black fiend, infernal!

                    While Highlandmen hate tolls an' taxes;
dead sheep   While moorlan herds like guid, fat braxies;
                    While Terra Firma, on her axis,
                                        Diurnal turns,
                    Count on a friend, in faith an' practice,
                                        In Robert Burns.

Here again we note the deftness of the signing off. The use of words
like 'terra firma', 'axis', and 'diurnal', is, of course, humorous rather than
pretentious in intention and effect: there is a deliberate inflation of the
vocabulary which, in juxtaposition to the pedestrian 'tolls and taxes',
sounds a note of cheerful exaggeration; and this gives way in the last line
to the simple profession of friendship.

The poem has a 'Postscript', which gives a humorous and ironical
discussion of a local theological dispute; here Burns's treatment of the
matter as an argument among shepherds about the reasons for the moon's
waxing and waning successfully conveys his attitude of amused contempt.

The 'Epistle to John Rankine' is, at least to the modern reader, the
least attractive of the verse letters in the Kilmarnock volume, for the
sexual slang in which he braggingly recounts his affair with Elizabeth
Paton (which produced his first illegitimate child) does not wear well.
The fact is that the atmosphere of male boasting of success in sexual
adventures is not very agreeable outside the climate of youthful male

conviviality in which it flourishes. Yet it is interesting that the notice of the Kilmarnock volume which appeared in the *English Review* of February, 1787, mentioned this poem 'in which [Burns] disguises an amour under the veil of partridge shooting', with the 'Address to the Deil', as a 'masterpiece' in the humorous line.

There remain a number of miscellaneous poems which deserve mention. 'On a Scotch Bard Gone to the West Indies', one of the latest poems written for the edition, was the product of Burns's preparations for going to Jamaica. Its lively and cheerful tone (contrasting so sharply with some of the more lugubrious poems he wrote about his own condition at this time) strengthens the impression already recorded that Burns was never, in spite of all the active steps he took to book passage on this ship and on that, wholly serious in his intention of emigrating. Here we have the playful side of Burns at its best, a rousing, entertaining, fast-moving piece, put into the mouth of a fictitious brother poet who is supposed to be lamenting the departure of the 'Scotch bard'. How much more persuasive his account of his misfortunes is in this poem than in the self-dramatizations of 'To a Mountain Daisy' and 'To Ruin';

	He saw Misfortune's cauld nor-west
	Lang mustering up a bitter blast;
jilt	A jillet brak his heart at last,
	Ill may she be!
	So, took a birth afore the mast,
	An' owre the sea.

staff	To tremble under Fortune's cummock,
meal and	On scarce a bellyfu' o' drummock,
water	Wi' his proud, independent stomach,
	Could ill agree;
rolled his	So, row't his hurdies in a hammock
buttocks	An' owre the sea.

Standing twenty-fifth among the thirty-six poems in the Kilmarnock volume is, oddly enough, the 'Dedication' to the poet's friend and landlord, Gavin Hamilton. Presumably intended at first to take its appropriate place at the beginning of the book, it was eventually relegated to a less conspicuous position perhaps because Burns felt, in the words of Scott Douglas, that 'its author's freedom of sentiment and lack of restraint for matters orthodox would stagger its cautious and circumspect typographer. It was accordingly slipped into the book near the close, in fellowship with 'The Louse', and some subjects less dainty in character than those first presented to the reader.'

The 'Dedication' really belongs with Burns's ecclesiastical satires, for, after an opening in which Burns characteristically protests that he has no intention of flattering his friend and benefactor, there soon emerges a discussion of the relation between 'sound believing' and decent moral behaviour. In lively rhymed octosyllables, divided into irregular verse paragraphs which aptly fit the development of the theme, Burns flashes out his ironical descriptions of the orthodox Calvinists whom Hamilton had offended. Burns is especially outraged at the orthodox Calvinist notion that human good works were, in the corrupt state of man since the Fall, no better in the sight of God than utter filth; he held that a man, whatever his theological beliefs, is to be praised if he is 'social, friendly, and honest' and to be blamed if he is uncharitable and censorious. He agreed with the eighteenth-century advocates of a 'moral sense' that man was by nature able to recognize and so pursue virtue and that his 'carnal inclination' to do good was the most secure foundation for ethics. He never doubted where he stood in the argument between faith and good works – he was with good works every time; and he lost no opportunity of attacking those who put 'sound believing' above active morality:

> That he's the poor man's friend in need,
> The gentleman in word and deed,
> It's no through terror of damnation:
> It's just a carnal inclination,
> And och! that's nae regeneration![5]

> . . . Vain is his hope, whase stay an' trust is,
> In *moral* Mercy, Truth and Justice!

coin	No – stretch a point to catch a plack;
	Abuse a brother to his back;
window	Steal thro' the winnock frae a whore,
	But point the rake that taks the door;
whinstone	Be to the poor like onie whunstane,
grindstone	And haud their noses to the grunstane;
	Ply ev'ry art o' legal thieving;
	No matter – stick to sound believing.

As in 'Holy Willie's Prayer', Burns is pretending to agree with his opponents and in ironically stating their creed as his own makes it sound as preposterous as possible:

Learn three-mile prayr's and half-mile graces,
palms   Wi' weel-spread looves, an' lang, wry faces;
Grunt up a solemn, lengthen'd groan,
And damn a' parties but your own;
I'll warrant then, ye're nae deceiver,
A steady, sturdy, staunch believer.

This section of the poem culminates in a mock denunciation of the opponents of orthodoxy in the very tones of contemporary preaching. Burns then turns back to Hamilton, with an apology for the digression, and moves the poem easily into a benediction on his patron and his family.

But Burns could not leave the poem there, with grateful poet invoking blessings on generous patron; his perpetual sensitivity to social distinctions made it necessary for him either to bring himself up to Hamilton's level or bring Hamilton down to his; and, surprisingly enough, he chose the latter course. 'As things are, I can end this poem by saying formally, "your humble servant",' he virtually says; 'but if only you were as poor and unfortunate as myself, I could address you without constraint as friend and brother.'

But if (which Pow'rs above prevent)
That iron-hearted carl, want,
Attended, in his grim advances,
By sad mistakes and black mischances
While hopes, and joys, and pleasures fly him,
Make you as poor a dog as I am,
Your humble servant then no more;
For who would humbly serve the poor?
But, by a poor man's hopes in Heav'n!
While recollection's pow'r is given,
If, in the vale of human life,
The victim sad of fortune's strife,
I, thro' the tender gushing tear,
Should recognize my Master dear,
If friendless, low, we meet together,
Then, Sir, your hand – my Friend and Brother!

Burns always found it difficult to compliment a social superior without constraint.

Finally, something must be said about 'To a Louse', in its way one of the most remarkable of all Burns's poems, and in so many respects the antithesis of 'To a Mountain Daisy'. Where in the daisy poem he laboured to produce a histrionic moral emotion, in 'To a Louse', perhaps better than anywhere else, he shows his ability to direct an apparently casual 'occasional' poem to a didactic conclusion, this conclusion expressed with all the simple gnomic quality of a country proverb. The poem is alive with bright descriptive touches and an all-embracing humour. The opening, with its exclamatory suddenness, carries us right into the situation:

crawling   Ha! whare ye gaun, ye crowlin ferlie!
wonder
              Your impudence protects you sairlie:
strut   I canna say but ye strunt rarely,
                     Owre gauze and lace;
              Tho' faith, I fear, ye dine but sparely
                     On sic a place.

Not only do we see the louse crawling in the unconscious lady's bonnet, but we see the poet himself watching it with exaggerated indignation. A note of social satire creeps in as the poem continues:

              Ye ugly, creepin, blastit wonner,
              Detested, shunn'd, by saunt an' sinner,
foot   How daur ye set your fit upon her,
                     Sae fine a Lady!
              Gae somewhere else and seek your dinner,
                     On some poor body.

This theme is developed at some length, the contrast between the vulgarity of the louse and the social pretensions of the lady on whose bonnet it is creeping produces ever greater mock outrage on the poet's part, until he finally, with effective abruptness, drops the pose of the disturbed onlooker and turns to address the lady herself. As soon as she is named – by the simple country name, 'Jenny' – she ceases to be a fine lady and becomes just a girl to whom the poet is addressing a friendly remark; the note of amusement is not dropped, but it has become kindly:

              O Jenny, dinna toss your head,
abroad   An' set your beauties a' abroad!
              Ye little ken what cursed speed
                     The blastie's makin!
those   Thae winks and finger-ends, I dread,
                     Are notice takin!

And so the poem ends, on a simple, proverbial note:

> O wad some Pow'r the giftie gie us
> To see oursels as others see us!
> It wad frae monie a blunder free us
>   An' foolish notion:
> What airs in dress an' gait wad lea'e us,
>   An' ev'n Devotion!

The nine brief epitaphs which are inserted at the end to pad out the volume are exercises in a contemporary fashion which need not detain us, and the handful of songs, inserted for a similar purpose, will be discussed in our final chapter, which treats of Burns as a song writer. We have looked carefully enough at the Kilmarnock volume to see that it displayed a new Scottish poet, of astonishing liveliness and verve, whose genius was nourished by the poetic traditions of his own people and whose work was sometimes enriched and more often corrupted by an intermittent effort to absorb the English poetic tradition of his age and to appeal to the genteel taste of his time. If to the contemporary genteel reader in Edinburgh or London it was the latter aspect which most appealed, history joins with criticism in considering the former as representing the real Burns and the true poet. Yet the verdict of history, distorted by a sentimental patriotism and by the genteel tradition itself, has not been as clear as it should be: although it has accepted 'To a Louse' it has also accepted and more than accepted 'The Cotter's Saturday Night' and other poems which appeal to a false Scots pride. The more one considers the forces working against Burns's integrity as a poet – forces which for the most part are still with us – the more one is astonished to realize that as his career developed his poetic integrity strengthened rather than weakened. The Kilmarnock volume was Burns's bid for the approval of the literati. It did win their approval, though for what we should consider the wrong reasons, and thus released Burns from any further obligation to please anyone but himself. That he regarded himself thus freed rather than more tightly bound is a tribute to his character as well as to his genius.

4

THE OMITTED POEMS

THE KILMARNOCK volume was far from representing Burns's total output up to the middle of 1786. Ever since his youthful song for Nelly Kilpatrick he had been sporadically turning his experiences into poetry, and during the second half of 1785 and the first part of the following year he was producing at a remarkable rate. If we look through any chronological arrangement of Burns's poems, we are impressed by the abundance and variety, if not always by the quality, of this early work. Sometimes he writes purely in the English tradition, as in the very early song, 'I Dream'd I Lay Where Flowers Were Springing'; sometimes he writes in swinging ballad style, as in the 'The Ronalds of the Bennals', in which young Robert flaunts his proud poverty before the two relatively wealthy Ronald girls, one of whom had rejected Gilbert's proposal of marriage; sometimes he writes in the very different style of the eighteenth-century street ballad in language that might have been used by Prior, as in 'No Churchman Am I for to Rail and to Write'; sometimes he captures the purest tone of folk song, as in 'Indeed Will I, Quo' Findlay' or (though the folk strain here is of a different, more lyrical, order) in 'Green Grow the Rashes, O'. There are studied expressions of melancholy, epigrams, satires, verse letters, songs of many kinds. Burns had plenty to choose from when he selected the poems for the Kilmarnock edition.

From this abundant store Burns 'waled a portion with judicious care'. The volume was to be a bid for recognition by the genteel world, and though he appeared in the character of a Scottish poet, and a rustic, he had no intention of offending the taste or morals of people like Dr. Blacklock or Hugh Blair if he could avoid it without compromising his own integrity. He would not alter poems he had written in order to make them more amenable to genteel taste, but he would, if necessary, omit them. He sought the advice of John Ballantine, the Ayr banker, and of Robert Aiken, and he let himself be guided by them in making the selection. The more violent satirical poems had to go. 'Holy Willie's Prayer' was altogether too devastating an attack on what some people might still take to be religion, and Burns appears from the beginning to have regarded the poem as unprintable: he did not offer it for Blair's criticism, and his references to it when he sent copies to his friends usually suggest that he considers it unsuitable for publication. 'The Twa Herds' and 'The Ordination', though less powerful, discussed living personalities and were therefore dangerous; 'Death and Dr. Hornbook' made fun of a friend in a manner that would not have been easy to laugh off, although Burns thought it inoffensive enough to include in the 1787 edition; the 'Address to Beelzebub' was a bitter and biting satire, aimed at Mr. M'Kenzie of Applecross and Mr. Macdonald of Glengary who, in order to keep Highlanders as impoverished menials on their lands, supposedly prevented them from emigrating from Scotland to Canada. Other poems were too trivial, bawdy, or imperfect for inclusion. 'The Jolly Beggars' – which was almost certainly written by this time – was such an obvious challenge to organized society, and indeed to all human institutions, that its omission was clearly necessary.

'The Twa Herds' is a rollicking attack on the orthodox clergy, in which Burns takes brilliant advantage of what he described as 'a bitter and shameless quarrel between two Rev. gentlemen, Moodie of Riccarton and Russell of Kilmarnock'. The quarrel concerned parochial boundaries and seems to have raged with remarkable violence. This is the poem he refers to in his autobiographical letter as 'the first of my poetic offspring that saw the light', but by this he must have meant that it circulated in manuscript, for there is no trace of its having been published before 1796. This 'burlesque lamentation on a quarrel between two rev^d Calvinists' apparently achieved considerable fame locally; 'with a certain side of both clergy and laity it met with a roar of applause', as Burns proudly told Dr. Moore. But it was another matter to submit it to the approval of the literati.

The device of presenting the quarrel in pastoral terms is simple enough, but it is extraordinarily effective in heightening the absurdity of the situation and reducing the two protagonists to ridiculous proportions The proper names, however, mean nothing to the modern reader, and the fact that the poem requires glossing can perhaps be held against it. It is essentially an 'occasional' poem, written to take advantage of a heaven-sent opportunity to deride the 'auld lichts' and indirectly champion the new. Even without knowledge of the background (which would have to include some understanding of the controversy about patronage) the modern reader can sense the happy thrusts at opponents, the cheerful opportunism which dominates the mood of the poem:

> Sic two – O, do I live to see't? –
> Sic famous two sud disagree't,
> An' names like villain, hypocrite,
>   Ilk ither gi'en,
> While New-Light herds wi' laughin spite
>   Say neither's liein!

'The Ordination' is even more local in its interest; it is full of references to specific persons, places, and situations, and it requires, for a full understanding, considerable knowledge of Ayrshire church politics of the time as well as knowledge of the general Scottish ecclesiastical situation. Here again Burns was taking advantage of a particular incident – the ordination of the Reverend James Mackinlay to the Laigh (Low) Kirk in Kilmarnock. The poem is a mock celebration of the triumph of orthodoxy represented by the choice of Mackinlay for the position:

> Curst 'Common-sense', that imp o' hell,
>   Cam in wi' Maggie Lauder:
> But Oliphant aft made her yell,
>   An' Russell sair misca'd her:
> This day Mackinlay taks the flail,

slap   An' he's the boy will blaud her!

cleft stick   He'll clap a shangan on her tail,

pelt   An' set the bairns to daud her
>   Wi' dirt this day.

Maggie Lauder was the wife of an earlier minister of the Laigh Kirk; Oliphant and Russell were successively 'auld licht' ministers at another Kilmarnock church. But one hardly needs to know these details in order to appreciate the essential point being made – that after an earlier rule by Moderates, orthodox Mackinlay is going to restore the good old faith and drive out heresy. The crude physical images in which orthodoxy's triumph is painted makes orthodoxy itself seem absurd, while the meaningless spite with which its proponents pursue their enemies helps to degrade the character of the orthodox. The very stanza form – the same as that used in 'The Holy Fair' – suggests rollicking secular celebration rather than theological fervour, and the contrast between the form and the ostensible theme is deliberate and effective.

> Nae mair by 'Bable's streams' we'll weep,
>   To think upon our 'Zion';
> And hing our fiddles up to sleep,
>   Like baby-clouts a-drying!
> Come, screw the pegs wi' tunefu' cheep,
gut strings   And o'er the thairms be tyin;
elbows jerk   Oh, rare! to see our elbucks wheep,
>   And a' like lamb-tails flyin,
>   Fu' fast this day!

Orthodoxy's triumph becomes more feverish – and more absurd:

> See, see auld Orthodoxy's faes
foes
flogging   She's swingein thro' the city!
> Hark, how the nine-tail'd cat she plays!
very   I vow it's unco pretty:
> There, Learning, with his Greekish face,
>   Grunts out some Latin ditty;
> And Common-sense is gaun, she says,
>   To mak to Jamie Beattie
>   Her plaint this day.

The poem concludes in an atmosphere of drunken swagger, with the 'auld licht' champions drinking confusion 'to every new-light mother's son'.

'Death and Doctor Hornbook' shows Burns making fun of John Wilson, parish schoolmaster at Tarbolton and also – in order to eke out his slender income – keeper of a small grocery shop where he sold drugs and dispensed medical advice. According to Gilbert, the poem was composed at a sitting the day after Burns and Wilson had had a minor quarrel at a Masonic meeting. The satire is developed by means of a story in which the poet meets Death and in which Death complains that he is being forced out of business by 'Jock Hornbook', whose medicines are killing off far more people than he (Death) can kill. The interest and value of the poem, however, lie less in this rather crude satire than in the lively narrative style in which the story is told. The 'Standard Habbie' verse form is less suited for sustained narrative than are the rhymed octosyllables Burns was to use so effectively in 'Tam o' Shanter', but in 'Death and Doctor Hornbook' Burns uses it for narrative with remarkable effect.

The opening sets the tone – humorous, ironic, extravagant:

Some books are lies frae end to end,
And some great lies were never penn'd:
known   Ev'n Ministers they hae been kenn'd,
                In holy rapture,
lie; vent   A rousing whid, at times, to vend,
                        And nail't wi' Scripture.

But this that I am gaun to tell,
Which lately on a night befel,
Is just as true's the Deil's in hell
                Or Dublin city:
That e'er he nearer comes oursel
great   'S a muckle pity.

The chuckling irony of '*even* ministers . . .'; the happy ambiguity of 'as
true's the Deil's in hell – or Dublin city'; and the dry reflection that
follows – these are deftly contrived effects, and take the reader into the
poem before he knows what has happened.

    The actual narrative now commences, and Burns is careful to provide
the sceptical reader with an alternative explanation of the strange
encounter which he can accept if he prefers: he had been drinking, and
was not quite steady on his feet when he left the public house and went
out into the moonlight:

village ale;   The Clachan yill had made me canty,
jolly
drunk   I was na fou, but just had plenty;
staggered now   I stacher'd whyles, but yet took tent ay
and then; care
clear   To free the ditches;
knew   An' hillocks, stanes, an' bushes kenn'd ay
                        Frae ghaists an' witches.

He *was* able to distinguish hillocks, stones, and bushes from ghosts and
witches – that crazy yet confident remark renders the semi-drunken
state of mind to perfection. The following verse has just that air of
solemnity and deliberation which we associate with the same state:

                      The rising Moon began to glowr
away over   The distant Cumnock hills out-owre:
                      To count her horns, wi' a' my pow'r
                              I set mysel;
                      But whether she had three or four,
                              I cou'd na tell.

The encounter with Death is described with a cheerful nonchalance which, while not underestimating the eeriness of the situation, makes clear that the poet was in a mood to accept anything that might happen to him with genial curiosity. His greeting to Death strikes this note at once:

mowing   'Guid-een', quo' I; 'Friend! hae ye been mawin,
sowing   When ither folk are busy sawin?'

When he learns that the stranger is Death,

                                        . . . Quoth I, 'Guid faith,
heed;   Ye're maybe come to stap my breath;
fellow   But tent me, billie;
advise;   I red ye weel, tak core o' skaith,
harm
large knife   See, there's a gully!'

But they soon shake hands and agree to be friends, and then Death begins to complain about the state of business:

                  'Ay, ay!' quo' he, an' shook his head,
                  'It's e'en a lang, lang time indeed
cut   Sin I began to nick the thread,
                              An' choke the breath:
                  Folk maun do something for their bread,
                              An' sae maun Death.

well-nigh   'Sax thousand years are near hand fled
                  Sin' I was to the butching bred,
                  An' mony a scheme in vain's been laid,
stop; scare   To stap or scar me;
                  Till ane Hornbook's ta'en up the trade,
worst   An' faith, he'll waur me.

village   'Ye ken Jock Hornbook i' the Clachan,
scrotum into   Deil mak his king's-hood in a spleuchan!
a tobacco   He's grown sae weel acquaint wi' Buchan,
pouch   And ither chaps,
children   The weans haud out their fingers laughin,
poke   An' pouk my hips.'

This picture of children sporting safely around Death because Dr. Hornbook, having read his Buchan's *Domestic Medicine* and other such works, has made them immune to disease is amusing and good natured enough, and done with a lively precision of imagery; but the poem does not sustain this tone of comic exaggeration of Hornbook's skill. After Death has complained, in the most vivid and specific manner, of Dr. Hornbook's cures and the uncanny skill of the man, his picture of the doctor's knowledge and methods becomes more and more absurd and fantastic, preparing the poem for the sudden turn by which it appears that Death's real grievance is not that Hornbook cures those marked down for death but that his medicines kill so many more that Death is cheated out of his lawful prey. The note of mockery grows ever stronger before this turn:

> 'Ev'n them he canna get attended,
> *known* Altho' their face he ne'er had kend it,
> *cabbage-* Just shit in a kail-blade and send it,
> *leaf*
> As soon's he smells't,
> Baith their disease, and what will mend it
> At once he tells't.

> *knives* 'And then a' doctor's saws and whittles,
> Of a' dimensions, shapes, an' mettles,
> A' kinds o' boxes, mugs, an' bottles,
> He's sure to hae;
> Their Latin names as fast he rattles
> As A B C.

> 'Calces o' fossils, earth, and trees;
> True Sal-marinum o' the seas;
> The Farina of beans and pease,
> He has't in plenty;
> Aqua-fontis, what you please,
> He can content ye.

The turn comes immediately after this. The poet is moved to express pity for Johnnie Ged, the gravedigger, who will be ruined for lack of work, but Death tells him not to worry:

> *groaned;* The creature grain'd an eldritch laugh,
> *weird* And says 'Ye needna yoke the pleugh,
> Kirk-yards will soon be till'd eneugh,
> Tak ye nae fear:
> *ditch* They'll a' be trench'd wi mony a sheugh,
> In two-three year.

in a
straw bed

oath

cloth

'Whare I kill'd ane, a fair strae-death,
By loss o' blood, or want o' breath,
This night I'm free to tak my aith,
       That Hornbook's skill
Has clad a score i' their last claith,
      By drap and pill.'

He proceeds to give examples of Hornbook's success in killing off his patients, rising to this damning generalization:

sample

'That's just a swatch o' Hornbook's way,
Thus goes he on from day to day,
Thus does he poison, kill, an' slay,
      An's weel paid for't;
Yet stops me o' my lawfu' prey,
      Wi' his damn'd dirt!'

The poem concludes in a mock-ominous strain:

next;
wager
deserts

'But hark! I'll tell you of a plot,
Tho' dinna ye be speakin o't;
I'll nail the self-conceited Sot,
      As dead's a herrin:
Niest time we meet, I'll wad a groat,
      He gets his fairin!'

The poem now dies away on a simple, matter-of-fact note, recalling the beginning of the narrative:

beyond;
twelve

But just as he began to tell,
The auld kirk-hammer strak the bell
Some wee short hour ayont the twal,
      Which rais'd us baith:
I took the way that pleas'd mysel,
      And sae did Death.

'Death and Doctor Hornbook' is a slight enough piece, an amusing squib at best; but it is done with remarkable skill. Burns's control over the narrative never falters, he manipulates the tone and combines comic and ironic touches with real art, while his handling of imagery and the ease with which he moulds the 'Standard Habbie' verse form to suit his purpose at each stage in the narration show a technical ability of very high order.

The 'Address to the Unco Guid' is another product of Burns's *annus mirabilis* – the year immediately preceding the publication of the Kilmarnock volume. It is difficult to see why it was not published in that volume, for it does not attack specific persons, its satire is general, its morality inoffensive. Burns included it in the Edinburgh edition of 1787. It is not, in fact, as fine a poem as some of the more bitter satires, though it has good (and quotable) lines, and a fine, flowing movement. Its movement is perhaps a little *too* smooth, its plea for suspending our judgment of others a little too facile. But it might be argued that this excessive facility is an effect deliberately aimed at in order to suggest the easy, tolerant moral attitude as opposed to the crabbed, censorious habit of mind. It opens well:

> O ye wha are sae guid yoursel
>   Sae pious and sae holy,
> Ye've nought to do but mark and tell
>   Your Neebours' fauts and folly!
> Whase life is like a weel-gaun mill,
>   Supply'd wi' store o' water,
> The heapet happer's ebbing still,
>   An' still the clap plays clatter.

faults (gloss for "fauts")
well-going (gloss for "weel-gaun")
hopper (gloss for "happer")

The poem proceeds to attack self-righteousness directly and objectively (rather than let it expose itself by speaking for itself, as in 'Holy Willie's Prayer'). There are numerous generalizations, some with the force of epigrams, but all couched in relatively abstract terms:

> Ye see your state wi' theirs compar'd,
>   And shudder at the niffer,
> But cast a moment's fair regard,
>   What maks the mighty differ;
> Discount what scant occasion gave,
>   That purity ye pride in,
> And (what's aft mair than a' the lave)
>   Your better art o' hiding.

exchange (gloss for "niffer")
rest (gloss for "lave")

The tendency towards generalization sometimes leads to the most conventional kind of eighteenth-century personification:

> See Social-life and Glee sit down,
> All joyous and unthinking,
> Till, quite transmugrify'd, they're grown
> Debauchery and Drinking:
> O would they stay to calculate
> Th' eternal consequences;
> Or, your more dreaded hell to state,
> Damnation of expences!

A sudden hit below the belt, as it were, redeems the poem when it is about to sink into a collection of abstract moral aphorisms; the last two lines of this stanza provide a rapid and welcome change of tone:

> Ye high, exalted, virtuous Dames,
> Ty'd up in godly laces,
> Before ye gie poor Frailty names,
> Suppose a change o' cases;
> A dear-lov'd lad, convenience snug,
> A treacherous inclination—
> *ear*   But, let me whisper i' your lug,
> *maybe*   Ye're aiblins nae temptation.

It broadens out again in the last two stanzas, where Burns is working in a purely English didactic tradition, and doing so effectively:

> Then gently scan your brother Man,
> Still gentler sister Woman;
> *little*   Tho' they may gang a kennin wrang,
> To step aside is human:
> One point must still be greatly dark,
> The moving *Why* they do it;
> And just as lamely can ye mark,
> How far perhaps they rue it.

(One notices how the internal rhymes in the first and third lines reinforce the note of equanimity and gentleness.)

> Who made the heart, 'tis *He* alone
> Decidedly can try us,
> He knows each chord its various tone,
> Each spring its various bias:

> Then at the balance let's be mute,
>   We never can adjust it;
> What's *done* we partly may compute,
>   But know not what's *resisted*.

Both in stanza form and idiom much of this poem is reminiscent of eighteenth-century English moral poetry. We can think of nothing in English to put beside 'The Holy Fair' or 'Death and Doctor Hornbook' or 'Holy Willie's Prayer'; but beside the 'Address to the Unco Guid' we can without too much extravagance put some of the poems of Gray and Cowper.

'Holy Willie's Prayer' – which was first printed anonymously in an eight-page pamphlet in 1789, together with 'quotations from the Presbyterian Eloquence' – is without doubt the greatest of all Burns's satirical pieces. This poem, together with 'The Twa Herds', 'The Holy Fair', 'The Address to the Deil', 'The Ordination', and 'The Kirk's Alarm', constitutes – in the words of Henley and Henderson – 'What is certainly the most brilliant series of assaults ever delivered against the practical bigotry of the Kirk.' But 'Holy Willie's Prayer' stands apart from the others as far more universal in its implications. The reader needs no glosses, as he does to understand fully 'The Ordination' and 'The Kirk's Alarm', and Holy Willie defines his own character as the poem proceeds so that it becomes irrelevant whether or not Burns was drawing a real person. Burns did, however, supply an 'argument' in one of the manuscripts of the poem, and it is of some interest:

Holy Willie was a rather oldish bachelor elder, in the parish of Mauchline, and much and justly famed for that polemical chattering which ends in tippling orthodoxy, and for that spiritualized bawdry which refines to liquorish devotion. In a sessional process with a gentleman in Mauchline – a Mr. Gavin Hamilton – *Holy Willie* and his priest, Father Auld, after full hearing in the Presbytery of Ayr, came off but second best, owing partly to the oratorical powers of Mr. Robert Aiken, Mr. Hamilton's counsel; but chiefly to Mr. Hamilton's being one of the most irreproachable and truly respectable characters in the country. On losing his process, the muse overheard him at his devotions as follows.

The device of having Holy Willie condemn himself by reciting a prayer overheard by the reader is a simple one, but it enables Burns to achieve a crushing indictment of the Calvinist doctrine of election by showing the kind of hypocrisy such a belief forces on one who considers himself among the elect. The point of the poem is not simply that Holy Willie is a hypocrite; it is that some kind of unconscious hypocrisy is made inevitable by the views he professes. If you imagine you are pre-destined to salvation you become both self-righteous and morally reckless; if, on the other hand, you believe that your lot is cast with the great majority of predestinately damned, then it does not matter how you behave. Either way your character is ruined.

The poem never degenerates into farce or burlesque; the liturgical note is maintained throughout, but it becomes more monstrous as the poem progresses and the character of the speaker reveals itself, until, with that final 'Amen, Amen', the whole religious tradition of which Holy Willie is the spokesman dissolves itself in irony. The first verse, with its slow movement and deliberate psalmlike opening, makes a point about the complacency of the speaker with powerful suddenness. The reader follows the solemn, religious diction until he finds himself, unaware, caught up in the calm statement that man's ultimate fate is arranged by God without reference to his behaviour:

> O thou that in the heavens does dwell!
> Wha, as it pleases best thysel,
> Sends ane to heaven & ten to hell,
>> A' for thy glory!
> And no for ony gude or ill
>> They've done before thee.

That 'ane to heaven an' ten to hell', following so quietly and confidently on the invocation, is out almost before we grasp what has been said; and having absorbed this shock, we move, equally unsuspecting, into the two last lines, with their calm denial of the efficacy of good works.

But Burns keeps a firm control over the poem; these sudden illumina-tions of the moral absurdity of the speaker's beliefs do not check the steady flow of prayer, and we can almost imagine the organ swelling in accompaniment (though Holy Willie himself would have disapproved of 'kists o' whistles') as he continues:

> I bless & praise thy matchless might,
> When thousands thou hast left in night,
> That I am here before thy sight,
>> For gifts & grace,
> A burning & a shining light
>> To a' this place.

Again, we start off with a conventional religious line and suddenly find ourselves in the midst of an appalling self-righteousness. The significance of the second line does not fully hit us until we have come to the end of it; but we are left no time for exclamation, for the poem pushes steadily on, developing the self-righteous note.

The third stanza, again echoing conventional religious phraseology, opens on a note of humility; but how deftly Burns has introduced that note in order to expose the absurdity of the doctrine of predestined damnation!

> What was I, or my generation,
> That I should get such exaltation?
> I, wha deserv'd most just damnation,
>   For broken laws
> Sax thousand years ere my creation,
>   Thro' Adam's cause.

The apparent humility moves at last invisibly into self-congratulation; after painting a vivid picture of the pains of hell to which he might well have been consigned 'when from my mither's womb I fell', he proceeds, in the fifth stanza, to congratulate himself that, by the arbitrary favour of God, he has become a light unto the nations:

> Yet I am here, a chosen sample,
> To shew thy grace is great & ample:
> I'm here, a pillar o' thy temple
>   Strong as a rock,
> A guide, a ruler & example
>   To a' thy flock.

The doctrine here is quite orthodox. A few are predestined to salvation by the freely vouchsafed grace of God, not because of any good they have done or may do, but in order to demonstrate that 'thy grace is great and ample'. It is only this relentless note of the purest self-righteousness that suggests the irony; the language is biblical, the sentiment in itself unimpeachable. Yet the quiet, complacent stanza tears the whole doctrine apart.

In the sixth stanza the poem takes a new turn, and the note of confession succeeds the note of praise:

troubled

But yet – O Lord – confess I must –
At times I'm fash'd wi' fleshly lust;
And sometimes too, in warldly trust
    Vile Self gets in;
But thou remembers we are dust,
    Defil'd wi' sin.

This seems to be the note of true humility and repentance, but the specification of the sins of 'fleshly lust' in the next two stanzas reveal the speaker as an expert fornicator, whose excuse is that he was drunk. By this time Holy Willie has become a monster of hypocrisy, yet the responsibility is less his than that of the creed he professes.

last night;
knowest

O Lord – yestreen – thou kens – wi' Meg –
Thy pardon I sincerely beg!
O may't ne'er be a living plague,
    To my dishonor!
And I'll ne'er lift a lawless leg
    Again upon her.

drunk

would;
meddle with

Besides, I farther maun avow,
Wi' Leezie's lass, three times – I trow –
But, Lord, that friday I was fou
    When I cam near her;
Or else, thou kens, thy servant true
    Wad never steer her.

The peculiar effect of having Holy Willie call himself 'thy servant' while confessing in bawdy detail to sordid acts of lust projects the irony to the point where it becomes immensely comic.

Holy Willie does not remain long in the confessional mood; the next stanza makes it clear that the confession was only the preliminary to another orgy of complacency, and we are left gasping at the way in which apparent humility again turns out to be self-righteousness:

Maybe thou lets this fleshly thorn
Buffet thy servant e'en & morn,
Lest he o'er proud & high should turn,
    That he's sae gifted;
If sae, thy hand maun e'en be borne
    Untill thou lift it.

By the end of this stanza Holy Willie has proved to himself that his fleshly lusts are trials deliberately sent by God to prevent him from considering himself too superior to others, and the conclusion – that he is therefore resigning himself humbly to the will of God by enjoying those lusts – is suggested by one deft phrase, perfectly proper and conventionally pious in itself, but monstrously absurd in the light of what has preceded it. Yet this monstrosity and this absurdity are never allowed to interfere with the placid flow of the prayer; Burns shows no awareness that by this time Holy Willie's creed has exploded in cosmic irony, and he increases the effect by his apparent indifference.

The next six verses are directed against the enemies of Calvinist orthodoxy, in particular against Gavin Hamilton, and against Robert Aiken, who represented Hamilton in his fight with the Kirk Session and in the appeal from the Kirk Session's findings to the Presbytery. They maintain the poem on a high level of complacency and self-righteousness, and by sounding a note of moral indignation almost reminiscent of the Hebrew prophets make the speaker appear even more absurd. Here is personal spite and envy masquerading as prophetic fervour, and the result is ironical in the extreme:

> Lord mind Gaun Hamilton's deserts!
> *cards*   He drinks, & swears, & plays at cartes,
> Yet has sae mony taking arts
>   Wi' Great & Sma',
> Frae God's ain priest the people's hearts
>   He steals awa.

> And when we chasten'd him therefore,
> *disturb-*   Thou kens how he bred sic a splore,
> *ance*   And set the warld in a roar
>   O' laughin at us:
> Curse thou his basket and his store,
>   Kail & potatoes.

Holy Willie's righteous indignation turns out to be spiteful rage at having been made a fool of, as well as having been defeated in legal argument:

> O Lord, my God! that glib-tongu'd Aiken,
> My vera heart and flesh are quakin
> To think how we stood sweatin, shakin,
>   An' piss'd wi' dread,
> *hanging;*   While he, wi' hinging lip an' snakin,
> *sneering*   Held up his head.

This brief descent into vulgar colloquial diction must not be allowed to spoil the liturgical tone of the poem, and in the two concluding verses Burns is careful to make the hymn music swell out to a resounding climax:

> Lord, in thy day o' vengeance try him!
> Lord, visit him that did employ him!
> And not pass in thy mercy by them;
>> Nor hear their prayer;
> But for thy people's sake destroy them,
>> And dinna spare!

> But Lord; remember me & mine
> Wi' mercies temporal & divine!
> That I for grace & gear may shine,
>> Excell'd by nane!
> And a' the glory shall be thine!
>> Amen! Amen!

wealth

This expression of personal spite and personal complacency in rousing religious language marks the climax of the poem not only in terms of its structure but also in terms of the development of the irony. Such cunning touches as 'grace *and gear*' are remarkably felicitous; once again, we hardly notice what the creature has said, so authentic is the religious tone, until he has moved on to the next part of his utterance. Having had his personal enemies destroyed and himself made conspicuous for both spiritual superiority and material prosperity, he is content to give the glory to God. The impertinence, the coolness of the proposition he makes to the Almighty is staggering; and when this preposterous prayer crashes to its final close with the sounding twofold 'Amen', we are utterly overcome by this combination of self-interest and apparent piety. We have even a kind of admiration for the man who can combine the two with an air of such complete conviction. But there is certainly nothing left of his creed by the time the poem comes to an end.

Students of English poetry who consider Browning the pioneer and most successful practitioner of the dramatic monologue might well consider Burns's claim to the distinction on the basis of this one poem, in which, with perfect dramatic appropriateness, a character damns himself and his doctrine before the reader's eyes without being in the least aware that he has done so.

In a satire as magnificent as this, any comment by the critic seems naive and irrelevant. Burns, though a craftsmanlike and often subtle poet, is never a difficult one. 'Holy Willie's Prayer' reveals itself at once as a tremendous indictment of a kind of religion and of a kind of person. It needs to be read aloud with a good Scots accent and an uninhibited pulpit eloquence in order to achieve its full effect, but even the reader unfamiliar with the sound of Scots speech can appreciate the poem's stature in a silent reading. It is one of the very few perfect satirical short poems in Scots or English.

'The Jolly Beggars' seems to have been written fairly early in Burns's career, though it is impossible to fix the exact date. There is fairly clear evidence that Burns planned to include it in the Edinburgh edition of 1787 but was dissuaded by Hugh Blair. According to Robert Chambers, writing in the middle of the nineteenth century, the 'cantata' was the product of an actual adventure, the details of which were narrated to Chambers long after Burns's death by the poet's friend John Richmond:

> The poem is understood to have been founded on the poet's ob-servation of an actual scene which one night met his eye, when, in company with his friends John Richmond and James Smith, he drop-ped accidentally at a late hour into the humble hostelry of Mrs Gibson, more familiarly named Poosie Nansie, already referred to. After witnessing much jollity amongst a company who by day appeared as miserable beggars, the three young men came away, Burns professing to have been greatly amused with the scene, but particularly with the gleesome behaviour of an old maimed soldier. In the course of a few days, he recited a part of the poem to Richmond, who informed me that, to the best of his recollection, it contained, in its original complete form, songs by a sweep and a sailor, which did not afterwards appear.

Burns himself professed later to have forgotten all about the piece. Writing to George Thomson in September, 1793, he remarked:

> I have forgot the Cantata you allude to, as I kept no copy, indeed did not know that it was in existence: however, I remember that none of the songs pleased myself, except the last – something about,

> > 'Courts for cowards were erected,
> > Churches built to please the priest.'

'The Jolly Beggars' was never published in Burns's lifetime; it first saw the light as a chapbook published by Stewart and Meikle in Glasgow in 1799. Whether Burns was sincere in his statement to Thomson that he had completely forgotten it may be doubted; it is difficult to believe that he could have completely forgotten such a remarkable work, and it is possible that the political atmosphere of 1793 suggested caution in any reference to this wildly radical cantata. It was certainly not the kind of piece that his genteel friends and admirers would have approved of.

Burns probably got the first suggestion for the cantata from a piece in Ramsay's *The Tea-Table Miscellany* entitled 'Merry Beggars', which introduced six beggars, each speaking a verse. It opens thus:

> *First beggar.*
> I once was a poet at London,
>   I kept my heart still full of glee;
> There's no man can say that I'm undone,
>   For begging's no new trade to me.
> *Tol derol, &c.*

The third beggar is a soldier:

> Make room for a soldier in buff,
>   Who valiantly strutted about,
> Till he fancy'd the peace breaking off,
>   And then he most wisely sold out.

The fifth is a fiddler:

> I still am a merry gut-scraper,
>   My heart never yet felt a qualm;
> Tho' poor, I can frolic and vapour,
>   And sing any tune by a psalm.

The first beggar reappears at the end to announce the chorus, which all repeat:

> Whoe'er would be merry and free,
>   Let him list, and from us he may learn;
> In palaces who shall you see
>   Half so happy as we in a barn?
> *Tol derol, &c.*

The Tea-Table Miscellany also contains a poem entitled 'The Happy Beggars', with six female beggars making similar professions.

The idea of becoming a beggar always had a certain fascination for Burns; it represented a gesture of freedom and escape, the worst that could happen to anybody for whom society found no room and a relief from all obligation to the genteel tradition:

> The last o't, the warst o't,
> Is only but to beg.

Henley and Henderson, in their notes to the cantata in the centenary edition, have traced the 'Jovial Mumper' in Scots and English literary tradition with alarming thoroughness, and there is no doubt that in writing 'The Jolly Beggars' Burns was indirectly influenced by such pieces as 'The Gaberlunzie Man' and 'The Jolly Beggar' and by a long line of songs and poems in goliardic vein which goes far back into the Middle Ages. It is, however, enough to realize that Burns was working here in a literary tradition, and that he adapted that tradition brilliantly to his own purposes.

'This irresistible presentation of humanity caught in the act and summarized for ever in the terms of art' is Henley and Henderson's description of 'The Jolly Beggars', and it can stand beside Matthew Arnold's 'puissant and splendid production' as an apt and quotable epitome of its qualities. The cantata has an abandon, a fierce and almost anarchistic acceptance of man at his lowest social level, which makes it remarkable even among Burns's works. The dramatic elements in it are of the crudest; yet we are projected into the scene with a violence and a completeness far greater than that achieved in many more satisfactory dramatic works. The cantata is essentially a collection of swaggering songs held together by brief intermittent recitative and introduced by a description of the setting. It opens with the characteristic contrast between winter exterior and cosy interior which we have noted as a feature of Scottish literature generally and which is to be found in 'Tam o' Shanter' and in several of the verse epistles. The stanza here is the old Scottish verse form used by Montgomerie in 'The Cherry and the Slae':

withered; earth	When lyart leaves bestrow the yird,
bat	Or wavering like the Bauckie-bird,
	Bedim cauld Boreas' blast;
lash	When hailstanes drive wi' bitter skyte,
	And infant Frosts begin to bite,
rime	In hoary cranreuch drest;
company	Ae night at e'en a merry core
lawless,	
vagrant	O' randie, gangrel bodies,

revel   In Poosie-Nansie's held the splore,

spare rags   To drink their orra dudies:

                  Wi' quaffing, and laughing,

roistered   They ranted an' they sang;

                  Wi' jumping, an' thumping,

                  The vera girdle rang.

The second stanza introduces the soldier, 'in auld red rags', who sits by the fire with his 'doxy' ,who in turn is warm 'wi' usquebae an' blankets'. The combination of raggedness and comfort which is an important part of the setting reminds one of the old Scots proverb, 'the clartier [dirtier] the cosier'. Burns is deliberately reducing the comforting elements to the most primitive (and the most ungenteel) level – whisky, sex, and swagger; and these are far removed from the conventional wine, woman, and song of the eighteenth-century drinking song.

The element of swagger represents independence in its lowest social form. To detect this note in the songs sung by the various characters is not, therefore, to discern a fault. Sir Herbert Grierson has remarked on 'the inferior swaggering note in the tradition of Durfey's *Pills to Purge Melancholy*' in some of the songs; but Burns was surely conscious of what he was doing and introduced this note deliberately as dramatically appropriate. The soldier's song is crude and boastful, but it has a fine popular ring to it, and it is set to the simple and lively air, 'Soldier's Joy',

      I am a son of Mars, who have been in many wars,

        And show my cuts and scars wherever I come:

      This here was for a wench, and that other in a trench

        When welcoming the French at the sound of the drum.

                          Lal de daudle, etc.

The 'Lal de daudle, etc.' of the printed text conveys no idea of the dancing liveliness of the chorus as sung; it is a simple enough tune, a development of the air to which the verse goes, at a higher pitch, and it seems to call for a general clapping of hands or stamping of feet at the first and third beat of every measure:

After an account of his career as a soldier, the singer, in the fourth and fifth verses, turns to his present situation:

> And now, tho' I must beg with a wooden arm and leg
> And many a tatter's rag hanging over my bum,
> I'm as happy with my wallet, my bottle, and my callet
> As when I us'd in scarlet to follow a drum.
> What tho' with hoary locks I must stand the winter shocks,
> Beneath the woods and rocks oftentimes for a home?
> When the tother bag I sell, and the tother bottle tell,
> I could meet a troop of Hell at the sound of a drum.
>
> > Lal de daudle, etc.

The swaggering gesture is fixed with precision in this final stanza, and the *recitativo* proceeds to link up the soldier's expression of views with the whole social atmosphere of the group before introducing the next character:

rafters	He ended; and the kebars sheuk
shook	
above	Aboon the chorus roar;
rats	While frighted rattons backward leuk,
inmost hole	An' seek the benmost bore:
tiny; corner	A fairy fiddler frae the neuk,
	He skirl'd out Encore!
dear	But up arose the martial chuck,
	An' laid the loud uproar.

And there follows immediately the soldier's 'doxy', who moves the atmosphere even further away from any sort of respectability or gentility with her bold, lilting, amorality:

> I once was a maid, tho' I cannot tell when,
> And still my delight is in proper young men.
> Some one of a troop of dragoons was my daddie:
> No wonder I'm fond of a sodger laddie!
>
> > Sing, lal de la, etc.

The song – which goes to a lively traditional tune in six-eight time and has a fine, dancing chorus – lists the sexual career of the singer in a manner which does not so much flout or attack ordinary social conventions as ignore them, as though in the world of real, elemental living they did not exist. The last verse returns the theme to an atmosphere of conviviality:

> And now I have lived – I know not how long!
> And still I can join in a cup and a song;
> But whilst with both hands I can hold the glass steady,
> Here's to thee, my hero, my sodger laddie.

The toast, the ultimate convivial gesture, concludes this song as it concludes the cantata as a whole. This ragged group is united, not by convention, but by sporadic enthusiasms which derive from the personalities of the members. At the end they find a common enthusiasm in renouncing organized society.

The camera now moves from the soldier and his doxy, to focus on another couple:

tinker-hussy	Poor Merry Andrew, in the neuk,
	Sat guzzling wi' a Tinker-hizzie;
cared not;	They mind't na wha the chorus teuk,
took	Between themsels they were sae busy:
	At length wi' drink an' courting dizzy,
staggered	He stoiter'd up an' made a face;
	Then turn'd, an laid a smack on Grizzie,
then	Syne tun'd his pipes wi' grave grimace.

This is the professional fool, and he takes cognizance of society only to laugh at it. Unlike the previous singer, he does not express the spontaneous amorality of one above or below social standards but the sophisticated scorn of the disillusioned jester. The song is set to an old English air, 'Auld Sir Symon', which had long been popular in both England and Scotland. It is slow moving and has a distinctly melancholy undercurrent which lends a note of almost wistful irony to the words:

> Sir Wisdom's a fool when he's fou;
>   Sir Knave is a fool in a session:
> He's there but a prentice I trow,
>   But I am a fool by profession.
>
> My grannie she bought me a beuk,
>   An' I held awa to the school:
> I fear I my talent misteuk,
>   But what will ye hae of a fool?

> For drink I wad venture my neck;
>   A hizzie's the half of my craft:
> But what could ye other expect
>   Of ane that' avowedly daft?

In the fifth verse the irony is heightened:

> Poor Andrew that tumbles for sport
>   Let naebody name wi' a jeer:
> There's even, I'm tauld, i' the Court
>   A tumbler ca'd the Premier.

The conclusion strikes a deft balance between satire and self-mockery:

> And now my conclusion I'll tell,
>   For faith! I'm confoundedly dry:
> The chiel that's a fool for himsel,
>   Guid Lord! he's far dafter than I.

A short narrative section then introduces a 'raucle carlin', a female vagabond and thief, who, in a most unlugubrious elegy for her dead Highland lover, evokes mock-Jacobite undertones. There are traces of more than one earlier folk song in this piece, and the opening lines of the chorus may be traditional. It is set to an old reel tune, 'O, an Ye Were Dead, Guidman', though today it is more often sung to the tune, 'The White Cockade', which fits the words equally well. The note of gaiety in the melody (the tune as printed in the *Caledonian Pocket Companion*, 1752, has the instruction, 'Cheerily': it is in D major) predominates over the elegiac nature of the theme and leaves little doubt that when the singer sought comfort in 'a hearty can' she did not seek in vain.

> A highland lad my Love was born,
> *lowland* The lalland laws he held in scorn:
> But he still was faithfu' to his clan,
> My gallant, braw John Highlandman.

> Chorus
> Sing hey my braw John Highlandman!
> Sing ho my braw John Highlandman!
> There's not a lad in a' the lan'
> Was match for my John Highlandman.

The words need the music to emphasize the rhythm, to keep each line firm and steady.

The two final stanzas show the turn from grief to bacchanalian comfort:

> But Och! they catch'd him at the last,
> And bound him in a dungeon fast,
> My curse upon them every one,
> They've hang'd my braw John Highlandman.

> And now a Widow I must mourn
> The pleasures that will ne'er return;
> No comfort but a hearty can,
> When I think on John Highlandman.

There is a pause at this point, at which we can imagine the company banging their cans while they roar out the chorus; and then the narrative is resumed, this time in 'Standard Habbie' verse form, in a change of key:

markets;
toddle

buxom

blown it

> A pigmy Scraper wi' his Fiddle,
> Wha us'd to trystes an' fairs to driddle,
> Her strappan limb an' gausy middle
>   (He reach'd nae higher)
> Had hol'd his heartie like a riddle,
>   An' blawn't on fire.

haunch

> Wi' hand on hainch, and upward e'e,
> He croon'd his gamut, one, two, three,
> Then in an *arioso* key,
>   The wee Apollo
> Set off wi' *allegretto* glee
>   His *giga* solo.

The fiddler's song is set to a tripping reel tune. Its tone is rather different from the coarse heartiness of the earlier songs, for the fiddler is a professional, and there is a delicacy (not, of course, moral but purely technical) about his utterance:

each; wipe

rest

> Let me ryke up to dight that tear;
> An' go wi' me an' be my dear,
> And then your every care an' fear
>   May whistle owre the lave o't.

Chorus

I am a fiddler to my trade,
An' a' the tunes that e'er I play'd,
The sweetest still to wife or maid
  Was *Whistle Owre the Lave O't*.

Burns wrote more than one set of verses to this tune, in every instance
taking the last line of each verse from an older Scots song whose title it
was. David Herd, in his *Ancient and Modern Scottish Songs*, printed the
following two stanzas under the title, 'Whistle o'er the Lave O't':

My mither sent me to the well,
  She had better gane hersell,
I got the thing I dare nae tell,
  Whistle o'er the lave o't.

My mither sent me to the sea,
  For to gather mussles three;
A sailor lad fell in wi' me,
  Whistle o'er the lave o't.

In sending another song of his with the same refrain and tune to George
Thomson in October, 1794, Burns remarked that 'the music [is] said to
be by a John Bruce, a celebrated violin-player, in Dumfries about the
beginning of this century'.

Though the version printed by Herd and the song, 'First When
Maggie Was My Care', which Burns wrote later to the same tune, are
both ironical and even shameless in feeling, the fiddler's song has a note
of tenderness which is an important part of the change of mood which
temporarily comes over 'The Jolly Beggars' at this point. The song is the
sunniest in the whole cantata, and has far less swagger. Its cheerfulness
comes from an almost pastoral freedom from care:

harvest
homes; we'll At kirns an' weddins we'se be there,
An' O, sae nicely's we will fare!
We'll bowse about till Daddie Care
  Sing *Whistle Owre the Lave O't*.

bones; pick
stone fence Sae merrily the banes we'll pyke,
An' sun oursels about the dyke;
An' at our leisure, when ye like,
  We'll – whistle owre the lave o't!

tickle; gut

> But bless me wi' your heav'n o' charms,
> An' while I kittle hair of thairns,
> Hunger, cauld, an' a' sic harms
> May whistle owre the lave o't.

This almost timid, pastoral note has no permanent place in such a swaggering company, and it is dramatically appropriate that the fiddler should be bullied out of his courtship by the tinker, a 'sturdy caird' who despises the 'poor gut-scraper'. The tinker does his courting boldly and boastfully:

> My bonie lass, I work in brass,
>   A tinkler is my station;
> I've travell'd round all Christian ground
>   In this my occupation;
> I've taen the gold, an' been enrolled
>   In many a noble squadron;
> But vain they search'd when off I march'd
>   To go an' clout the caldron.
>
> Despise that shrimp, that wither'd imp,
>   With a' his noise an' cap'rin,
> An' take a share wi' those that bear
>   The budget and the apron! . . .

The melody is that of an old tinker song, 'Clout the Cauldron', a simple tune that echoes the steady beating of the tinker's hammer. There is a version of 'Clout the Cauldron' in *The Tea-Table Miscellany*:

> Have you any pots or pans,
>   Or any broken chandlers?
> I am a tinkler to my trade,
>   And newly come frae Flanders,
> As scant of siller as of grace,
>   Disbanded, we've a bad run;
> Gar tell the lady of the place,
>   I'm come to clout her caldron.

The *recitativo* which follows, telling of the tinker's success in his courtship and of subsequent events, opens with a phrase that has been criticized as artificial and out of place in this context:

tinker

> The caird prevail'd: th' unblushing fair
>   In his embraces sunk,
> Partly wi' love o'ercome sae sair,
>   An' partly she was drunk. . . .

But the intention here is clearly ironical. The use of a conventional poetic diction emphasizes the unconventional nature of the situation. The conventional phrase, after all, would be 'the blushing fair', and 'th' unblushing fair' points up with deliberate irony the difference between such a situation in genteel life and in Poosie Nansie's. The lines

> Partly wi' love o'ercome sae sair,
>   An' partly she was drunk

are humorous in the same obvious way that we find in 'The Holy Fair':

> How mony hearts this day converts
>   O' sinners and o' lasses!

and

> There's some are fou o' love divine;
>   There's some are fou o' brandy.

The culminating figure in the miniature drama is the poet, whose description has a certain gravity of utterance, put into that traditional Scots stanza which Burns used in 'The Holy Fair' and elsewhere:

> He was a care-defying blade,
>   As ever Bacchus listed!
> Tho' Fortune sair upon him laid,
>   His heart she ever miss'd it.
> He had no wish but – to be glad,
>   Nor want but – when he thristed;
> He hated nought but – to be sad,
>   An' thus the Muse suggested
>   His sang that night.

The poet is moved into the centre of the stage in a way the other characters were not; his mixture of stoicism and hedonism provides an attitude in which the attitudes of all the previous spokesmen can be subsumed, and his song mingles contemptuous pride with professions of love 'to a' the fair' which deliberately flout the attitudes of conventional love poetry. The tune is an adaptation of an old reel tune, and goes with great spirit but not too fast. The phrase 'For a' that, an' a' that' (which is also the title of the tune) was a favourite one of Burns and used by him effectively in a number of poems including, of course, 'Is There for Honest Poverty?' Here it adds a note of fine contempt for all conventionality:

> I am a Bard, of no regard
>   Wi' gentle folks an' a' that,
> *staring* But Homer-like the glowrin byke,
> *crowd*   Frae town to town I draw that.

> Chorus
> For a' that, an' a' that,
>   An' twice as muckle's a' that,
> I've lost but ane, I've twa behin',
>   I've wife eneugh for a' that.

There is a magnificent independence in the second verse:

> *pond* I never drank the Muses' stank,
> *stream*   Castalia's burn, an' a' that;
> *foams* But there it streams, an' richly reams –
>   My Helicon I ca' that.

The internal rhyme helps to suggest the proud snapping of the fingers at conventional society, while the use of the Scots word 'stank' in connection with the Muses produces in us exactly the kind of shock that is most effective at this point – the shock of recognizing that a beggar can also be a poet, that a 'Bard of no regard wi' gentle folks' can be 'Homer-like', that the Muses can flourish as much among poor rustics as among the elegant classical scholars of the city. The entire Petrarchan tradition of love poetry is implicitly dismissed in such lines as

> Great love I bear to a' the fair,
>   Their humble slave an' a' that

where the phrase 'an' a' that' at first seems merely the regular repetition of what by this stage in the song is an expected refrain, but it is no sooner read (or sung) that it is recognized as a sneer at those poets who are mere slaves of literary convention. The bard is a lover of the sex all right, and he will accept the traditional formulation of the lover's attitude, but only as a prelude to action, as it were –

> But clear your decks, an' here's the Sex!
> I like the jads for a' that.

The final chorus has a careless gallantry about it:

> For a' that, an' a' that,
>   An' twice as muckle's a' that,
> My dearest bluid, to do them guid,
>   They're welcome til't for a' that!

The bard becomes the symbol of the group, as we return to the stanza form of the introductory verses and step back to view the entire gathering:

walls

> So sung the Bard, and Nansie's waws
> Shook with a thunder of applause
>   Re-echo'd from each mouth!

emptied
their bags
cover; tails
burning
thirst
company

> They toom'd their pocks, they pawn'd their duds,
> They scarcely left to coor their fuds,
>   To quench their lowan drouth.
> Then owre again the jovial thrang
>   The Poet did request

untie;
choose

> To lowse his pack an' wale a sang,
>   A ballad o' the best.
> He, rising, rejoicing
>   Between his twa Deborahs,
> Looks round him an' found them
>   Impatient for the Chorus.

The concluding song marks the high point both of conviviality and of anarchism. It is one of the supreme statements of nonconventionality in literature. Accepting society, but only in the sense of freely chosen companionship, it rejects all social institutions and all attempts to impose conventional patterns on human behaviour. To have such a song sung by a group of beggars over the 'smoking bowl' on a winter evening in a humble hostelry emphasizes its effect. The meaning of 'The Jolly

Beggars' is greater than the sum of the meaning of the various songs; the setting provides its own amplification, while the cumulative effect of the introduction of the characters and their songs is a significant part of the total meaning. It is interesting that the lines which remained in Burns's head long after, when he professed to have forgotten almost everything about the cantata, represented the final and most extreme repudiation of social institutions:

> Courts for cowards were erected,
>   Churches built to please the priest!

This concluding chorus, in which all the characters join, goes to the tune of an English drinking song, 'Jolly Mortals, Fill Your Glasses'. There are, in fact, two eighteenth-century English tunes with this title, but it seems clear from the way in which the words fit the music that Burns's song was intended to fit the older tune, a deliberate, almost marchlike melody in common time, with something of the quality of a hymn tune about it; it is precisely suited for this kind of final chorus, for though as a tune it lacks character it has exactly the right kind of emphasis.

This song is English both in diction and inspiration, but this is no defect. The simple stanza form is perfectly manipulated, the language is direct and forceful, the imagery unforced and appropriate, and the occasional generalizations in standard English diction add a fitting note of solemnity, as though this is a profession of faith, which the song needs if it is to bring the cantata fittingly to a close.

> See the smoking bowl before us!
>   Mark our jovial, ragged ring!
> Round and round take up the chorus,
>   And in raptures let us sing:

> Chorus

> A fig for those by law protected!
>   Liberty's a glorious feast,
> Courts for cowards were erected,
>   Churches built to please the priest!

The song moves to its climax in the fifth stanza, with its almost aphoristic profession:

Life is all a variorum,
  We regard not how it goes;
Let them prate about decorum,
  Who have character to lose.

There follows the resounding conclusion, in which the hymnlike quality
of the song is emphasized:

Here's to budgets, bags, and wallets!
  Here's to all the wandering train!
Here's our ragged brats and callets!
  One and all, cry out, Amen!

The repetition of the chorus brings 'The Jolly Beggars' to a close.

We have already noted that in 'The Jolly Beggars' the whole is
greater than the sum of the parts. A world, an attitude, a way of life have
been cumulatively distilled as the cantata moves to its close, and the critic
is at a loss to define the process of distillation. One can, of course, note
the vividness, the life and colour and exuberance which run through the
cantata. We can quote Carlyle: 'The blanket of the Night is drawn
asunder for a moment; in full, ruddy, flaming light, these rough tatterde-
malions are seen in their boisterous revel; for the strong pulse of Life
vindicates its right to gladness even here; and when the curtain closes,
we prolong the action, without effort; the next day as the last, our *Caird*
and our *Balladmonger* are singing and soldiering; their 'brats and callets'
are hawking, begging, cheating; and some other night, in new combina-
tions, they will wring from Fate another hour of wassail and good cheer.'
But there is more to it than this: 'The Jolly Beggars' appeals to
humanity's 'unofficial self' (to employ the useful phrase coined by George
Orwell) to a degree extremely rare in literature. One side of any
adequate human personality always demands anarchy, the repudiation
of all conventions and social institutions, just as another side always
demands set forms and rituals. 'The Jolly Beggars' isolates this first
side – gives it gloriously triumphant expression – while not shirking any
of its implications. Squalor, beggary, lust, drunkenness are all here, but
so are conviviality, comradeship, independence, courage. There is no
idealization of the peasant, as there is to some degree in Wordsworth,
nor is the beggar made into pure symbol, as in Yeats. There is nothing
either doctrinaire or mythopoeic about Burns as a poet; he uses poetic
devices to make life speak for itself, not to impose a philosophical or
mythological pattern on it. And virtues are not isolated from their

necessary vices. The ultimate implications of anarchism are poverty and insecurity, but also certain kinds of nobility. Man as anarchist may be lustful and squalid, but he is also heroic. At the other extreme is man as a dweller in the anthill. Civilization may demand a mean between these extremes, but there can be no doubt regarding which extreme exhibits man as more richly human. Henley and Henderson's description, 'humanity caught in the act', remains, 'after all the refinements of subtilty and the dogmatism of learning' (to use Dr. Johnson's famous phrase), perhaps the most apt summing up of 'The Jolly Beggars'.

We may be surprised that Burns included so few songs in the Kilmarnock volume. It is true that he was not at this period devoting nearly as much time and energy to song writing as he was later to do, but he had produced several charming songs by 1786, enough for a generous representation. The reason for the negligible number of songs in this volume is probably to be found in Burns's concern for the taste of the genteel audience to whom the volume was addressed; such an audience, although it enjoyed songs and was perfectly prepared to buy songbooks, would hardly have considered them literature proper. Burns probably felt that he would reveal a naiveté in taste if he showed a preference for songs over other kinds of poetry, just as we know he felt that it was a sign of musical ignorance and backwardness that he preferred folk melodies to symphonic music. As we shall see later, he did the bulk of his great work in rescuing and recreating Scottish song anonymously and without pay as a contributor to collections of Scottish songs edited by others. It did not occur to him that he could claim greater poetic stature as a song writer than as a practitioner of other kinds of verse. For all his interest in song, he does not appear seriously to have associated his songs with his ambition to be a Scottish poet recognized by the genteel world.

5

'CALEDONIA'S BARD, BROTHER BURNS'

BURNS SET out for Edinburgh on November 27, 1786, to follow up the success of his poems there with a personal appearance. His immediate practical intention in going to the capital was to arrange for the publication of a second edition and to see what chances there were of a position in the Excise, but of course he was also eager to confront the genteel world whose approbation he so desired, in spite of his pride and his contempt for mere gentility. He was on the defensive from the first, anxious that no one should think that he had come to sponge or to curry favour, determined that everyone should realize that, as he wrote to Sir John Whitefoord on December 1, he was not 'the needy, sharping author, fastening on those in upper life, who honour him with a little notice of him or his works'. He had a difficult role to play, and the testimony of those before whom he played it is almost unanimous that he played it extremely well.

Once in Edinburgh, he lodged with his friend John Richmond in Baxter's Close, in the Lawmarket; from these headquarters he sallied forth to meet the polite world of Edinburgh. On December 7 he was writing to Gavin Hamilton:

> For my own affairs, I am in a fair way of becoming as eminent as Thomas a Kempis or John Bunyan; and you may expect henceforth to see my birthday inserted among the wonderful events, in the Poor Robin's and Aberdeen Almanacks, along with the black Monday, & the battle of Bothwel bridge. – My Lord Glencairn & the Dean of Faculty, Mr H. Erskine, have taken me under their wing, and by all probability I shall soon be the tenth Worthy, and the eighth Wise Man, of the world.

A week later, he wrote to John Ballantine that he had been introduced 'to a good many of the noblesse', and added, 'but my avowed Patrons & Patronesses are, the Duchess of Gordon – the Countess of Glencairn, with my lord & lady Betty – the Dean of Faculty – Sir John Whiteford'. He was able to boast, too, that 'I have likewise warm friends among the Literati, Professors Stewart, Blair, Greenfield, and M^r McKenzie the Man of feeling'.

Edinburgh at this time was in a lull between the two major phases of its Golden Age; the age of David Hume was over, that of Walter Scott and Francis Jeffrey had not yet begun. But Burns met almost all the literati who were still active, and he saw all that was to be seen of the lively social life which was in no degree interrupted by the intellectual lull. The Earl of Glencairn, a liberal and intelligent nobleman just ten years Burns's senior, offered his friendship and admiration from the first, and was, in fact, the only peer with whom Burns remained on the best of terms; Glencairn died in 1791. The beautiful and brilliant Duchess of Gordon graced the rustic poet with her social approval – this was tantamount to giving him the entrée into Edinburgh society – and encouragement. Henry Erskine, Dean of the Faculty of Advocates and both a social and an intellectual leader in the Edinburgh of the period, similarly acknowledged Burns; with three such patrons no house or salon in Scotland could be closed to him. 'The man will be spoiled, if he can spoil', wrote Mrs. Cockburn after Burns had been in Edinburgh only a few weeks: 'but he keeps his simple manners, and is quite sober'.

Professor Dugald Stewart (who had had Burns to dinner at his country house, Catrine Bank, near Mauchline, in October, 1786) wrote a long account of Burns in Edinburgh to Dr. Currie when the latter was preparing his edition of Burns's works. 'His manners', wrote Stewart, 'were then, as they continued ever afterwards, simple, manly, and independent; strongly expressive of conscious genius and worth; but without anything that indicated forwardness, arrogance, or vanity. He took his share in the conversation, but not more than belonged to him; and listened with apparent attention and deference, on subjects where his want of education deprived him of the means of information.' But there is a significant addition: 'If there had been a little more of gentleness and accommodation in his temper, he would, I think, have been still more interesting.' Stewart was one of many who were struck by Burns's conversational ability in society: 'Nothing was more remarkable among his various attainments, than the fluency, and precision, and originality of his language, when he spoke in company, more particularly as he aimed at purity in his turn of expression, and avoided more successfully than most Scotchmen, the pecularities of Scottish phraseology.' Stewart agreed with Mrs. Cockburn that the treatment Burns received in Edinburgh might well have spoiled him utterly:

The attentions he received during his stay in town from all ranks and descriptions of persons, were such as would have turned any head but his own. I cannot say that I could perceive any unfavourable effect which they left on his mind. He retained the same simplicity of manners and appearance which had struck me so forcibly when I first saw him in the country; nor did he seem to feel any additional self-importance from the number and rank of his new acquaintance. His dress was perfectly suited to his station, plain and unpretending, with a sufficient attention to neatness. If I recollect right, he always wore boots; and, when on more than usual ceremony, buck-skin breeches.

Professor Stewart also remarked on Burns's intelligence – an aspect of the poet which is often ignored by literary critics but which is often mentioned by contemporary observers. Mrs. Maria Riddell, in a remarkable memoir of the poet which she wrote for the *Dumfries Journal* after his death, went so far as to say that Burns's chief claim to distinction did not lie in his poetry but in his conversation. 'If others have climbed more successfully to the heights of Parnassus', wrote Mrs. Riddell (as reprinted by Dr. Currie), 'none certainly outshone Burns in the charms – the sorcery I would almost call it, of fascinating conversation; the spontaneous eloquence of social argument, or the unstudied poignancy of brilliant repartee. . . . I believe no man was ever gifted with a larger portion of the *vivida vis animi:* the animated expressions of his countenance were almost peculiar to himself. The rapid lightnings of his eye were always the harbingers of some flash of genius. . . .' There can be no doubt that Burns was able to hold his conversational end up in any Edinburgh drawing room.

Walter Scott, then a boy of sixteen, met Burns at the house of Dr. Adam Ferguson, and many years later gave Lockhart his recollection of the meeting:

I think his countenance was more massive than it looks in any of the portraits. I would have taken the poet, had I not known what he was, for a very sagacious country farmer of the old Scotch school; that is, none of your modern agriculturalists, who keep labourers for their drudgery, but the *douce guidman* who held his own plough. There was a strong expression of sense and shrewdness in all his lineaments: the eye alone, I think, indicated the poetical character and temperament. It was large, and of a cast which glowed (I say literally *glowed*) when he spoke with feeling or interest. I never saw such another eye in a human being, though I have seen the most distinguished men of my time. His conversation expressed perfect self-confidence, but without the least intrusive forwardness; and when he differed in opinion, he did not hesitate to express it firmly, yet at the same time with modesty.

In spite of his triumphs, Burns was worried and insecure. 'Various concurring circumstances have raised my fame as a Poet to a height which I am absolutely certain I have not merits to support; and I look down on the future as I would into the bottomless pit'. So he wrote to Aiken on December 16, and about the same time he wrote to the Reverend William Greenfield an even more illuminating letter:

Never did Saul's armour sit so heavy on David when going to encounter Goliah, as does the encumbering robe of public notice with which the friendship and patronage of some 'names dear to fame' have invested me. – I do not say this in the ridiculous idea of seeming self-abasement, and affected modesty. – I have long studied myself, and I think I know pretty exactly what ground I occupy, both as a Man & a Poet; and however the world, or a friend, may sometimes differ from me in that particular, I stand for it, in silent resolve, with all the tenaciousness of Property. – I am willing to believe that my abilities deserved a better fate than the veriest shades of life; but to be dragged forth, with all my imperfections on my head, to the full glare of learned and polite observation, is what, I am afraid, I shall have bitter reason to repent. –

I mention this to you, once for all, merely, in the Confessor style, to disburthen my conscience, and that – 'When proud fortune's ebbing tide recedes' – you may bear me witness, when my bubble of fame was at the highest, I stood, unintoxicated, with the inebriating cup in my hand, looking forward, with rueful resolve, to the hastening time when the stroke of envious Calumny, with all the eagerness of vengeful triumph, should dash it to the ground.

He was fully aware that in Edinburgh he was acting a part, that he was being trotted around the drawing rooms of the city to be on exhibition like 'the learned pig in the Grassmarket'. He knew that it was not the quality of his poetry but the fact that he was a 'Heaven-taught plough-man' that accounted for his social triumphs, and he wondered uneasily how long it would last.

'With what uncommon penetration and sagacity', wrote Henry Mackenzie in his long review of the Kilmarnock edition in the *Lounger* of December 9, 'this Heaven-taught ploughman, from his humble and unlettered station, has looked upon men and manners'. The critics had seized the bait Burns had held out to them in the Preface, and praised him (in the words of the October *Edinburgh Magazine*) as 'a striking example of native genius bursting through the obscurity of poverty and the obstructions of laborious life', as a 'rusticus abnormis sapiens', as (in the words of the December *Monthly Review*) a 'humble bard' whose 'simple strains, artless and unadorned, seem to flow without effort from the native feelings of the heart'. It was partly Burns's own fault that he appeared in Edinburgh largely as a novelty and a curiosity, but knowledge of this fact did not make him any more comfortable.

His pride and sensitivity made him sometimes unduly suspicious of the conventional forms of social courtesy. He found it especially difficult to suffer fools gladly and to see people who had expressed an admiration for him being equally courteous and complimentary to people of rank but of no mind. The combination of high rank and stupidity enraged him, because it showed him that rank had its privileges regardless of character or ability. As a result he occasionally exercised his genius for repartee in a manner which shook those who had come to gaze patronizingly on him as a gifted rustic. With the ladies he sometimes made blunders; his country upbringing had not taught him to distinguish the various degrees of social flirtation, or the immense gulf between a gentle pressure when shaking hands and an attempt to steal a kiss behind the door. In the country, one thing led to another fairly simply and directly, but, as he soon discovered, the sex life of Edinburgh ladies of rank, though perhaps no more moral fundamentally, was certainly much more circumscribed by convention and conditioned by class consciousness. It was humiliating never to be able to discover whether the obstacles he met with were specially raised for him because he was considered a forward ploughman or whether they existed for everybody. He soon learned to go to a lower social stratum for sexual as well as for general social relaxation. The Edinburgh gentry, when they discovered this, were not pleased, although in strict logic they might have been expected to be. Strict logic, however, has never governed the laws of social behaviour.

Burns's Masonic connections helped to enlarge the area of his social life. He was assumed a member of the Canongate Kilwinning Lodge on February 1, 1787, but his greatest Masonic triumph had occurred the previous month, when at a meeting of the Grand Lodge of Scotland he heard the Grand Master give the toast, 'Caledonia, and Caledonia's Bard, Brother Burns'. Masonry was a great solvent of class distinctions, and some of the members of the Canongate Kilwinning Lodge were also members of convivial organizations which were socially far removed from the world of the literati or the Duchess of Gordon. One such organization, the Crochallan Fencibles, proved particularly congenial to Burns; he was introduced to it by its founder, the printer William Smellie, and joined happily in its bawdy songs and relaxed social atmosphere as a relief from the formal genteel functions where he had to be on his best behaviour. Thus Burns came into contact with the Edinburgh that Fergusson had known and celebrated.

Burns can have had little time for writing poetry while he was being lionized in Edinburgh. The lively and amusing 'Address to a Haggis' is one of the few good vernacular poems written at this time; it appeared in the *Caledonian Mercury* on December 19, and in the *Scots Magazine* for January. The 'Address to Edinburgh' was a 'duty' poem, written in December as a more or less official expression of gratitude to the city which had received him so hospitably; it, too, was published in the *Caledonian Mercury*, so that the Edinburgh public could see that he had done his duty by the city. It is a frigid, artificial poem in stilted neoclassic English. Edinburgh is hailed as 'Edina! Scotia's darling seat!' and the firm of Edinburgh plumbers and sanitary engineers who in a later generation adopted the name 'Edina' for their version of a necessary but hardly a poetic kind of seat were demonstrating, if somewhat crudely, real critical insight.

But if Burns wrote the 'Address to Edinburgh' to please the literati, he did not often accept their advice. In March, 1787, he wrote to Mrs. Dunlop (an aristocratic lady in her late fifties who had been redeemed from boredom and unhappiness by her discovery of the Kilmarnock poems and as a result had begun a correspondence with Burns which continued throughout the rest of his life; she became the poet's sincere friend and self-appointed adviser): 'I have the advice of some very judicious friends among the Literati here, but with them I sometimes find it necessary to claim the privilege of thinking for myself.' It was as well that he did, for advice to abandon the vernacular and choose themes from classical mythology, however well meant, showed a complete misunderstanding of Burns's genius.

In spite of the social strain he was continually under in Edinburgh, the evidence is clear that he played his part well, though there were occasional moments of tactlessness and anger. He made new friends in a new world, and though some of these friends did him more harm than good – the irascible William Nicol, for example, Latin master at the High School, who became one of Burns's cronies – on the whole it was good for him to have his circle of acquaintance thus enlarged. The Earl of Glencairn introduced him to William Creech, the publisher, who became Burns's literary agent; if the financial terms agreed on between Burns and Creech for the publication of the second edition of his poems were not as good as they might have been, and if Creech was dilatory in paying Burns what was due him for this edition, the fault was hardly Glencairn's. As early as December 7 Burns was able to report to Gavin Hamilton another happy result of Glencairn's patronage: 'Through my Lord's influence it is inserted in the records of the Caledonian Hunt, that they universally, one & all, subscribe for the 2ᵈ Edition.' The Caledonian Hunt was an exclusive and influential group, and their support meant a great deal. It was to 'the noblemen and gentlemen of the Caledonian Hunt' that Burns dedicated his second edition, the Edinburgh edition of 1787.

His genteel friends were not, however, keen on the idea that he should seek a job in the Excise. A ploughman poet was a ploughman poet, after all, and his duty was to stay on a farm. Patrick Miller – who first introduced himself to Burns by leaving anonymously 'ten guineas for the Ayrshire Bard in Mʳ Sibbald's hand' – came forward with the offer of a farm for rent. 'My generous Friend, Mʳ Peter Miller, brother to the Justice Clerk, has been talking with me about the lease of some farm or other in an estate called Dasswinton which he has lately bought near Dumfries', Burns reported to John Ballantine in January. But he added: 'Some life-rented, embittering Recollections whisper me that I will be happier anywhere than in my old neighbourhood, but Mʳ Miller is no Judge of land; and though I dare say he means to favour me, yet he may give me, in his opinion, an advantageous bargain that may ruin me.' Burns's foreboding proved to be justified.

One must distinguish between the friends Burns made in Edinburgh who were in a sense patrons – not only Glencairn and the Duchess of Gordon, but literary and intellectual lights such as Dugald Stewart, Henry Mackenzie, Hugh Blair, and others of the literati – and those whom he could meet without social constraint and with whom he could relax happily beyond the shadow of genteel good taste. The most important of the latter group was William Nicol, who was to be Burns's companion on his second Highland tour and whose egotism and bad manners dragged Burns away from the company of the Duke and Duchess of Atholl at Blair Athol and, later in the same trip, from that of the Duke and Duchess of Gordon at Castle Gordon, thus ending his relationship with both families and perhaps ruining his chances of getting the kind of job he was looking for. But Nicol had something that Burns needed: he was convivial, lively, and independent; he had a gift for bawdry and for lively vernacular conversation; and he was democratic to the point of insolence. Nicol, coarse and offensive though he often was, must have been a refreshing change from the atmosphere of studied gentility in which Burns spent so much of his time in Edinburgh. The only extant letter by Burns written in pure Scots throughout – and done with a verve and sparkle which show what a gift Burns had for comic prose narrative in the vernacular – was addressed to Nicol. Other friends in the second category were Robert Ainslie, young Edinburgh law student with whom Burns soon struck up a cheerful intimacy; William Smellie, printer of the Edinburgh edition and stalwart of the Crochallan Fencibles; and Peter Hill, at that time clerk in William Creech's office.

Burns's immediate purpose in coming to Edinburgh was to arrange for the publication of a second edition of his poems, and he got down to this immediately. 'I am nearly agreed with Creech to print my book', he wrote to Ballantine on December 13, and a month later he wrote to the same correspondent that 'I have this day corrected my 152^d page'. In coming to an arrangement with Creech, Burns asked the advice of Henry Mackenzie, who, thinking of writing as a gentlemanly hobby rather than a means of livelihood, agreed that a hundred guineas for the copyright of the poems would be a fair bargain. This agreement was arrived at when the 1787 Edinburgh edition was almost ready for distribution, and it gave Creech the right to put out further editions for his own benefit solely. The 1787 edition itself was of course sold by subscription, with Burns paying Creech to act as his agent and Smellie to do the printing and carry the cost of the binding and similar expenses; he himself was to keep what was left of the subscription money. Dr. Snyder has calculated that Burns's gross receipts from the sale of the subscription copies and of the copyright must have been £855. A year later Burns wrote to Dr. Moore that he expected to net about £400. He had made something over £50 from the Kilmarnock volume.

Burns had no very clear idea at this time of how he wanted to earn his livelihood in the future. He naturally wanted to continue his career as a poet, but he seems never seriously to have contemplated making his living by his pen. 'The appelation of, a Scotch Bard, is by far my highest pride; to continue to deserve it is my most exalted ambition', he wrote to Mrs. Dunlop on March 22, the day when he finished correcting his proof sheets. 'I have no greater, no dearer aim than to have it in my power, unplagu'd with the routine business, for which Heaven knows I am unfit enough, to make leisurely pilgrimages through Caledonia; to sit on the fields of her battles; to wander on the romantic banks of her rivers; and to muse by the stately tower or venerable ruins, once the honoured abodes of her heroes.' He added, however: 'But these are all Utopian ideas.' Later on, in the same letter, he wrote:

> I guess that I shall clear between two and three hundred pounds by my Authorship; with that sum I intend, so far as I may be said to have any intention, to return to my old acquaintance, the plough, and, if I can meet with a lease by which I can live, to commence Farmer. – I do not intend to give up Poesy: being bred to labour secures me independance, and the Muses are my chief, sometimes have been my only enjoyment.

Mrs. Dunlop's solution of the problem was that Burns should obtain a commission in the army, but Burns was probably not serious in replying that were the profits from his poems sufficient (presumably to buy a commission), 'with rapture I would take your hint of a military life, as the most congenial to my feelings and situation of any other.' His earlier gesture towards joining the army as a way of escape had certainly not meant the purchase of a commission, but, as we have seen, had been associated in his mind with the idea of becoming a beggar – a last resort in the struggle for existence.

The Edinburgh edition was published on April 21, 1787; it contained a new preface, in the form of a dedication to the Caledonian Hunt, a list of subscribers (which occupied thirty-seven pages), a much fuller glossary than the brief one in the Kilmarnock edition, and almost a hundred more pages of poetry than the earlier volume. It was substantially the Kilmarnock volume with new poems added, and some minor changes in the spelling of Scots forms in the old poems. These new poems were for the most part, however, poems which he had already written before the publication of the Kilmarnock edition and which he included now because he thought they would be congenial to the taste of his new patrons. They add little to the value of the book.

There were twenty-two poems in the Edinburgh edition which had not been included in the Kilmarnock volume. The best of these we have already discussed in the chapter on the poems omitted in 1786. 'Death and Doctor Hornbook', 'The Ordination', and 'Address to the Unco Guid' now appear for the first time, and it is difficult to see why they were found suitable for the Edinburgh edition and rejected from the Kilmarnock. Five religious pieces – 'Stanzas in Prospect of Death', 'O Thou Dread Power', 'Paraphrase of the First Psalm', 'Prayer under the Pressure of Violent Anguish' and the 'Ninetieth Psalm Versified' – show Burns writing in conventional neoclassic English with no spark of genius or even of originality. There remain 'The Brigs of Ayr', 'The Calf',

'Tam Samson's Elegy', 'A Winter Night', 'To Miss Logan', 'Address to a Haggis', 'Address to Edinburgh', and seven songs. In these poems, interesting though they are, there is nothing to suggest powers that were not demonstrated by the Kilmarnock volume, except one of the songs; for here is 'Green Grow the Rashes, O', a superb piece and one of the best of Burns's songs.

'The Brigs of Ayr' is, however, also worth examination. It was written in the late summer or early autumn of 1786; Burns encloses the poem, together with warm words of friendship and compliment, in a letter to John Ballantine in October. The idea for a dialogue between two bridges Burns almost certainly derived from Fergusson, who has several poems of this kind – the 'Mutual Complaint of Plainstanes and Causey', 'A Drink Eclogue' (a dialogue between a bottle of brandy and a bottle of whisky, with the last word by the landlady), and 'The Ghaists' (a dialogue between the ghosts of two seventeenth-century Edinburgh merchants). Of these poems the two latter employ the heroic couplet, the verse form of 'The Brigs of Ayr', while the first uses the octosyllabic couplet. But 'The Brigs of Ayr' is as much English as Scots in its inspiration; in fact, it reflects a combination of both influences to a degree uncommon in Burns's poetry. On reading the introductory dedication to Ballantine, one would imagine that here is a poem squarely in the tradition of mid-eighteenth-century English verse; yet, as the theme develops and the echoes of Fergusson grow, one begins to see, in the kind of humour, the imagery, and the whole atmosphere of the poem, a clear connection not only with the old Scottish flyting tradition but also with the broader tradition of humorous, realistic Scots poetry.

The introductory poem shows a competence – one could hardly call it more than that – in handling a conventional English form:

> The simple Bard, rough at the rustic plough,
> Learning his tuneful trade from ev'ry bough
> (The chanting linnet, or the mellow thrush,
> Hailing the setting sun, sweet, in the green thorn bush;
> The soaring lark, the perching red-breast shrill,
> Or deep-ton'd plovers grey, wild-whistling o'er the hill):
> Shell he – nurst in the peasant's lowly shed,
> To hardy independence bravely bred,
> By early poverty to hardship steel'd,
> And train'd to arms in stern misfortune's field –
> Shall he be guilty of their hireling crimes,
> The servile, mercenary Swiss of rhymes? . . .

In sentiment, in turn of phrase, in the handling of the couplet, this is in the tradition of eighteenth-century English poetry which literary historians have labelled 'pre-Romantic'. It is worth noting that Burns is pre-Romantic when he follows eighteenth-century English poetry most closely; when he works in the Scottish tradition his poetry falls outside all such categories.

The account of the conversation between the spirits of the two bridges, preceded by a description of the poet's wandering forth at night and being startled by overhearing the strange dialogue, moves steadily away from the style of the introduction into a racy, realistic, satiric idiom. The auld brig's opening remarks show this new idiom at once:

> *'no small*
> *beer'*   I doubt na, frien', ye'll think ye're nae sheep-shank,
> *stretched*
> *across*   Ance ye were streekit owre frae bank to bank
> *when*   But gin ye be a brig as auld as me,
>   Tho' faith, that date I doubt, ye'll never see;
> *wager a*
> *farthing*   There'll be, if that day come, I'll wad a boddle,
>   Some fewer whigmeleeries in your noddle.

This characteristically Scottish version of the ancients-versus-moderns debate continues in the same vein, with the oblique satire on human character emerging as the poem proceeds, to produce a lively and amusing *débat* – though hardly as effective as 'The Twa Dogs', a poem very similar to it. Burns shows his characteristic ability to employ racy, conversational idiom without shattering the verse form or losing the added point provided by the discipline of the verse:

> *cuckoo*   Conceited gowk! puff'd' up wi' windy pride!
>   This mony a year I've stood the flood an' tide;
> *eld;*   And tho' wi' crazy eild I'm sair forfairn,
> *worn out*   I'll be a Brig when ye're a shapeless cairn!
>   As yet ye little ken about the matter,
>   But twa-three winters will inform ye better.

At this point in the second speech of the auld brig, the poem moves – quite naturally and without our realizing that there is a change in style until the section is over – into a set description of the River Ayr in spate, where, in spite of the Scots forms, the inspiration is as much English as Scots:

When heavy, dark, continued, a'-day rains,
Wi' deepening deluges o'erflow the plains,
When from the hills where springs the brawling Coil,
Or stately Lugar's mossy fountains boil,
Or where the Greenock winds his moorland course,
Or haunted Garpal draws his feeble source,
thaws   Arous'd by blustering winds an' spotting thowes,
melted   In mony a torrent down the snaw-broo rowes;
snow rolls
spate   While crashing ice, borne on the roaring speat,
away   Sweeps dams, an' mills, an' brigs, a' to the gate;
And from Glenbuck, down to the Ratton-key,
Auld Ayr is just one lengthen'd, tumbling sea;
crash   Then down ye'll hurl, deil nor ye never rise!
muddy   And dash the gumlie jaups up to the pouring skies.
splashes
A lesson sadly teaching, to your cost,
That Architecture's noble art is lost!

The last four lines (in spite of the alexandrine, which is pure eighteenth-century English in the way it is handled) return the poem to the flyting mood again, and this mood is sustained by the new brig's reply:

lost the   Fine architecture, trowth, I needs must say't o't!
way   The Lord be thankit that we've tint the gate o't!

The poem returns to the neoclassic idiom in the conclusion, with a description of the Genius of the Stream arriving to silence the clamour. He is followed by a crowd of allegorical figures – 'Sweet Female Beauty hand in hand with Spring', Rural Joy, 'Summer, with his fervid-beaming eye', Plenty (with, of course, her horn), Winter, Hospitality, Courage, Benevolence, Learning and Worth (keeping step together) and

Last, white-rob'd Peace, crown'd with a hazel wreath,
To rustic Agriculture did bequeath
The broken, iron instruments of death:
At sight of whom our Sprites forgat their kindling wrath.

This company seems rather absurd after the lively and robust quarrelling of the bridges; but the Edinburgh literati must have liked it. What has happened here is precisely what happened in 'The Vision' (to which, incidentally, Burns added new verses in this edition): a failure of inspiration or a doubt as to how to end the poem leads him to fall back on the English tradition he learned from Masson and his later reading. In this tradition, though he could be skilful, he seems to have had no basis for self-criticism, no means of distinguishing frigidity from liveliness or competent versifying from living poetry.

'Green Grow the Rashes, O' was entered without the final verse in the Commonplace Book in August, 1784. Burns was here rewriting an old song, current in several versions. In a letter to Richmond on September 3, announcing the birth of Jean's twins, he had quoted, as we have seen, a lively and thoroughly bawdy version. Another old version was printed by Herd:

> Green grows the rashes – O,
> Green grows the rashes – O:
> The feather-bed is no sae saft
> As a bed among the rashes.
>
> We're a' dry wi' drinking o't,
> We're a' dry drinking o't;
> The parson kist the fidler's wife,
> And he cou'd na preach for thinking o't
> *Green grows*, &c.
>
> The down-bed, the feather-bed,
> The bed among the rashes – O;
> Yet a' the beds is na sae saft
> As the bellies o' the lasses – O.

There are two other versions, both thoroughly bawdy, in *The Merry Muses of Caledonia*, the collection of indecent songs which Burns assembled for the private use of himself and his chosen cronies. The version Burns sent to Richmond contains elements of both.

Burns's complete recasting of these coarse old fragments into a finished song which, while retaining the abandoned mood of the original, adds to it a note of tenderness and at the same time a leavening of wit, is characteristic of his method as a song writer. His version expresses the complete abandon to the moment's emotion which is the theme of so many of his best songs; its delicacy of phrasing and aptness of expression produce a peculiar sense of inevitability which has kept the song universally popular. One might mention, too, its apt fitting to the tune, an old one, of which a rudimentary form exists in an early seventeenth-century manuscript under the title, 'A dance: Green grow the rashes'. It was one of the first of Burns's songs to be printed with the music; it so appeared in the *Scots Musical Museum*, 1787.

Burns version opens and closes with his 'purified' form of the chorus:

> Green grow the rashes, O;
> Green grow the rashes, O;
> The sweetest hours that e'er I spent,
> Are spent among the lasses, O.

He then builds the song up to a gradual climax of extravagance and ends with a deft compliment to the lasses (a fine, skilfully phrased adaptation of an idea he probably found, more elaborately expressed, in Pope):

> There's nought but care on ev'ry han',
>   In every hour that passes, O:
> What signifies the life o' man,
>   An' 'twere na for the lasses, O.

worldly

> The warly race may riches chase,
>   An' riches still may fly them, O;
> An' tho' at last they catch them fast,
>   Their hearts can ne'er enjoy them, O.

quiet

> But gie me a cannie hour at e'en,
>   My arms about my Dearie, O;
> An' warly cares, an' warly men,

topsy-turvy

>   May a' gae tapsalteerie, O!

sober

> For you sae douse, ye sneer at this,
>   Ye're nought but senseless asses, O:
> The wisest Man the warl' saw,
>   He dearly lov'd the lasses, O.

> Auld Nature swears, the lovely Dears
>   Her noblest work she classes, O:
> Her prentice han' she try'd on man,
>   An' then she made the lasses, O.

This has all the qualities of a good song. It distills a single mood; yet it has structure, working up to a climax. It is thoroughly singable; indeed, it sings itself, even without the tune. The phrasing is deft, and even witty: yet the ideas do not stand out from the poem to distract attention from the simple, emotional quality. Although the poem in a sense constitutes a profession of faith, there is nothing rhetorical or sententious about the utterance; the maintaining of the lilt (helped by the repetition of that final 'O' in every second and fourth line) is adroitly done and helps to remind us continuously that this is a song, not a recitation. All in all, this apparently simple lyric is the consummate singing presentation of man *qua* lover; in this particular direction, art can go no further.

The three remaining songs are less interesting. 'Composed in Spring' (beginning 'Again rejoicing Nature sees') was said by Burns to have been constructed around a chorus which was 'part of a song composed by a gentleman in Edinburgh, a particular friend of the author's', but the chorus may well be by Burns himself, and the girl referred to there as 'Menie' may originally have been Jean. If this is so, the song is a lament for the loss of Jean Armour, but it remains, except for the chorus, an imitative and stilted poem. 'The Gloomy Night is Gathering Fast' was written in anticipation of Burns's departure for Jamaica; it is a somewhat melodramatic farewell to Scotland and not comparable in originality, liveliness, or skill to 'On a Scotch Bard Gone to the West Indies'. Finally there is 'No Churchman Am I', a competent imitation of a swaggering English drinking song which appears to have been written for the Tarbolton Bachelors, with an additional verse composed for a Masonic gathering.

The Edinburgh edition, with its imposing list of subscribers (printed against Burns's wish – he had to pay for those thirty-seven pages of printing – but on the insistence of some of his Edinburgh friends) and its equally imposing 'Dedication to the Noblemen and Gentlemen of the Caledonian Hunt', established his fame as a poet throughout Britain and beyond.[1] Cadell and Davies immediately brought it out in London; pirated editions soon appeared in Dublin and Belfast; and it was not long before there were printings in Philadelphia and New York. On the whole it can be fairly said that Burns was known and judged as a poet in his lifetime by the poems in this Edinburgh volume of 1787; the only other important poem, apart from the songs, published while Burns was still alive was 'Tam o' Shanter', which first appeared in 1791 and which was included in the 1793 edition.

The most important part of Burns's mission in Edinburgh had thus been successful. He had published his second edition there, under the very best auspices. The reviews were favourable (though the Edinburgh edition started the minority protest against Burns's licentiousness), the city had acclaimed him, he had made his mark. He was not, however, successful in obtaining the kind of government sinecure for which he had hoped and to which it was perfectly proper for poets in those days to aspire. Instead, he had an appointment with Patrick Miller to look over a farm of his with a view to leasing it. In spite of misgivings, he was not reluctant to return to farming, and he certainly did not want to spend any more time being patronized and sometimes resented in Edinburgh now that his book was out. 'When you kindly offered to accomodate [*sic*] me with a Farm', he wrote to Miller shortly before leaving Edinburgh, 'I was afraid to think of it, as I knew my circumstances unequal to the proposal; but now, when by the appearance of my second edition of my book, I may reckon on a middling farming capital, there is nothing I wish for more than to resume the Plough'. But first he wanted to spend a short time exploring the Scotland whose poet he had declared himself to be.

Although his Edinburgh visit had been a success, it had not been without its moments of strain and difficulty. His pride and sensitivity made him constantly on the lookout for insults, and he once almost quarrelled with Glencairn when he found him being too cordial to a blue-blooded nincompoop. There were other difficulties. He was loaded with well-meant but unacceptable advice, and he had to learn how to refuse it without giving offence. Something of his problem can be seen in a letter he wrote to Mrs. Dunlop at the end of April. Mrs. Dunlop had the most genteel of tastes and chiefly admired poems like 'The Cotter's Saturday Night'. She had little sympathy with the more robust side of Burns's genius. This was not the last time Burns had to write in this strain:

> Your criticisms, Madam, I understand very well, and could have wished to have pleased you better. – You are right in your guesses that I am not very amenable to counsel. – Poets, much my superiors, have so flattered those who possessed the adventitious qualities of wealth and power that I am determined to flatter no created being, either in prose or verse, so help me God. – I set as little by kings, lords, clergy, critics, &c. as all these respectable Gentry do by my Bardship. – I know what I may expect from the world, by and by; illiberal abuse and perhaps contemptuous neglect: but I am resolved to study the sentiments of a very respectable Personage, Milton's Satan – 'Hail horrors! hail, infernal world!'

The mood in which Burns left Edinburgh can perhaps best be summed up by the letter he wrote to Hugh Blair two days before his departure:

. . . I often felt the embarrassment of my singular situation: **drawn** forth from the veriest shades of life to the glare of remark; and honored by the notice of those illustrious names of my country whose works, while they are applauded to the end of time, will ever instruct and mend the heart. However the meteor-like novelty of my appearance in the world might attract notice, and honor me with the acquaintance of the permanent lights of genius and literature, those who are truly benefactors of the immortal nature of man, I know very well that my utmost merit was far unequal to the task of preserving that character when once the novelty was over; I have made up my mind that abuse, or almost even neglect, will not surprise me in my quarters.

He left Edinburgh in the early morning of May 5, to make a trip through the Border country, so celebrated in Scottish ballad and folklore, before returning to Ayrshire. He was accompanied during most of the journey by Bob Ainslie, who proved a most congenial companion. At Coldstream Burns crossed the Tweed into England – his first step outside his native land – but he returned to Scotland the next day. The travellers then made their way through the historic Border towns of Jedburgh, Melrose, and Selkirk. From Selkirk he wrote to William Creech, his publisher, enclosing a poem lamenting Creech's absence (he was then in London). The piece, which was not published in Burns's lifetime, is a lively impromptu in the form of a mock lament in the 'Habbie Simson' tradition, and shows Burns in the best of poetic spirits:

mother hen [*Auld Reekie* *is Edinburgh*.[	Auld chuckie Reekie's sair distrest, Down droops her ance weel burnish'd crest,
trimmed	Nae joy her bonie buskit nest
at all	Can yield ava: Her darling bird that she lo'es best, Willie, 's awa.

The refrain 'Willie's awa' concludes each verse, as the poem proceeds to paint a humorous picture of Creech's importance to Edinburgh:

louts, milk- *sops, dupes*	Now gawkies, tawpies, gowks and fools, Frae colleges and boarding schools,
summer *toad-*	May sprout like simmer puddock-stools
wood	In glen or shaw;
dust	He wha could brush them down to mools, Willie's awa!

-*chamber*   The brethren o' the Commerce-Chaumer
woeful   May mourn their loss wi' doolfu' Clamour;
                        He was a dictionar and grammar
                                Amang them a';
                        I fear they'll now mak mony a stammer,
                                  Willie's awa!

The concluding verse of this twelve-stanza poem well illustrates the lighthearted skill with which Burns could handle complicated rhymes, and the humorous effect he could achieve with them:

ruffle   May never wicked fortune touzle him!
                        May never wicked men bamboozle him!
pate;   Until a pow as auld's Methusalem
old as
cheerfully   He canty claw!
scratch   Then to the blessed, New Jerusalem
                                Fleet wing awa!

From Selkirk they travelled east again to the coast. At Eyemouth Burns was given a royal reception by the St. Abb Masonic Lodge. Later he crossed to England again (Ainslie by now having returned to Edinburgh) and went as far south as Newcastle, then moved westwards to Carlisle, from which city he wrote to Nicol the most perfect piece of pure Scots prose to be found in his extant letters:

Kind, honest-hearted Willie,
    I'm sitten down here, after seven and forty miles ridin, e'en as forjeskit and forniaw'd as a forfoughten cock, to gie ye some notion o' my landlowper-like stravaguin sin the sorrowfu' hour that I sheuk hands and parted wi' auld Reekie. –
    My auld, ga'd Gleyde o' a meere has huchyall'd up hill and down brae, in Scotland and England, as teugh and birnie as a vera devil wi' me. – It's true, she's as poor's a Sang-maker and as hard's a kirk, and tipper-taipers when she taks the gate first like a Lady's gentlewoman in a minuwae, or a hen on a het girdle, but she's a yauld, poutherie Girran for a' that; and has a stomach like Willie Stalker's meere that wad hae digested tumbler-wheels, for she'll whip me off her five stimparts o' the best aits at a down-sittin and ne'er fash her thumb. – When ance her ringbanes and spavies, her crucks and cramps, are fairly soupl'd, she beets to, beets to, and ay the hindmost hour the tightest. – I could wager her price to a thretty pennies that, for twa

or three wooks ridin at fifty mile a day, the deil-sticket a five gallopers acqueesh Clyde and Whithorn could cast saut in her tail. . . .

The reader who does not know the meaning of all the Scots words used here can nevertheless get a vivid impression of the colour and verve of this prose style.

From Carlisle he proceeded to Dumfries, where he received the freedom of the burgh, and thence to Patrick Miller's estate, where he looked over a farm Miller was proposing to lease to him, and finally, on June 9, he was back at Mossgiel. He had left six months before, an Ayrshire rhymster with only a local reputation, and returned now 'Caledonia's Bard, brother Burns'. The local boy had made good.

6

BETWEEN TWO WORLDS

BACK AGAIN at Mossgiel, Burns was restless and fretful. 'I cannot settle to my mind', he wrote to James Smith. 'Farming, the only thing of which I know anything, and heaven above knows but little do I understand of that, I cannot, dare not risk on farms as they are. If I do not fix, I will go for Jamaica. Should I stay in an unsettled state at home, I would only dissipate my little fortune, and ruin what I intend shall compensate my little ones for the stigma I have brought on their names.' The Armour family were all 'servile compliance' now that the poet had returned with his fame established, and Burns found this disgusting. But it did not prevent him from renewing his association with Jean – though with no thought at this time of marriage – who soon became pregnant again.

He had hopes of settling on Patrick Miller's farm. He wrote to Nicol: 'From my view of the lands, and his [Miller's] reception of my Bardship, my hopes in that business are rather mended; but they are but slender.' He was now finding it more difficult than ever to come to terms with life, to reconcile his genius with his social position, and to determine his relation to the society of his time. In the same letter to Nicol he wrote:

I never, my friend, thought Mankind very capable of anything generous; but the stateliness of the Patricians in Edin^r, and the servility of my plebeian brethren, who perhaps formerly eyed me askance, since I returned home, have nearly put me out of conceit altogether with my species. – I have bought a pocket Milton, which I carry perpetually about with me, in order to study the sentiments – the dauntless magnanimity; the intrepid unyielding independence; the desperate daring, and noble defiance of hardship, in that great personage, Satan.

He was soon off again, this time on a tour of the Argyllshire Highlands. We know he was at Arrochar, at the head of Loch Long, and at Inveraray. On June 30 he was writing to James Smith presumably from Loch Lomondside, and the picture he gives in the letter of his entertainment 'at a Highland gentleman's hospitable mansion' makes clear why he was so discontented with the prospect of settling down as a humble tenant farmer again, and at the same time reflects his enthusiasm for Scottish song and dance:

> . . . Our dancing was none of the French or English insipid formal movements; the ladies sung Scotch songs like angels, at intervals; then we flew at Bab at the Bowster, Tullochgorum, Loch Erroch Side, &c. like midges sporting in the mottie sun, or craws prognosticating a storm in a hairst day. When the dear lasses left us, we ranged round the bowl till the good-fellow hour of six; except a few minutes that we went out to pay our devotions to the glorious lamp of day peering over the towering top of Benlomond.

This 'stravaguin' around the countryside, being entertained by hospitable gentlemen and their attractive daughters, suited him admirably and fostered his muse; but he could not live this way indefinitely. 'I have yet fixed on nothing with respect to the serious business of life', he remarked in the same letter. 'I am, just as usual, a rhyming, mason-making, raking, aimless, idle fellow. However, I shall somewhere have a farm soon.'

He was at Mossgiel again in July, and early in August he returned to Edinburgh, in an endeavour to settle his business with Creech and to plan a Highland trip with Nicol. Burns and Nicol set off in a chaise (Nicol's idea) on August 25. This journey, which took them to Linlithgow, Stirling, Crieff, Aberfeldy, Blair Athol, up through Strathspey to Aviemore and north to Inverness, was the most ambitious and, as far as his poetry was concerned, the most fruitful of Burns's expeditions. From Inverness they went by Forres to Elgin, thence along the southern shore of the Moray Firth to Banff, down the east coast from Peterhead through Aberdeen and Stonehaven to Montrose and finally back to Edinburgh, by way of Dundee, Perth, and Kinross, crossing the Forth at Queensferry. This itinerary took Burns through a substantial part of Scotland – the Perthshire Highlands, with their scenic beauty and historical associations, including Loch Tay, the Pass of Killicrankie where 'Bonny Dundee' was killed while leading his men to a Jacobite victory, and the River Tummel, scene of Jacobite marchings; Culloden Moor, where the Jacobite Rebellion was finally crushed; the historic towns of Inverness and Elgin, the latter with its picturesque ruined cathedral; the thriving fishing towns by the Moray Firth and the North Sea, with their folk traditions and work songs, for which Burns always had a ready ear; Aberdeen with its literary and intellectual atmosphere; Arbroath, with its ruined abbey; 'the rich harvests and fine hedge rows' of the Carse of Gowrie; and the 'fine, fruitful, hilly, woody country round Perth.' Burns had an eye for the historic monuments; he mentions in the journal he kept during the trip that he saw the field of Bannockburn and 'the hole where glorious Bruce set his standard', and at Linlithgow he saw 'the room where the beautiful injured Mary Queen of Scots was born'; he mentions also Castle Cawdor, 'where Macbeth murdered King Duncan' and even 'the bed in which King Duncan was stabbed'; 'the muir where Shakespeare lays Macbeth's witch meeting'; and at Scone 'Queen Mary's bed, the hangings wrought with her own hands.'

But as a rule it was not on these obvious historical themes that he wrote his poetry. The most characteristic poetic products of this trip are to be seen in the reworked folk songs that were not published until much later: songs on the birks of Aberfeldy; a local Aberdeenshire piece like 'Theniel Menzies' Bonie Mary'; a song with a Perthshire setting like 'Blythe Was She'; a song from Buckie, a bustling fishing town on the Moray Firth, 'Lady Only, Honest Lucky'. It is interesting to trace the place names in these and other songs which are the products of Burns's travels; one could in fact chart his journey precisely by tracing the localities (and sometimes even the dialect) in the songs he wrote at this time. A scrap of a fisherman's work song, a fragment celebrating a local alewife, a local beauty in some local beauty spot, a hint, an old chorus, a tradition, a gust of life somehow preserved in a fragmentary rhyme – all these were grist to Burns's mill, all these he transmuted into finished songs, and found for them their appropriate airs. By using his travels for his songs in this way, Burns developed from the Ayrshire bard into the poet of Scotland. 'I am such an enthusiast', Burns wrote to George Thomson in January, 1793, 'that in the course of my several peregrinations through Scotland, I made a pilgrimage to the individual spot from which the song took its rise. – Lochaber, & the braes of Ballenden, excepted, so far as the locality, either from the title of the air, or the tenor of the Song, could be ascertained, I have paid my devotions at the particular shrine of every Scots Muse.'

On this journey with Nicol Burns was entertained by the Duke and Duchess of Atholl at Blair Atholl and by the Duke and Duchess of Gordon at Gordon Castle. These were the occasions on which Nicol made himself offensive by dragging Burns away prematurely. Burns also met his relatives in Stonehaven and Montrose; he was glad to find his cousin Robert Burness 'one of those who love fun, a jill, a punning joke, and have not a bad heart'.

After a brief period in Edinburgh he set out on yet another trip. He travelled this time with Dr. James Adair, a friend of Dr. Lawrie, the Loudon minister. The travellers went to Harvieston, in Clackmannanshire (where Burns had already paid a brief visit) and spent some time with relatives of Gavin Hamilton. Burns's chief purpose in making this fourth excursion seems to have been to visit Peggy Chalmers, daughter of an Ayrshire gentleman farmer and related by marriage to Hamilton. She, too, lived at Harvieston, and Burns seems to have thought of making this attractive and accomplished girl his wife: but, though he retained her friendship, she married another. She inspired some of his less effective love songs.

Dr. Adair wrote Dr. Currie an account of this trip, in which he described excursions he and Burns made from Harvieston 'to visit various parts of the surrounding scenery, inferior to none in Scotland, in beauty, sublimity, and romantic interest.' Dr. Adair described also a visit from the ninety-year-old Mrs. Bruce, supposedly a lineal descendant of Robert Bruce, whose Jacobite proclivities delighted Burns and were the occasion of some harmless drinking of treasonable toasts and confusion to the House of Hanover. This visit was one of many encouragements Burns received in his tendency to 'sentimental Jacobitism', which proved so fruitful for his muse. On this trip, also, Burns visited John Ramsay of Ochtertyre, who advised him to write a play and then to produce some 'Scottish Georgics'. Ramsay reported that when he had asked Burns 'whether the Edinburgh Literati had mended his poems by their criticisms' Burns had replied that 'these gentlemen remind me of some spinsters in my country, who spin their thread so fine, that it is neither for weft nor woof.' He added that 'he had not changed a word except one, to please Dr. Blair.' This was the celebrated change of 'salvation' to 'damnation' in 'The Holy Fair'.

Burns was back in Edinburgh before the end of October, determined to settle with Creech but finding the publisher an exceedingly difficult man to bring to the point. During this second winter in Edinburgh he was no longer a social lion; the novelty of the ploughman poet had worn off, and he was left largely to his own devices. He was more unsettled than ever about his plans for the future; reluctant to settle down again at Mossgiel, yet having no other positive alternative. He kept suggesting to his friends that they might help him get a position in the Excise, and when he met Robert Graham of Fintry, commissioner of Excise, at Blair House he felt he could appeal to him, both as a 'patron of his rhymes' (as he terms him in a verse epistle of 1788) and a fellow Mason, for help in obtaining an appointment. But it was some time before anything materialized.

He also found other interests in Edinburgh. Writing on October 25 to the Reverend John Skinner, 'the old, venerable author of Tullochgorum', one of Burns's favourite songs, Burns revealed what was perhaps his chief interest at this time, and what was to become ever more so:

There is a work going on in Edinburgh, just now, which claims your best assistance. An engraver in this town has set about collecting and publishing all the Scotch songs, with the music, that can be found. Songs in the English language, if by Scotchmen, are admitted, but the music must be all Scotch. . . . I have been absolutely crazed about it, collecting old stanzas, and every information remaining respecting their origin, authors, &c., &c.

The engraver was James Johnson, whom Burns had first met in Edinburgh the previous April, when Johnson was about to bring out the first volume of his *Scots Musical Museum*. Johnson was a humble and ill-educated lover of Scottish songs, who, having invented a cheap but not particularly attractive process for printing music by using stamped pewter plates, embarked on the publication of what was originally announced as a 'Collection of Scots, English and Irish Songs in two neat 8vo volumes'. Under Burns's influence, Johnson changed the title and enlarged the scope of his project, until eventually the *Scots Musical Museum* ran into six volumes. When Johnson originally asked Burns for assistance he did not presumably realize what a congenial task he was offering the poet. As the months went by, Burns took over more and more of the editorial duties, until by the middle of 1787 he was in fact though not in title the real editor of the collection. His letters to Johnson give some indication of the assiduity and enthusiasm with which he tracked down Scottish songs and threw himself into the business of collecting, editing, restoring, rewriting, and creating. The great body of Burns's poetic output between early 1787 and late in 1792 went into the *Museum*. Burns refused to accept a fee of any sort for this work; it was work for Scotland, not to establish his own fame as a poet. In all the careful investigating and creating which he did for Johnson and, later, for George Thomson's *Select Scottish Airs*, he worked less as Robert Burns than as the embodied spirit of Scottish song. As a result, he was not anxious to claim authorship for his own productions or to distinguish between the original fragment on which he may have based a song and his own additions and reworking; thus to this day it is not always possible to separate Burns's original work from traditional material.

That Burns's interest in Scottish song suddenly became his chief enthusiasm and that throughout the remainder of his life he was primarily a song writer can be attributed to this meeting with Johnson. If he had not met Johnson at this time and found in his *Museum* a medium for the publication of restored and original Scots songs, he might well have turned more and more to the genteel productions suitable for publication in the magazines read by the literati. It was not, as some writers have claimed, Dr. Blacklock who saved a genius for Scotland; it was humble James Johnson.

Though much of Burns's poetic efforts were from now on given to song writing and restoring, he seems never to have regarded these activities as those of a professional poet, for which he deserved adequate compensation. To the modern mind there is no reason at all why he should not have tried to make poetry his livelihood, and if he had tried the chances are that he would have succeeded; he could at least have added substantially to his income and thus relieved himself of considerable worry and distracting effort. But the idea of receiving payment for his poems now seems to have become positively repugnant to him. The whole business of the Edinburgh edition, with its protracted negotiations and Creech's long delay in paying Burns his due, seems to have produced an actual physical revulsion. Burns had put himself up in the market place once, and the experience was too humiliating ever to be repeated. Thereafter he regarded his poetry, as he was later to put it to George Thomson, as 'either *above* or *below* price'. The cavalier way in which he allowed Creech to publish the 1793 edition without suggesting any payment at all for the new poems in it and his refusal to write for the newspapers on any commercial basis are part of the same pattern.

During this second winter in Edinburgh Burns became acquainted also with Mrs. James M'Lehose, an attractive and sentimental woman of Burns's own age, who was living apart from her husband. The story of the strange hothouse relationship between the poet and Mrs. M'Lehose ('Sylvander' and 'Clarinda', as they came to call themselves in their heatedly sentimental correspondence) stands out like a mockingly artificial exercise in Burns's otherwise stern biography. For the first time in his life Burns found himself having a real affair with a genteel woman, a respectable, conventional woman – yet a woman of sensibility withal – who enjoyed his advances but who dared not allow them to go beyond a certain point. After a preliminary exploration by letter, when he was confined indoors with 'a bruised limb', he soon saw what the rules of the game were, and by following them with passion and skill worked himself (and her) up into a fine emotional state, a kind of verbal sexuality, in which state they embraced with reasonable chastity and then proceeded to consummate their love in discourse. No wonder Burns found it necessary to satisfy his more physical sexual needs with less genteel and less accomplished Edinburgh women before he returned to another of these emotional orgies. Clarinda's discovery of these other friends, together with the shock of Burns's eventual acknowledgment of Jean as his wife, temporarily estranged them, and permanently ended this phase of the relationship. The relationship is important for Burns's literary life in that it demonstrated how far he could go in writing a certain type of sentimental English love letter (the Clarinda-Sylvander correspondence is really a remarkable tour de force on Burns's side) and produced a handful of love lyrics, most of which are fairly conventional exercises in neoclassic idiom. The final song to Clarinda, however – written in 1791 after Clarinda had got over her anger with Burns and was preparing to sail to the West Indies to rejoin her husband – is among his masterpieces of its kind; in it, with the skill so characteristic of his love poetry at its best, he reduces everything to one basic and overpowering emotion – the emotion of having loved and now having to part. 'Ae Fond Kiss, and Then We Sever' completely transcends the Sylvander-Clarinda affair (as few of his other lyrics to her do) to become a distillation, a quintessential statement, of this elemental situation.

In the midst of his affair with Clarinda, Burns remained unsettled and anxious. In January, 1788, he wrote to Graham of Fintry asking him to support his application 'to be admitted an Officer of Excise', and in February he wrote in similar terms to the Earl of Glencairn; neither application brought an immediate result, though he seems to have been given reason to expect an eventual appointment. In February he was back at Mossgiel, writing to Clarinda that he had seen Jean (soon to bear twins again) and that in comparison 'with my Clarinda' he found her 'the expiring glimmer of a farthing taper beside the cloudless glory of the meridian sun. – Here was tasteless insipidity, vulgarity of soul, and mercenary fawning; there, polished good sense, heaven-born genius, and the most generous, the most delicate, the most tender Passion. – I have done with her, and she with me'. Ten days later he wrote to Robert Ainslie in very different terms, boasting of having had relations with Jean once again ('till she rejoiced with joy unspeakable and full of glory') but complimenting himself on his prudence in making her swear 'never to attempt any claim on me as a husband'. These two letters show

Burns at his worst; it is difficult to acquit him of having behaved like a cad. But it is equally difficult to believe that he was telling the truth in this letter, especially when we remember that Jean was within a week or two of giving birth to twins. A plausible explanation, which puts the business in a somewhat better light, is that Burns had already decided to marry Jean and that he wrote as he did to Mrs. M'Lehose and Ainslie to throw them off the scent until after he had acknowledged the marriage and received his Excise instructions. If Mrs. M'Lehose had found out too soon that Burns was not sincere in his protestations to her, she might easily have made trouble for him in Edinburgh.

The Excise appointment moved slowly, and Burns became more and more inclined to accept Patrick Miller's offer of a lease on his farm. Back in Edinburgh in the middle of March, he wrote to Peggy Chalmers: 'Yesternight I completed a bargain with Mr Miller, of Dalswinton, for the farm of Ellisland, on the banks of the Nith, between five and six miles above Dumfries. I begin at Whitsunday to build a house, drive lime, &c.; and heaven be my help! for it will take a strong effort to bring my mind into the routine of business'. Having made up his mind, he had no further reason to remain in Edinburgh, and he left for Ayrshire again on March 24. On April 28 he wrote to James Smith from Mauchline that he had 'lately and privately' given Jean Armour 'a matrimonial title to my corpus'. His period of wandering and experiment were at an end; he had come back to farming, and to Jean. It remained to be seen how the Ellisland farmer and exciseman, settled now in conventional domesticity with his wife and child,[1] would continue in his role as poet.

Fortunately, Burns's association with James Johnson (and later, as we shall see, with George Thomson) helped to focus his song-writing activities and to guarantee that, whatever his personal problems, he would continue his great work in this field. He did, in fact, continue it enthusiastically for the rest of his life; his last song, 'Fairest Maid on Devon Banks', was written nine days before his death. But what other kinds of poetry had he been writing during those undecided months between the publication of the Edinburgh edition and his settling at Ellisland? Had his Edinburgh experience changed the direction of his genius in any way?

Edinburgh did, of course, have some effect on his poetry. It encouraged him, for one thing, to throw off brief 'occasional' poems, descriptions of people, compliments to young ladies, album pieces of one kind or another. These vary a great deal in merit; the best of them are witty and graceful, as such pieces should be, but the majority are of no great poetic interest. Early in 1787 Burns threw off these lines about the printer, William Smellie, who had introduced him to the Crochallan Fencibles:

> Shrewd Willie Smellie to Crochallan came;
> The old cock'd hat, the grey surtout, the same;
> His bristling beard just rising in its might,
> 'Twas four long nights and days to shaving night;
> His uncomb'd grizzly locks, wild staring, thatch'd
> A head for thought profound and clear, unmatch'd;
> Yet tho' his caustic wit was biting-rude,
> His heart was warm, benevolent, and good.

There is nothing characteristically Scottish or characteristicallyBurnsian about this; it shows the poet functioning as a rhymster for all occasions, and Burns had a facility in things of this sort that enabled him to please friends by ready verse descriptions and compliments. Sometimes these brief poems were in Scots, as is his verse about William Dunbar, 'one of the worthiest fellows in the world':

As I cam by Crochallan,
peeped   I cannilie keeket ben;
inside
Rattlin, roarin Willie
    Was sittin at yon boord-en,
Sittin at yon boord-en',
    And amang gude companie;
Rattlin, roarin Willie,
    You're welcome hame to me!

Sometimes he used a traditional Scots stanza for an impromptu of this kind, as in his 'Extempore in the Court of Session', describing Hay Campbell, the Lord Advocate, and Harry Erskine, Dean of the Faculty of Advocates:

LORD ADVOCATE
He clench'd his pamphlets in his fist,
    He quoted and he hinted,
Till, in a declamation-mist,
lost   His argument he tint it:
He gapèd for't, he grapèd for't,
    He fand it was awa, man;
But what his common sense came short,
    He ekèd out wi' law, man.

MR ERSKINE

Collected, Harry stood awee,
   Then open'd out his arm, man;
His Lordship saw wi' ruefu' e'e,
   And ey'd the gathering storm, man:
Like wind-driv'n hail it did assail,

waterfall   Or torrents owre a lin, man;
The BENCH sae wise lift up their eyes,
   Hauf-wauken'd wi' the din, man.

One might cite, as other examples of versifying to fit the occasion, his inscription for Robert Fergusson's headstone (which he was responsible for erecting) and his lines inscribed under Fergusson's portrait – neither especially impressive, and both probably thrown off rapidly. In the same general category, though even more obviously impromptus, are the scraps of original verse with which he sprinkled his correspondence at this time. Writing a farewell to Dr. Fyffe, the Edinburgh surgeon, before leaving the city, he concluded:

Now, God in heaven bless REEKIE's town
   With plenty, joy and peace!
And may her wealth and fair renown
   To latest times increase!!! – Amen.

Similarly, in writing to 'the Right Worshipful St. James's Lodge, Tarbolton', to apologize for not being able to join his masonic brethren there at their quarterly meeting, he concluded:

Within your dear Mansion may wayward Contention
   Or withered Envy ne'er enter
May Secrecy round be the mystical bound,
   And brotherly Love be the Centre!!!

All this is mere versifying, but it shows Burns aware that, as a known poet, he had a duty to rhyme wherever possible. Of course, he had always been prone to make extempore rhymes of this sort, but his Edinburgh experience seems to have made him take such efforts rather more seriously.

Perhaps the best of these scraps of minor versifying are the spontaneous poems of compliment or abuse in which he did not have his eye so closely on the insipid album pieces of the period. The 'Epigram at Roslin Inn' has a spontaneity and a warmth that make it the perfect impromptu compliment:

> My blessings on ye, honest wife!
>   I ne'er was here before;
> Ye've wealth o' gear for spoon and knife –
>   Heart could not wish for more.
> *trouble*   Heav'n keep you clear o' sturt and strife,
>   Till far ayont fourscore,
> And while I toddle on thro' life,
>   I'll ne'er gae by your door!

The use of 'toddle' in the second-last line, and indeed the whole image evoked by those two lines, has the fine folk simplicity, the sudden searchlight on an elemental fact about life, which Burns achieved so often and so successfully in his songs. Beside the compliment to the Roslin landlady we may put this carefully turned insult to an Edinburgh artist, whom he found engaged on a painting of Jacob's dream:

> Dear ——, I'll gie ye some advice,
>   You'll tak it no uncivil:
> You shouldna paint at angels mair,
>   But try and paint the devil.
> *ticklish*   To paint an Angel's kittle wark,
>   Wi' Nick, there's little danger:
> Ye'll easy draw a long-kent face,
>   But no sae weel a *stranger*.

Burns came to be so facile at this sort of thing that he turned out several abusive pieces merely for the fun of it, as well as complimentary pieces that did not come from the heart. While visiting Inveraray on his West Highland excursion he vented his annoyance at a neglectful innkeeper who was more intent on serving the Duke of Argyll's guests than on attending to the wants of the poet, in two fine abusive stanzas:

> Whoe'er he be that sojourns here,
>   I pity much his case,
> Unless he come to wait upon
>   The Lord their God, 'His Grace'.

> There's naething here but Highland pride
>   And Highland scab and hunger:
> If Providence has sent me here,
>   'Twas surely in an anger.

Though this may have arisen out of genuine personal indignation, the same can hardly be said for the insulting lines about the House of Hanover which he wrote 'on seeing the royal palace at Stirling in ruins':

> . . . The injured Stewart line is gone,
> A race outlandish fills their throne:
> An idiot race, to honour lost –
> Who know them best despise them most.

This sort of thing got him into trouble more than once.

If his acceptance at Edinburgh as 'Caledonia's Bard' encouraged him to consider that his proper function was to throw as many impromptu rhymes around as possible – and who is to say that such a conception was wrong? – it also encouraged him to write more formal poems of compliment in the genteel manner, which are among his least interesting works. His 'Address to Wm. Tytler, Esq. of Woodhouselee' (sent to Tytler, the author of *An Historical and Critical Enquiry into the Evidence against Mary Queen of Scots,* 'with an impression of the author's portrait') is about as bad as this kind of poem can be:

> Reveréd defender of beauteous Stuart,
>   Of Stuart, a name once respected;
> A name, which to love was the mark of a true heart,
>   But now 'tis despised and neglected.

> Tho' something like moisture conglobes in my eye,
>   Let no one misdeem me disloyal;
> A poor friendless wand'rer may well claim a sigh,
>   Still more, if that wand'rer were royal. . . .

Then there were poems composed by way of duty, such as the 'Elegy on the Death of Sir James Hunter Blair', a distinguished Edinburgh citizen who had been very cordial to Burns when the poet was introduced to him. 'That I have lost a friend is but repeating after Caledonia', he wrote to Bob Aiken on Blair's death in July, 1787; and since the loss was Scotland's it was the duty of Scotland's poet to express in verse the appropriate emotions. 'The performance is but mediocre', Burns wrote later, 'but my grief was sincere'. The poem, however, sought to express not his own grief but Caledonia's; it is tricked out with the fanciest

neoclassic devices he could think of, and the result is unhappy. A duty
poem of a different kind was written by Burns in response to a request
of a group of Jacobites to write them a 'Birthday Ode for 31st December, 1787'. Here he attempts to whip up Jacobite feeling in an ode
modelled on Gray, and the effect is no more successful than his earlier
attempt at the ode form, 'A Winter Night'. A final example of a duty
piece that Burns could have composed only after his Edinburgh experience is his elegy on the death of Robert Dundas. Writing of this elegy
some years later, he explained: 'My very worthy & most respected
friend Mr Alexr Wood, Surgeon, urged me to pay a compliment in the
way of my trade to his Lordship's memory. – Well, to work I went, &
produced a copy of Elegiac verses, some of them I own rather commonplace, & others rather hidebound.' The poem is written in heroic
couplets, and its forced and turgid quality can be gauged by four
lines:

> Ye dark, waste hills, ye brown unsightly plains,
> Congenial scenes, ye soothe my mournful strains:
> Ye tempests, rage! ye turbid torrents roll!
> Ye suit the joyless tenor of my soul.

Burns never forgave the Dundas family for not acknowledging this
poem, a copy of which he sent them together with a letter.

From these examples it will be seen that Burns's acceptance of a kind
of unofficial poet-laureateship of Scotland had certain unhappy results.
However, though he could produce artificial exercises of this kind
when he felt the occasion demanded, he did not regard the activity as
more than a small and unimportant part of his work as a poet. These
exercises did not corrupt his style or make him any less able to write, in
either Scots or English, the sort of poetry in which his real genius could
best express itself.

We can see the real Burns at work in the epistle 'To the Gudewife of
Wauchope-House', written in February, 1787, in answer to a rhyming
letter from Mrs. Elizabeth Scott of Wauchope. The poem has the
swinging ease we see in the best of his verse letters and shows the ability
to sound a note of spontaneous conversation in a skilfully contrived old
Scots stanza that we have noticed before in pieces of this type. The
poem is of interest biographically, too, for it is a verse account of his
early affair with Nelly Kilpatrick, which inspired his first poem, and of
his subsequent poetic ambitions. The patriotic ambition is as strong as
the poetic:

> E'en then, a wish (I mind its pow'r),
> A wish that to my latest hour
>   Shall strongly heave my breast,
> That I for poor auld Scotland's sake
> Some usefu' plan or book could make,
>   Or sing a sang at least. . . .

This is the Scottish patriotism that produced all the work for Johnson's *Scots Musical Museum* and Thomson's *Select Scottish Airs*, rather than the sense of duty that produced the elegy for Sir James Hunter Blair.

'To the Gudewife of Wauchope-House' works up to a fine climax – no one could take leave of a correspondent in verse more effectively than Burns – which combines conversational ease with formal benediction:

> For you, no bred to barn and byre,
> Wha sweetly tune the Scottish lyre,
>   Thanks to you for your line!
> The marl'd plaid ye kindly spare,
> By me should gratefully be ware;
>   'Twad please me to the nine.

proud I'd be mair vauntie o' my hap,

crupper   Douce hingin owre my curple,
> Than onie ermine ever lap,
>   Or proud imperial purple.
>   Farewell, then! lang hale, then,
>   An' plenty be your fa'!
>   May losses and crosses

door   Ne'er at your hallan ca'!

We have only to put this poem beside the 'Epistle to Robert Graham, Esq. of Fintry' to see the difference between Burns working in a tradition and in an idiom which he had made completely his own, and Burns writing in order to impress an influential friend of whom he is asking a favour. Burns was seeking Graham's help in obtaining the Excise appointment. The explanation is not that the latter poem is written in English and the former in Scots; for Burns could handle certain kinds of English with perfect ease and mastery (as we shall see, some of his best songs are almost entirely in standard English). The difference lies in the poetic tradition in which the poet is working rather than in the language – or one might say in the *diction* rather than in the language –

and also in the emotional tone. In the epistle to Graham, Burns was carefully playing a part, trying to say what would impress and avoid what would offend, and at the same time to refrain from saying anything that would injure his own pride. The result is a curiously stilted poem in which the tone keeps changing from outright flattery to too much protesting of independence, the whole plodding along in end-stopped heroic couplets.

Most of Burns's poetic activity during this period was spent on his songs, which come more and more to predominate among his poems. The abundance and variety of these are amazing: from trivial verses in the folk idiom written to fit a particular tune, such as 'What Will I Do Gin My Hoggie Die?' and 'To the Weaver's Gin Ye Go', to the most perfect rebuilding of an old song from a fragment of its chorus, such as 'I'm O'er Young to Marry Yet'; from songs celebrating localities he visited, such as 'The Birks of Aberfeldy', to formal poems of compliment like some of his verses to Peggy Chalmers. With his parting gift to Clarinda – a pair o' wineglasses – he wrote a formal piece in the purest genteel idiom:

> Fair Empress of the poet's soul.
>   And Queen of poetesses;
> Clarinda, take this little boon,
>   This humble pair of glasses. . . .

This was how he had addressed her from the beginning:

> Clarinda, mistress of my soul,
>   The measur'd time is run!
> The wretch beneath the dreary pole
>   So marks his latest sun.

But on his reconciliation with Jean and his final recognition of her as his wife, he wrote two very different songs:

directions

> Of a' the airts the wind can blaw,
>   I dearly like the west,
> For there the bony Lassie lives,
>   The Lassie I lo'e best:

roll

> There's wild-woods grow, and rivers row,
>   And mony a hill between;
> But day and night my fancy's flight
>   Is ever wi' my Jean.

And the magnificent note of sheer exultation in the other song he wrote
about her at this time makes all the Clarinda songs except 'Ae Fond Kiss
and Then We Sever' look like mere exercises:

> I hae a wife o' my ain,
>   I'll partake wi' naebody.
> I'll tak Cuckold frae nane,
>   I'll gie Cuckold to naebody.
>
> I hae a penny to spend,
>   There, thanks to naebody;
> I hae naething to lend,
>   I'll borrow frae naebody.
>
> I am naebody's lord,
>   I'll be slave to naebody;
> I hae a gude braid sword,
>   I'll tak dunts frae naebody.
>
> I'll be merry and free,
>   I'll be sad for naebody;
> Naebody cares for me,
>   I care for naebody.

knocks

The different kinds of skill represented by these two songs and 'Ae Fond
Kiss' sufficiently indicate Burns's versatility as a song writer.

Thus Burns when he agreed to take the Ellisland farm was as much a
poet as ever. His problem was to find time for both farming and writing
poetry, and, when his excise appointment came through in the Autumn
of 1789, to combine farming and composing with the strenuous activities of a gauger. His difficulties were increased by the lack of a house on
the farm; he had to have one built before he could bring Jean and young
Robert there, and this was a slow business. He spent much of the
remainder of 1788 moving between Ellisland and Mauchline, lodging
when at Ellisland in a tumble-down hut a mile from his farm. At
Mauchline he took the course of instruction for prospective excisemen.
Altogether, this was a strenuous period; his new emotional readjustment
to Jean as his wife, his quarrel with Clarinda, his decision to take a farm
about which he was very dubious, the problems of building the farmhouse, worry about whether and when the excise job would come

through – all this distracted him both mentally and physically, and left him little leisure or energy for poetry.

The Ellisland farm, at a rental of £50 annually for the first three years and £70 thereafter, was not in fact a good bargain. The soil was poor and neglected; as Patrick Miller, the landlord, admitted years later: 'When I purchased this estate about five and twenty years ago, I had not seen it. It was in the most miserable state of exhaustion and all the tenants in poverty.' Burns signed the lease against his better judgment, partly because he did not like to refuse Miller, who, Burns realized, acted largely out of friendship and with the best of intentions. After the first poor harvest Burns was discouraged and began to think seriously of giving the farm up.

Jean joined her husband in December – not yet at the new farmhouse, which was still unfinished, but at another makeshift lodging in Nithsdale. It was not until late spring, 1789, that the Burnses moved into the farmhouse. During the preceding period of moving about and worrying, Burns had striven hard to keep active and cheerful. His frame of mind is well indicated in a letter he wrote to Alexander Cunningham the previous July:

> For my own Biographical story, I can only say with the venerable Hebrew Patriarch; 'Here am I, with the Children God has given me!' I have been a Farmer since Whitsunday, & am just now building a house – not a Palace to attract the train-attended steps of pride-swoln Greatness; but a plain, simple Domicile for Humility & Contentment. – I am, too, a married man, – This was a step of which I had no idea when you & I were together. – On my return to Ayr-shire, I found a much-lov'd Female's positive happiness, or absolute Misery among my hands; and I could not trifle with such a sacred Deposite. – I am, since, doubly pleased with my conduct. . . . – When I tell you that Mrs Burns was once, *my Jean*, you will know the rest. – Of four children she bore me, in seventeen months, my eldest boy is only living. – By the bye, I intend breeding him up for the Church; and from an innate dexterity in secret Mischief which he possesses, & a certain hypocritical gravity as he looks on the consequences, I have no small hopes of him in the sacerdotal line. –

The suggestion that he married Jean out of affection and good nature is probably true enough. He was fond of her, he liked the idea of being married and settling down with his family; but the fact remains that, for all Jean's ability to sing his songs, she shared none of his wider intellectual interests and had not the remotest inkling of the real nature of his abilities and achievement. It was only a limited side of himself that he could show to Jean. He could not talk with her as he could to Peggy Chalmers, he could not even allow her to meet his genteel friends, for she was unable to adjust to their world as he could. She was virtually illiterate, good natured, affectionate, hard working. In a narrowly domestic setting in the farmhouse she fitted admirably; but Burns had larger interests and wider horizons. There was thus something schizophrenic about Burns's position at this time. One side of him wanted simply 'a happy fireside clime, wi' weans an' wife', and the other wanted that larger world of ideas, of books and culture, of philosophy and literature, which Jean could never have entered. It must be emphasized that Burns was not only a vernacular poet who did some of his best work in his native folk tradition; he was also a brilliant conversationalist, intelligent, quick witted, curious, easily assimilating new knowledge and making effective use of it in jest or earnest. As always, he needed friends among whom to perform, and after his Edinburgh experiences and his excursions through Scotland he needed them more than ever, and his standard was higher than ever. Thus, though he worked desperately hard at his farming while Jean looked after the dairy, his interests and ambitions were divided.

Burns received his commission as exciseman after taking the six weeks' course in the summer of 1788. But this was merely the equivalent of a certificate of competence; it did not mean that he had a position in the Excise and drew pay for it. It did mean, however, that he was eligible for such a position. During the farming difficulties of 1789 he decided to try for an excise post while remaining on the farm, and with the help of Graham of Fintry was successful in being appointed exciseman in charge of the 'Dumfries first Itinerary', a district covering twelve parishes. For a salary of £50 a year, it was now his duty to inspect this district regularly with a view to ensuring that there was no smuggling of liquor or other dutiable commodities and that all measures used in their legal handling were accurate. The position involved riding some two hundred miles weekly, over bad roads and very often in bad weather, and he carried out his duties conscientiously, although, as might be guessed, they had an increasingly harmful effect on his health. Under these circumstances it was impossible for Burns to do much work on the farm, and the emphasis was now put on dairy farming, which Jean supervised – when she was not bearing children. She bore Robert another son in August.

Clearly, this was not a way of life to encourage the production of poetry. He was throughout his stay at Ellisland overworked and troubled; passionately devoted though he was to the ideal of domestic life, his own did not altogether satisfy him, and he suffered recurring moods of depression and confusion. In the summer of 1790 he was making love to Anne Park in the Globe Tavern, Dumfries, who bore him a son in March, 1791 – only nine days before Jean herself gave birth to another boy, William Nicol. Good natured and tolerant as ever ('Oor Rab should hae had twa wives', was her comment on her husband's failing), Jean reared Anne's child with her own. But Burns needed more than good nature and tolerance, and the split between his domestic life and his social and intellectual needs kept widening.

He was a good exciseman. In July, 1790, his salary was increased to seventy-five pounds a year, on his promotion to the Dumfries '3rd, or Tobacco, Division'. The following January he was listed among those recommended for promotion to the position of examiner and eventually of supervisor, but as these promotions went by seniority, Burns had to wait till his turn came.

During this period he was in continual correspondence with Mrs. Dunlop who, out of sympathy though she was with one side of his poetic ambitions, was nevertheless a genuine friend, well-wisher, and admirer, with a protective maternal feeling for him. She may have been sometimes a little tedious and sometimes irritatingly insistent on giving advice, but she was intelligent and interested, and Burns could discuss with her subjects that he could not talk about at all with Jean.

We know nothing, or next to nothing [he wrote Mrs. Dunlop on New Year's Day, 1789] of the substance or structure of our Souls, so cannot account for those seeming caprices in them; that one should be particularly pleased with this thing, or struck with that, which on Minds of a different cast shall make no extraordinary impression. – I have some favourite flowers in Spring, among which are the mountain daisy, the hare-bell, the foxglove, the wild brier-rose, the budding birk, & the hoary hawthorn, that I view and hang over with particular delight. – I never hear the loud, solitary whistle of the Curlew in a Summer noon, or the wild, mixing cadence of a troop of grey-plover in an Autumnal-morning, without feeling an elevation of soul like the enthusiasm of Devotion or Poesy. – Tell me, my dear Friend, to what can this be owing? Are we a piece of machinery, which, like an Eolian harp, passive, takes the impression of the passing accident? Or do these workings argue something within us above the trodden clod? . . .

There were also other friends to whom Burns eagerly turned for social and intellectual intercourse. Less than a mile north of Ellisland, at Friar's Carse, lived Robert Riddell, a retired army captain with some cultural pretensions, among which was an interest in Scots song. He and the poet became intimate soon after Burns had settled at Ellisland. Riddell gave Burns the key to a 'hermitage' he had erected on his grounds, and Burns went there whenever he could to meditate and compose poetry. It was at Friar's Carse that the celebrated bacchanalian contest of October 16, 1789, took place; duly written up by Burns in his poem, 'The Whistle'. Burns later prepared for Riddell two manuscripts of the utmost importance for students of the poet's life and mind: the first is the interleaved copy of the *Scots Musical Museum*, containing numerous notes in Burns's hand, and the second is the Gledriddell Manuscripts (really two separate manuscript books), containing Burns's transcripts of a selection of his poems and letters. Burns also co-operated with Riddell in the founding of the Monkland Friendly Society, whose chief function was to provide a circulating library of serious modern works for its members. The members were mostly the tenant farmers of the neighbourhood, and Burns, who, in Riddell's phrase, 'was so good as to take the whole charge of this small concern', thus rendered a notable public service. Through Robert Riddell, Burns later came to know his younger brother Walter and Walter's wife Maria, an attractive young woman with whom Burns struck up a warm friendship and with whom he continued a lively correspondence until they were separated by an unfortunate quarrel (resulting from a drunken prank at a party, in which it appears that Burns may have been deliberately encouraged by the men to drink more than he could hold and then take part in a burlesque of the 'Rape of the Sabines' in which he chose Maria as his Sabine). It was also through Robert Riddell that Burns met Francis Grose, the antiquary, in 1789.

Looking after his farm, riding[2] around the country performing his excise duties, making time when he could to dine, talk, or correspond with such friends as the Riddells and Mrs. Dunlop, dropping in occasionally at the Globe Tavern in Dumfries to visit Anne Park, writing anxious and helpful letters to his shiftless younger brother William, who was proving something of a problem, and at the same time keeping up a correspondence with friends and acquaintances in Edinburgh and elsewhere – it was a full and strenuous life, and one which tended to emphasize the split between peasant and man of letters. Things were not made any easier by the realization that Ellisland could not be made to pay unless he sank into it much more capital than he could possibly raise.

In 1791 he decided to give up his lease on the farm. His feelings had been gradually cooling towards his landlord, Patrick Miller, and Miller, who had found a purchaser for the farm, was quite glad to let Burns go. In November, 1791, he moved with his family to Dumfries to live on his scanty salary as an exciseman and on what capital he had left from his settlement with Creech and his sale of the Ellisland stock and crops.

In spite of the continuous demands on his time at Ellisland, and in spite, too, of bouts of serious illness, Burns seems to have done a considerable amount of reading at this period. Peter Hill had by now set up as a bookseller on his own, and Burns's letters to him contain numerous orders for books – Smollett's novels, Elizabethan and seventeenth-century drama (Shakespeare, Ben Jonson, Otway, Dryden, Congreve, Wycherley, Vanbrugh, among others); more recent dramatic works including those of Sheridan; the plays of Molière and 'any other good Dramatic Authors in their native language. . . . I mean Comic Authors chiefly, tho' I should wish Racine, Corneille, & Voltaire too.' In the same letter he orders a number of literary, historical, and theological works for the Monkland Friendly Society, and, for himself, 'An Index to the Excise Laws, or an Abridgment of all the Statutes now in force relative to the Excise, by Jellinger Symons.' He also orders a family Bible for 'an honest Country neighbour of mine'.

His interest in Scots song never flagged, and some of his best songs are the product of this period. There are also some lively 'occasional' pieces, some epigrams, and a few formal poems of compliment. The quantity of his production at Ellisland was not very great, but the quality is high. One need only mention 'Auld Lang Syne' and 'John Anderson, My Jo' among the songs, and, among the nonlyrical poems, 'Tam o' Shanter'.

'Tam o' Shanter' was written in 1790 for Captain Grose, the antiquary, and first appeared[3] in Grose's *Antiquities of Scotland*, a work 'chiefly meant to illustrate and describe the ancient castles and monasteries of Scotland'. 'The Antiquarian and the Poet', wrote Gilbert Burns later to Dr. Currie, 'were "unco pack and thick thegither". Robert requested of Captain Grose, when he should come to Ayrshire, that he would make a drawing of Alloway Kirk, as it was the burial-place of his father, and where he himself had some claim to lay down his bones, when they should be no longer serviceable to him; and added, by way of encouragement, that it was the scene of many a good story of witches and apparitions, of which he knew the Captain was very fond. The captain agreed to the request, provided the poet would furnish a witch-story, to be printed along with it.' 'Tam o' Shanter' duly appeared in the second volume of the *Antiquities*, published in 1791; it was included as a long footnote to Captain Grose's description of Alloway Kirk. 'This church', the footnote begins, 'is also famous for being the place wherein the witches and warlocks used to hold their infernal meetings, or sabbaths, and prepare their magical unctions; here too they used to amuse themselves with dancing to the pipes of the muckle-horned Deel. Diverse stories of these horrid rites are still current: one of which my worthy friend Mr. Burns has here favoured me with in verse.'

The plot of 'Tam o' Shanter' is genuine folklore. 'This poem is founded on a traditional story', wrote Gilbert to Dr. Currie, and Robert, writing to Grose in June, 1790, gives three witch stories connected with Alloway Kirk, of which he calls two 'authentic', and says of the third that, 'though equally true, [it] is not so well identified as the two former with regard to the scene'. The second of these three anecdotes was the story of Tam o' Shanter, and it is interesting to compare Burns's prose summary with the poem which he made of it. Here is his first account of the story, in his letter to Grose:

On a market-day, in the town of Ayr, a farmer from Carrick, and consequently whose way lay by the very gate of Aloway kirk-yard, in order to cross the river Doon, at the old bridge, which is about two or three hundred yards farther on than the said gate, had been detained by his business till by the time he reached Aloway it was the wizard hour, between night and morning.

Though he was terrified with a blaze streaming from the kirk, yet as it is a well known fact, that to turn back on these occasions is running by far the greatest risk of mischief, he prudently advanced on his road. When he had reached the gate of the kirk-yard, he was surprised and entertained, through the ribs and arches of an old gothic window which still faces the highway, to see a dance of witches merrily footing it round their old sooty blackguard master, who was keeping them all alive with the power of his bagpipe. The farmer stopping his horse to observe them a little, could plainly descry the faces of many old women of his acquaintance and neighbourhood. How the gentleman was dressed, tradition does not say; but the ladies were all in their smocks; and one of them happening unluckily to have a smock which was considerably too short to answer all the purpose of that piece of dress, our farmer was so tickled that he involuntarily burst out, with a loud laugh, 'Weel luppen, Maggy wi' the short sark!' and recollecting himself, instantly spurred his horse to the top of his speed. I need not mention the universally known fact, that no diabolical power can pursue you beyond the middle of a running stream. Lucky it was for the poor farmer that the river Doon was so near, for notwithstanding the speed of his horse, which was a good one, against he reached the middle of the arch of the bridge, and consequently the middle of the stream, the pursuing, vengeful hags were so close at his heels, that one of them actually sprung to seize him: but it was too late; nothing was on her side of the stream but the horse's tail, which immediately gave way to her infernal grip, as if blasted by a stroke of lightning; but the farmer was beyond her reach. – However, the unsightly, tailless condition of the vigorous steed was to the last hours of the noble creature's life, an awful warning to the Carrick farmers, not to stay too late in Ayr markets. –

'Tam o' Shanter' is Burns's most sustained single poetic effort, as well as the only example among his poems of this kind of narrative poetry. It was written at a time when he was beset with all kinds of difficulties and worries, after a spell of scanty production. And it showed him a master of verse narrative as no Scots poet had been since the fifteenth century. The speed and verve of the narration, the fine, flexible use of the octosyllabic couplet, the effective handling of the verse paragraph demonstrate a degree of craftsmanship that few other users of this verse form have achieved. Matthew Prior, who also used octosyllabic couplets for narrative poetry, had something of this ease and fluency, but Prior's verse tales have a city swagger about them, a deliberate air of a man about town displaying his humour and familiarity, as well as a looseness of structure and little concern for the verse paragraph, which put them far below 'Tam o' Shanter' in literary quality.

The opening of the poem marks the characteristically Scottish contrast between the wild weather outside and the snug fireside within. This introductory section, describing Tam drinking happily at the inn, has a structure of its own, and moves to a climax at the end of the seventh verse paragraph. The first twelve lines give us first a brief but vivid impression of market day at a country town, with the evening closing in, and then an equally vivid picture of the farmer's wife waiting suspiciously at home for his return:

packman	
fellows	When chapman billies leave the street,
thirsty	And drouthy neebors, neebors meet,
	As market-days are wearing late,
road	An' folk begin to tak the gate;

ale
drunk;
very
not
gaps in
walls

> While we sit bousing at the nappy,
> An' getting fou and unco happy,
> We think na on the lang Scots miles,
> The mosses, waters, slaps, and styles,
> That lie between us and our hame,
> Whare sits our sulky sullen dame,
> Gathering her brows like gathering storm,
> Nursing her wrath to keep it warm.

There is a pause here, before Burns proceeds to nail the general description down by applying it to Tam o' Shanter, in four sturdy lines:

found

> This truth fand honest Tam o' Shanter,
> As he frae Ayr ae night did canter,
> (Auld Ayr, wham ne'er a town surpasses,
> For honest men and bonny lasses).

The parenthetical remark about 'auld Ayr' and its inhabitant adds just the note of familiarity, of personal knowledge, that the mood of the poem requires. This is an anecdote told by someone who knows the hero and his environment; Tam becomes one of us, and the casual note of compliment to Ayr puts the reader, as it were, up at the bar, having a drink with the narrator.

The perspective shifts a little in the lines that follow. After another pause (and it should be noted how effectively Burns places his pauses and varies his tempo) the narrator takes the reader by the arm and moves with him to the rear of the pub, from which they look at the back of the unconscious Tam as he drinks at the bar with his cronies, and remind themselves of his faults and of his waiting wife:

taken; own
rogue
chattering;
babbler

> O Tam! had'st thou but been sae wise,
> As ta'en thy ain wife Kate's advice!
> She tauld thee weel thou was a skellum,
> A blethering, blustering, drunken blellum;
> That frae November till October,
> Ae market-day thou was nae sober.

And as the narrator lets himself go in depicting Tam's wife's view of Tam (which becomes as it proceeds also our view of him), he breaks out with a somewhat beery generalization:

makes;   Ah, gentle dames! it gars me greet,
weep   To think how mony counsels sweet,
               How mony lengthen'd sage advices,
               The husband frae the wife despises!

The narrator is lost for a moment in contemplation of the stupidity of men (of other men, that is). And all the time Tam, growing more and more unconscious of the demands of domesticity, morality, or even self-preservation, is drinking happily at the bar with his cronies:

               But to our tale: Ae market-night,
               Tam had got planted unco right;
               Fast by an ingle, bleezing finely,
frothing   Wi' reaming swats, that drank divinely;
ale   And at his elbow, Souter Johnny,
cobbler   His ancient, trusty, drouthy crony;

Then comes the climax of good fellowship:

               Tam lo'ed him like a vera brither;
               They had been fou for weeks thegither.

Here there is another pause, and then the narrator again describes how the hour is growing later and the night wilder:

               The night drave on wi' sangs and clatter;
               And ay the ale was growing better:
               The landlady and Tam grew gracious,
               Wi' favours, secret, sweet, and precious:
               The Souter tauld his queerest stories;
               The landlord's laugh was ready chorus:
roar   The storm without might rair and rustle,
               Tam did na mind the storm a whistle.

And then we come to the climax of this interior and to the end of the first section of the poem:

               Care, mad to see a man sae happy,
               E'en drown'd himsel amang the nappy:
loads   As bees flee hame wi' lades o' treasure,
               The minutes wing'd their way wi' pleasure:
               Kings may be blest, but Tam was glorious,
               O'er a' the ills o' life victorious!

The picture of the jovial interior is expanded, in a blaze of happy sympathy, into a celebration of Tam's mood. The double rhymes ('happy' and 'nappy'; 'treasure' and 'pleasure') help to give the impression of a grand, carefree, snap of the fingers, while the final rhyming of 'glorious' with 'victorious' sounds a slightly drunken organ note which swells the climax of this account of Tam's state of mind.

There is a long pause now, and the echoes of that 'glorious' and 'victorious' die away in the reader's ears. Then, in a most interesting transitional passage, the tone is suddenly changed, and the narrator, using standard English and talking with deliberate sententiousness, brings the cold world of reality into this warm atmosphere. First, we have a series of deliberately poetic generalizations about the transitory nature of human pleasures, and the application is then punched home with a proverbial statement in simple, direct language and a return to Scots diction and to Tam:

> But pleasures are like poppies spread,
> You seize the flow'r, its bloom is shed;
> Or like the snow falls in the river,
> A moment white – then melts for ever;
> Or like the borealis race,
> That flit ere you can point their place;
> Or like the rainbow's lovely form
> Evanishing amid the storm.—
> Nae man can tether time or tide;
> The hour approaches Tam maun ride;
> That hour, o' night's black arch the key-stane,
> That dreary hour he mounts his beast in;
> And sic a night he taks the road in,
> As ne'er poor sinner was abroad in.

Mr. Edwin Muir cites the eight lines in standard English as proof of his thesis that ever since the end of the Middle Ages the Scot, because of the peculiar linguistic and cultural situation in which he found himself, has had to feel in Scots and think in English. But it would have been easy for Burns to have found a number of Scots proverbial lines which would have expressed the thought conveyed by the lines about the poppies and the borealis. The point here is not, surely, that the poet is introducing *thought* and must therefore employ standard English, but that he is being deliberate, cold, and formal, in order to contrast the unwelcome truth about pleasure with Tam's cosy feeling about it. The English in these lines is a deliberately 'fancy' English, piling up simile after simile as though to draw attention to the literary quality of the utterance. Mr. Muir's explanation of these lines takes no account of this very conscious poetic diction – he sees it simply as English. Burns is seeking a form of expression which will set the sternness of objective fact against the warm, cosy, and self-deluding view of the half-intoxicated Tam, and he wants to do this with just a touch of irony. What more effective device than to employ a deliberate neoclassic English poetic diction in these lines?

The next verse paragraph builds up the storm scene until it reaches the point where the name of the Devil can be introduced. The climactic couplet which concludes it rings out as a warning of supernatural terrors to come:

> That night, a child might understand,
> The Deil had business on his hand.

We return to Tam and follow him as he rides 'thro' dub and mire', crooning to himself to keep his courage up but not forgetting to look round

> wi' prudent cares,
> Lest bogles catch him unawares: . . .

And so he approaches the haunted kirk:

owls

> Kirk-Alloway was drawing nigh,
> Whare ghaists and houlets nightly cry. –

We now move, after a pause, to another paragraph, in which Kirk-Alloway is introduced as a climax of a series of horrors:

> By this time he was cross the ford,
> *smothered*   Whare, in the snaw, the chapman smoor'd;
> *birches;*   And past the birks and meikle stane,
> *big*   Whare drunken Charlie brak's neck-bane;
> *furze*   And thro' the whins, and by the cairn,
> Whare hunters fand the murder'd bairn;
> And near the thorn, aboon the well,
> Whare Mungo's mither hang'd hersel. –
> Before him Doon pours all his floods;
> The doubling storm roars thro' the woods;

> The lightnings flash from pole to pole;
> Near and more near the thunders roll:
> When, glimmering thro' the groaning trees,
> Kirk-Alloway seem'd in a bleeze.

Tam hears the sound of 'mirth and dancing' coming from the kirk, and at this point Burns pauses, and breaks into an exclamation of wonder at the boldness which whisky can inspire. This interruption effectively keeps the reader in suspense and gives him an excuse to dismiss, if he so wishes, all that Tam saw as the product of the man's drunken imagination. (It is to be noted that Burns nearly always provided this 'out' in his supernatural scenes: yet before the poem is over we find that he has made all details *but one* (Maggie's loss of her tail) capable of rational explanation. This set the formula used ever since in tales of the supernatural.)

> Inspiring bold John Barleycorn!
> What dangers thou canst make us scorn!

Thus inspired, Tam presses forward, in spite of the reluctance of Maggie his mare:

> And, wow! Tam saw an unco sight!

This sharp, sudden, exclamatory line is very different in movement from the slower exclamation about the effects of whisky,

> Inspiring bold John Barleycorn!

In the later line he is not halting the narrative to make a generalization but pressing forward into his tale in a mood of sudden excitement and astonishment. There follows immediately the eerie catalogue of what Tam saw:

	Warlocks and witches in a dance;
brand	Nae cotillion, brent new frae France,
	But hornpipes, jigs, strathspeys, and reels,
	Put life and mettle in their heels.
window	A winnock-bunker in the east,
seat	There sat auld Nick, in shape o' beast;
shaggy dog	A towzie tyke, black, grim, and large,
	To gie them music was his charge:
made	He screw'd the pipes and gart them skirl,
rattle	Till roof and rafters a' did dirl. –

Coffins stood round, like open presses,
That shaw'd the dead in their last dresses;
weird trick   And by some devilish cantraip slight
Each in its cauld hand held a light. –
By which heroic Tam was able
To note upon the haly table,
irons   A murderer's banes in gibbet airns;
Twa span-lang, wee, unchristen'd bairns;
rope   A thief, new-cutted frae a rape,
mouth   Wi' his last gasp his gab did gape;
Five tomahawks, wi' blude red-rusted;
Five scymitars, wi' murder crusted;
A garter, which a babe had strangled;
A knife, a father's throat had mangled,
Whom his ain son o' life bereft,
stuck; haft   The grey hairs yet stack to the heft;
Wi' mair o' horrible and awefu',
Which even to name wad be unlawfu'.

The note of superstitious terror is exaggerated here almost to the point of absurdity, and certainly to the point where some kind of humorous effect is achieved. Here is the devil of folklore, Auld Nick, surrounded by all his traditional properties. The objects described are so monstrously horrible that they are not quite real, like the setting of an eighteenth-century Gothic novel, and so a note of comic mockery emerges, as though Burns is gently laughing at people who could believe in such things. Yet this note does not lessen the suspense. Tam all this while has remained motionless on his mare, watching the incredible scene, and the longer the description the more interested we become in finding out how Tam has reacted. But Burns deftly increases our suspense with another exclamation, one of a series planted effectively at intervals throughout the poem:

these; girls   Now, Tam, O Tam! had thae been queans,
A' plump and strapping in their teens,
greasy   Their sarks, instead o' creeshie flannen,
Been snaw-white seventeen hunder linnen!
these   Thir breeks o' mine, my only pair,
That ance were plush, o' gude blue hair,
buttocks   I wad hae gi'en them off my hurdies,
lasses   For ae blink o' the bonnie burdies!

But wither'd beldams, auld and droll,
lean; wean   Rigwoodie hags wad spean a foal,
leaping;   Lowping and flinging on a crummock,
staff   I wonder didna turn thy stomach.

We return to Tam, whose discerning eye has picked out one of the witches as a 'winsome wench and wawlie', though Burns makes clear in a parenthetical description of her that once she grew to her full witch status she would do serious damage in the countryside. For a moment, however, the picture of Nannie dancing is human and strangely touching:

short shift;   Her cutty sark, o' Paisley harn,
coarse cloth   That while a lassie she had worn,
                 In longitude tho' sorely scanty,
proud   It was her best, and she was vauntie. –
                 Ah! little kend thy reverend grannie,
bought   That sark she coft for her wee Nannie,
                 Wi' twa pund Scots ('twas a' her riches),
                 Wad ever grac'd a dance of witches!

The suggestion of a fall from an earlier happy, human state gives a momentary flash of pathos to the narrative; but it is modified by humour and not sustained long enough to threaten the mood of the poem as a whole.

The next verse paragraph describes Nannie's furious dancing, the verse getting faster and faster, carrying the reader along with a rush, until he becomes identified with Tam as he shouts applause. And with that shout the scene changes abruptly:

then   Till first ae caper, syne anither,
lost   Tam tint his reason a' thegither,
                 And roars out, 'Weel done, Cutty-sark!'
                 And in an instant all was dark:
                 And scarcely had he Maggie rallied,
                 When out the hellish legion sallied.

It is interesting that the change is described without taking a new paragraph: to begin a new paragraph after Tam's shout would be to suggest a pause between the shout and the resulting change, whereas the effect of sudden alteration is desired. So Burns describes the beginning of the witches' attack without taking breath and only after he has got the attack going does he pause. The next paragraph continues and elaborates the description of the pursuing witches and the fleeing Maggie:

fret
shepherds;
hive

unearthly
yell

> As bees bizz out wi' angry fyke,
> When plundering herds assail their byke; ...
> So Maggie runs, the witches follow,
> Wi' mony an eldritch skreech and hollow.

At this moment of suspense Burns deliberately tantalizes the reader again by holding up the narrative while he wags his finger and shakes his head at Tam. The poet's mock-sympathetic confidence in his hero's doom has comic implications, which are reinforced by the imagery:

deserts

> Ah, Tam! Ah, Tam! thou'll get thy fairin!
> In hell they'll roast thee like a herrin!

Maggie pushes on; the verse – after that sudden slowing down – gains speed again, until Tam and his mare gain the bridge, and safety, for witches cannot cross running water. But Nannie, pressing close behind, had removed poor Maggie's tail:

intent

whole

clutched

> For Nannie, far before the rest,
> Hard upon noble Maggie prest,
> And flew at Tam wi' furious ettle;
> But little wist she Maggie's mettle –
> Ae spring brought off her master hale,
> But left behind her ain grey tail:
> The carlin claught her by the rump,
> And left poor Maggie scarce a stump.

There is an abrupt pause at this point. The story is now told, but the poet's tone indicates that something more is to come. And, after the expectant pause, it does come – a mock moral, a deliberately absurd oversimplification of the meaning of the tale to make it a warning against drinking and wenching:

> Now, wha this tale o' truth shall read,
> Ilk man and mother's son, take heed:
> Whene'er to drink you are inclin'd,
> Or cutty-sarks run in your mind,
> Think, ye may buy the joys o'er dear,
> Remember Tam o' Shanter's mare.

And on that note of 'Remember!' – like the speech of the ghost in *Hamlet* – the poem comes to an end.

Among the many qualities of 'Tam o' Shanter' which show Burns's technical skill in handling this kind of verse narrative – the effective use of the octosyllabic couplet, the variations in tempo, the use of the verse paragraph, and the placing of the pauses – perhaps the most remarkable is his handling of the *tone* of the poem. The tone is at once comic and full of suspense, shrewd yet irresponsible, mocking yet sympathetic; there is a fine balance here between mere supernatural anecdote and the precisely etched realistic picture, and it is maintained throughout the poem. 'Tam o' Shanter' is the work of a virtuoso. Yet it is the only verse narrative of its kind that Burns wrote, the product (if tradition is to be trusted) of one day's truancy from the work and worries of his farm and his excise duties during one of his most troubled periods. Clearly, with a little leisure and a little relief from the 'carking cares' that continually pressed on him, many other new aspects of his poetic genius might have been as profitably explored. It is easy to see why Burns, wiser than his Edinburgh advisers, continually longed for a government job which would leave him with some time of his own.

His friendship with Grose produced also that lively and amusing piece, 'On the Late Captain Grose's Peregrinations thro' Scotland, Collecting Antiquities of that Kingdom', which first appeared in the *Edinburgh Evening Courant* of August 27, 1789; it was reprinted in four other periodicals before it was published in the 1793 edition of Burns's poems. This good-humoured and boisterous poem is in Burns's best vein:

> Hear, Land o' Cakes, and brither Scots,
> Frae Maidenkirk to Johnny Groats! –
> If there's a hole in a' your coats,
> > I rede you tent it:
> A chield's amang you, taking notes,
> > And, faith, he'll prent it.

advise; look to fellow

print

> If in your bounds ye chance to light
> Upon a fine, fat, fodgel wight,
> O' stature short, but genius bright,
> > That's he, mark weel –
> And wow! he has an unco slight
> > O' caulk and keel.

dumpy

skill chalk and ruddle

After this vigorous opening, with its friendly mockery, Burns proceeds to describe the antiquary haunting some 'auld, houlet-haunted biggin'

or deserted kirk and then makes magnificent fun of his antiquarian habit
of collecting old relics:

abundance	He has a fouth o' auld nick-nackets:
iron	Rusty airn caps and jingling jackets,
would keep;	Wad haud the Lothians three in tackets,
shoenails	
twelvemonth	A towmont gude;
porridge-	And parritch-pats, and auld saut-backets,
pots;	
salt boxes	Before the Flood.

	Of Eve's first fire he has a cinder;
-shovel	Auld Tubalcain's fire-shool and fender;
	That which distinguished the gender
	O' Balaam's ass;
	A broom-stick o' the witch of Endor,
	Weel shod wi' brass.

besides;	
smartly	Forbye, he'll shape you aff fu' gleg
kilt	The cut of Adam's philibeg;
cut; throat	The knife that nicket Abel's craig
	He'll prove you fully,
clasp knife	It was a faulding jocteleg,
cabbage	Or lang-kail gullie. –
knife	

The poem concludes with the usual complimentary turn:

	Now, by the Pow'rs o' Verse and Prose!
	Thou art a dainty chield, O Grose! –
	Whae'er o' thee shall ill suppose,
	They sair misca' thee;
	I'd take the rascal by the nose,
befall	Wad say, Shame fa' thee.

Burns also composed an epigram on Grose, no better and no worse
than most specimens of this literary form in that period, and a swinging
impromptu (based on an old song) occasioned by ignorance of the
Captain's whereabouts when he wished to address a letter to him. He
sent the letter, enclosed in an envelope on which the verses were written,
to an Edinburgh customs officer, a friend of Grose's. The verses themselves are not, of course, great poetry; but they illustrate perfectly that
gift for zestful impromptu which Burns possessed in such great measure:

know

Ken ye ought o' Captain Grose
　　　　Igo & ago,
Is he amang his friends or foes?
　　　　Iram coram dago.

Is he South, or is he North?
　　　　Igo & ago
Or drowned in the river Forth?
　　　　Iram coram dago.

creatures

Is he slain by Highland bodies?
　　　　Igo & ago,
And eaten like a weather-haggis?
　　　　Iram coram dago.

Is he to Abram's bosom gane?
　　　　Igo & ago,
holding;
belly
Or haudin Sarah by the wame?
　　　　Iram coram dago.

Whare'er he be, the Lord be near him!
　　　　Igo & ago,
meddle
with
As for the deil, he daur na steer him,
　　　　Iram coram dago.

But please transmit th' inclosed letter,
　　　　Igo & ago,
Which will oblidge your humble debtor,
　　　　Iram coram dago.

have old
stones

So may ye hae auld stanes in store,
　　　　Igo & ago,
The very stanes that Adam bore;
　　　　Iram coram dago.

So may ye get in glad possession,
　　　　Igo & ago,
The coins o' Satan's Coronation!
　　　　Iram coram dago.

There is no point in analyzing a poem of this kind; its qualities of liveliness, humour, good-natured mockery and spontaneity are evident enough. Burns's ability to throw off this sort of thing with such ease and frequency shows not only that he had poetry in his very bones but also that he had made himself complete master of his craft.

At Ellisland, in spite of all distractions, Burns maintained his interest in liberal theology and lost no opportunity of furthering its cause against that of the 'unco guid'. In the summer of 1789 he supported the Reverend Dr. William M'Gill of Ayr, accused of heresy for his *Practical Essay on the Death of Jesus Christ*, against the orthodox, with a spirited ballad, 'The Kirk's Alarm'. This poem was privately circulated among his friends, for he felt that publication would be dangerous. 'If I could be of any service to D^r McGill', he wrote to John Logan, 'I would do it though it should be at a much greater expense than irritating a few bigotted Priests; but as I am afraid, serving him in his present embarras is a task too hard for me, I have enemies enow, God knows, tho' I do not wantonly add to the number'. 'The Kirk's Alarm' requires elaborate annotation for the modern reader, because almost every verse contains a reference to a different character concerned in the controversy and because the full flavour of the satire can be savoured only by those who have made themselves familiar with the references. Nevertheless, the opening verses will give a good idea of the poem's character and of the point at issue:

> Orthodox! orthodox! wha believe in John Knox,
>   Let me sound an alarm to your conscience:
> A heretic blast has been blown in the West,
>   That 'what is no sense must be nonsense',
> Orthodox! That 'what is no sense must be nonsense'.
>
> Doctor Mac! Doctor Mac! you should streek on a rack,
>   To strike evil-doers wi' terror:
> To join Faith and Sense, upon any pretence,
>   Was heretic, damnable error,
> Doctor Mac! 'Twas heretic, damnable error.

This is a hard-hitting satire, with a strong popular flavour and a cunning use of an appropriate stanza form. The 'bob-and-wheel' device, which has a long history in English and Scots poetry, was not unknown in eighteenth-century English poetry (Gay used it in *The Beggars' Opera*), and a simpler form of the same stanza was common in drinking songs and political squibs and ballads of the seventeenth and eighteenth centuries.

Burns also wrote election ballads during the parliamentary contests of 1790 and of 1795, but these, which confine themselves to local issues and personalities and never reach out to any wider theme, are of little interest and of no great poetic merit, although the second of the 1795 ballads, 'Fy, Let Us A' to Kirkcudbright' (a parody of 'The Blythsome Bridal'), has a speed and liveliness which almost compensate for the incomprehensibility of the allusions to the modern reader. More general political satires – 'Ode to the Departed Regency Bill', and 'A New Psalm for the Chapel of Kilmarnock' – were contributed to the London *Morning Star*, whose editor, Peter Stuart, admired Burns and sought his contributions. The former of these is another of Burns's none too success-ful attempts at the ode form as practised by such English writers as Gray; but the latter is a clever parody of the Scottish metrical Psalter, something in the mood of 'Holy Willie's Prayer' but much milder both in tone and method. It is supposed to be a song of thanksgiving 'devoutly sung' on the occasion of the King's recovery 'in a certain chapel not fifty leagues from the market-cross' of Kilmarnock:

> O, sing a new song to the Lord!
> Make, all and every one,
> A joyful noise, ev'n for the King
> His restoration!
>
> The sons of Belial in the land
> Did set their heads together.
> 'Come, let us sweep them off,' said they,
> 'Like an o'erflowing river!' . . .
>
> Th' ungodly o'er the just prevail'd;
> For so Thou hadst appointed,
> That Thou might'st greater glory give
> Unto Thine own anointed!
>
> And now thou hast restored our State,
> Pity our Kirk also;
> For she by tribulations
> Is now brought very low!
>
> Consume that high-place, Patronage,
> From off Thy holy hill;
> And in Thy fury burn the book
> Even of that man M'Gill!

> Now hear our prayer, accept our song,
>   And fight Thy chosen's battle!
> We seek but little, Lord, from Thee:
>   Thou kens we get as little!

This is a very precise parody of the language and versification of the Scottish metrical Psalter, even to the pentasyllabic pronunciation of words like 'restoration' and 'tribulation'. The opening line, of course, is the opening of Psalm 96.

Burns further displayed his interest in public affairs by drawing up a remarkable plea, addressed to William Pitt, on behalf of the distillers of Scotland, then suffering from 'a most partial tax laid on by the House of Commons, to favour a few opulent English Distillers'. The letter appeared, signed 'JOHN BARLEYCORN – Praeses', in the *Edinburgh Evening Courant* of February 9, 1789. It is Burns in his full-dress, public English prose style, carefully wrought, weighted and balanced:

> Sir,
> While pursy Burgesses crowd your gate, sweating under the weight of heavy Addresses, permit us, the quondam Distillers in that part of G— B— called Sc— to approach you, not with venal approbation, but with fraternal condolence; not as what you are just now, or for some time have been [Pitt's resignation was expected imminently], but as what, in all probability, you will shortly be. – We will have the merit of not deserting our friends in the day of their calamity, and you will have the satisfaction of perusing at least one honest Address. . . .

– and so on in the same vein for about a thousand more words, in which he makes his point with wit, passion, and dignity. On public occasions like these the formal epistolary style Burns had learned from his reading with Murdoch served him in good stead; here, indeed, was the right occasion for employing this side of his skill.

Burns's political activity was not confined to writing election ballads and producing poems and letters on public affairs. Like so many other liberal-minded Scotsmen and Englishmen, he was stirred by the French Revolution, and he allowed himself to give expression to sentiments about it which alienated his more conservative genteel friends. The course which the revolution took, however, made the support of its principles against persons who opposed them more than a matter of polite difference of opinion; and as hysteria and reaction mounted in

Britain after the execution of Louis XVI and even more so after Britain and France went to war in 1793, it became increasingly dangerous to be suspected of active sympathy with the revolutionary cause – particularly so for a man like Burns, already to some degree a public figure, and, what was really more to the point, a government servant. His earlier Jacobite utterances had sometimes been reckless, though rarely wholly serious – his considered attitude towards Jacobitism, the English Revolution of 1688, and the American Revolution of 1776 were expressed with admirable clarity and historical understanding in a letter he wrote to the *Edinburgh Evening Courant* in November, 1788 – but even here his recklessness had already done him some harm.

Burns's letter to the *Edinburgh Evening Courant* was a public statement of his position on some of the most important political issues of the day. He insists on putting the Stuarts in their historical context and not judging them by standards which were unknown to their age. 'At that period the science of government – the true relation between King and subject, like other sciences, was but just in its infancy, emerging from the dark ages of ignorance and barbarism. The Stuarts only contended for prerogatives which they knew their predecessors enjoyed, and which they saw their contemporaries enjoying; but these prerogatives were inimical to the happiness of a nation and the rights of subjects.' After explaining how constitutional monarchy came to be established in Britain and after acknowledging its superiority to the method of government favoured by the Stuarts, he discusses the Jacobite rebellions of 1715 and 1745 with a combination of disapproval and sympathy. 'That they failed, I bless my God most fervently; but cannot join in the ridicule against them'. He then moves to more burning ground:

Man, Mr. Printer, is a strange, weak, inconsistent being – Who would believe, Sir, that in this our Augustan age of liberality and refinement, while we seem so justly sensible and jealous of our rights and liberties, and animated with such indignation against the very memory of those who would have subverted them, who would suppose that a certain people, under our national protection, should complain, not against a Monarch and a few favourite advisers, but against our whole legislative body, of the very same imposition and oppression, the Romish religion not excepted, and almost in the very same terms as our forefathers did against the family of Stuart! I will not, I cannot, enter into the merits of the cause; but I dare say, the American Congress, in 1776, will be allowed to have been as able and as enlightened, and, a whole empire will say, as honest, as the English

Convention of 1688; and that the fourth of July will be as sacred to their posterity as the fifth of November is to us.

Earlier in the letter Burns had used the phrase 'the rights of man' – a phrase considered by Dr. Currie incendiary enough to make him delete it from his printed text. By that time the French Revolution and its aftermath had raised even more fundamental questions.

It was one thing to call for moderation in discussing the errors of the Stuarts; it was another to utter sentiments favourable to the French Revolution in a time of mounting hysteria – Jacobins were at this time a more active danger than Jacobites. It was Burns's attitude towards the French Revolution that estranged him from Mrs. Dunlop in January, 1795 – a breach which was healed only when Burns was literally on his deathbed. It was this, too, that caused his superiors in the Excise to inquire sharply into his conduct and opinions, with the result that Burns, confused and frightened at the prospect of being deprived of his position and thus being without any means of supporting his family, had to make a somewhat humiliating recantation. But in spite of the fact that Burns was forced to take this distasteful step – an act which, as Professor DeLancey Ferguson has well argued, 'shook his self-confidence as nothing else had ever done' – the spirit of 1789 did combine in Burns's mind and art with that of 1688 and even, in an odd way, with that of 1745, to encourage him as the poet of democracy and of the rights of man. Scottish patriotism and a zest for liberty and fraternity always went together for Burns, and the combination produced some of his most celebrated songs.

THE SONGS

BURNS LIVED in Dumfries from November 1791 until his death in July 1796. This bustling town – the most important in southwestern Scotland – afforded him something of the cultural and social activity he had known at Edinburgh, and with less strain on his temper and his pride, for here he was a resident and an exciseman with a job to do, as well as a poet, whereas in the capital he had been a visiting celebrity on exhibition. Here, in spite of troubles arising out of his tactless political utterances, his quarrel with Maria Riddell and Mrs. Dunlop's estrangement, and the final and fatal recurrence of his rheumatic heart disease which brought with it an almost hysterical fear of getting into debt (a fear which shadowed his last days), he managed to stabilize his life in some degree, and to produce some of his finest songs. He made new friends – and we have seen how important male companionship was to Burns. Among these were Dr. William Maxwell, who had been in France during the French Revolution and who had returned fervent in its support; John Syme, with whom Burns made a tour of Galloway in June, 1794; Alexander Findlater, Supervisor of the Dumfries Excise district; John Lewars, a fellow exciseman, whose sister Jessie helped to nurse Burns in his last illness and who was the subject of one of Burns's finest songs; James Gray, a teacher in the Dumfries Burgh School, who has left a pleasant picture of his visit to the Burns home, where he found the poet reading and explaining to his children 'the English poets from Shakespeare to Gray' and 'directing the studies of the eldest son'. These and other friends were men to whom Burns could go for good conversation and cheerful society. If on certain social occasions he drank more than was good for him, such were the manners of the time and the country. Burns was not, in fact, an unusually heavy drinker for the period; he did not have a good head for liquor and it took less to affect him than it often did others. The view that in his last years he had become a drunkard is derived from Dr. Currie, Burns's first biographer, who never knew Burns personally and collected information about him from those who did not understand the intolerable social tensions amid which Burns lived in his last years. It was the view of patronising gentlemen, indignant that Burns presumed to indulge in excesses beyond his station, that is largely reflected in Currie. In any case, drink had nothing to do with Burns's death.

It is worth noting that Burns was on good terms with his superiors in the Excise and that when he was denounced to the Excise Board by an informer as unpatriotic he was exonerated after a friendly and informal trial at which (in addition to the supervisor who conducted it) both Findlater and Syme were present; he was, however, warned to be more circumspect in the future. All the evidence goes to show that, although Burns had enemies, he was a respected citizen in Dumfries, well liked and well thought of by friends and colleagues. When, in 1793, he applied to the Lord Provost, Bailies, and Town Council of Dumfries for the right to have his children educated in the Burgh schools without paying 'the high School-fees which a Stranger pays', citing the fact that he had been made an Honorary Burgess some years before, his request was immediately granted. It looked as though Burns might at last find a way of life that would reconcile the different aspects of his mind and ambitions, and that the lively country town of Dumfries represented the kind of compromise between Ayrshire and Edinburgh which he needed. Had it not been for ill-health, which affected his spirits as well as his body, he might have adjusted reasonably well in Dumfries to a life of poetry, excise service, and social and intellectual activity.

In 1793, Creech brought out a new edition of his poems, in two volumes, for which Burns received nothing except several complimentary copies. It is true that Burns had sold Creech outright the copyright of the poems printed in the 1787 volume, but this new edition contained twenty new poems (some fifty printed pages) including 'Tam o' Shanter'. Apart from 'Tam' the 1793 volume contained little new material of interest. The first new piece, entitled 'Written in Friars-Carse Hermitage on Nith-Side' is a somewhat artificial study in English meditative verse, suggesting, in cadence and sometimes in imagery, the much briefer 'How Sleep the Brave' of Collins:

> Thou whom chance may hither lead,
> Be thou clad in russet weed,
> Be thou deckt in silken stole,
> Grave these counsels on thy soul.

The next new poem is an 'Ode, Sacred to the Memory of Mrs. ——— of———' (Mrs. Oswald of Auchencruive), a savage attack on the deceased lady in the inappropriate form of an ode, complete with strophe, antistrophe, and epode. In a letter to Dr. Moore enclosing the poem, written at Ellisland in March, 1789, Burns gives some explanation of the virulence of his feeling:

> The inclosed Ode is a compliment to the memory of the late Mrs Oswald of Auchencruive. – You, probably, knew her personally, an honor of which I cannot boast; but I spent my early years in her neighbourhood, and among her servants and tenants I know that she was detested with the most heartfelt cordiality. – However, in the particular part of her conduct, which roused my Poetic wrath, she was much less blameable. – In January last, on my road to Ayrshire, I had put up at Bailie Whigham's in Sanqhuar, the only tolerable inn in the place. – The frost was keen, and the grim evening and howling wind were ushering in a night of snow and drift. – My horse & I were both much fatigued with the labours of the day, and just as my friend the Bailie and I, were bidding defiance to the storm over a smoking bowl, in wheels the funeral pageantry of the late great Mrs Oswald, and poor I am forced to brave all the horrors of the tempestuous night, and jade my horse, my young favourite horse whom I had just christened Pegasus, twelve miles farther on, through the wildest moor & hills of Ayrshire, to New Cumnock, the next Inn. – The powers of Poesy & Prose sink under me, when I would describe what I felt. – Suffice it to say, that when a good fire at New Cumnock had so far recovered my frozen sinews, I sat down and wrote the inclosed Ode.

There is a note of schoolboy spleen in the poem, understandable in the light of its origin. The opening stanza will suggest something of this quality:

> Dweller in yon dungeon dark,
> Hangman of creation, mark!
> Who in widow weeds appears,
> Laden with unhonoured years.
> Noosing with care a bursting purse,
> Baited with many a deadly curse.

And the strophe begins:

View the wither'd beldam's face –
Can thy keen inspection trace
Aught of Humanity's sweet melting grace?
Note that eye, 'tis rheum o'erflows,
Pity's flood there never rose. . . .

The poem ends with the suggestion that Mrs. Oswald, for all her wealth, goes to Hell, while 'the cave-lodged beggar . . . expires in rags, unknown, and goes to Heaven'. If proof were needed that Burns functioned best as a satirist when he was working in the Scottish tradition, this poem provides it.

It does not follow that whenever Burns wrote in Scots he wrote well. The 'Elegy on Capt. M—— H——' (Matthew Henderson), though in Scots and in the 'Standard Habbie' stanza form, is a lifeless performance – almost a literal rendering into Scots of the most artificial kind of neo-classic poetic diction; and the 'Epitaph' which follows is of no great interest or poetic distinction, though there is a certain ingenuity in the rhymes. The 'Lament of Mary Queen of Scots on the Approach of Spring' was (as he wrote to Dr. Moore in February, 1791) 'begun while I was busy with Percy's Reliques of English Poetry', which accounts for its not unsuccessful fusion of folk elements with the tone of neoclassic elegy. Some of the stanzas have a ring of the ballads about them:

I was the Queen o' bonnie France,
    Where happy I hae been;
Fu' lightly rase I in the morn,
    As blythe lay down at e'en:
And I'm the sov'reign of Scotland,
    And monie a traitor there;
Yet here I lie in foreign bands
    And never-ending care.

The final verse combines the two notes:

O! soon, to me, may summer-suns
    Nae mair light up the morn!
Nae mair, to me, the autumn winds
    Wave o'er the yellow corn!
And in the narrow house o' death
    Let winter round me rave;
And the next flowers, that deck the spring,
    Bloom on my peaceful grave.

The next new poem in the 1793 volume is the Epistle to Robert Graham of Fintry which has been already discussed, and this is followed by a 'Lament for James, Earl of Glencairn', Burns's friend and patron, who died in January, 1791. Burns had a genuine affection for Glencairn, being fully sensible of what he owed him; he named his fourth son, born in 1794, James Glencairn Burns. Genuineness of emotion, however, does not always guarantee good poetry; the lament is an unimpressive collocation of sound sentiments and conventional elegiac devices which comes to life only in the final verse, where Burns suddenly strikes a folk note with remarkable directness and simplicity, and the effect is impressive:

> The bridegroom may forget the bride,
>   Was made his wedded wife yestreen;
> The monarch may forget the crown
>   That on his head an hour has been;
> The mother may forget the child
>   That smiles sae sweetly on her knee;
> But I'll remember thee, Glencairn,
>   And a' that thou has done for me!

After a few lines in couplets to Sir John Whitefoord, sent to him by Burns with the lament for Glencairn, the reader comes to 'Tam o' Shanter', the great prize piece of the 1793 edition. Two slight and uninteresting pieces follow – 'On Seeing a Wounded Hare' and 'Address to the Shade of Thomson' – and the next new poem is that fine description of Captain Grose which we have discussed in the previous chapter. Some complimentary lines to Miss Cruickshank follow – she was the young daughter of the poet's friend, William Cruickshank of the High School, Edinburgh – which have the conventional elegance of an album piece; they were 'written on the blank leaf of a Book, presented to her by the Author'. A brief song to an unknown 'Anna' comes next, then some rather frigid verses on the death of John M'Leod. The 'Humble petition of Bruar Water to the Noble Duke of Athole', which follows, is an interesting 'occasional' piece, the result of his stay with the Duke on his northern tour. 'On scaring some Waterfowl in Loch-Turit' is the product of the Stirlingshire trip of October, 1787; it reads like a copybook piece, as do the lines 'Written with a Pencil over the Chimney-Piece, in the Parlour of the Inn at Kenmore, Taymouth', another product of his travels. The lines 'Written with a Pencil, Standing by the Fall of Fyers, Near Loch-Ness' are yet another attempt of the travelling poet to do his duty.

We then come to a rather unexpected poem: 'On the Birth of a Posthumous Child, Born in Peculiar Circumstances of Family-Distress'. It is a simple poem in Scots, with an unforced emotion expressing itself with an almost biblical directness:

> May He who gives the rain to pour,
> And winds the blast to blaw,
> Protect thee frae the driving shower,
> The bitter frost and snaw.

Finally, there is 'The Whistle', an account of the bacchanalian contest held at Friar's Carse, at which the man who remained sober enough to blow the whistle after his companions had drunk themselves under the table was to keep the whistle as a trophy. The contestants were Sir Robert Lowrie, Robert Riddell, and Alexander Ferguson of Craigdarroch, who proved the victor. The poem, a lively but crude ballad, meant to be sung, is prefixed by an amusing prose note by Burns giving the history of the whistle from the time when it was brought to Scotland by 'a matchless champion of Bacchus' who came over with Anne of Denmark, the Danish queen of James VI. The poem is in standard English, in that jingling tradition which survived so long in English verse. The last two verses will sufficiently indicate its tone of rather shabby conviviality:

> Next uprose our Bard, like a prophet in drink: –
> 'Craigdarroch, thou'lt soar when creation shall sink!
> But if thou would flourish immortal in rhyme,
> Come – one bottle more – and have at the sublime!
>
> 'Thy line, that have struggled for freedom with Bruce,
> Shall heroes and patriots ever produce:
> So thine be the laurel, and mine be the bay;
> The field thou hast won, by yon bright god of day!'

It will be seen, then, that, except for 'Tam o' Shanter' and 'Green Grow the Rashes, O', neither the 1787 nor the 1793 volume added materially to Burns's stature as a poet. The Kilmarnock volume remained the essential core of subsequent editions in the poet's lifetime, the chief evidence to contemporaries of Burns's poetic abilities, and his chief claim to fame as a published poet. But to say this is to ignore the songs, which, ever since Burns's meeting with Johnson during his first

Edinburgh visit, claimed most of his poetic energies. It is in his songs that his growth as a poet after 1786 can chiefly be traced, as it is his songs that have spread his reputation throughout the world. An account of Burns's poetry without a full discussion of his achievement as a song writer is like *Hamlet* without the Prince of Denmark, or, what is even less excusable, water without whisky.

But before we discuss Burns's better-known songs, there is an aspect of his art which claims some consideration, though editors and biographers have hitherto fought shy of it. Burns was a master of bawdry and produced for the private edification of his friends some of the finest examples of that underground art ever to have reached the expert in what is politely classified as *curiosa*. His interest, however, was not that of the timidly prurient representative of respectability who goes secretly to obscene literature in order to indulge in sexual fantasies and so exploit his own frustrations. Burns enjoyed sex with a huge enjoyment; it was for him one of the most exciting elements – perhaps *the* most exciting – in human experience, and while he explored its emotional aspects in some of the most tender and passionate love lyrics ever written, he also produced with equal gusto and with equal skill remarkable lyrical comments on the purely physical aspect of the relation between the sexes.

There has always been a tradition of lyrical obscenity among the Scottish peasantry, a tradition which Puritanism could drive underground but never stamp out. The old medieval goliardic tradition – the tradition of the wandering scholars, the songs of drinking and love-making that have been handed down, not by the peasantry, but through the universities – has also remained alive in Scotland to a greater degree than in most European countries. A student who proceeds today from a Scottish to an English university will find in the latter a much sparser repertoire of bawdy songs, and many of those that are known will be Scots. (Anybody who has heard one hundred and fifty-six verses of 'The Ball of Kirriemuir', sung at Balliol will appreciate this point.) Academic and popular obscenity came together at more than one point in Scottish history, and both traditions were available to Burns, for all his lack of formal education. His experience with the Crochallan Fencibles at Edinburgh must have rounded out his education in these matters that had been so effectively begun in the Ayrshire countryside.

Nevertheless, the folk tradition was more important for Burns than the academic, in this as in other spheres. In the erotic folk poetry of Scotland there is an amazing variety of picturesque imagery, as well as a hilarious ingenuity in handling the most elemental of all themes. Sex is handled not with earnest obscenity but with lively humour:

> She let him in sae cannily,
> She let him in sae privily,
> She let him in sae cannily,
> To do the thing, you ken, jo.
>
> But ere a' was done, and a' was said,
> Out fell the bottom of the bed;
> The lassie lost her maidenhead,
> And her mither heard the din, jo.

This is from an old song, 'Let Me in This Ae Night', which Burns worked over more than once and from which he made an effective dramatic love lyric with no trace of obscenity (it is generally entitled 'O Lassie, Are Ye Sleepin Yet?'). But when Burns 'purified' obscene songs he did not as a rule forget the original versions but worked on them in a different way for a different audience. *The Merry Muses of Caledonia* preserves many of the results of this side of his activity.

A great deal of nonsense has been talked about *The Merry Muses* – a title, incidentally, which was preserved in a number of inaccurate nineteenth-century editions which included any other bawdy songs the printer could lay his hands on. Editor after editor has apologized for, concealed, or made sententious remarks about this side of Burns's poetic and editorial activity, and the impression is generally given either that Burns preserved a few old songs of this kind as examples of the originals which he worked from and purified or that they represented a monstrous aberration which no decent man should dwell on. The simple fact is that Burns, like many other men before and since, enjoyed this sort of thing, was extremely skilful at it, and quoted examples of it to close friends and correspondents whenever he was in the mood. A succession of nineteenth-century editors suppressed, distorted, rewrote, and apparently sometimes even destroyed his letters in order to obscure his love of a bawdy song and his frank and robust attitude to carnality. In a letter to John M'Murdo, written from Dumfries in December, 1793, Burns wrote, according to Dr. Currie, who first transcribed the letter:

> I think I once mentioned something of a collection of Scots songs I have for some years been making: I send you a perusal of what I have got together. I could not conveniently spare them above five or six days, and five or six glances of them will probably more than suffice you. A very few of them are my own. . . .

As long as the manuscript of this letter remained untraced, Currie's text was accepted as authentic. It was used by Professor Ferguson in his edition of Burns's letters. But the original manuscript has since turned up and has been examined by Professor Ferguson, who reports that the sentence 'A very few of them are my own' does not appear in Burns's letter to M'Murdo. 'That sentence', he comments, 'is one of Currie's most brazen and successful interpolations'. The collection referred to in the letter is, of course, *The Merry Muses*, and by his interpolation Currie was trying to dissociate Burns from the collection as much as possible. As a matter of fact, the majority of the poems in *The Merry Muses* are traditional, or improvements of traditional pieces, and it would thus be true to say that a minority of them are Burns's own. But a fair number are by Burns himself, and his hand can be suspected in many of the others.

Burns's letters to Robert Cleghorn, a member of the Crochallan Fencibles and evidently a connoisseur of bawdry, contain the fullest evidence of this side of his talent. Here is a typical one, dated October 25 (probably 1793):

> I have just bought a quire of Post, & I am determined, my Dear Cleghorn, to give you the maidenhead of it. – Indeed that is all my reason for, & all that I can propose to give you by, this present scrawl. – From my late hours last night, & the dripping fogs & damn'd east-wind of this stupid day, I have left me as little soul as an oyster. – 'Sir John, you are so fretful, you cannot live long'. – 'Why, there is it! Come, sing me a BAUDY-SONG to make me merry!!!' –

> Act Sederunt of the Session – A Scots Ballad –

> Tune – O'er the muir amang the heather –

>> In Edinburgh town they've made a law,
>> In Edinburgh at the Court o' Session,
>> That standin' p——ks are fautors a',
>> And guilty o' a high transgression.

>> Decreet[1] o' the Court o' Session,
>> Act Sederunt o' the Session,
>> That standin' p——ks are fautors a',
>> And guilty o' a high transgression.

And they've provided dungeons deep,
    Ilk lass has ane in her possession,
Until the fautors wail and weep,
    There shall they lie for their transgression.

Decreet o' the Court o' Session,
    Act Sederunt o' the Session.
The rogues in pouring tears shall weep,
    By Act Sederunt o' the Session.-

Well! the Law is good for Something, since we can make a B——dy song out of it. - (N.B. I never made anything of it in any other way -) There is, there must be, some truth in original sin. - My violent propensity to B——dy convinces me of it. - Lack a day! if that species of Composition be the Sin against 'the Haly Ghaist', 'I am the most offending soul alive.' - Mair for taiken, A fine chiel, a hand-wail'd friend & crony o' my ain, gat o'er the lugs in loove wi' a braw, bonie, fodgel hizzie frae the English-side, weel-ken'd i' the burgh of Annan by the name o' Bonnie Mary; & I tauld the tale as follows.- N.B. The chorus is auld –

and here Burns gives another bawdy song, which concludes the letter.

The ingenuity of imagery which characterizes the song quoted here is characteristic both of Burns's own bawdy poetry and of Scottish folk bawdry in general. There is another kind of bawdiness in Burns which has nothing to do with the folk tradition. This can be illustrated by a passage from a letter he wrote to George Thomson in January, 1795:

Some years ago, when I was young, & by no means the saint I am now, I was looking over, in company with a belle lettre friend, a Magazine Ode to Spring, when my friend fell foul of the recurrence of the same thoughts, & offered me a bet that it was impossible to produce an Ode to Spring on an original plan. - I accepted it, & pledged myself to bring in the verdant fields, - the budding flowers, - the chrystal streams, - the melody of the groves, - & a love-story into the bargain, & yet be original. Here follows the piece, & wrote for music too!

    Ode to Spring – Tune, The tither morn. –

    When maukin bucks, at early f——s,
        In dewy grass are seen, Sir,
    And birds, on boughs, take off their m——s,
        Amang the leaves sae green, Sir;

Latona's sun looks liquorish on
   Dame Nature's grand impètus,
Till his p——go rise, then westward flies
   To r——ger Madame Thetis.

Two more stanzas follow, in which Burns takes off the conventional ode to Spring of the period with remarkable skill. By keeping the tone and imagery of a characteristic sentimental piece in the genteel tradition, and at the same time describing in meticulous detail and with outrageous obscenity the love making of Dame Nature and Madame Thetis and of Damon and Sylvia, he passes a critical comment on the whole tradition of odes to Spring. This is obscenity used ironically for purposes of literary criticism.

There is no need to go through all of Burns's obscene poems in order to demonstrate his skill and felicity in this branch of his art, but mention must at least be made of 'The Court of Equity', 'When Princes and Prelates', and 'The Patriarch'. The first of these describes the sitting of a mock court, presided over by Burns and composed in addition of his friends Smith and Richmond, to try the case of 'Coachman Dow and Clockie Brown', who are accused of acts which 'stain the fornicator's honour'. The poem, in lively octosyllabic couplets, has a wonderful time with Scots legal phraseology and with the technical terms of clockmaking. The vigour and ingenuity of the language used to describe the actual offences are remarkable:

> First, Clockie Brown, there's witness borne,
> And affidavit made and sworn,
> That ye hae wrought a hurly-burly,
> In Jeanie Mitchell's turlie-whurlie,
> And graizl'd at her regulator,
> Till a' her wheels gang glitter-clatter;
> And, further still, you cruel Vandal –
> A tale might e'en in hell be scandal –
> That ye hae made repeated trials,
> Wi' drogs and draps in doctors' vials,
> Mixed, as ye thought, in fell infusion,
> Your ain begotten wean to poosion;
> And yet ye are sae scant o' grace,
> As daur to lift your brazen face;
> And offer here to tak' your aith,
> Ye never lifted Jeanie's claith;

> But though ye should yoursel' manswear,
> Laird Wilson's sclates can witness bear,
> Last Mauchline February Fair,
> That Jeanie's masts ye laid them bare,
> And ye had furled up her sails,
> And was at play at heads and tails.

This is scurrilous stuff, but it is full of life and full of wit. Sandy Dow, whose crime was simple fornication, is let off more easily than Clockie [i.e., clockmaker] Brown:

> Your crime – a manly deed we trow it,
> For men, and men alone, can do it,
> And he's nae man that won't avow it;
> Therefore, confess, and join our core,
> And keep reproach outside the door,
> For in denial persevering,
> Is to a scoundrel's name adhering;
> The best o' men hae been surprised,
> The doucest women been advised,
> The cleverest lads hae had a trick o't,
> The bonniest lassies ta'en a lick o't,
> Kings hae been proud our name to own,
> As adding glory to their crown,
> The rhyming sons o' bleak Parnassus,
> *mad*   Were aye red-wud about the lasses. . . .

'When Princes and Prelates' (entitled 'Poor Bodies Hae Naething but Mow [copulation]' in *The Merry Muses*) is written to the tune of 'The Campbells Are Coming', and makes the point, with numerous lively illustrations, that the most exalted personages engage in this basic activity. It ends with a toast to the King and Queen which must be unique among loyal toasts:

> Then fill up your glasses,
> Ye sons of Parnassus,
> This toast I'm sure you'll allow, allow,
> Here's to Geordie our King,
> And Charlotte his Queen,
> And lang may they live for to mow, mow, mow.

Chorus
And why shouldna poor bodies mow, mow, mow?
And why shouldna poor bodies mow?
The rich they hae siller, and houses, and land,
Poor bodies hae naething but mow.

'The Patriarch' is a less interesting and probably an earlier poem, but it is worth noting as another of the poems in which Burns sets exalted personages (in this case biblical figures) in a realistic context of physical love-making and thus brings out humorously the contrast between social or moral pretensions and actual behaviour. Other writers may talk of the democracy of the grave; Burns found it more amusing to contemplate the democracy of sex.

Of the simple erotic folk poems which Burns turned into charming and tender love lyrics, it can be said only that Burns's transformation of them did not mean that he did not enjoy them in their original form or that he recognized an impassable barrier between the bawdy and the tenderly protective. Burns saw this aspect of life steadily and saw it whole, as his letter to Richmond on the birth of twins makes clear. Part of the charm of such songs as 'O, Wha My Babie Clouts Will Buy' derives from this combination of enjoyment of sex and of its consequences; Burns did not have to deny or forget the physical aspects of sex in order to be able to rejoice in his fatherhood or to write passionate love songs, and there are indeed undertones of the purely physical in the most 'respectable' of his love lyrics. It is this which makes him so superior as a love poet to both the neoclassic celebrators of Chloe and Celia and such Romantic poets as Shelley.

The crowning glory of Burns's achievement is, by common consent, his songs; yet he was little known as a song writer in his lifetime. Only a handful of songs appeared in the Kilmarnock and Edinburgh editions, and of these perhaps two gave real indication of his stature as a song writer. 'Green Grow the Rashes, O', which appeared in the Edinburgh edition, we have already had occasion to discuss. Of the three songs in the Kilmarnock volume, only 'Corn Rigs' is worth examination, and that is one of Burns's finest. Written to a lively old Scots tune (though the tune has been claimed also for the north of England) and suggested by an 'old chorus' (which Ramsay had used in a not too successful song – adversely criticized by Burns – at the end of *The Gentle Shepherd*,) 'Corn Rigs' is as perfect an expression of the mood of simple surrender to the moment of physical passion as exists in any literature. The lightly

etched-in country setting, the swinging lilt of the chorus (with its
rhythm of the reel), the happy, assured quality of the double rhymes,
and the gradual movement, through a description of the successive
phases of the action to the final climactic affirmation, show such mastery
of this kind of lyric expression that Henley and Henderson refused to
believe that the song could be as early as Burns said it was in his autobiographical letter to Dr. Moore.

As with all Burns's songs, the reader must remember that it was
written to a tune and meant to be sung; the very movement of the verse
suggests this:

> It was upon a Lammas night,
>> When corn rigs are bonie,
> Beneath the moon's unclouded light,
>> I held awa to Annie:

careless

> The time flew by wi' tentless heed,
>> Till 'tween the late and early,
> Wi' sma' persuasion she agreed
>> To see me thro' the barley.

> Chorus
> Corn rigs, an' barley rigs,
>> An' corn rigs are bonie:
> I'll ne'er forget that happy night,
>> Amang the rigs wi' Annie.

The magnificent abandon of the final verse, with its reckless affirmation,
ends the poem on a triumphant note:

> I hae been blythe wi' comrades dear;
>> I hae been merry drinking;

possessions

> I hae been joyfu' gath'rin gear;
>> I hae been happy thinking:
> But a' the pleasures e'er I saw,
>> Tho' three items doubl'd fairly,
> That happy night was worth them a',
>> Amang the rigs o' barley.

A modern critic has remarked of this verse that it 'is a mere effusion of
thoughtless emotion, with a commonplace judgment tagged on to it

exalting feeling at the expense of everything else',[2] which may be true
but is quite beside the point; it is not the profundity of the philosophy
but the ability to recapture the experience that is so remarkable, and few
will deny that Burns recaptures it to perfection, and, further, that in
expressing it in this form he gives it at the same time a precision and a
significance wholly lacking in the experience outside art. If one went
through Burns's songs paraphrasing their philosophy, one would indeed
have a sad collection of moral or other platitudes; but a love song is not
to be judged by the depth or originality of its ethics. This seems an
obvious enough point, but it is worth making in view of the charges
against Burns made by one of Scotland's foremost critics.

We have already noted Burns's meeting with James Johnson in April,
1787, and his subsequent undertaking to furnish Johnson with songs for
his *Scots Musical Museum*, which eventually led to Burns's becoming the
virtual editor of the work. Johnson had no qualifications for this undertaking except enthusiasm, and even that eventually began to wane, so
that Burns had to keep prodding him. Stephen Clarke, the Edinburgh
organist who was in charge of the musical arrangement of the airs, was
both lazy and careless and held the work up many times by his indolence
and on at least one occasion by his losing several irreplaceable old songs
which Burns had sent him. Burns's part in the *Museum* was therefore
much greater than that of contributing poet; he kept the project going,
enlarged its scope, 'collected, begged, borrowed, and stole' songs from
all quarters, many of which he reshaped before sending to Johnson, and
in addition contributed a vast number of his own.

The first volume of the *Museum* was almost ready to go to press when
Johnson and Burns met, so that, published in 1787, it contained only two
songs by Burns, 'Green Grow the Rashes, O' and 'Young Peggy Blooms
Our Bonniest Lass'. Volume two appeared in 1788, with a hundred
songs of which forty were Burns's. Burns, too, wrote the preface to this,
as well as to the next two volumes. 'Ignorance and Prejudice may perhaps affect to sneer at the simplicity of the poetry or music of some of
these pieces,' he wrote; 'but their having been for ages the favourites of
Nature's Judges – the Common People, was to the Editor a sufficient
test of their merit.' The third volume appeared in 1790, with a 'flaming
Preface'. 'Consciousness of the well-known merit of our Scottish Music',
Burns wrote, 'and the national fondness of a Scotch-man for the productions of his own country, are at once the Editor's motive and apology
for this Undertaking.' Over fifty songs in this volume were by Burns.
Volume four appeared in 1792, with about half of its hundred songs by

Burns, and the fifth volume – Burns having in the meantime undertaken to help also with George Thomson's *Select Scottish Airs* – not until 1796, after the poet's death, although Burns had worked hard on it and had seen it well advanced towards publication before he died. It is significant that after Johnson was left on his own, even though he had plenty of material on hand left over from previous volumes, he took almost seven years to bring out the sixth and final volume.

The vast majority of his own contributions to the *Museum* were never publicly acknowledged by Burns. The index to the third volume cites him as author of six of the songs, and six songs are similarly all with which he is credited in the index to volume four;[3] fifteen songs are given to him in the index to volume five. In the sixth volume Burns is credited with twenty-six songs in the index and the text. He arranged a rough code to indicate his own work to those in the know, marking his own songs 'R', 'B', or 'X' and marking with a 'Z' old songs which he had altered or reshaped. But it is impossible to use this key to identify Burns's contributions; many songs which are clearly his are not marked with any of these letters, while the sign 'Z' can mean anything from virtual total composition through every degree of patching and remodelling to the slightest kind of editorial handling. The fact is that Burns did not wish the extent of his original work to be known to the public. 'There is no reason for telling everybody this piece of intelligence,' he wrote to Mrs. Dunlop after admitting that in 'a good many' of the songs 'little more than the Chorus is ancient.'

There is extant a manuscript in Burns's hand headed 'List of Songs for 3ᵈ Volume of the Scots Musical Museum'. It contains a list of ninety-four titles, after thirty-four of which the words 'Mr. Burns's old words' are written. The phrase might at first sight be taken to mean that these were songs that Burns was merely transmitting, without having worked on them himself, but in fact wherever an earlier version is extant we can see that Burns has remodelled the songs considerably and sometimes completely rewritten them. The sixth song on Burns's list is 'White Cockade', which duly appears in the third volume of the *Museum*. If the *Museum* text (among those described as 'Mr. Burns's old words') be put beside an older version of this song (for example, the version printed by David Herd, where it will be found as 'My Love Was Born in Aberdeen') it will be seen that Burns, by altering the last two lines of each stanza, has made a Jacobite song out of a song which had previously no Jacobite associations, and set it to a spirited reel tune. The original version went to the tune 'Over the Hills and Far Away', used by Gay in *The Beggars' Opera*. This is only one example, and the change here, though significant, is slighter than many of the changes which we know to have been made when an old song became 'Mr. Burns's old words'. 'John Anderson My Jo' is described in the same phrase, but is in fact, as we shall see, a completely new version of an old bawdy song of the same title. Sometimes a song described as 'Mr. Burns's old words' in this manuscript list is definitely credited to Burns in reprints of the *Museum* made by Johnson after Burns's death: 'My Wife She Dang Me', 'The Gallant Weaver', 'For A' That and A' That' (not the well-known 'Is There for Honest Poverty', with a similar chorus) are among the songs described in the manuscript as 'Mr. Burns's old words' and later described by Johnson as 'written for this work by Robert Burns'.

Ten of the ninety-four songs in the manuscript list are claimed by Burns as his own, with the phrase 'Mr. Burns's words' or some similar indication. Two are definitely known from other sources to be original poems by Burns though not so claimed here. Opposite eleven of the titles it is noted that Burns sent or gave the words or the old words. Songs so described are occasionally by other poets (Lapraik, for example), occasionally traditional, and sometimes apparently remodelled in some degree by Burns. (Opposite one item, Burns writes: 'Mr. Burns gave the ballad & corrected it with his own hand.') Altogether, of these ninety-four songs – most of which appear in the *Museum*, though some in later volumes than the third – forty-seven are demonstrably either by Burns or altered by him,,and others may have received his editorial attention. Yet many of these forty-seven have never been included in collected editions of Burns's poems.

It is clear from this manuscript list, which was apparently intended for Johnson and is full of suggestions concerning where the best texts of older poems were to be found, that Burns was editor, adapter, arranger, and creator for Johnson's *Museum* to an extent that he never publicly admitted. After the poet's death Johnson did what he could to give Burns credit for his own poems, when he added to some of the songs as listed on the title page the words, 'Written for this work by Robert Burns'; but only a fraction of Burns's original work is so indicated. During Burns's lifetime the songs in the *Museum* were (except for some indications of authorship in the index) all printed anonymously. Oddly enough, though his patriotic enthusiasm for collecting and creating Scottish songs made him quite willing to remain anonymous himself, he felt that Johnson needed the spur of personal fame. He wrote him in November, 1788: 'Perhaps you may not find your account, *lucratively*, in this business; but you are the Patriot for the Music of your Country; and I am certain, Posterity will look on themselves as highly indebted to your Publick spirit. – Be not in a hurry, let us go on correctly; and your name shall be immortal.'

Some of Burns's most characteristic contributions to the *Museum* were songs written to Scottish dance tunes which are not known to have had words to them previously. The number of traditional song tunes was limited, though Burns added to it by discovering new ones and having them taken down from the singing of country people. James Dick, in the preface to his edition of Burns's songs, estimated that 'in all the various collections published up to 1787 there were not two hundred different Scottish airs printed with verses', and he adds that 'of these Johnson had utilized a good proportion in the first volume of the *Museum*'.[4] The result was that Burns turned his hand to setting words to airs which had hitherto only been known as dance tunes. In doing so he often changed the tempo in order to bring out the full quality of the tune. His ear was remarkably sensitive to rhythms of dance music and to the potentialities of dance melodies as airs for songs. By slowing down a fast-tripping reel tune, often in a minor key, he was able to bring out an elegaic quality that was concealed in a faster tempo. Activity of this kind required a fineness of ear and a peculiar genius for wedding words to music very rare among poets. Many a composer has successfully written music for existing words, but the poet who successfully writes words for existing tunes is much less easy to find.

Burns's association with George Thomson was in many ways less satisfactory than that with Johnson. Unlike the humble Johnson, Thomson was educated and genteel, anxious to refine Scots out of Scots songs and to substitute conventional neoclassic inanities. He never frankly confessed this motive to Burns (he knew that if he did Burns would certainly have nothing to do with the project) but approached him with tact, after having secured a letter of introduction from Alexander Cunningham. His plan, he wrote Burns in September, 1792, was to bring out a collection of 'the most favourite of our national melodies', with accompaniments arranged by Joseph Pleyel, 'the most agreeable composer living'. He was distressed because some charming melodies were 'united to mere nonsense and doggerel', while others had words 'so loose and indelicate as cannot be sung in decent company'. To remove this reproach', he flatteringly added, 'would be an easy task to the author of "The Cotter's Saturday Night".' (Had he been more sensitive to the nature of Burns's genius, he would have realized that it was not the author of 'The Cotter's Saturday Night' who should be appealed to where song writing was involved but that rather different character, the author of 'Green Grow the Rashes, O'.) Thomson ended with a frank appeal for Burns to write 'twenty or twenty-five songs, suitable to the particular melodies which I am prepared to send you'. He would pay 'any reasonable price you shall please to demand for it.'

Burns did not pause to scrutinize the implications of Thomson's letter, but replied at once from Dumfries with immense enthusiasm:

I have just this moment got your letter. – As the request you make to me will positively add to my enjoyments in complying with it, I shall enter into your undertaking with all the small portion of abilities I have, strained to their utmost exertion by the impulse of Enthusiasm. – Only, don't hurry me: 'Deil tak the hindmost' is by no means the Cri de guerre of my Muse. – Will you, as I am inferiour to none of you in enthusiastic attachment to the Poetry & Music of old Caledonia, &, since you request it, have chearfully promised my mite of assistance, will you let me have a list of your airs, with the first line of the verses you intend for them, that I may have an opportunity of suggesting any alteration that may occur to me – you know 'tis in the way of my trade – still leaving you, Gentlemen, the undoubted right of Publishers, to approve, or reject, at your pleasure in your own Publication? – I say, the first line of the verses, because if they are verses that have appeared in any of our Collections of songs, I know them & can have recourse to them. Apropos, if you are for *English* verses, there is, on my part, an end of the matter. – Whether in the simplicity of *the Ballad*, or the pathos of *the Song*, I can only hope to please myself in being allowed at least a sprinkling of our native tongue. English verses, particularly the works of Scotsmen, that have merit, are certainly very eligible. – Tweedside; Galashiels, viz. Ah, the poor shepherd's mournful fate &c. Gilderoy, viz. Ah, Chloris! could I now but sit, except, excuse my vanity, you should for Gilderoy prefer my own song, 'From thee, Eliza, I must go' &c. all these you cannot mend; but such insipid stuff as, 'To Fanny fair could I impart' &c. usually set to The Mill, Mill, O, 'tis a disgrace to the Collections in which it has already appeared, & would doubly disgrace a Collection that will have the very superior merit of yours. – But more of this in the farther prosecution of the Business, if I am to be called on for my strictures & amendments – I say, amendments, for I will not *alter* except where I myself at least think that I *amend*. –

As to any remuneration, you may think my Songs either *above*, or *below* price; for they shall absolutely be the one or the other. – In the honest enthusiasm with which I embark in your undertaking, to talk of money, wages, fee, hire, &c. would be downright Sodomy of

Soul! – A proof of each of the Songs that I compose or amend, I shall receive as a favour. – In the rustic phrase of the Season, 'Gude speed the wark!'

This is a remarkable outburst, and after receiving it Thomson saw that he could count on the poet for much more than improved words for some twenty or twenty-five melodies. It was not long before Thomson, under the influence of Burns's enthusiasm, decided to make a radical alteration in his plans, which had not in fact been as definite as he had pretended in his letter. 'The number of songs which I had originally in view was limited, but I now resolve to include every Scotch air and song worth singing, leaving none behind but mere gleanings', he wrote in January, 1793.

Burns's second letter to Thomson indicates the difference in attitude between the two men: 'Let me tell you', he began abruptly, 'that you are too fastidious in your ideas of Songs & ballads'. Burns was from now on to be fighting continually against Thomson's 'improving 'zeal; with patience but firmness he explained in letter after letter that he would not eliminate some roughness or Scotticism from a song, that he had written a song for the tune he named, not the tune chosen by Thomson, that Thomson had missed some characteristic rhythmic quality which any alteration would eliminate. It is surprising that Burns never lost his temper; the explanation may be that Thomson does not seem to have argued back in defence of his position but made, without comment, many of the changes he wanted, so that a great number of the pieces sent by Burns appear in the *Select Scottish Airs* either set to a tune different from that which Burns intended or with some other change made by Thomson. Occasionally Burns gave in and rewrote a song to please Thomson – as when he rewrote 'Scots Wha Hae' by padding out the last line of each verse in order to enable the song to go to the air chosen by Thomson; fortunately, when the exact words and tune Burns had originally intended were eventually discovered, public opinion forced Thomson to print them.

Burns's correspondence with Thomson provides a fascinating record of his interest in and knowledge of Scots song and Scots music. If any proof were required that Murdoch's description of the young Burns as lacking an ear for music was wholly wrong, these letters give that proof. Burns's sensitivity to the qualities of a melody were remarkable; he could distinguish the subtlest variations between different versions of the same tune and note what effect the slightest change had on its charac-ter. It is clear that Burns did not have a good singing voice, but it is equally clear that he had an excellent ear. There is fairly convincing evidence that he learned to play the fiddle, and it is probable that he used his instrument to assist him in transcribing melodies he had heard. He could certainly read music; he quotes two bars of music in a letter to Thomson. He speaks in these letters with the greatest precision and assurance of crochets and quavers and different kinds of tempo and of the kind of accompaniment required by a specific kind of song.

How much musical education Burns received cannot be determined. The 'sang schools' established in Scotland in the sixteenth and seventeenth centuries did not survive into Burns's day, but some rudiments of musical teaching in connection with congregational singing in Church were maintained. Burns's interest in dancing – which he shared with the Scotland of his day, for eighteenth-century Scotland danced as it has never danced since – must have further cultivated his sense of rhythm and melody. Dancing in Burns's time was equally popular in rustic barns and in city assembly rooms. Currie, writing a few years after Burns's death, vividly described the dancing of Scottish rustics:

. . . The School is usually a barn, and the arena for the performers is generally a clay floor. The dome is lighted by candles stuck in one end of a cloven stick, the other end of which is thrust into the wall. Reels, strathspeys, country-dances, and hornpipes, are here practised. The jig, so much in favour among the English peasantry, has no place among them. The attachment of the people of Scotland of every rank, and particularly of the peasantry, to this amusement, is very great. After the labours of the day are over, young men and women walk many miles in the cold and dreary night of winter, to these country dancing-schools; and the instant that the violin sounds a Scottish, fatigue seems to vanish, the toil-bent rustic becomes erect, his features brighten with sympathy; every nerve seems to thrill with sensation, and every artery to vibrate with life. These rustic performers are indeed less to be admired for grace, than for agility and animation, and their accurate observance of time. Their modes of dancing, as well as their tunes, are common to every rank of Scotland, and are now generally known.

In the Assembly Rooms of Edinburgh, Aberdeen, and other Scottish cities elegant ladies and gentlemen of the highest social pretensions danced, under suitable chaperonage, the same dances that their humbler fellow countrymen danced in barns, and with the same liveliness and enthusiasm. Throughout Burns's life Scotland was humming with dance music, much of which Burns turned into song.

The letters to Thomson provide a running commentary on Scottish song that is as illuminating today as when the letters were written. They show Burns the conscientious craftsman, speaking with the assurance and the technical understanding of one who thoroughly knows his job. 'Every seventh line ends with three syllables', he writes to Thomson about his song, 'O Saw Ye Bonie Lesley', in place of the two in the other lines, but you will see in the sixth bar of the second part, the place where these three syllables will always recur, that the four semiquavers usually sung as one syllable will with the greatest propriety divide into two – thus' (and here he writes out two bars of music). The letters are full of such observations as: 'Duncan Gray is that kind of light-horse gallop of an air, which precludes sentiment.' Frequently we find a firm but courteous refusal to make any alteration: 'I cannot alter the disputed lines in the Mill Mill O. – What you think a defect, I esteem as a positive beauty: so you see how Doctors differ.' 'Dainty Davie – I have heard sung, nineteen thousand, nine hundred, & ninety-nine times, & always with the chorus to the low part of the tune; & nothing, since a Highland wench in the Cowgate once bore me three bastards at a birth, has surprised me so much as your opinion on this subject.' He tries his best to convince Thomson's ear of the points he makes:

I agree with you, as to the air, Craigieburnwood, that a chorus would in some degree spoil the effect; & shall certainly have none in my projected song to it. – It is not, however, a case in point with Rothemurche: there, as in 'Roy's wife of Aldivaloch', a chorus, to my taste, goes well enough. – As to the chorus going first, you know it is so with 'Roy's Wife' also. – In fact, the first part of both tunes, the rhythm is so peculiar & irregular, & on that irregularity depends so much of their beauty, that we must e'en take them with all their wildness, & humour the verse accordingly. – Leaving out the starting-note, in both tunes, has I think an effect that no regularity could counterbalance the want of. – Try

> { O Roy's Wife &c.
> { O Lassie wi' the lint-white locks –

and compare with

> { Roy's Wife of Aldivaloch –
> { Lassie wi' the lint-white locks –

does not the tameness of the prefixed syllable strike you? – In the last case, with the true furor of genius, you strike at once into the wild originality of the air; whereas in the first insipid business it is like the grating screw of the pins before the fiddle is brought in tune. – This is my taste; if I am wrong, I beg pardon of the Cognoscenti. –

Burns spared no pains in collecting folk melodies and transmitting them to Thomson with appropriate words. 'I have still several M.S.S. Scots airs by me, which I have pickt up, mostly from the singing of country lasses. – They please me vastly, but your learned lugs [ears] would perhaps be displeased with the very feature for which I like them.' Further on in the same letter he asks: 'Do you know a fine air, called Jackie Hume's lament? – I have a Song of considerable merit, to that air, . . . I'll inclose you both the Song & tune, as I had them ready to send to Johnson's Museum. – I send you likewise, to me a beautiful little air, which I had taken down from viva voce.' Perhaps the most beautiful of all Scottish song melodies, 'Ca' the Yowes to the Knowes', was discovered by Burns.

Burns was equally interested in the history of the melodies he collected. 'Mr Clarke says that the tune is positively an old Chant of the ROMISH CHURCH', he wrote to Thomson of 'The Grey Goose & the Gled', 'which corroborates the old tradition, that at the Reformation, the Reformers burlesqued much of the old Church Music with setting them to bawdy verses.' Some of the tunes which Burns used were, in fact, derived from old ecclesiastical chants, and in slowing down the tempo Burns was instinctively restoring something of their original quality. Burns handled more recent tunes the same way. 'The Caledonian Hunt's Delight', for example, a reel tune composed by 'Mr. James Millar, Writer in Edinburgh', was slowed down by Burns to the somewhat plaintive melody (marked 'Slow & tender' in the *Museum*) for which he wrote what is now the best known of his several versions of 'Ye Banks and Braes o' Bonnie Doon' (he wrote other songs to this tune as well).

Burns would never write words for a melody until he had made himself completely familiar with it. Discussing the tune, 'Laddie, Lie Near Me', he wrote to Thomson:

. . . I do not know the air; & untill I am compleat master of a tune, in my own singing, (such as it is) I never can compose for it. – My way is: I consider the poetic Sentiment, correspondent to my idea of the musical expression; then chuse my theme; begin one Stanza; when that is composed, which is generally the most difficult part of the business, I walk out, sit down now & then, look out for objects in

Nature around me that are in unison or harmony with the cogitations of my fancy & workings of my bosom; humming every now & then the air with the verses I have framed: when I feel my Muse beginning to jade, I retire to the solitary fireside of my study, & there commit my effusions to paper; swinging, at intervals, on the hind-legs of my elbow-chair, by way of calling forth my own critical strictures, as my pen goes on. –

In spite of the constant irritation provided by Thomson's fatuous suggestions, Burns thoroughly enjoyed himself in this work. 'You cannot imagine', he wrote to Thomson in April, 1793, 'how much this business of composing for your publication has added to my enjoyments. – What with my early attachment to ballads, Johnson's Museum, your book, &c. Ballad-making is now as compleatly my hobby-horse, as ever Fortification was Uncle Toby's; so I'll e'en canter it away till I come to the limit of my race, (God grant that I may take the right side of the winning-post!) & then chearfully looking back on the honest folks with whom I have been happy, I shall say, or sing, 'Sae merry as we a' hae been' – & then, raising my last looks to the whole Human-race, the last voice of Coila shall be – 'Good night & joy be with you a'!' ('Good Night and Joy Be with You A'' was the song used in Scotland in parting at the end of a festivity, until it was superseded by Burns's 'Auld Lang Syne'. But Burns's words, sung throughout the world, are not sung to the air for which Burns wrote them; Burns had originally written them for a different though related air, to which it is set in the *Museum*.)

Thomson despised Johnson and his *Scots Musical Museum* and sometimes retained songs by Burns which he did not intend to use, simply to prevent them from falling into Johnson's hands. Burns, who does not seem to have realized Thomson's attitude on this matter, would request Thomson to return to him songs that he did not wish to use, so that he could give them to Johnson; but Thomson would generally prefer to keep them by him, though unused. These and other tricks made Thomson a much less faithful transmitter than Johnson of Burns's songs and of his intentions with respect to their musical setting; but since Burns's differences with Thomson produced that host of letters in which he commented in detail on about a hundred Scottish songs, defending and explaining his views of their rhythm, diction, musical potentialities, and other aspects, we cannot altogether regret that Thomson was not as complaisant as Johnson.

The first 'set' of Thomson's collection appeared in 1793 (the Preface is dated May 1), with the title *A Select Collection of Original Scottish Airs;* it contained twenty-five airs. The remaining sets were published after Burns's death, and Thomson was free to make what use he liked of the material he had received from Burns. The complete work made five handsome volumes, far superior as a piece of bookmaking to the shabbily produced pages of the *Museum.* On the publication of the first set, Thomson sent Burns a copy, with a letter of thanks and a five-pound note in token of his appreciation. 'Do not return it', he wrote, 'for, by Heaven! if you do, our correspondence is at an end.' To which Burns replied:

I assure you, my dear Sir, that you truly hurt me with your pecuniary parcel. – It degrades me in my own eyes. – However, to return it would savour of bombast affectation; But, as to any more traffic of that D^r & C^r kind, I swear, by that HONOUR which crowns the upright Statue of ROBT BURNS'S INTEGRITY! – On the least motion of it, I will indignantly spurn the by-past transaction, & from that moment commence entire Stranger to you! –

In August of the same year Thomson, not receiving from other expected sources (chiefly John Wolcot, the English versifier who wrote under the name of Peter Pindar) the English songs which, as he wrote Burns, he stood pledged to furnish along with every Scottish song, appealed to Burns to help him out. 'I certainly have got into a scrape if you do not stand my friend', he wrote. 'A couple of stanzas to each air will do as well as half a dozen'. Burns, forgetting that he earlier refused to have anything to do with Thomson's project if Thomson wanted *English* verses, cheerfully replied:

You may readily trust me, my dear Sir, that any exertion in my power, is heartily at your service. – But one thing I must hint to you, the very name of Peter Pindar is of great Service to your Publication; so, get a verse from him now & then, though I have no objection, as well as I can, to bear the burden of the business.

'Bear the burden of the business' is precisely what Burns did, both for Thomson and for Johnson. He sent Thomson song after song, and let him take what he would out of that abundance. In his second letter to Thomson he had made his position on that score clear:

... Now, don't let it enter into your head, that you are under any necessity of taking my verses. – I have long ago made up my mind as

to my own reputation in the business of Authorship; & have nothing
to be pleased, or offended at, in your adoption or rejection of my
verses. – Tho' you should reject one half of what I give you, I shall be
pleased with your adopting t'other half; & shall continue to serve you
with the same assiduity.

Through personal troubles and sharply declining health Burns
'continued to serve with the same assiduity', almost until the day of his
death. 'Alas! my dear Thomson', he wrote some three months before
he died, 'I fear it will be some time ere I tune my lyre again! . . . – Almost ever since I wrote you last, I have known Existence by the pressure
of the heavy hand of Sickness; & have counted time by the repercussions
of PAIN!' Yet in a week or two later he was writing again to Thomson
about 'an air which I have long admired' which he was in the process of
composing verses for. On June 1, less than two months before his death,
he was writing to Johnson, asking about the progress of the fifth volume
of the *Museum* and apologizing for having been prevented by illness
from doing more for the collection 'for some time past'. But he rallied
to sound a note of optimistic encouragement to the dilatory Johnson:
'In the meantime, let us finish what we have so well begun'. On July 4,
when he was at Brow, on the Solway Firth, in a last fantastic attempt to
recover his rapidly waning strength by sea bathing, he wrote to Thomson:

I rec^d your songs: but my health being so precarious nay dangerous-
ly situated, that as a last effort I am here at a sea-bathing quarters. – Besides my inveterate rheumatism, my appetite is quite gone, & I am so
emaciated as to be scarce able to support myself on my own legs. –
Alas! is this a time for me to woo the Muses? However, I am still
anxiously willing to serve your work; & if possible shall try. . . . – You
will see my alterations & remarks on the margin of each song. . . .

There is only one further letter of Burns's to Thomson, and this was
written on his deathbed, in a mood of sudden panic:

After all my boasted independence, curst necessity compels me to
implore you for five pounds. – A cruel scoundrel of a Haberdasher to
whom I owe an account, taking it into his head that I am dying, has
commenced a process , & will infallibly put me in to jail. – Do, for
God's sake, send me that sum, & that by return of post. – Forgive me
this earnestness, but the horrors of a jail have made me half distracted.

– I do not ask all this gratuitously; for upon returning health, I hereby promise & engage to furnish you with five pounds' worth of the neatest song-genius you have seen. – I tryed my hand on Rothiemurche this morning. – The measure is so difficult, that it is impossible to infuse much genius into the lines – they are on the other side. Forgive me!

'I tryed my hand on Rothiemurche this morning'. He knew he was dying – he died nine days later – yet he was still discussing songs and projecting more work on them. This is surely the final proof that Johnson and Thomson were catalysts who released in Burns an enormous creative and critical energy in the field of song writing, an energy unparalleled in degree or quality in either English or Scottish literature. It was in the employment of this energy that he found not only relief from pain and sickness and misunderstanding by both friends and enemies but also release from his split personality – from the basic and perpetual conflict between Rab Mossgiel and Caledonia's Bard, between the son of William Burnes and the Caledonian Hunt's Delight, between the lover of Jean Armour and the correspondent of Clarinda, between the peasant and the man of letters. In doing so he produced some of the finest songs in any language.

We have already discussed several of Burns's earliest songs and noted his remarks on Scottish song in the Commonplace Book. It remains for us to single out a few of the more interesting songs which appeared in the *Museum* and the *Select Scottish Airs* and to say something of their quality.

The first of Burns's songs in volume two of the *Museum* is: 'When Guilford Good Our Pilot Stood', which appeared in the Edinburgh Edition with the note 'Tune: Gilliecrankie': it is set to a different tune in the *Museum*, since 'Killicrankie' had already been used. 'To the Weaver's Gin Ye Go', a trivial song based on an old chorus, interesting chiefly as an illustration of Burns's improvizations for tunes that lacked words, is the next one of his, and is more interesting as a song. 'The chorus of this song is old', he wrote in the interleaved *Museum* he presented to Robert Riddell, 'the rest of it is mine. – Here, once for all, let me apologize for many silly compositions of mine in this work. Many beautiful airs wanted words; in the hurry of other avocations, if I could string a parcel of rhymes together any thing near tolerable, I was fain to let them pass. He must be an excellent poet indeed, whose every performance is excellent.' The tune is characteristically Scottish, with that mixture of liveliness and plaintiveness that distinguishes so many reel tunes; all that need be said about Burns's words is that, trivial though they are, they sound the authentic folk note and show how effortlessly Burns could, as it were, reproduce the folk mind.

'Whistle, an' I'll Come to Ye My Lad' appears both in the *Museum* and in *Select Scottish Airs*, the version Burns sent to Thomson being somewhat altered. The tune, an original and spirited air in six-eight time, fascinated Burns, and for this reason, after having produced one version for Johnson, he rewrote the song for Thomson. 'Is Whistle & I'll Come to You, My Lad – one of your airs?' he wrote to Thomson in August, 1793. 'I admire it much; & yesterday I set the following verses to it.' As with so many of Burns's songs, its quality cannot be judged by the words alone; it is meant to be sung, and the words fit the curve of the tune precisely, echoing its tripping notes with appropriate verbal devices, so that simply looked at as a set of words it loses much of its liveliness. The repetition of the key line in the chorus is prevented from sounding like mere reiteration by the way the tune develops; the last line rises to a climax under the influence of the music, so that the whole chorus can be recognized as mounting to a high pitch of resolution. The words alone (we quote the later version) scarcely achieve this, though they have a fine swing to them:

> O whistle, and I'll come to you, my lad,
> O whistle, and I'll come to you, my lad;
> Tho' father and mother and a' should gae mad,
> O whistle, and I'll come to you, my lad.

Again, the repetition of the last line of each verse loses much of its effect without the music, where the development of the tune takes the verse home in the second repetition, giving new significance and assurance to the utterance:

watch   But warily tent, when ye come to court me,
-gate; ajar   And come na unless the back-yett be a-jee;
then   Syne up the back-style, and let naebody see,
              And come, as ye were na coming to me,
              And come, as ye were na coming to me.

The song that follows this in the Museum is one of the most perfect examples of Burns's reshaping of an old fragment. 'I'm O'er Young to Marry Yet' is based on an old and ubiquitous folk theme. 'The chorus of this song is old – the rest of it, such as it is, is mine', wrote Burns in the interleaved *Museum*. It is set to a lively reel tune (which is not, however, the melody to which it is now generally sung).

only child	I am my mammy's ae bairn,
strange	Wi' unco folk I weary, Sir,
	And lying in a man's bed,
afraid;	I'm fley'd it make me irie, Sir.
eerie	

> I'm o'er young, I'm o'er young,
>   I'm o'er young to marry yet;
> I'm o'er young, 'twad be a sin
>   To tak me frae my mammy yet.

> Hallowmass is come and gane,
>   The nights are lang in winter, Sir;
> And you an' I in ae bed.
>   In trowth, I dare na venture, Sir.

> I'm o'er young, etc.

	Fu' loud and shrill the frosty wind
woods	Blaws thro' the leafless timmer, Sir;
way	But if ye come this gate again,
older be by	I'll aulder be gin simmer, Sir.
summer	

> I'm o'er young, etc.

The lilting rhythms, the archness of tone, the neatly turned climax not only demonstrate Burns's craftsmanship as a song writer but show how perfectly he could reproduce the best qualities of genuine folk song. The trick of ending every second line of the verse with 'Sir' is hard to achieve by the conscious artist without giving the effect of awkward imitation of the antique, but in this poem (as in many of Burns's songs where he ends the line with monosyllables such as 'O') there is nothing of the synthetic folk element that we get in many of the nineteenth-century ballad imitations; the diction flows with a happy directness and a fine dramatic feeling, while the monosyllable 'Sir' provides just what the poem needs to bring the rhythms of the reel into the diction and fit the piece perfectly to its tune. All these monosyllabic line endings in Burns's songs help to reproduce the effect of the dance tune in the actual spoken rhythms, as well as to fit the words to the precise curve of the melody.

'The Birks of Aberfeldy' (described in Johnson's later printing of the *Museum* as having been 'written for this work by R. Burns') is a more conventional effort, a product of one of his tours in 1787; but it is worth noting as deriving from Burns's interest in Scottish topography, his desire to celebrate Scottish places in song. It is based on an old song, 'The Birks of Abergeldie', to whose fine melody Burns set his words. Except for the chorus, there is little of the folk element in Burns's version, which consists of a rather formal description of the scenery and works up to the kind of climax we have noted in many of his poems:

> Let Fortune's gifts at random flee,
> They ne'er shall draw a wish frae me,
> Supremely blest wi' love and thee
> In the birks of Aberfeldy.

The ending of each verse with the phrase 'the birks of Aberfeldy' is achieved with a certain amount of deftness, and the song as a whole has the charm of a well-turned set piece; but the melody rather than the words has kept it popular in Scotland.

Another popular piece, also described as 'written for this work by Robert Burns', is 'McPherson's Farewell', deriving ultimately from a broadside purporting to give the last words of a notorious robber and murderer hanged at Inverness at the beginning of the century. Burns's lines (wholly original, except for a suggestion in the chorus) have a fine swagger to them; they are in a rhetorical tradition equally removed from the folk tradition of 'I'm O'er Young to Marry Yet' and the album tradition of 'The Birks of Aberfeldy'. The song goes to a rather unusual slowed-down reel tune known as early as 1710 as 'McFarsence's Testament' and entitled 'McPherson's Farewell' in eighteenth-century collections of Scottish airs before the *Museum*. The quality of the song is summed up in the chorus:

went
lively tune

> Sae rantingly, sae wantonly,
> Sae dauntingly gae'd he.
> He play'd a spring, and danc'd it round,
> Below the gallows-tree.

The next of Burns's songs in the second volume of the *Museum* is 'The Highland Lassie O', a love song to Mary Campbell; its biographical interest we have noted in an earlier chapter. The chorus is in the purest folk tradition:

> Within the glen sae bushy, O,
> Aboon the plain sae rashy O,
> I set me down wi' right gude will
> To sing my Highland Lassie O.

The verses are an interesting blend of simple folk elements and neoclassic elegance, demonstrating how easily Burns could move from one to the other – from a line like 'O were yon hills and valley mine', which has the real folk ring, to 'By secret truth and honour's band', which derives from a very different source. The total effect, however, is not as incongruous as might be expected; the poem as a whole emerges as a formal but not unpleasing expression of exuberant love. It is less happily fitted to its tune than are most of Burns's songs.

These first five of Burns's songs in volume two of the *Museum* – to ignore the opening ballad – will perhaps show something of the range of Burns as a song writer and the extremes of folk idiom and neoclassic expression between which he so freely moved. It would be interesting as well as pleasant for the present writer, to go through all of Burns's songs in this way, discussing their idiom, their relation to older songs, the tunes to which they are set, and their quality as song-poems. But such a procedure would demand a substantial volume of its own. All that can be done within the limits of such a study as this is to pick out from the vast quantity of remaining songs those which most demand discussion and appreciation, and by commenting on them to endeavour to round out our picture of Burns as a song writer.

The criticism of song lyrics is not easy. The analytic technique which demonstrates subtlety and paradox in the organization is inapplicable to poems which are meant to be sung and which are often written in order to recapture folk emotion. Modern criticism, which does so well with John Donne or an ode of Keats, is singularly ill equipped for an appraisal of Burns's songs. In this venture our only guide can be Arnold's instruction to see the object in itself as it really is, and a determination to account for its appeal as honestly and sensitively as possible.

Many of Burns's most successful songs are written in standard English just tipped with Scots. These are not, however, the songs in which he recaptures a folk emotion but the more formal songs of love or compliment which he learned to turn with skill fairly early in his career. They must be distinguished again from the songs written in a conventional neoclassic diction echoing a conventional neoclassic emotion – such as several of those written to Clarinda. 'Mary Morison', an early song, yet one of his finest, is a good example of this 'middle' kind of song: the language is English with a tipping of Scots; the diction is formal but not conventional, with the feeling personal and the turn of thought wholly original; and the structure is a simple and most effective movement from general compliment to specific recollection and on to a climax of appeal. The tripartite structure is particularly suitable to a love song of this kind; it prevents the song from turning into a mere list of compliments which move to no particular goal (and many contemporary love songs were just that) and at the same time provides for a repetition of the tune three times – usually the ideal number if the audience is to appreciate, without becoming wearied, its full quality and the deftness with which different words are successively fitted to it.

'Mary Morison' was first printed in volume four of Currie's edition in 1800, and later in the fifth volume of Thomson's *Scottish Airs*. Burns sent it to Thomson in March, 1793, noting that 'the song is one of my juvenile works. – I leave it among your hands. – I do not think it very remarkable either for its merits, or demerits'. Burns marked this copy with an instruction to set it to the tune of 'Duncan Davison', a song which appeared in the second volume of the *Museum*; it is a rather ordinary reel tune. Thomson set it to another tune, 'The Glasgow Lasses', although today it is always sung to yet a third – the tune of the song, 'The Miller', which also appeared in the second volume of the *Museum*; though this last was not the tune for which Burns wrote the song, nevertheless it suits the words admirably.

The poem opens with a simple gravity of utterance which sets the key for the whole:

> O Mary, at thy window be,
>   It is the wish'd, the trysted hour:
> Those smiles and glances let me see,
>   That make the miser's treasure poor:
endure the How blythly wad I bide the stoure,
turmoil A weary slave frae sun to sun;
>   Could I the rich reward secure,
> The lovely Mary Morison.

The stanza form, not uncommon in older Scottish poetry, is handled with great sureness. The key to the stanza is the turn on the fifth line, where the repetition of the rhyme of the fourth and second lines turns the stanza over, as it were, to start on a new tack; the second rhyming word of the first part of the verse becomes the first rhyming word of the second. To mould the thought of the poem to such a structure requires considerable skill, and Burns achieves this end successfully in each of the three verses. In the first, the pause after the opening four lines of compliment precedes the rising emotion of the next four lines, in which the poet, after taking a new breath, moves from compliment to passion. Similarly, in the second stanza the poet lulls himself almost into a stupor of admiration by the end of the first four lines, and then explains and amplifies his feeling in the second part:

last night

> Yestreen when to the trembling string,
>   The dance gaed thro' the lighted ha',
> To thee my fancy took its wing,
>   I sat, but neither heard or saw:

fine

the other

>   Tho' this was fair, and that was braw,
> And yon the toast of a' the town,
>   I sigh'd, and said among them a',
> 'Ye are na Mary Morison.'

In the third and last stanza the note changes from confession to appeal, the emotion riding to a climax in the first four lines and turning adroitly on the fifth to ebb into an almost elegiac mood:

> O Mary, canst thou wreck his peace,
>   Wha for thy sake wad gladly die!
> Or canst thou break that heart of his,

fault

>   Whase only faut is loving thee.
> If love for love thou wilt nae gie,
> At least be pity to me shown;

cannot

>   A thought ungentle canna be
> The thought o' Mary Morison.

In such a song as 'Mary Morison' Burns combines formality with simplicity; we can see him here combining what he had learned from English poets with the influence of the native Scots tradition. A similar song in this respect is 'Go, Fetch to Me a Pint o' Wine', which appeared in the third volume of the *Museum* and later (with the wrong tune) in Thomson's fifth volume. Burns did not at once claim the complete song as his (it was not ascribed to him in the *Museum*): 'the first half stanza of the song is old, the rest is mine', he wrote in the interleaved *Museum*, and it is probable that the first line of some early ballad gave him the suggestion. In September, 1793, he wrote to Thomson: 'It is a song of mine, & I think not a bad one.' The song as we have it is clearly his, and it is one of his most brilliant performances. It depends less on the melody for its full effect than do certain of his other most successful songs. Indeed, he was not too happy about the tune by James Oswald to which he originally set it, and later suggested to Thomson that he should set it to 'Woes my Heart that We Should Sunder', for 'it precisely suits the measure of this air.' But Thomson ignored this instruction, and set it to 'The Old Highland Laddie', to which it is now sung.

Burns has managed to infuse into this song the whole atmosphere of medieval romance and martial ballad, combining a note of ceremony and even pageantry, on the one hand with a genuine folk feeling and on the other with a tone of formal compliment.

> Go, fetch to me a pint o' wine,
> *cup*   And fill it in a silver tassie;
> That I may drink before I go
>   A service to my bonie lassie.
> The boat rocks at the Pier o' Leith,
>   Fu' loud the wind blaws frae the Ferry,
> The ship rides by the Berwick-law,
> And I maun leave my bony Mary.
>
> The trumpets sound, the banners fly,
>   The glittering spears are rankèd ready,
> The shouts o' war are heard afar,
>   The battle closes deep and bloody:
> It's not the roar o' sea or shore,
>   Wad mak me langer wish to tarry;
> Nor shouts o' war that's heard afar,
>   It's leaving thee, my bony Mary!

The domiciling of different kinds of imagery in a single emotional context is superbly done. The elemental formality of the opening two lines is set suddenly against a realistic picture of a stormy embarkation at Leith, with the specification of place names ('the Pier o' Leith', 'Berwick-law' – a conspicuous hill overlooking the Firth of Forth near North Berwick) that is an effective trick of the ballads. The second stanza conjures up all the panoply of ceremonial warfare; that single line

> The glittering spears are rankèd ready

is an absolute epitome of the medieval heroic phase of Scottish history. From the panoply of war we move to its horror ('deep and bloody') and the final turn of the poem comes when both the horror of battle and the dangers of the storm are put aside as nothing compared with 'leaving thee, my bony Mary'. Paraphrase, as so often in poetry, sounds merely silly, and even analysis of the structure or imagery of a poem of this kind does not tell us very much. This is a love poem set in an atmosphere of history – history with all its ceremony and violence – and of nature, with all *its* violence; and through it all the opening gesture of drinking a health 'in a silver tassie' works as a unifying image, a grave salute to love in the midst of natural and human warfare.

A poem which depends for its effect even less on the music is 'Thou Ling'ring Star with Less'ning Ray', sometimes entitled 'To Mary in Heaven' and in the *Scots Musical Museum* (volume three) entitled 'My Mary, Dear Departed Shade'. This poem is written wholly in English, and in a rhetorical tradition far removed from that which produced the most characteristic of Burns's songs. Because of its connection with 'Highland Mary', to whose death it refers, it has had perhaps more attention than it intrinsically deserves; it is a skilful but strained production, and the emotion is wrought up to a pitch that verges on hysteria. Biographically, it is of the greatest interest, for it makes clear that Burns had some reason to be remorseful about his relations with Mary, while the tone of solemn commemoration in which she is referred to makes it extremely difficult for us to accept the tradition – passed from Burns's friend John Richmond to James Grierson and from him to Joseph Train – that Mary was little better than a common prostitute. The poem was sent to Mrs. Dunlop in November, 1789, with a strangely morbid and even hysterical letter. It is essentially a spoken poem (the tune, by 'Miss Johnston of Hilton', to which it was set is conventional and characterless) and lends itself to declamatory recitation.

The same might be said of the well-known 'Is There for Honest Poverty?' for this song has come to be known as a recitation rather than a song. But in fact it is a good song, set to a lively reel tune to which a variety of songs had been sung earlier in the century (Burns had written his song, 'Tho' Women's Minds like Winter Winds' to this tune; it appeared in volume three of the *Museum*). It was first published in 1799 in a Stewart and Meikle Chapbook, then in Currie's edition in 1800, and after that in the fourth volume of Thomson's *Scottish Airs* in 1805. It is a rhetorical poem, testifying to the effect on Burns of the French Revolution and its ideological currents, and it owes its popularity to its effectiveness as a series of slogans. The sententiousness of versified political and moral utterance is less to the taste of the present generation of literary critics, but it must be said for this poem that it represents a legitimate and in its way impressive use of the poetic medium, even though it exhibits few if any of Burns's distinguishing characteristics as a poet. The poem has a well contrived structure, moving from the generalization about 'honest poverty' through specific illustrations of the difference between virtue and social rank to a final climactic generalization which is at once a prayer and a prophecy:

> Then let us pray that come it may,
> As come it will for a' that,
> That sense and worth, o'er a' the earth,
> May bear the gree, and a' that.
> For a' that, and a' that,
> Its comin yet for a' that,
> That man to man, the warld o'er,
> Shall brothers be for a' that.

have the
first place

The poem has an immense rhetorical *élan*, heightened by the use of the traditional refrain, 'for a' that and a' that'. Slogan poetry may not be the highest kind of literary art, but a poem like this gets itself remembered and quoted, and that is surely important.

Nevertheless, it is refreshing to turn from this kind of poetic oratory to the fine folk spirit of such a song as 'Merry Hae I Been Teethin a Heckle' (flax comb), a refurbished folk song which appeared in the third volume of the *Museum* set to a spirited pipe tune, 'Lord Breadalbine's March'. The seemingly effortless creation of a mood of rustic content, with (as so often in Burns) undertones implying a completely anarchistic view of life, requires no critical analysis for its appreciation:

flax comb
> O merry hae I been teethin a heckle,
> An' merry hae I been shapin a spoon:

patching
> O merry hae I been cloutin a kettle,
> An' kissin my Katie when a' was done.

drive
> O, A' the lang day I ca' at my hammer,
> An' a' the lang day I whistle and sing,

lass
> O, A' the lang night I cuddle my kimmer,
> An' a' the lang night as happy's a king.

The final verse has the note of total abandonment to the moment with which so many of Burns's more folklike love poems end:

Come to my arms, my Katie, my Katie,
　　An' come to my arms and kiss me again!
Drunken or sober here's to thee, Katie!
　　And blest be the day I did it again.

Or we may turn to such a song as 'What Will I Do Gin My Hoggie
(young sheep) Die', a simple bubbling over of a rustic folk theme:

What will I do gin my Hoggie die,
　　My joy, my pride, my Hoggie. . . .

Most interesting of all to students of Burns's relation to the folk
tradition are the snatches of old work songs he picked up on his tours of
the Scottish countryside and shaped into finished pieces:

men　　　　　　　Up wi' the carls of Dysart,
　　　　　　　　　　And the lads o' Buckhiven,
women　　　　　　And the Kimmers o' Largo,
　　　　　　　　　　And the lasses o' Leven.

　　　　　　　　　　Hey ca' thro' ca' thro'
much to do　　　　For we hae mickle a do,
　　　　　　　　　　Hey ca' thro' ca' thro'
　　　　　　　　　　For we hae mickle a do.

We hae tales to tell,
　　And we hae sangs to sing;
We hae pennies to spend,
　　And we hae pints to bring.

　　　　　　　　　　Hey ca' thro', &c.

We'll live a' our days,
　　And them that comes behin',
Let them do the like,
wealth　　　　　　And spend the gear they win.

　　　　　　　　　　Hey ca' thro', &c.

This is a Fife song – the places mentioned are all Fife fishing towns –
based on something that Burns picked up as he came through Fife on

his way back from his Highland tour in September, 1787. Burns probably picked up the tune, too, which apparently was not printed before
it appeared with this song in the fourth volume of the *Museum*. It is a
charming little pipe tune in compound triple time, which fits the words
like a glove.

A week before he picked up the fragment of 'Hey Ca' Thro' ' in Fife,
he passed through another fishing town, Buckie, on the Moray Firth,
and left us this recollection of the local scene:

> A' the lads o' Thornie-bank
> When they gae to the shore o' Bucky,
> They'll step in and tak a pint
> Wi' Lady Onlie, honest lucky.

> Chorus
> Lady Onlie, honest lucky,
> Brews gude ale at shore o' Bucky;
> I wish her sale for her gude ale,
> The best on a' the shore o' Bucky'

kerchief

> Her house sae bien, her curch sae clean,
> I wat she is a dainty Chuckie!

glowing coal

> And cheary blinks the ingle gleede
> O' Lady Onlie, honest lucky.

> Lady Onlie, etc.

Lively scraps such as this demonstrate Burns's irrepressible faculty for
song making and his ability to make his voice the anonymous voice of
the folk.

Drinking, making love, working, or simply the weather are the subjects of these numerous songs Burns based on older fragments. As an
example of the last of these subjects, we might take 'Up in the Morning
Early', which appeared in the second volume of the *Museum* set to the
old air 'Cold and Raw' (known in the seventeenth century as 'Stingo').
'The chorus of this is old; the two stanzas are mine', wrote Burns in the
interleaved *Museum*.

> Cauld blaws the wind frae east to west,
> The drift is driving sairly;

sorely
shrill

> Sae loud and shill's I hear the blast,
> I'm sure it's winter fairly.

> Up in the morning's no for me,
>   Up in the morning early;
> When a' the hills are cover'd wi' snaw,
>   I'm sure it's winter fairly.

Burns uses other kinds of folk themes, too – the young girl refusing to marry an old man ('An Auld Man Shall Never Daunton Me'), the old *mal marié* theme ('Whistle o'er the Lave O't'), simple abuse ('Sic a Wife As Willie Had'), and sometimes unclassifiable themes, as in the little song, 'Hey, the Dusty Miller', a refurbishing of an old fragment whose theme reminds us of the importance of the miller in an agricultural society. The miller figures largely in folk literature, but in this song he has lost his significance as an object of satire and eventually emerges as a lover. The song appeared in the second volume of the *Museum*, set to an old reel tune:

> Hey, the Dusty Miller,
>   And his dusty coat,
> He will win a shilling,
>   Or he spend a groat.
> Dusty was the coat,
>   Dusty was the colour,
> Dusty was the kiss
>   That I got frae the Miller. . . .

One must not forget, either, Burns's Jacobite songs, which dealt with what had by this time become essentially a folk theme. 'Charlie He's My Darling' has the purest folk feeling and manages, in fact, to combine with the Jacobite theme a number of other folk elements:

> 'Twas on a monday morning,
>   Right early in the year,
> That Charlie came to our town,
>   The young Chevalier.
>
> An' Charlie he's my darling,
>   My darling, my darling,
> Charlie he's my darling,
>   The young Chevalier.
>
> As he was walking up the street,
>   The city for to view,
> O there he spied a bonie lass
>   The window looking thro'. . . .

Another Jacobite song, based on a seventeenth-century street ballad, distils briefly but effectively the patriotic association of local customs with local pride:

> Bannocks o' bear meal,
> Bannocks o' barley,
> Here's to the Highlandman's
> Bannocks o' barley.

broil
> Wha, in a brulzie,
>   Will first cry a parley?
> Never the lads
>   Wi' the bannocks o' barley.

> Bannocks o' bear meal, etc.

Nothing illustrates how far removed from contemporary politics the Jacobite theme had become by the last decade of the eighteenth century more effectively than the way in which Burns treats it in his songs; the theme had, in fact, become associated with local and national patriotism, with themes of love, nostalgia, parting, and almost anything except actual contemporary political rebellion. Although the process of domiciling Jacobitism among the folk themes of Scotland was far advanced before Burns came on the scene, it was he who finally assured that this absurd and anachronistic rebellion was transmuted into a source of legitimate emotion for all Scotsmen.

Of Burns's drinking songs, perhaps the best is the well-known 'Willie Brew'd a Peck o' Maut'. 'The air is Masterton's; the song mine', wrote Burns in the interleaved *Museum*. 'The occasion of it was this. – Mr Wm Nicol, of the High School, Edinr, during the autumn vacation being at Moffat, honest Allan, who was at that time on a visit to Dalswinton and I went to pay Nicol a visit. We had such a joyous meeting that Mr Masterton and I each in our own way should celebrate the business.' The song is in the purest bacchanalian tradition, wholly lacking in the self-conscious swaggering note found in so many of the English drinking songs of the century; it is a frank celebration of drunkenness, derived from a specific social occasion and anchored solidly in experience. The sublime understatement of the chorus is both psychologically sound and structurally appropriate.

> O Willie brew'd a peck o' maut,
>   And Rob and Allan cam to see;

livelong
> Three blyther hearts, that lee lang night,
>   Ye wad na found in Christendie.

drunk   We are na fou, We're nae that fou,
drop; eye   But just a drappie in our e'e;
                The cock may craw, the day may daw,
brew   And ay we'll taste the barley bree.

            Here are we met, three merry boys,
            Three merry boys I trow are we;
            And mony a night we've merry been,
            And mony mae we hope to be!

            We are na fou, etc.

            It is the moon, I ken her horn,
sky; high   That's blinkin in the lift sae hie;
entice   She shines sae bright to wyle us hame,
            But by my sooth she'll wait a wee!

Few poets have had Burns's skill at distilling a mood of total abandonment to the pleasures of the moment.

Of the patriotic songs, by far the best known is 'Scots Wha Hae', which, in spite of being inspired by the old air 'Hey Tuttu Taitie', supposed to be the tune to which Bruce's army marched into battle at Bannockburn, is more in the eighteenth-century rhetorical style (inspired equally by the Scottish War of Independence and the French Revolution) than in the Scottish folk tradition. Burns wrote to Thomson at the end of August, 1793, that the thought that this may have been the air played at Bannockburn 'warmed me to a pitch of enthusiasm on the theme of Liberty & Independence, which I threw into a kind of Scots Ode, fitted to the Air, that one might suppose to be the gallant ROYAL SCOT's address to his heroic followers on that eventful morning.' He added in a P.S.: 'I shewed the air to Urbani, who was highly pleased with it, & begged me to make soft verses for it; but I had no idea of giving myself trouble on the subject, till the accidental recollection of that glorious struggle for Freedom, associated with the glowing ideas of some other struggles of the same nature, *not quite so ancient*, roused my rhyming Mania.' We have seen how Thomson persuaded Burns to change the song to allow him to set it to another tune, although public opinion later forced Thomson to print the original version set to the air Burns had written it for. But, while the song does go effectively to the rather tricky old tune, it is, like 'Is There for Honest Poverty', essentially a rhetorical poem of slogans and exhortations. The Scots in the poem is

not integral,[5] or even particularly helpful, and by the last two stanzas it
has been given up and the poem is revealed as an English sentimental
poem on liberty in the eighteenth-century sense:

> By oppression's woes and pains!
> By your sons in servile chains!
> We will drain our dearest veins,
>   But they shall be free!
>
> Lay the proud usurpers low!
> Tyrants fall in every foe!
> Liberty's in every blow!
>   Let us do, or die!

The oblique patriotism of the Jacobite love poems produces a far more
individual note:

> It was a' for our rightfu' king
>   We left fair Scotland's strand;
> It was a' for our rightfu' king,
>   We e'er saw Irish land, my dear,
>   We e'er saw Irish land.

Burns modelled this grand song on an earlier street ballad, 'Mally
Stewart', which suggested the effective repetition in the last two lines
coupled by 'my dear'. The song appeared in the fifth volume of the
Museum set to a simple and thoroughly appropriate seventeenth-century
ballad tune. It is remarkable how effectively the Jacobite and patriotic
notes can be handled when they have been, as here, so muted as to fall
into place as an elegiac background for a love lyric. The skill with which
Burns achieves this muting is remarkable. He begins the second stanza
with a striking evocation of the mood of the Lost Cause and proceeds
immediately to link patriotism with love and to introduce the plangent
theme of exile:

> Now a' is done that men can do,
>   And a' is done in vain:
> My Love and Native Land fareweel,
>   For I maun cross the main, my dear,
>   For I maun cross the main.

The third verse derives more directly than anything else in the poem
from a version of the old ballad:

He turn'd him right and round about,
    Upon the Irish shore,
gave   And gae his bridle reins a shake,
    With adieu for evermore, my dear,
        With, adieu for evermore!

This is the central stanza of the poem, on which the whole pivots. We are held by this romantic figure of the horseman bidding an eternal farewell to his love, and in the last two verses the poem turns into a personal love elegy:

The soger frae the wars returns,
    The sailor frae the main,
But I hae parted frae my Love,
    Never to meet again, my dear,
        Never to meet again.

When day is gane, and night is come,
    And a' folk bound to sleep;
I think on him that's far awa,
livelong   The lee-lang night, & weep, my dear,
        The lee-lang night & weep.

It is the girl speaking at the end, bringing the poem to an effective close on a note of simple grief. In structure, imagery, handling of verse form, cadence of the individual line as well as of the stanza as a whole, and control of the emotion, this is among the very finest of Burns's songs, and one of the great lyrics in the language. His inspiration here is patriotism, Jacobitism (associated with the themes of love and exile), and the folk tradition; beside the magical blending of such elements the patriotic exhortations of 'Scots Wha Hae' sound strident and crude.

The variety of Burns's love songs is remarkable. There are hardly two which follow the same pattern. There are many poems in which a profession of love is linked with description of nature, but each poem has its own way of making the connection; Burns never seems to have exhausted his resources here. The second version of 'Ca' the Yowes to the Knowes' begins by distilling a mood of complete pastoral peace, then, with this as a background, pronounces a simple benediction on the beloved, and ends with a profession of love almost heartbreaking in its intensity – yet with never a trace of sentimentality or self-indulgent emotion. The parts of the song are bound together by the traditional pastoral chorus. The earlier version, which has the same chorus, is really quite a different poem, much more folklike in idiom and situation, and preserving a considerable amount of the folk poem on which it was based. Burns never claimed the first version as wholly his, for he wrote of it in the interleaved *Museum:* 'This beautiful song is in the true old Scotch taste, yet I do not know that ever either air or words, were in print before.' The melody, one of the loveliest in all Scottish song, was discovered by Burns. 'I am flattered at your adopting "Ca' the Yowes to the Knowes", as it was owing to me that ever it saw the light', he wrote to Thomson in September, 1794. 'About seven years ago, I was well acquainted with a worthy little fellow of a Clergyman, a Mr Clunzie, who sung it charmingly; & at my request, Mr Clarke took it down from his singing. – When I gave it to Johnson, I added some Stanzas to the song & mended others [the first version had appeared in the third volume of the *Museum*], but still it will not do for *you*. – In a solitary stroll which I took today, I tried my hand on a few pastoral lines following up the idea of the chorus, which I would preserve.' The result was something memorable:

ewes; hillocks	Ca' the yowes to the knowes,
	Ca' them whare the heather growes,
brook runs	Ca' them whare the burnie rowes,
	My bonie dearie.

	Hark, the mavis' evening sang
	Sounding Clouden's woods amang;
a-folding	Then a faulding let us gang,
	My bonie dearie.

Two stanzas follow, depicting town and country silent in the moonlight, then comes the benediction:

Ghaist nor bogle shalt thou fear;
Thou'rt to love and heaven sae dear,
Nocht of ill may come thee near,
    My bonie dearie.

The concluding is a profession of love:

Fair and lovely as thou art,
Thou hast stown my very heart;
I can die – but canna part,
    My bonie dearie.

But the words are meant for the music, and the song must be judged as a song. Thomson, characteristically, printed it with the wrong tune.

A very different use of images from nature is found in 'A Red Red Rose', a simple love song based on folk materials, first published in the fifth volume of the *Museum*. Nowhere in literature has that combination of swagger and tender protectiveness so characteristic of the male in love been so perfectly captured, and it is all done by simple similes and simple exaggeration:

> O my Luve's like a red, red rose,
>   That's newly sprung in June.
> O my Luve's like the melodie
>   That's sweetly play'd in tune.
>
> As fair art thou, my bonie lass,
>   So deep in luve am I;
> And I will love thee still, my Dear,
>   Till a' the seas gang dry.

go

The note of protective male tenderness is often sounded in Burns's love poetry, though it is by no means the dominant note. He can think of love as passion, possession, or mere abandonment to physical desire, but he returns again and again to this protective note, and he sounds it most effectively in one of the very last songs he wrote, 'Oh Wert Thou in the Cauld Blast'. This was written for Jessie Lewars, sister of John Lewars, Burns's fellow exciseman. Jessie helped to nurse him in his final illness, and a few weeks before his death she played for him on her piano her favourite air, 'Lenox Love to Blantyre' (also known as 'The Wren'). Having mastered the melody, the dying poet wrote to it this song for her:

> O wert thou in the cauld blast,
>   On yonder lea, on yonder lea;
> My plaidie to the angry airt,
>   I'd shelter thee, I'd shelter thee:
> Or did misfortune's bitter storms
>   Around thee blaw, around thee blaw,
> Thy bield should be my bosom,
>   To share it a', to share it a'.
>
> Or were I in the wildest waste,
>   Sae black and bare, sae black and bare,
> The desart were a paradise,
>   If thou wert there, if thou wert there.

quarter

blow
shelter

Or were I monarch o' the globe,
  Wi' thee to reign, wi' thee to reign;
The brightest jewel in my crown,
  Wad be my queen, wad be my queen.

Burns used all his resources as a song writer to reverse the real roles of himself and his nurse, and in doing so evoked with a passionate simplicity the mood of love as protection.

There are other, less well known, love songs that deserve discussion, but it must suffice to mention only one of these, 'The Posie', one of the least known and one of the most beautiful. It first appeared in the fourth volume of the *Museum*, set to one of the finest of eighteenth-century melodies. The words, which move with a splendid lilt, fit the music perfectly.

O luve will venture in where it daur na weel be seen,
O luve will venture in where wisdom ance has been,
But I will down yon river rove, amang the woods sae green,
And a' to pu' a posie to my ain dear May. . . .

Finally, we must mention 'John Anderson My Jo', a poem of love in old age, in which Burns's feeling for domesticity and companionship fuses with the love theme to produce a very different kind of love song. The title and the stanza form are traditional, but the poem as Burns produced it is wholly original. The version of 'John Anderson My Jo' which appears in *The Merry Muses* represents the kind of older poem Burns had to work with; it is an amusing but wholly obscene poem, in which a lustful woman reproaches her aging husband for having lost something of his earlier sexual potency. Burns's poem illustrates how perfectly he could express a 'great commonplace'; it is the old *ubi sunt* theme linked to that of love and expressed through a specific situation. It is the wife addressing the husband:

	John Anderson, my jo, John,
acquainted	When we were first Acquent;
	Your locks were like the raven,
smooth	Your bony brow was brent;
bald	But now your brow is beld, John,
	Your locks are like the snaw;
head	But blessings on your frosty pow,
	John Anderson my Jo.

John Anderson my jo, John,
together   We clamb the hill thegither;
cheerful   And mony a canty day John,
        We've had wi' ane anither:
    Now we maun totter down, John,
        And hand in hand we'll go;
    And sleep thegither at the foot,
        John Anderson my Jo.

Burns avoids sentimentality in a poem of this kind by avoiding generalizations and by projecting the emotion through a concrete situation. He learned to do this from the folk tradition, and he developed a skill in the handling of images which helped him enormously in the task of providing for common emotions a local habitation and a name. Nowhere is this better illustrated than in 'Auld Lang Syne', which projects perfectly a mood of remembered friendship with almost no use of generalization. Nothing can be further removed from Dante's

        nessun maggior dolore,
    che ricordarsi del tempo felice
    nella miseria

than Burns's

waded   We twa hae paidl'd in the burn,
noon   Frae morning sun till dine;
broad   But seas between us braid hae roar'd,
        Sin auld lang syne,

yet the two poets are talking about the same thing – remembrance of past happiness. Burns did not work through an intellectual and moral system as Dante and Milton did, and he was therefore incapable of writing good reflective or philosophical poetry. It is the concrete experience that he uses to project significance; when he tries the generalization he either fails or is forced into a rhetorical tradition in which he is not really at home, and certainly not at his best.

We have already noted Burns's impressive handling of the dramatic monologue in 'Holy Willie's Prayer'. The dramatic quality of his songs is to be discerned everywhere. Although Burns was more influenced by the folk-song tradition than by the parallel but distinct ballad tradition, he was able to carry over into his songs the dramatic quality for which the Scottish ballads are famous. Again and again in his poems the situation is projected through a dramatic utterance, as so many of his opening lines witness: 'O, mirk, mirk in this midnight hour', 'O, open the door some pity to show', 'O, saw ye my dear, my Philly', 'O lassie, are ye sleepin yet?' Many of these opening lines are traditional, but in his own development of the poem Burns sustains and enriches the dramatic quality with remarkable skill. He rarely talks *about* a situation; instead, he projects it directly by speaking *from* it, as it were. The Jacobite songs in particular have this quality.

'Auld Lang Syne', the best known and most often sung of all Burns's songs, reminds us that Burns is as much the poet of friendship between men as of love between the sexes. That it speedily took the place of Scotland's older parting song 'Good Night and Joy Be with You All' and that it has become the traditional song among English-speaking peoples for bidding farewell to the old year and hailing the new are evidence of the success with which Burns was able to present the theme of 'ricordarsi del tempo felice' through a context of remembered friendship. The song very cunningly combines a note of present conviviality with a poignant sense of the loss of earlier companionship brought by time and distance; such a note is just right for New Year's Eve, when the mind hovers between retrospect and anticipation and we think equally of days gone for ever and days to come. But of course 'Auld Lang Syne' is more than a New Year's song: it is one of the great expressions of the tragic ambiguity of man's relation to time, which 'mixes memory with desire', carrying away old friendships and bringing new, turning childhood escapades into old men's recollections, making change the very condition of consciousness, and at the same time the creator and the destroyer of human experience. And all this is done in the purest folk idiom, with no abstract statements or generalizations, except for the chorus itself, which states in simple but powerful terms the question that lies at the heart of so much human emotion.

That the song as we have it is essentially Burns's cannot be doubted, though he never claimed authorship, and there is undoubtedly something preserved from an earlier version. We have only to set it beside the earlier extant poems of the same title to see the vast difference between Burns's version and what the song had become by the time Burns came to rework it. Here are the first two stanzas of the 'Auld Lang Syne' which appeared in Ramsay's *The Tea-Table Miscellany*:

> Should auld acquaintance be forgot,
>> Tho' they return with scars?
> These are the noble hero's lot,
>> Obtain'd in glorious wars:

Welcome, my VARO, to my breast,
  Thy arms about me twine,
And make me once again as blest,
  As I was lang syne.

Methinks around us on each bough,
  A thousand cupids play,
Whilst thro' the groves I walk with you,
  Each object makes me gay:
Since your return the sun and moon
  With brighter beams do shine;
Streams murmur soft notes while they run,
  As they did lang syne. . . .

This version (which also appears in David Herd's *Ancient and Modern Scottish Songs*) is clearly a sophisticated version far removed from what must have been the original folk song from which the title and the first line are derived. Watson's *Choice Collection* also has a version, which does not, however, get us very much nearer to the real thing:

Should old Acquaintance be forgot,
  And never thought upon,
The Flames of Love extinguished,
  And freely past and gone?
Is thy kind Heart now grown so cold
  In that Loving Breast of thine,
That thou canst never once reflect
  On Old-long-syne?

Where are thy Protestations,
  Thy Vows and Oaths, my Dear,
Thou made to me, and I to thee,
  In Register yet clear?
Is Faith and Truth so violate
  To the Immortal Gods Divine
That thou canst never once reflect
  On Old-long-syne?

Henley and Henderson quote from a unique broadside, which was Watson's source, entitled 'An Excellent and proper new ballad, entitled *Old Long Syne*. Newly corrected and amended, with a large and new

edition of several excellent love lines'. This title, as Henley and Henderson observe, proves the existence of an older version, which Burns may
have known. It differs from Watson's version in having a refrain:

> On old long syne
sweetheart On old long syne, my jo,
> On old long syne:
> That thou canst never once reflect
> On old long syne.

But what we know of the history from this broadside to the version
printed by Ramsay and Herd hardly prepare us for the 'Auld Lang Syne'
Burns suddenly communicated to Mrs. Dunlop in a letter dated December 7, 1788. Burns made several changes later, but this is the earliest of
his versions:

> Should auld acquaintance be forgot,
> And never thought upon?
> Let's hae a waught o' Malaga,
> For auld long syne. –

> Chorus
> For auld lang syne, my jo,
> For auld lang syne;
> Let's hae a waught o' Malaga,
> For auld lang syne. –

pay for And surely ye'll be your pint-stoup!
> And surely I'll be mine!
> And we'll tak a cup o' kindness yet,
> For auld lang syne. –
> For auld &c.

> We two hae run about the braes,
pulled; And pou't the gowans fine;
daisies But we've wander'd mony a weary foot
> Sin auld lang syne. –
> For auld &c.

> We twa hae paidl't in the burn
> Frae morning sun till dine;
> But seas between us baith hae roar'd,
> Sin auld lang syne. –
> For auld &c.

companion
         And there's a han' my trusty fiere,
           And gie's a han' o' thine!
         And we'll tak a right gudewilly waught
           For auld lang syne!

He added: 'Light be the turf on the breast of the heaven-inspired Poet who composed this glorious Fragment! There is more of the fire of native genius in it, than in half a dozen of modern English Bacchanalians.'

Writing to Thomson in September, 1793, he enclosed a slightly different version, preceded by this remark: 'The air is but mediocre [not the tune to which it is now sung]; but the following song, the old song of the olden times, & which has never been in print, nor even in manuscript, until I took it down from an old man's singing; is enough to recommend any air –'

         Auld lang syne –

         Should auld acquaintance be forgot,
           And never brought to mind?
         Should auld acquaintance be forgot,
           And days o' lang syne?

         Chorus
         For auld lang syne, my Dear,
           For auld lang syne,
         We'll tak a cup o' kindness yet,
           For auld lang syne –

         We twa hae run about the braes,
           And pu't the gowans fine;
         But we've wandered mony a weary foot,
           Sin auld lang syne. –
         For auld lang syne &c.

         We twa hae paidlet i' the burn,
           Frae morning sun till dine:
         But seas between us braid hae roar'd,
           Sin auld lang syne. –
         For auld &c.

         And there's a hand, my trusty feire,
           And gie's a hand o' thine;

And we'll tak a right gude-willie waught,
    For auld lang syne. –
For auld &c.

And surely ye'll be your pint-stowp,
    And surely I'll be mine;
And we'll tak a cup o' kindness yet,
    For auld lang syne. –
For auld &c.

The song appeared in the fifth volume of the *Museum*, published at
the end of 1796 after Burns's death, and Burns probably saw it in proof.
In the *Museum* version the verse beginning

And surely ye'll be your pint-stowp

becomes the second verse, placed immediately after the chorus. There
are other minor variations from the version communicated to Thomson
in 1793. The last line of the first verse reads

And auld lang syne!

instead of

And days o' lang syne?

and the first line of the chorus ends with 'my jo' instead of 'my Dear'.
    In the interleaved *Museum* Burns appended a note to the twenty-fifth
song, which was the earlier 'Auld Lang Syne' as printed by Ramsay:
'The original and by much the best set of the words of this song is as
follows'. He then wrote out a version of the song which differs slightly
from all of those just cited, though it is closest to Johnson's. It has Johnson's order of the verses and has 'my jo' in the chorus, but agrees with
the version communicated to Thomson in reading

And days o' lang syne?

at the end of the first verse. The version which appeared in Thomson's
Scottish Airs, 1799, is, as we should expect, the same as that communicated to Thomson in 1793. Here for the first time it is set to the tune to
which it has since been sung. James Dick has presented evidence which
suggests, although it cannot prove, that Burns, who knew Thomson's

tune and who had referred to his own tune as 'mediocre', had been consulted and had approved the setting of the song to Thomson's tune.

Modern texts of the song tend to be a conflation of the *Museum* and the Thomson versions, and perhaps in a song of this kind that is no great matter. Its greatness lies in the linking of the central emotion to the idea of time and change through precise contrasts between past and present:

> We twa hae run about the braes,
>   And pu't the gowans fine
> But we've wandered mony a weary foot,
>   Sin auld lang syne.

The precision with which Burns captures the quality of a boy's holiday activity in this and the subsequent stanza is remarkable, and those who have in fact spent their boyhood in Scotland and their summers there running about the braes or 'paidling' in the burn cannot read or sing these verses without an immediate recall of the essential quality of those days. But their appeal is not simply to autobiography; the two activities are perfect symbols of lost youth in any context, and when they are juxtaposed to images suggestive of time and distance the effect is immediate. The sublimation of nostalgia for the past in present good fellowship brings the poem to a close (whichever version we take) with a formal social gesture, in the light of which everything falls into shape; past and present are held together for one tenuous moment by ritual, which is man's way of marking permanently the fleeting meanings of things. And as we think of Robert Burns, and of Scotland, and of the world outside Scotland which has taken his songs to its heart, we raise our glass across the crowded years to salute the Scots poet and farmer and exciseman, the pupil of Murdoch, the lover of Jean and Mary and Clarinda, the son of Agnes Broun and William Burnes, Rab Mossgiel and Caledonia's Bard, this brilliant and troubled peasant, assaulted on all sides by old traditions and new gospels, who almost single handed created a glorious Indian Summer for native Scottish literature and in doing so made himself known to peoples and to generations far removed from both the heady air of his disintegrating century and the split personality of his history-racked country; we salute him in his terms, which he has made ours:

> For auld lang syne, my dear,
>   For auld lang syne,
> We'll tak a cup o' kindness yet
>   For auld lang syne.

NOTES

CHAPTER ONE:

1. W. C. Mackenzie, *Andrew Fletcher of Saltoun* (Edinburgh: The Porpoise Press, 1935), p. 286.
2. It should be noted, however, that the glory was not evenly sustained throughout the period. When Burns arrived in Edinburgh in 1786 there was no one active among the literati who was really his intellectual equal. David Hume had been dead for a decade and Adam Smith was ill and living a retired life. Coming between the age of Hume and that of Walter Scott, in both of whom he would have met his mental equals, Burns was forced to consort with second-raters, and the result was not happy.
3. David Herd, ed., *Ancient and Mordern Scots Songs*, 2nd enlarged ed. (Edinburgh: printed by John Wotherspoon for James Dickson and Charles Elliott, 1776), II, 206. The first edition was published in Edinburgh in 1769.
4. Iain Ross, ed., *The Gude and Godlie Ballatis* (Edinburgh: The Saltire Society, 1939), p. 43.
5. *Ibid.*, p. 60.
6. *Ibid.*, p. 63.
7. The first edition was published in Dublin. Hutcheson, born in Ulster of Scottish parentage, was educated at Glasgow University and in 1729 returned to Glasgow as professor of moral philosophy there. An edition of the *Inquiry* was published in Glasgow in 1738.
8. Allan Ramsay, *The Tea-Table Miscellany*, 14th ed. (Glasgow: reprinted by John Crum, 1871), Preface.

CHAPTER TWO:

1. DeLancey Ferguson, *Pride and Passion: Robert Burns, 1759–1796* (New York: Oxford University Press, 1939), p. 41.
2. In all printed versions of the letters (including the standard Clarendon

Press edition) the initial is 'E' and not 'A'; but Professor Ferguson tells me that in the only extant manuscript of these letters the initial is 'A'. Apparently the substitution was deliberately made by Currie.

3. Irvine is the 'Gudetown' of John Galt's admirable novel, *The Provost*, which, though written in 1822, gives a picture of the town a generation earlier. Galt was a native of Irvine, and his description is full and vivid.

4. James Crichton-Brown, *Burns from a New Point of View* (London: Hodder & Stoughton, Ltd., n.d.), p. 66.

5. The original of this letter was unknown when Professor Ferguson edited the letters for the Clarendon Press, and the text in that edition is necessarily taken from Scott Douglas's edition. The Douglas text is both fragmentary and wilfully inaccurate, as can now be seen by reference to the original manuscript, which has since turned up. I owe a transcript of it to the kindness of Professor Ferguson, who notes at the end: 'Lot 13 in Armour sale, American Art Association–Anderson Galleries, New York, 22 April, 1937. Transcribed from the original holograph, by courtesy of Mr. David A. Randall, Charles Scribner's Sons, N.Y.'

6. Franklyn Bliss Snyder, *The Life of Robert Burns* (New York: The Macmillan Company, 1932), p. 144.

CHAPTER THREE:

1. The Holy Fair, 'a common phrase in the West of Scotland for a sacramental occasion', as Burns described it in his note to the poem in the Edinburgh edition, was a vast outdoor 'tent preaching' held annually in connection with the communion service. Some of the goings-on at these 'occasions' had already been the subject of adverse comment before Burns's poem. In the year of Burns's birth there was published in London a fierce attack on these outdoor 'sacred solemnities', entitled *Letter from a Blacksmith to the Ministers and Elders of the Church of Scotland, in which the Manner of Publick Worship in That Church is Considered, Its Inconveniences and Defects Pointed Out, and Methods of Removing Them Honestly Proposed*. Burns apparently drew on this pamphlet in 'The Holy Fair'.

2. In the Kilmarnock edition, the names of the ministers referred to in the poem are indicated only by asterisks, and 'God' is printed 'G——'.

3. The reading of the Kilmarnock edition was 'salvation', but Burns changed it in 1787 to 'damnation', acting on a somewhat guarded suggestion by Hugh Blair. Blair had not actually suggested 'damnation', but had noted that 'salvation' ought to be altered and added:

'The Author may easily contrive some other Rhyme in place of the word *Salv——n*'.

4. So Burns dates it. Gilbert Burns, however, said that Robert repeated the poem to him in the summer of 1784. But Gilbert's memory was not always accurate, and the winter landscape certainly suggests January.

5. Burns later omitted the line 'And och! that's nae regeneration!' at Hugh Blair's suggestion.

CHAPTER FOUR: There are no notes for this chapter.

CHAPTER FIVE:

1. The edition was a great success, and a second printing was immediately begun.

CHAPTER SIX:

1. Of two pairs of twins which Jean had borne by this time, only one boy, Robert, now survived. The others died soon after birth.

2. After his transfer to the Dumfries third division, where the distances to be covered were considerably less, he was able to dispense with his horse and go on foot.

3. This was its first appearance in a book. Actually, after considerable circulation in manuscript, it first appeared in *The Edinburgh Magazine* for March, 1791, and then in the *Edinburgh Herald* of March 18, 1791. Volume II of Grose's *Antiquities* appeared in April.

CHAPTER SEVEN:

1. Always pronounced in Scots law with the accent on the first syllable.

2. Edwin Muir, *Scott and Scotland* (London: George Routledge & Sons, Ltd., 1936), p. 27.

3. I have not seen the original issues, which are not easy to come by, and I cite these facts on the authority of James C. Dick, *The Songs of Robert Burns, Now First Printed with the Melodies for Which They Were Written . . .* (London: Henry Frowde, 1903), p. xxxvi. The edition of the *Museum* that I have used is the reprint edited by David Laing in 1853. Though (apart from the editorial matter) this edition uses the plates of an earlier printing done in Johnson's lifetime, it has many more attributions to Burns in the index to each volume than the original issues have.

4. Dick, *op. cit.*, p. xiii.

5. Sir James Murray has pointed out that the correct Middle Scots idiom for the opening words would be 'Scots that has'. But we hardly demand that kind of historical accuracy in a song.

INDEX

N.B. When authorship is known poems cited or quoted are placed under their respective authors; anonymous poems are placed under the heading 'Poems, songs and ballads'. When a poem is quoted an asterisk is placed against the title. Tunes are placed under that heading.

THE SALTIRE SOCIETY

The Society seeks to preserve traditional Scottish culture and to encourage new developments in numerous fields from architecture and engineering to literature and music. Branches are active in Aberdeen, Dumfries, Edinburgh, Glasgow, Helensburgh, Highland (based in Inverness), Kirriemuir, St. Andrews and South Fife. There are Saltire representatives in Ayr and London.

Further information from The Administrator,
The Saltire Society,
9 Fountain Close,
22 High Street
EDINBURGH EH1 1TF
Tel. 031 556 1836 Fax. 031 557 1675

SOME SALTIRE PUBLICATIONS

Complete list (and details of the Saltire Society, membership etc.) available from the:

The Saltire Society,
9 Fountain Close,
22 High Street,
Edinburgh EH1 1TF